Vygotsky's Developmental and Educational Psychology

Lev Vygotsky (1896–1934) was one of the most significant and influential psychologists of the twentieth century. Nevertheless, true appreciation of his theories has been hindered by a lack of understanding of the background to his thought.

Vygotsky's Developmental and Educational Psychology aims to demonstrate how we can come to a new and original understanding of Vygotsky's theories through knowledge of their cultural, philosophical and historical context. Beginning with the main philosophical influences of Marxist and Hegelian thought, this book leads the reader through Vygotsky's life and the development of his thought. Central areas covered include:

- The child
- Motivation and cognition
- The relevance of Vygotsky's theories to current research in developmental psychology.

This comprehensive survey of Vygotsky's thought will prove an invaluable resource for those studying developmental psychology or education.

Peter E. Langford is a freelance psychologist, previously affiliated to Birkbeck College, University of London, the University of Tasmania, and La Trobe University, Australia.

Vygotsky's Developmental and Educational Psychology

Peter E. Langford

Routledge
Taylor & Francis Group
LONDON AND NEW YORK

First published 2005 by Psychology Press

Published 2021 by Routledge
2 Park Square, Milton Park, Abingdon, Oxon OX14 4RN
605 Third Avenue, New York, NY 10017

Routledge is an imprint of the Taylor & Francis Group, an informa business

Typeset in Times by RefineCatch Limited, Bungay, Suffolk
Cover design by Hybert Design

British Library Cataloguing in Publication Data
A catalogue record for this book is available from the British Library

Library of Congress Cataloging-in-Publication Data
Langford, Peter (Peter E.)
Vygotsky's developmental and educational psychology / Peter E. Langford.–1st ed.
p. cm.
Includes bibliographical references and index.
ISBN 1-84169-271-9 (hardcover)
1. Vygotskiæi, L. S. (Lev Semenovich), 1896–1934. 2. Developmental psychology. 3. Educational psychology. I. Title.

BF109.V95L36 2005
155'.092–dc22

2005001734

ISBN 13: 978-1-84169-279-1 (hbk)

Contents

List of figures

Acknowledgements

I should thank the Psychology Department of the University of Tasmania for giving me time to pursue this research while on its staff. Some of my deepest debts are to the Psychology Press readers who provided invaluable advice on both the content and presentation of the book, particularly to Professor Elizabeth Robinson. Naturally, the remaining defects are my own responsibility.

I would also like to thank the librarians and staff of the following institutions for their unfailing helpfulness and courtesy. In Russia: Moscow State Library and East View, Moscow. In the UK: the British Library, Senate House Library, University of London and the Library of the School of Oriental and African Studies, University of London. In the USA: East View, New Jersey and Document Express, Stanford, CA. In Australia: the libraries of the University of Tasmania and La Trobe, Melbourne and Monash Universities and the State Library of Victoria.

1 Introduction

> The reaction on labour and speech of the development of the brain and its attendant senses, of the increasing clarity of consciousness, power of abstraction and of conclusion, gave both labour and speech an ever-renewed impulse to further development. This development did not reach its conclusion when man finally became distinct from the ape, but on the whole made further powerful progress, its degree and direction varying among different peoples and at different times, and here and there even being interrupted by local or temporary regression.
>
> (Engels, 1896)

This book is about L. S. Vygotsky, who, with Pavlov, was the most famous and influential Russian, or, strictly, Byelorussian, psychologist of the twentieth century. His influence has also tended to increase in the last 25 years, even though he died in 1934. However, introducing him is notoriously difficult, because there are a number of conflicting views about what his message was, as well as about what its merits were. This introduction outlines my interpretation of Vygotsky. A review of some other approaches to him is given in Chapter 8.

It was central to Vygotsky's work that he began from principles that he found in Marx to build a form of Marxist psychology. Today, for many in the West and elsewhere, this may lead to the conclusion that he built on foundations of sand and the whole edifice is probably both unstable and undesirable. However, Vygotsky built on some of Marx's principles, not all of them. So, in thinking about Vygotsky's Marxism, we need to think of some modified and extended aspects of Marxism, not about classical Marxism as a whole. Some of these are also aspects that Marxism has in common with some versions of the liberal philosophy of history (see Chapter 14).

Vygotsky: an interpretation

Vygotsky's development went through several periods. During 1918–20, he was committed to what was then called reflexology, in the Soviet Union.

This was similar to Western behaviourism, in that it argued that all human behaviour can be reduced to conditioned reflexes, but differed in giving attention to the physiology of such reflexes, as well as to behaviour. For the entire period 1921–27, he was engaged in moving away from this outlook, which proved a difficult task. Nearly all those who had, like him, set out to build a Marxist psychology in the Soviet Union, in this period, were committed to reflexology (most significantly Bekhterev, 1921, 1926a, 1926b) or to halfway-house versions, lying between it and Vygotsky's last ideas. A good example of the latter was Kornilov, the head of the key Moscow Institute of Psychology from 1924 to 1930, under whom Vygotsky worked in that period. This atmosphere seems to have slowed his move away from reflexology.

Vygotsky became a Marxist, in a general sense, shortly after the end of the First World War, but it was not until after 1920 that he began to think that Marxists should develop a special kind of psychology. From around 1928, he adopted several ideas about the construction of a Marxist psychology that marked a radical break with his previous thinking on the topic. He took from Marx and Engels two main items: Their theory that the historical development of the individual is determined by their role in the historical development of production; and the challenge they posed to somehow connect the historical development of the individual with the development of the child (a challenge made explicit by Engels, 1886).

Vygotsky assumes that there are developmental tasks that exist in both the development of the species and individual development, but that these are met in different ways. For this reason we can talk about an underlying map of development that applies to both history and the individual. This is primarily a map of the individual as they exist inside a social system, not the asocial individual who appears, for instance, in Piaget's approach to cognitive development.

The states of the developing social system are determined by three dimensions. The first is the levels of activity, that is to say the use of tools and practice, the social relations of work, signs and consciousness and the self. Signs here means anything that can communicate meaning, such as gestures, speech or writing. The first two of these levels show little consciousness, while as we move from these to the last, consciousness increases. The next dimension is motivation; the third is the relation between the inner and the outer, the main example of which is the relation between the inner and outer selves. The primary dimensions of developmental advance are the first two.

Each of the levels of activity contains four steps, ranging from least to most developed. Tools and practice, for instance, develop from the use of tools based on the human body and designed by imagination, to the scientific construction of machines based on abstract scientific concepts, with two steps in between these extremes. The development of motivation contains five steps. Four correspond to the steps in the levels, but there is an additional first step in infancy, before the levels appear, which is the appearance of the distinction between means and goals. The dimension of inner versus outer contains only two steps, as it only applies to the last two periods of development (after 7 years of age).

In both Vygotsky's last periods (1928–31) and (1932–34), the forces that push us across this developmental map, that is the dynamic model, differ, in some areas, in history and in the child. However, for introductory purposes we can concentrate on aspects that are similar. In the period 1928–31 he stresses long-term interactions between the levels, in both historical and child development. In its early stages, development is driven forward by the use of tools and practice. After this initial period, signs and self-consciousness become the main dynamic forces (Vygotsky, 1930k, 1931b). Finally, towards the end of the period he analyses, tools, practice and signs are synthesised in advanced concepts, ending the divorce between signs and practice (Vygotsky, 1931a, Ch. 3). Now it is such concepts that provide the dynamic impetus for development.

Vygotsky justifies this model on the grounds that it is required by two aspects of development: That it is social and that it is cognitive (Vygotsky, 1930k, pp. 40–44, 1931b, pp. 60–63). His justification for thinking that development is social is that fundamentally new psychological functions and forms of thought cannot emerge from natural, innate, functions after the first periods of development, because it is only those first periods that have primarily resulted from biological evolution. There are only two kinds of evolution: biological and social. Therefore, once biological development is over in its essentials, development after that must be mainly social, although minor biological aspects persist.

He then argues that after its earliest stage production was cognitive, that is it required relatively sophisticated concepts and problem solving. Even to reproduce such a system of production we need something that can transmit this sophistication to the new generation. This must involve signs: especially speech; but also other ways of transmitting meaning, such as diagrams. Forms of social influence other than the sign, that could transmit the results of cultural development to the child, especially imitation and learning through conditioning, are not candidates, because they do not transmit a cognitive approach to problems, which is needed for production after its initial period. As the central parts of culture after that time involve such higher forms of cognition, it is only signs, which can transmit meaning, that are able to do this.

Vygotsky did not invent this argument, which was advanced earlier in outline form by Durkheim (1912) and Levy-Bruhl (1910) and in much the same form that Vygotsky did by Mead (1909, 1910). However, none of these was later viewed as a 'real', i.e. specialist, psychologist, and so much of its later influence, within both developmental and general psychology, has been through Vygotsky. In this abbreviated form the argument contains some obvious weaknesses, that Vygotsky addressed and overcame (Chapters 5, 11). The most important rival argument can be found in Marx's later writings and assumed a particularly influential form at the hands of A. N. Leont'ev (1948,

1960, 1974). Leont'ev began his career working under Vygotsky's direction, but broke from him around 1928.

This alternative says that the transmission of practice through conditioning and imitation is followed by the child's becoming conscious of this practice and this renders it cognitive. Vygotsky's reply to this is outlined in Chapter 4.

Corresponding to the above shifts in the dynamic function of the levels, we find long-term shifts in motivation. In his penultimate period, in the early stages the child's goals are biological; next, the goals of the individual are socially determined by what other people think; finally these two things are synthesised in the interests of adolescence (Vygotsky, 1931a, Ch. 1).

These two dialectical sequences, formed by the levels and motivation, are interlinked. During development after infancy, the initial point for a cycle of development comes from a new form of social relations (Vygotsky, 1931a, Ch. 3). This leads to changes in motivation, which precipitate further changes in the levels, that is in signs, self-consciousness and practice (Vygotsky, 1931a, Ch. 1). The reason that motivation can play this dynamic role is that the cognitive attainments involved in moving between steps along the levels, such as the improvements in tools and practice just mentioned, depend on the child's achieving a certain motivational distance from situations. An infant will react immediately to what is around it and this prevents it from reflecting on what it experiences. To build machines using scientific concepts requires the capacity for considerable delay of gratification on the part of the machine's designer, in order to reap the rewards of its operation, once all the thought, planning and effort needed to make it are finished.

In the period 1932–34 this dynamic model changed, although many of the fundamentals remained. He now suggests that there are stages in development that encompass both the intellect and the personality. He now talks most about the dynamics of development within stages, rather than about long-term dynamics. The dynamics within stages are similar across all stages. Within each stage a cycle of developments moves from social relations, to stress on language and signs, to self-consciousness, then to changes in practice and the personality as a whole. Within this cycle some parts are dynamic and push the others along, while others are passive. The main dynamic forces are again signs and self-consciousness in the middle period of development (Vygotsky, 1932b, 1932d, 1933i, 1934c, Ch. 6). This sequence is similar to the one he had assumed operated on a short-term basis within the middle period of development in the earlier model.

The nature of motivation, like that of some of the levels, changes considerably from the earlier period, but its role in the dynamics of development changes little. Each cycle of development starts with a new kind of social relations. This leads immediately to changes in motivation (Vygotsky, 1933i, 1934f, 1934k), which in turn act to produce further changes in the levels. So motivation is still an additional dynamic force.

Although Vygotsky concentrates on stage dynamics in his last period, we can piece together his late stance on longer term dynamics from scattered comments (see Chapters 5 and 6). It is similar to his earlier view, except that he now assumes the infant and the child below 7 years have both social relations and self-consciousness.

Next, we come to Vygotsky's theory of knowledge. In the West, this is often seen as the central point in theories of cognitive development, in large part because Piaget successfully urged this idea. The approach adopted here interprets Vygotsky as a dialectical realist.

The term 'realist', as used here, is short for the approach that philosophers often call moderate realism. According to moderate realism, our knowledge gradually approximates to reality through some mechanism that helps it to do so, such as feedback from direct practice. In a familiar version, if an idea works in practice it is retained, if not it is rejected; this results in the idea approximating more and more closely to reality. Vygotsky often explicitly says he was a moderate realist (Vygotsky, 1925a, Ch. 1, 1927d, Chs 1, 4, 1930a, 1930b, 1930h, 1931b, Chs 1, 2, 1931d, 1932c, 1934c, Ch. 2).

Although the antirealist philosophy of constructivism is currently more popular in Western developmental psychology than realism, realism remains popular among philosophers and in other areas of psychology. One of the common justifications for realism is that if we reject it, we reject any capacity to reflect on the foundations of society and to change them. We are climbing aboard a car with no windscreen and no steering wheel. This is not just a rhetorical flourish, as the widespread and fashionable philosophy of postmodernism says precisely this: There is no such thing as valid social understanding, as everything we think we know about society is relative, and expresses our own nature and interests, not what really is, even in an approximate way.

The term 'dialectical', as applied to Vygotsky in this context, does not just mean that he used dialectical thinking in his theory in a general way. That would be to state the obvious. It refers to a particular aspect of dialectical thinking that Vygotsky applied to the way in which knowledge develops. This is that one side of the child's thinking may predominate in the development of realistic knowledge at one point, a reverse side later on, while ultimately the two merge in a higher synthesis.

Vygotsky's theory of knowledge is most clearly expressed in his analysis of the connection between speech and thought. Thought, as he uses the term, means a system for knowing about the world that is closely connected to practice. In broad outline his view of the long-term development of speech and thought remained the same throughout the period from 1928 until 1934.

In most of the first two periods, or stages, of development, practice predominates; in most of the next three it is signs (1930k, 1931b, Ch. 6, 1934c, 1934e). To reiterate, signs here means anything that can communicate meaning, such as gestures, speech or writing. Towards the end of the fifth period of development, advanced abstract concepts predominate, which are formed from the synthesis of practical thought and signs, including language (Vygotsky, 1931a, Ch. 3, 1933g). So the previous tendencies, emphasising first practice and then language and consciousness, are synthesised. This pattern of dialectical development, so called because it resembles a conversation, is taken from Hegel (especially Hegel, 1807, 1831).

We now need to know how the dialectic of practice and signs accomplishes the aim of knowing reality, thus being realist. For most of the first two periods, when practice is dominant, and towards the end of his five stages, when practice resumes at least an equal partnership with language, this is not a particular problem. For the most part he assumes that his readers are aware, that for many realist philosophers who stress practice, the feedback from practice corrects both the forms of thought and the particular uses made of them, bringing them into alignment with reality. This was, for instance, the view of Marx (1859, 1867, Ch, 7). At times he is more explicit (particularly in Vygotsky, 1931a, pp. 119–120), where he discusses Lenin's (1925) use of this idea favourably.

Vygotsky's view was that signs and language predominate in the acquisition of knowledge in the middle period of development. Their link with reality is mainly formed through the effect of sign use in providing the child with a means to overcome its one-sided perspectives on the world and adopt the view of a general observer, thus creating realistic knowledge (Vygotsky, 1931a, Ch. 3, 1931b, Ch. 6, 1934c, Ch. 7).

Finally, an ambiguous aspect of Vygotsky's views is the way he connects signs as the motor of development and signs as the origin of new forms of knowledge. Vygotsky, adopting what seems to be the most obvious stance, thinks that if something is most important in driving forward the knowledge system, it must be most important in the development of new forms of knowledge. So, first practice has these roles in infancy and part of early childhood, then we shift to signs and finally to advanced concepts. So, if a new kind of simple concept, meaning or advanced concept appears, it does so as a result of the action of whatever is pushing cognition forward at the time.

However, this is not the only picture we can form. The engine of development might be pushing something else forward, that is actually responsible for the development of new knowledge. So, the development of the child's speech might be powering the changes in its meanings, but it may be that this occurs through the intermediary of something else, such as the effects that speech has on the child's practice and use of tools, which in turn affect its understanding.

Although, particularly in the form suggested by A. N. Leont'ev (1982), this second interpretation of Vygotsky has been remarkably popular, it is both inherently unlikely and not what he actually says (see Chapter 8).

We should also consider one further issue. Gaining knowledge can mean not only the development of new forms of knowledge, but also the use of existing means to fill out the *content* of knowledge. However, whatever means are used to gather content must have previously emerged as new forms. In other words, there can be no content without forms. On this level, Vygotsky thinks that the development of new forms of knowledge is the more fundamental problem. However, he only admits this in relation to the development of fundamental units of meaning, particularly those found in words. On the broader issue of the relation between the fundamental meanings and statements and rules formed from them, he generally thinks that development of the units of meaning is more fundamental. This can be confusing, because he and others often refer to this second tendency as the priority of content over form in development.

Conclusions

Vygotsky's project was based on accepting that Marx had already founded a Marxist psychology, by claiming that the development of human capacities and personality depend on the development of the productive forces and that the historical development of production takes roughly the form Marx outlined. Vygotsky proposed to complete this by, among other things:

- showing how the development of the child differs from the historical development of human characteristics
- stressing that previous investigators had often underestimated the role of signs in development

His attempts to work out the implications of these ideas and to rid himself of his earlier reflexology went through three broad stages: 1921–27, when he was still feeling his way; 1928–31, when he announced a preliminary version of his own theory; 1932–34, when he refined his earlier ideas considerably.

Part I

The theory

2 Life and early work

Vygotsky's life

Vygotsky was born into a Jewish family in 1896 and spent most of his early life in Gomel' in Byelorussia. He showed signs of considerable precocity while still at school and in his senior years took a leading role in a discussion group on philosophical, literary and other topics. He wrote a substantial and impressive study of Shakespeare's *Hamlet* during this period (Vygotsky, 1914). His favourite philosopher was then, as later, Hegel (Vygodskaya & Lifanova, 1996). After the First World War he worked at Gomel' Teachers' College from 1918 to 1920, at which time he wrote most of the book *Pedagogical psychology* (1926c). The outlook adopted is that of reflexology, particularly that of Bekhterev, which is to say that it proposes to explain all human behaviour in terms of conditioned reflexes, similar to those that Pavlov (1897) had established in dogs and Thorndike (1902, 1911) in cats and other animals.

In Pavlov's best known experiment he regularly rang a bell before dogs were fed; being fed produced salivation. After repeating this several times, the dogs salivated to the bell, even if no food were given, showing that salivation had become associated with the bell. An application of this to education is that if students regularly associate schoolwork with threats that produce fear, they will come to associate schoolwork with fear. Alternatively, if they associate schoolwork with rewards, such as praise or prizes, that produce pleasure, then they will associate schoolwork with pleasure.

This sudden change from Shakespeare and Hegel to reflexology was to be partly reversed by the mid-1920s, when his psychology once again came under literary and philosophical influences, although it had other important aspects (Vygotsky, 1925a, 1925b, 1926c). This reversal began in the period from 1921 to 1924, when Vygotsky undertook his doctoral thesis at Moscow University, on the psychology of art, while still partly based in Gomel'. Although Vygotsky had become a Marxist shortly after the end of the First World War, it was not until this period at Moscow University that he took the idea of creating a specifically Marxist psychology seriously. It was one of the aims of his thesis to contribute to this.

In 1924 he was very ill for much of the year, with the tuberculosis that would finally kill him. In the same year, Kornilov, one of the most noted Marxist psychologists in the Soviet Union at that time, was in the process of recreating the Institute of Psychology in Moscow. One of the main aims of this change was to create a focus for distinctively Marxist work in psychology, in opposition to both the idealist psychology of Chelpanov (1917, 1924, 1925, 1926) and his students and the reflexology of Bekhterev (1904, 1921, 1926a, 1926b) and Pavlov (1897, 1926), which both Kornilov and Vygotsky by this time saw as incompatible with Marxism. The official title of Kornilov's approach was 'reactology' (Kornilov, 1922, 1928), which was in contrast to the 'reflexology' of Bekhterev and Pavlov. The main difference was that, while the reflexologists assumed that stimulus and response are mainly joined by associations, reactologists made no particular assumptions about the nature of such connections. This meant they were free to assume the connections were highly complex, thus allowing them more room for the study of higher mental processes, such as thinking, than reflexology.

Vygotsky so impressed Kornilov with his papers at the Second All-Union Congress on Psychoneurology, in 1924, that he immediately invited him to take up a junior position at the Institute of Psychology (Vygotsky, 1925b, 1926a). Alexander Luria, who was to become one of Vygotsky's chief collaborators, relates that he first encountered Vygotsky at this conference and was impressed by one of his papers. At the end of the reading, he went to introduce himself to the speaker and was surprised to find that the sheets from which Vygotsky had apparently read the paper were blank. He had read the paper verbatim from memory and the sheets were just a prop (Wertsch, 1985).

Vygotsky had a near photographic memory, as well as being able to read at over 600 words a minute (Wertsch, 1985). He read so fast that he moved his eyes diagonally from the top left to the bottom right of the page, instead of moving along each line, so his eye movements would not slow his progress.

Vygotsky accepted the invitation from Kornilov and soon moved to Moscow. Once there, he initially had difficulty in finding lodgings and for a while slept on a camp bed in the basement of the Experimental Psychology Institute. This also housed the Institute's archives. Although not everyone's bedtime reading, in a short time he had read most of them.

In 1924 he also married Rosa Smekhova. Their marriage was by all accounts a happy one and Rosa is reported to have helped him to endure the stresses of the political pressures he was to face in the ensuing years (Vygodskaya & Lifanova, 1996). Although Vygotsky's habit of working an 18-hour day was the sort of thing that would nowadays be considered a recipe for disaster in marriage, she shared his ideals and was apparently willing to tolerate the sacrifice of his lack of attention in the cause. They had two children, one of whom, Gita Vygodskaya, became an educationalist and wrote an interesting biography of her father (Vygodskaya & Lifanova, 1996).

The fact that his daughter's name is Vygodskaya, and that of her father

Vygotsky, is not entirely due to the Russian feminine ending, which would produce Vygotskaya. In the early 1920s, before he became a well-known writer, Vygotsky changed his name from Vygodsky, his family name, to Vygotsky. It is possible that he did this to make his name sound less Jewish. It is perhaps not too fanciful to see in this a precursor of Vygotsky's lifelong tendency to alter words, if it would please people. In his writings, it is sometimes noticeable that he adopts the jargon favoured by currently fashionable theories, rather than terminology that would seem more natural.

The picture that Vygotsky's daughter draws of her father in the family is one of an almost perfect father, who could solve the problems of fatherhood with the same extraordinary facility and calm that he solved the problems of diagnosing children with difficulties and plumbed the theoretical problems of Marxist psychology. This may be to some extent the perception of a devoted daughter, but some of the other glimpses we have of Vygotsky the man tend in the same direction.

However, Galperin, who knew Vygotsky in the early 1930s, has given us a different picture (Haenen, 1996). This is of a man who was forever struggling to avoid a descent into insanity and whose abnormally calm and distanced external demeanour masked the struggles within. It is possible to relate this to the picture that Storr (1972) has drawn of a certain type of creative theorist who has an underlying uncertainty about the existence of the world, which is schizoid in nature. Their compulsive interest in theories about the world and its inhabitants stems from a desire to gain intellectual reassurance that the world exists to counterbalance their underlying intuitive uncertainty. Einstein is supposed to have been an example of this; and from Galperin's description, Vygotsky may have been another. The widespread view that Vygotsky was an unusually stable character may have come from the tendency for those who knew him to feel they had to conform to the image of Vygotsky the saint that grew up around him. It is hard to see why Galperin would invent his version, especially as his own views owed so much to Vygotsky and he shows no sign of personal animosity towards him.

However, if Vygotsky was defending against some inner fear, his willpower and capacity for distancing were equal to the task, as he survived almost incredible pressures in the next decade, while continuing to produce material that showed little of the strains he was under until the last months of his life.

In 1925 Vygotsky completed his doctoral thesis at the University of Moscow, entitled *The psychology of art* (1925a), and submitted it for examination. He was too sick to offer the normal oral defence of the thesis, which was waived. The thesis was not published for many years. When it was finally published in book form, in 1968, it created something of a sensation, went through a number of editions and was translated into many languages. One reason for this is that, of his book-length publications, it is the most readable, although the content is also undeniably significant.

There has been speculation as to why Vygotsky did not publish this book during his lifetime. One theory has been that he outgrew the ideas it advanced

(Joravsky, 1989). Another was that the years 1925–30 were a time of acute paper shortage, as of everything else (Joravsky, 1989). The Soviet economy was ravaged by war and civil war in the years 1914–21, then racked by the economic crises of 1923–25 and 1929–31. During the second economic crisis there was mass starvation. However, both these points need to seen within the context that Vygotsky published the substantial book *Pedagogical psychology* in 1926, which had been written several years previously and adopted a reflexological point of view, a viewpoint far more remote from his concerns in the mid-1920s than *The psychology of art*. Probably it was a combination of the difficulty in finding a publisher for a non-textbook, in the prevailing conditions, and that *The psychology of art* was no longer on Vygotsky's main line of march. From 1928 this was to be the perfection of his general theory of development and its practical implications.

In 1925 Vygotsky also began to organise the Laboratory of Psychology for Abnormal Childhood in Moscow, attached to the Institute of Psychology. This passed through a change of name and sponsor in 1929, but Vygotsky remained involved until his death. After Vygotsky recovered from his illness in 1925, he threw himself into an astounding decade of Herculean work and growing fame. In most years, he published over a dozen articles, sometimes many more, and usually one or more books as well. Soon after he arrived at the Institute, he was joined by Alexander Luria and Alexei N. Leont'ev, who to begin with were his loyal lieutenants and with Vygotsky made up the 'troika' of the Vygotsky school, as it now became. He became a celebrated lecturer, whose lectures attracted overflowing audiences. As already mentioned, he also expanded his interests to include what is now called 'abnormal' or 'clinical' psychology, but was then generally termed 'defectology' in the Soviet Union. He proved to have an unusual gift for the diagnosis of clinical cases and those with an interest would often come to Moscow to see him make diagnoses. When Vygotsky went on a trip, his students were so enthusiastic that some even wrote poems in honour of his travels.

In dealing with this period of his life, a certain misconception can creep in. This is that, as a number of Vygotsky interpreters have said or implied, Soviet Russia in the 1920s was a kind of cultural playground, in which intellectuals and artists could do their own thing, before the clampdown that Stalin instituted in 1929 (e.g. Daniels, 1993; Wertsch, 1985). Were this the case, some of Vygotsky's poses would seem capricious and even born of a personal desire to play with perspectives on his work.

The truth is, however, quite different. Soviet Russia in the 1920s was a safer place to say things that could be construed as unorthodox than Russia in, say, the 1930s; but it was still a dangerous place, in which saying or writing the wrong thing could earn dismissal from a post or exile. The decisive internal political struggle of the early 1920s was within the Central Committee of the Communist Party. This committee, at least nominally, controlled the party as a whole. It was between the majority and the Left Opposition and took place in 1923–24 (Carr, 1954; Oxley, 2001). One of the issues between them was whether there could be minority factions within the Communist Party. A minority faction was defined as a distinct grouping, with distinct policies that did not coincide with those of the majority. The idea that there could be such factions was defeated by the majority, ably generalled by Stalin, who argued that factions led to splits. There should be only one party line, which all party members should abide by.

So, by 1924, the policy of a unified party line on political matters was reinforced. To back this up there were salutary expulsions of staff from the party newspaper *Pravda* and other institutions of those who had published material contrary to the party line. This was accompanied by the beginning of the application of Stalin's trademark tactics. These included smears against fellow party members, especially bringing against them past political affiliations, e.g. using the fact that Trotsky had been a Menshevik (i.e. a member of a socialist party opposed to the Bolsheviks); using the power of the central party apparatus to appoint party branch secretaries, thus making sure that the secretaries sent the right kind of delegates to conferences, especially those of the Central Committee; and the abuse of the Lenin levy. This last was a special wave of entry to the party in 1924, supposedly to commemorate Lenin's death in 1923. In fact, the accompanying purge of the party was used to disproportionately purge oppositionists and the levy took in mainly the young and uneducated, who were most likely to prove amenable to 'education'.

To fill out this picture, and to show the extent to which desperation ruled on all sides, it is worth mentioning Trotsky's tactics, prior to his joining and on behalf of the Left Opposition, in the struggle of 1923. These were in some ways almost as bad as those of the Stalinists. His paper on the party situation of 1923, which was instrumental in precipitating the crisis, was a call for youth to overthrow the now worn out and conservative old guard and take control with radical new policies. This was said to be necessary due to the situation in Russia at the time: The civil war was only recently over; the economy lay in ruins; starvation was rife; further foreign intervention threatened.

Whatever Trotsky's actual motives for this intervention, as far as the majority was concerned his combination of naivety and guile beggared belief. To think that the inexperience of youth would lead them out of the crisis, rather than into an even worse one, was incredible. To think that Trotsky lacked the ulterior motive of wishing to lead this new party of teenage communists by the nose was impossible. To imagine that the majority of the party, older and more experienced, should be put aside in favour of inexperienced youth, who lacked the years of painful struggle many had undergone, was more than either incredible or impossible: It deserved vigorous rejection.

After 1923 the party progressively increased its grip on areas of intellectual life that had thus far remained outside its influence. This was of direct concern for Vygotsky, who, although he became a Marxist shortly after the revolution of 1917, remained for his entire life outside the Communist Party. The probable reason for this was that, like a number of other notable Soviet Marxist intellectuals, he wanted both to retain a degree of independence and to remain clear of the heavy weight of political work that fell on the party member. The intellectual of this kind who most resembled Vygotsky, both in status and outlook, was A. Deborin, an influential Soviet philosopher, who edited the party's chief theoretical organ, *Under the banner of Marxism*, from 1925 to 1930. He was also, like Vygotsky, preoccupied with the connection between Hegel and Marx (Deborin, 1909, 1923, 1929). Both men had their wings seriously clipped in the repression of 1930, although both found that by minor adaptation and, in the case of Deborin, public self-criticism, they escaped the worst effects of the repression. The difference between them was that, while suppression of some of Deborin's minor writings occurred in 1930, this was the extent of his suppression. The suppression of Vygotsky began later in 1935–36, but this included his major published work *Thinking and speech* (1934c) and prevented the publication of his many other unpublished late writings, most notably the articles eventually collected in *Problems of child development* (Vygotsky, 1960).

The first significant organisation to feel the grip of the party was Protekult, which was a state-funded organisation for the promotion of proletarian education and culture. Two of the leading Soviet intellectuals of the time, Bogdanov and Lunacharsky, were in the leadership of Protekult in the early 1920s. They were noted for their heterodox views, advocating a version of futurism in which the socialist future would involve a radical break with the culture and education of the past (Sochor, 1988). This was at variance with the views of orthodox Marxists such as Lenin (1921) and Trotsky (1924), who thought socialist culture should build on the progressive features of the past, not discard them. The organisation was already under heavy attack by the party leaders by 1925, for deviations from the party line, and in that year was substantially reduced, but allowed to continue in rump form until the early 1930s (Carr & Davies, 1969–78, Vol. 1). So, in the interval 1925–28 the sword of Damocles hanging over the educational and cultural system was clearly visible. It was also visibly descending.

It was not only those who opposed Stalin from the left who were frightened by the time the year 1925 arrived. Zinoviev had been Lenin's personal secretary and one of the highest profile leaders of the 1917 revolution. From 1923 to 1927 he was head of the Communist International. Kamenev was a long-standing member of the Central Committee and Politburo and a key figure in the party.

But by 1925 both Zinoviev and Kamenev, who were not Left Oppositionists, announced themselves heartily fed up with suppressing their real opinions (Serge, 1968, p. 154). By the start of 1927 Zinoviev and his followers only remained within the party by recanting their real views, so as to be ready to seize back control from the Stalinists when the inevitable crisis to which current policies were leading took place (Serge, 1968, p. 154; Trotsky, 1934). But this was to little avail, as, by the end of 1927, he had been expelled from the party. Kamenev stayed on in much the same spirit during 1927, only to be expelled in the following year. Both men were allowed back into the party in 1929, following greater efforts to give lip service to Stalin and his policies, only to be expelled again in 1932, when they could hold their peace no more.

By 1928 things had gone so far that Trotsky and a number of other prominent party members had been exiled. In the same year a group of Vygotsky's followers, centred on A. N. Leont'ev, began moving from Moscow and the Institute of Psychology to Kharkhov in Ukraine, reasoning that they would be safer there than in the capital, where ideological sensitivities and deviations from the party line were likely to be more keenly felt and more severely dealt with (Joravsky, 1989). At the same time, Vygotsky's other chief lieutenant, Luria, took the extraordinary step of leaving his psychological research with Vygotsky in Moscow to enrol in a medical degree, apparently on the theory that medicine offered fewer ideological sensitivities than psychology (Graham, 1993). This was extraordinary, as Luria had already shown himself to be among the most promising of the younger generation of Soviet psychologists. He later back-pedalled from this extreme action by leading expeditions, planned by Vygotsky, to undertake psychological research in Soviet Central Asia in 1930–31 (Cole, 1996). These also, however, removed him from the eye of the storm.

These actions show the considerable fear that by 1928 already gripped those who might be in the firing line, although Vygotsky remained calmer and stayed on at the Institute of Psychology in Moscow. These events, ironically, took place at about the same time as the publication of Vygotsky (1928h), in which he announces his first version of his own theory of psychological development, inaugurating what I will call the third period of his development (1928–31). From this time until his final period, in which he revamped the earlier theory (1932–34), he continued working in Moscow, in the epicentre of a repression that assumed its full force in 1930.

In 1929 Stalin moved to decisively gain control of the Communist Party, by further purging the old guard and bringing in naive outsiders. He set 1930 as the year he would, among other things, take decisive ideological control of publications and cultural institutions that belonged to the state but that up to that time had not been fully controlled by it. Prior to that date, they had been under the immediate control of a mixture of party members and nonparty Marxists, such as Vygotsky and Deborin. As long as they stayed clear of controversy on current political issues, avoided banned opinions and advanced only theory of a reasonably orthodox kind, the nonparty Marxists were seen to be fulfilling a useful function. But for Stalin this was finally not enough. The nonaligned Marxists who studied, say, palaeontology or zoology comprised a dangerous reservoir of potential oppositionists. They could be Zinovievists or Trotskyites. They could also be wasting public funds on work with no immediate practical utility. So now there was, at least in theory, a party line in palaeontology, zoology and psychology.

This was thought to be useful in two ways. Anyone who refused to swallow the party line in their discipline was obviously unreliable and so should be expelled from their position; unless they were important, in which case some more thoroughgoing solution, such as exile, should be sought. Further, it made theories at least apparently useful and thus of benefit to the nation.

Although this was the implied doctrine, it was applied quite capriciously. There was no actual party line in psychology until the theories of Pavlov were declared such from 1949–54 (Joravsky, 1961, 1989). As far as psychology was concerned, it was left to opportunist groups of, usually, young psychologists, to set their sights on the alleged failings of one or more established workers and tear them down. So the party line only existed as a negative doctrine of what was not Marxist. Even this was not written down and could be expanded and contracted by enterprising groups hoping to profit from the downfall of others.

Although Vygotsky was under investigation from 1930, the investigation was painfully slow and had not been completed at the time of his death. In addition, his minder at the Institute of Psychology, whom he was given in 1930 when the Institute was investigated, V. N. Kolbanoskii, soon realised he was in the presence of genius and changed sides, in large measure accounting for Vygotsky's relatively charmed life from 1930 to 1934.

The years 1927–31 saw the publication in serialised parts of two books by Vygotsky, designed for use as a correspondence course: *Pedology of the school age* (1928g) and *Pedology of the adolescent* (1931a). The second of these contains much valuable material on the theory he developed in the period 1928–31. After 1928, it soon became clear that the movement of the group led by A. N. Leont'ev to Karkhov involved a theoretical split with Vygotsky's approach, as well as just a retreat to the safety of the provinces, with most of those going siding with A. N. Leont'ev. One notable exception was Lydia Bozhovich, who was to rank among the most important Soviet researchers in the Vygotskyan tradition. In response, Vygotsky wrote one of his most important texts: *History of the development of higher mental functions* (1931b). We can see the gulf opening between Vygotsky and A. N. Leont'ev by comparing their comments on an experiment by A. N. Leont'ev (1931) on the mediation of attention. Leont'ev (1931) considers the mediating aids given to the children to assist attention in the experiment (coloured cards) to be nonlanguage like, which is the obvious stance; but Vygotsky (1931b, 1931g) describes them as language like, which is in accord with his own theory. In his work, A. N. Leont'ev was to stress learning from direct practical experience, while Vygotsky continued to stress the influence of signs.

Vygotsky's (1931b) book more or less fully defined his position at the time on the matters dealt with. Two of his most important previous books had gone unpublished, namely *The psychology of art* (1926c) and *The historical meaning of the crisis in psychology* (1927c). Like these, his programmatic statement of 1931 went long unpublished, first appearing in radically abridged form in 1960 and in its full form in 1984. It appears that the main reason Vygotsky declined to publish it was that he believed it would be used to prove his ideological heterodoxy and thus to suppress his present and future work entirely (Joravsky, 1989).

In the years from 1928 to his death in 1934, Vygotsky was also under pressure from criticisms by his colleagues that his approach was nonMarxist. These were different from the kinds of criticism that young opportunists aimed at other psychologists (such as Kornilov), in that they were more measured and reasoned. In addition to A. N. Leont'ev, the most significant of the other critics was Sergei Rubinshtein (1934, 1935; Payne, 1968). After the Second World War, Leont'ev and Rubinshtein were to vie for control of Soviet psychology, gaining and losing it alternately.

A. N. Leont'ev and Rubinshtein agreed that Vygotsky put too much emphasis on language in the development of the child (A. N. Leont'ev, 1931, 1948; Rubinshtein, 1934, 1935, 1946, 1959). They thought that a Marxist psychology would stress the direct psychological effect of the use of tools in practice. They found this view in Marx's pronouncements on the subject (Marx, 1846a, 1859, Preface, 1867, Ch. 7, 1872, Afterword). Although Vygotsky agreed that tools are a significant element in development, they objected to his idea that throughout much of development dynamic psychological influence is exerted downwards from language and signs to practice.

Although Vygotsky had opposed Marx on this subject in the years before 1929, in that year there was a determination to bring intellectuals into line with party thinking. On many issues this thinking was less Marxist than Vygotsky. However, Vygotsky had chosen to amend Marx on a point where the politics of the hour decreed Marx had been right. The main reason was probably that in 1929–33 Stalin pursued an ultra-left political rhetoric and policy that glorified manual labour and decried the work of the mental worker. In the hysterical atmosphere that prevailed, theories like those of Rubinshtein and A. N. Leont'ev that praised manual labour and direct physical practice were more likely to be smiled on than one like Vygotsky's that praised words.

Vygotsky's leadership at the Psychological Institute in the 1920s was informal and Kornilov remained its titular head until 1930. It was no doubt for this reason that the main weight of repression in 1930 fell on Kornilov. It was his views rather than those of Vygotsky that were proscribed and he was removed from his post. However, although Vygotsky's minder, Kolbanoskii, soon developed an unanticipated attraction to Vygotsky's doctrines, this was not enough to prevent a gradual reduction in his activities there. Kolbanoskii, nonetheless, continued his support for Vygotsky beyond the grave by sponsoring the publication of one of his most important books, *Thinking and speech*, in 1934 (Joravsky, 1989). Without this rather selfless sponsorship, it is doubtful that this would have been published at all until the Khrushchev thaw of the 1950s.

Stalin's political and cultural policies in the period 1929–33 had lurched to the left, which had probably magnified distaste for Vygotsky's views, as Stalin's propaganda had involved the glorification of manual labour. There was a further change in the line in 1933, following the accession of Hitler to power in Germany. Stalin realised, too late, that this had been materially assisted by the previous ultra-left policy, under which the large German Communist Party had, on Soviet insistence, refused to form an alliance with the German Social Democrats against Hitler. After this, in 1934, Vygotsky was regarded with more favour and was even offered another job, but his health would not sustain him for much longer (Joravsky, 1989).

Between 1930 and 1934 Vygotsky remained based in Moscow, travelling extensively to give lectures, writing furiously, working 20-hour days, smoking as much as ever and increasingly disturbed at the falling away of his erstwhile disciples. He met two fellow geniuses: Kurt Lewin, the famous German psychologist, who was by that time a refugee from Hitler; and the Russian film director Sergei Eisenstein, often considered the greatest, certainly the most influential, of all film directors. Vygotsky had long animated discussions with Lewin, the traces of which can be found in his writings from the period. To Eisenstein we owe a two-sentence description of Vygotsky, which ends: 'From under this strange haircut peered the eyes of one of the most brilliant psychologists of our time, who saw the world with celestial clarity.'

Vygotsky died of tuberculosis on 11 June 1934 at a sanatorium in Moscow. His last words were 'It is enough', presumably meaning, among other things, that his life's work in psychology had turned out to be enough. Despite the grim atmosphere around him and despite the fact that only part of his final theoretical contribution had been published or had any imminent prospect of being so, he could still think this. This was an example of that calm self-confidence he so often displayed: One day his work would be made known and understood because of its significance. Whatever the truth of Galperin's claim that underneath his calm and distance Vygotsky maintained only a tenuous grip on sanity, here, as on many previous occasions, it was the calm that prevailed.

From 1930 to 1936 an investigation of his writings was carried out, with a view to suppression if necessary. Finally, in 1935 and 1936, they were declared heterodox and the book *Thinking and speech*, his most significant publication, suppressed. This did not mean, as is sometimes said, that he became an unperson whose name could not be mentioned (e.g. Joravsky, 1989). Paragraph-length asides about him were quite common in the Soviet psychological literature of the 1930s and 1940s (e.g. Leont'ev, 1948; Rubinshtein, 1935, 1946). But his books were withdrawn from library shelves and there could be no new publications or republications. In addition, it was expected that references to him would condemn at least some of what had been condemned in him, even though commentators were at liberty to say positive things about his work. Such comments were often of a kind that most other psychologists would have been flattered to receive, paying tribute to the foundational role of Vygotsky in Soviet psychology. However, they then usually go on to say how grossly mistaken he was on key issues and how far Soviet psychology had travelled beyond him.

The nature of two of the charges that were brought against Vygotsky, resulting in the suppression of his writings until 1954, are illuminating (Graham, 1993). First, in 1935, it was decided that Vygotsky had defied party policy towards the peasantry by asserting their cultural level was lower than that of the cities. It seems strange that this policy, which began in the period 1929–33, should be so solicitous of the feelings of the peasantry, when that was a period when the peasants were being subjected to forced appropriation of their produce and forced collectivisation of their land, largely against their will. But political correctness in speech and writing is often, as in this case, accompanied by compulsion and worse in practice.

Second, in 1936 the Central Committee passed a decree banning 'pedology', because some of its practitioners asserted such things as that educational potential is limited by genetic potential (as Vygotsky did in Vygotsky, 1931d, 1931f, 1934e). Pedology was an international movement in the 1920s and 1930s that applied psychology to education.

The implication, in both cases, is that science should be replaced by politics and politics is not about the truth but about what it is politically expedient to say. In other words, Vygotsky was, in an all too real sense, a victim of political correctness.

That both the condemned propositions can be found in the works of Marx and Engels seems not to have deterred the inquisitors one whit. If we follow their line of reasoning, Marx's and Engels's *Communist manifesto* (1848) would have been suppressed, as it says that part of the progressive role of capitalism was to end 'rural idiocy'. Marx's *Critique of the Gotha programme* (1875) would have been dealt with likewise, as in Part 1, Section 3, it clearly says that people are mentally unequal due to natural inheritance. This provides an illustration of how far from orthodox Marxism and the writings of Marx the Soviet regime had progressed by the 1930s.

After the death of Stalin, in 1953, Vygotsky was no longer a banned author. However, this only led immediately to the republication of a relatively small selection of his works in 1956 and 1960, although this did include four of the most significant of the late works. *Thinking and speech* was republished as part of a 1956 volume called *Collected psychological studies*, which also included 'The problem of mental retardation' (1935e); the collection of articles *Problems of child development* appeared in 1960, with the collection *Mental development of children in the process of teaching* included in the same volume. This was followed by *The psychology of art* in 1968 and a number of papers in edited collections and journals. It was not, however, until the *Collected works* in Russian in 1982–84 that the full scope of his writings became apparent, even to the Russian public. It had been apparent somewhat earlier to the leading Soviet commentators, when the *Collected works* were begun around 1972, as most of them were on the editorial board or otherwise connected with the publication. Some, like D. B. Elkonin and L. Bozhovich, had accessed them even earlier (Bozhovich, 1968; Elkonin, 1971).

The publication of the *Collected works* and of the other works published before 1982–84 put most of Vygotsky's essential writings in the public domain in Russian. However, some remained either unpublished or buried in obscure periodicals. One was the article 'The socialist transformation of man', first republished from a now obscure journal, in an English translation, in *The Vygotsky reader* (1994). A further collection of late writings, *Lectures on pedology*, comprising articles from 1932–34 and a series of lectures given in 1934 did not appear in Russian until 2001.

The publication of Vygotsky in other languages has, in general, followed that in Russian, at a somewhat later date.

Early work: 1914–27

Vygotsky's work before 1928 is not covered in detail in the remainder of the book, as before that time there was no original general theory and it is that theory that most people are interested in and that seems most important. The Vygotsky who is portrayed in most writing about him is the Vygotsky of 1928–34, that is the last two periods of his life, and that is the subject of the remainder of this book. However, he went through a number of distinct phases in his thinking before this and produced at least two book-length works of lasting influence, *The psychology of art* (1925a) and *The historical meaning of the crisis in psychology* (1927c). So some orientation to his early work is desirable.

We have already seen that in his first period of work in psychology, 1918–20, he adopted the viewpoint of reflexology. Vygotsky's later intellectual path was away from this to ways of thinking that were more cognitive and traditional. We can place the start of his second period in 1921, when he was already working on his PhD thesis at Moscow University. It ended in 1927, the year before the announcement of the first version of the general theory.

One key idea of the period 1922–27 was that reflexology was too limiting and new psychological ideas were needed that could be discovered from the use of the Marxist method in empirical studies (Vygotsky, 1925a, 1927d). It was thus a result of the interaction between his increasing commitment to Marxism and his previous attachment to reflexology. In the monograph *The historical crisis of psychology* (1927d), probably written in 1926 or 1927, he takes the work he did in *The psychology of art* as one of his key examples of how the application of a new, Marxist, method to factual material will give psychology new content.

Vygotsky's stance at this time was that the only existing psychological theories or hypotheses that could be saved from the psychology of the past were those advanced by materialists (Vygotsky, 1925a, 1927c, 1927d). Part of this would be the concepts of reactology, that is Kornilov's theory, and part would be drawn from other materialist views, but the ideas of idealist philosophers and psychologists were declared off limits. This stance is, in fact, a peculiar one for an avowed Marxist like Vygotsky to hold, as it is contrary to Marx's own attitude. Marx and Engels believed that the full flowering of their outlook, including their psychology, would originate from, among other things, the process of turning Hegel into a materialist. This meant that it depended on using not just an idealist philosopher but one of the most idealist philosophers of modern times.

To begin with, Vygotsky ignored this contradiction, probably because some aspects of the Russian revolutionary tradition stressed a narrow materialism, rather than a more rounded interpretation of Marxist philosophy as a whole. A central contributor to this narrow tradition was, until the mid-1920s, often thought to be Lenin, who until then was mainly judged by his only major philosophical publication, *Materialism and empiriocriticism* (1909), which is a defence of philosophical materialism. In psychology the only developed theory that claimed to be Marxist was the reflexology of Bekhterev (1904, 1921, 1926a, 1926b), a kind of mechanical materialism.

Marxists, since Marx, have distinguished between mechanical and dialectical materialism (Marx, 1872, Afterword). Up until 1928 Vygotsky remained under the influence of the mechanical materialism found in reflexology. Materialism is the belief that the world and human beings themselves consist of one substance, matter, whose properties can be known. Mechanical materialism claims that the properties of matter are similar to those studied in the science of mechanics. One key quality of these is that there is no development. A system of mechanical bodies remains moving under the same mechanical laws that existed at the start of time and will exist at the end of time. The laws of motion and the way forces interact always remain the same. Dialectical materialism, which is Marx's philosophical view, by contrast, says that a system of matter in motion may, as a result of the conflict between tendencies within itself, develop new laws that were not there at the start. The main point of this distinction is to say that society is not like mechanics, always subject to the same laws. It is like the dialectical model and develops new laws. Marxists regard the attempts of thinkers, such as Hobbes, James Mill and many economists, to deal with society on the model of mechanics, as ideological, as they suggest that fundamentally society has always been and always will be the same. It is a contention of Marxism that over the centuries society has altered fundamentally.

Up until 1927 the combination of Lenin's militant materialism and the elements of mechanical materialism in the Russian revolutionary tradition retained considerable hold on Vygotsky. However, the year 1925 saw the publication of parts of a previously unpublished work by Lenin, his *Philosophical notebooks* (1925). This was published in the party's theoretical journal, *Under the banner of Marxism*, at the instigation of Deborin, its editor, and created something of a sensation, as it showed Lenin as not just a materialist, but a dialectical materialist, with a deep interest in Hegel. Hegel had, before Marx, elaborated many of the features of dialectical thinking. Lenin's notebooks are quoted or cited many times in Vygotsky's writings (especially in his key works, Vygotsky, 1931b, 1934c, 1935e). One theme Lenin dilates on is that one cannot understand Marx correctly without an understanding of Hegel, because without that there is the probability of a mechanical materialist reading of Marx. To drive this home, he even says that Plekhanov, often called the father of Russian Marxism, and well known for his advocacy of Hegel, leaned to mechanical rather than dialectical materialism (Plekhanov, 1895, 1897, 1922a, 1922b, 1922c).

As if this were not enough to convey his message, Lenin also says that Hegel was closer to Marx than the Marxists who were mechanical materialists, because 'intelligent idealism is closer to Marxism than stupid materialism' (Lenin, 1925). Hegel had been an idealist who thought the world is composed of ideas; this contrasted with Marx's view that the world is made of matter. However, Hegel's manner of thinking, embodied in his dialectics, brought him close to Marx, who used the same manner of thinking. Taken literally, Lenin's comment is wrong, since intelligent idealism and stupid materialism, from his perspective, both have one main point wrong; but its intent is to shock, and to turn attention towards the importance of dialectics, through the paradoxical nature of what it says.

Marxists, who were stupid, that is mechanical, materialists, did not think entirely in terms of mechanical concepts but they did so in some parts of their thinking. The key example Lenin has in mind is their idea that society will gradually get more and more socialistic, until a certain mark is reached and then socialism has arrived. This is like the mechanical processes of rolling a ball down an inclined plane or filling a glass with water until it is full. This left them unprepared for the sudden lurch to reaction in the First World War, when the working class widely supported the war, followed by the sudden lurch to socialist revolution in Russia after the war. Such sudden jumps in development are typical of dialectical, but not of mechanical, processes.

Two other newly available manuscripts that may also have alerted Vygotsky to his mistake were those of Marx: *The German ideology* (1846a) and *Economic and philosophical manuscripts of 1844* (1844). Although not published until 1932 and 1938, respectively, these were widely circulated among the Moscow intelligentsia in the late 1920s by Ryazanov, who had obtained them in Germany (Carr & Davies, 1969–78, Vol. 2). Vygotsky cites the former frequently, (especially in Vygotsky, 1930h). Both show the Hegelian roots of Marx's doctrines more clearly than Marx's later writings, especially the latter (Colletti, 1969, 1974, 1992; Tucker, 1974).

For these and other reasons, 1928 began a radical change in Vygotsky's programme, marking the start of the third period of his work. Now the new psychology was to come in large part from the works of Marx, Hegel and a number of other writers from the Marxist tradition, regardless of whether they were materialist or idealist. This was to be checked and amended by applications of the empirical method that Marx adapted from Hegel (Marx, 1872, Afterword). The use made of Hegel was an important part of this programme. The way in which he was to be used stemmed from the slogan that Marxism is Hegel turned on his head or, rather, on his feet. This well-known slogan appears several times in the writings of Marx and Engels

(Engels, 1878, Ch. 1, 1886; Marx, 1872, Afterword). It means that much of the content of Hegel's idealist doctrine is true but it needs to be transformed from idealism to materialism. For instance, instead of saying that history is governed by the evolution of ideas, we should say it is controlled by the evolution of the productive forces. But once we have done that, we find that the evolution of ideas, as driven by that of the productive forces, is very similar to the evolution of ideas according to Hegel.

This slogan of Marx and Engels is, of course, flagrantly at variance with the programme pursued by Vygotsky in his second period from 1921 to 1927, which banned the recycling of idealist concepts transformed into a materialist format. Now he began to embrace it, as usual with startling rapidity.

Although Vygotsky vacillates in what he says about his new programme, this was its overall thrust, if we attend to what he *did* rather than what he *said* from 1928 to 1934. The greatest alteration to it came in 1933, when he changed a number of key ideas. This project is the topic of the remainder of the book.

Conclusions

Vygotsky was both unusually gifted and also, probably as a result, possessed a calm, although possibly also brittle, self-confidence. Throughout the 1920s and early 1930s, whatever the uncertainties beneath the surface, he developed his ideas with a quiet persistence, despite the huge upheavals in Soviet society, as well as increasing resistance, although he was hurt by defections from his cause by a number of erstwhile friends and colleagues. The underlying reason for much of the resistance was that he held that signs and self-consciousness dominate the psychological aspects of gaining knowledge, during much of development, as opposed to tools. This was contrary to the ideas of Marx.

His early ideas went through three periods: From 1914 to 1917 his interests were primarily literary and philosophical. In the first period of work in psychology, from 1918 to 1921, he adopted the viewpoint of reflexology, which claims that all human behaviour can be understood in terms of conditioned reflexes. In the second, from 1922 to 1927, he increasingly realised the inadequacies of this viewpoint and thought that a combination of the application of the Marxist method to new data and of adopting ideas from the materialist psychologies of the past would enable a new Marxist psychology to emerge.

By 1928 he realised the contradictory nature of this approach and adopted a revised strategy. The cornerstone of this was the idea, taken from Marx, that the historical development of human capacities occurred as part of the development of production. It also involved heavy reliance on ideas taken from idealist philosophers, especially Hegel, recycled in a materialist form.

3 Biological and historical development, 1928–31

According to Vygotsky, in this period of his work, the development of the human species consisted of two parts: biological development, to produce the original human biological type through biological evolution, and cultural development, to transform early tribal society into modern industrial societies.

Vygotsky argues that biological development was over by the time human social evolution began (Vygotsky, 1930k, 1930n, 1931b, Chs 1–3). This can be challenged on the basis that there was probably an evolution of social characteristics between, say, *homo habilis* (one of our predecessors lying between ape and *homo sapiens*) and the present. Because of the definition of social evolution used, this is denied the name social evolution. However, even if biological and social evolution overlapped, as implied by Engels (1896), this is not a fundamental problem for Vygotsky, whose main point is that biological evolution stopped long ago and that the enormous social evolution since tribalism has occurred since the end of biological evolution, which is largely uncontroversial.

Outline of the underlying model

The states through which the individual's social system can pass are determined by three overall dimensions. These provide a map of the places that the individual can go in development. The first is the levels of activity: use of tools and practice; the social relations of work; signs, including language, and consciousness; and self-consciousness. The first two of these lack consciousness of their own; as we move from these to the last, consciousness increases. The next dimension is the kind of motivation the individual has; the third is the relation between inner and outer aspects of the personality, especially the self. The primary dimensions of developmental advance are the first two.

Each of the levels of activity contains four steps, ranging from least to most advanced. Tools and practice, for instance, develop from the use of tools based on the human body, designed by intuitive estimation, to the construction of machines using abstract scientific concepts, with two steps in between. Motivation advances along five steps, with an extra step in infancy, compared to the levels, which have then not yet formed. It goes through two steps where the goals of the individual are largely biological, then through two steps where they are determined by what other people think and on to a final state where they are generated by a synthesis of the biological and the social. The inner and outer pass through only two steps, as the distinction does not appear until midway through development.

In order to pass through the places specified by this map of development we need developmental dynamics, which specifies the motive forces that drive the individual and their social system forwards (or, in some cases, backwards). Unlike some developmental theorists, Vygotsky does not offer a picture where everything involved in development pushes it forward. Rather, at particular points he pictures some activities and functions as being dynamic and driving the system forward, while others are sluggish and lack forward dynamism. If the latter are to move forward, they need to be pushed along by the former. Furthermore, the dynamic activities and functions are not always the same ones throughout development; although a function may be dynamic at one point, at another it can become sluggish and lacking in dynamism.

In this period, his dynamic model stresses long-term shifts of emphasis along the first dimension, that is the levels. To begin with, during biological development and tribalism, development is driven forward by practice. After this initial period, signs and self-consciousness take over as the dynamic forces in development (Vygotsky, 1930k, 1931b, pp. 23, 62–63). The word 'signs', here, has the broad meaning of anything that can communicate meaning, such as gestures, speech or writing. Finally, towards the end of the period of development he focuses on, in modern capitalism, practice and signs are synthesised in advanced concepts, overcoming the divorce between language and practice (Vygotsky, 1931a, Ch. 3). Now such concepts provide the dynamic impetus for development.

It is a distinctive feature of Vygotsky's theory that signs provide the main dynamism for the historical development of production in its middle period, roughly between tribalism and capitalism. This distinguishes him in particular from Marx, who changed his emphasis, but at no stage advocated a stress on signs. He believed in his later period that top-down influences from consciousness emerge directly from the practice of production, with language only becoming a significant dynamic force in the final period, roughly coinciding with the rise of capitalism, when production came to be based on science (Engels, 1878, Part 2; Marx, 1867, Chs 7, 15). This was the starting point for the view of Vygotsky's rival, A. N. Leont'ev (1948, 1960, 1974).

Marx even says in *The German ideology* (1846a, Part 1) that: 'Consciousness can never be anything other than conscious existence, and the existence of men is their actual life-process.' Taken literally this means that human consciousness can never be in advance of human action, which is absurd. Marx's intention is clearly to counter the views of the Left Hegelians, against whom this book is directed, and who maintained that consciousness was by far the most dynamic factor in history. Marx's statement is overkill, but it is symptomatic of his general desire to adopt an ultra-materialist stance on the topic.

Vygotsky's main arguments in favour of his stance are considered in more detail in the next chapter. In brief, he argued that if the historical development of human capacities is not based on biological evolution, it must be based on cultural evolution (Vygotsky, 1930k, 1931b, Ch. 3). Further, even early in historical development the culture of production needed cognitive sophistication and this could only develop and be passed on through the transfer of meaning by signs.

Turning to the dynamics of motivation, progress along the levels and in motivation are linked. After the close of biological development, the first point in a cycle of development is a new form of social relations (Vygotsky, 1931b, Ch. 3). This results in changes in motivation, which lead to changes in signs, self-consciousness and practice (Vygotsky, 1931a, Ch. 1). This is because the individual needs to achieve motivational distance from situations in order to move along the levels, such as the improvements in tools and practice just mentioned. An animal usually reacts to what is around it without thinking and this prevents it from reflecting on what it experiences. To build machines by using scientific concepts we need to be able to delay gratification. The machine's designer, to reap the rewards of its operation, must be able to delay his reward from the project for a long period.

Peculiarities of species development

Each of the steps forward in the levels corresponds to its opposite number on the other levels and in motivation. Motivation has its first step early in development, before the levels are formed, during biological evolution. If we are at step 1 in tools, at the start of historical development, then this has a natural fit with being at step 1 in social relations, signs, and self-consciousness, and step 2 in motivation. Step 2 in the levels corresponds to step 3 in motivation, and so on.

In the development of the child, according to Vygotsky, there is a tendency for the levels and motivation to move forward in a lockstep manner. The levels start at step 1, motivation is at step 2; then the levels move to step 2, motivation to step 3, and so on. We know that for Marx (1859) and Vygotsky (1930h) there are seven stages of historical development or modes of production: tribal, state slavery, private slavery, feudal, capitalist, socialist, communist. By lockstep progress through the steps in motivation and the levels, after infancy, we get only four periods. However, Vygotsky (1931a, Ch. 6) mentions two more periods of individual development: youth (said in Vygotsky, 1933i, to be 17–25) and maturity (some period after 25 years). This could imply two more steps along each level. He may, possibly, even have intended one more. So, after biological beginnings, we can count seven historical periods and at least seven periods in child development.

However, this does not dispose of the problem, particularly because progress in history was irregular. For instance, there was a jump from all levels being at 1 to all levels being at 3 during the shift from tribalism to state slavery, at least for part of the population. By contrast, Marx thought that between classical, private slavery and the feudal system the level of co-operation in work fell back considerably, almost to 1 again, because the land was tilled by individual families of serfs and the town guilds revived handicraft methods of producing things. One reason for this was that it helped overcome the economic disorder that followed the end of the Roman Empire (Marx, 1846a, 1867, Ch. 13). Large-scale enterprises with a complicated division of labour are easily disrupted by war and plunder, especially if they involve the organisation of transport. Individuals working for themselves and either consuming their own products or selling onto a local market are less easily disrupted.

This is close to saying that, under feudalism, development along all the levels and in motivation went back to the level of tribalism. However, neither Marx nor Vygotsky said that the whole mode of production went back to tribalism, as this would have made feudalism just a reversion to tribalism, while they clearly regarded it as something separate.

What Marx seems to have had in mind here is that there were aspects of the development of production lying outside the areas we have so far been considering and that Vygotsky concentrated on. It was these that made forms of production, that otherwise seemed similar, different. The most obvious of these was the ownership of production. Although the level of cooperation in work under feudalism often fell back to that involved in tribalism, the ownership of the means of production was different, as they were now jointly owned under feudal relations of ownership, rather than by the collective ownership of a tribe. This, in turn, paved the way for the individualistic ownership found under capitalism.

Vygotsky seems to have thought that there were certain aspects of the historical development of production, as viewed by Marx, that dropped out in the development of the individual child; the most significant of which was these legal relations between owners, workers and the means of production. These are what Marx calls the relations of production and are supposed to rest on the more fundamental relations of work or cooperation in production, although they are not the same.

Vygotsky's decision to slough off the legal relations of production in dealing with the child has two obvious bases: The modern child's legal relations do not resemble the historical relations of production; for Marx the legal relations are less fundamental than the relations of work.

Biological development

Vygotsky (1930n, 1931b) took over his view of the stages in biological development from Karl Buhler (1913, 1918). Although Buhler was not the first to suggest this sequence, he had provided an authoritative collation of material on the topic to which Vygotsky could turn. According to this, there were three such stages:

- instinct
- associative learning
- thought

Before associative learning arose, animals were dominated by instinct, conceived as a tendency to react in an automatic and innate manner to specific stimuli. A sea anemone, for instance, will close up if pricked or otherwise irritated. This helps to protect its most delicate features, which are its tentacles.

In the next stage, conditioning is possible. Here we find that the stimulus and the response are not inherently linked but must be brought together. For instance, Pavlov's (1897) dogs regularly heard a bell before feeding. When the food was in their mouths they instinctively salivated, but as time went by they also salivated to the sound of the bell. So the bell was originally separated from the response of salivation but now, through a process that is highly adaptive from a biological point of view, the two are brought together. Yet there is still no deliberate goal-seeking motivation in this process, as the salivation is not a goal that is sought but, from a psychological point of view, just happens through passive associations.

Natural, biological thought, which constitutes the third stage, was believed to be the particular domain of the apes, studied with such charming insight by Kohler (1917), in studies Vygotsky is always keen to rehearse. However, thought is also found lower in the animal kingdom in animals such as the dog and the rat; although for Vygotsky, in them it is subordinate to conditioned reflexes.

Although Vygotsky does not trouble much about which animals can achieve what, he seems to have followed contemporary opinion in placing the beginning of conditioned reflexes (the predominant form of associative learning) in lower mammals and he concurs with Pavlov that dogs are the perfect example of an animal dominated by conditioned reflexes (Vygotsky, 1931b, Ch. 3). Here he had Pavlov's experiments with dogs in mind, but he would no doubt have had much the same opinion of that other staple of later studies on conditioning, rats: the natural foe and equal of the dog.

This picture of the capacities of animals is somewhat dated, in that conditioning has by now long been convincingly demonstrated in simpler animals such as fish, hydra and several unicellular organisms (D. A. Lieberman, 1993). In addition, there is a tendency to attribute somewhat more capacity for thought to dogs, rats and even certain insects, such as hunting wasps and jumping spiders, than Vygotsky implies (e.g. Greenberg & Haraway, 2002; Hinde; 1966 Thorpe, 1956). Yet here, he would no doubt have commented that the fact that such animals can show thought does not show they are dominated by it.

These facts are not threatening to the theory, as the theory is about the order in which the capacities appear in a particular branch of evolution, not which animals can do what. Facts might disconfirm this theory, if it could be shown that an animal could evolve to a higher stage, without its ancestors having first been at the necessary lower stages. There is still no evidence for this.

During the three biological stages, cognition and motivation become progressively separated. In instinct, a stimulus pattern innately produces a response pattern, as when some species of young birds instinctively open their mouths, at the sight of the shape and colour of the parents' beaks or the human infant instinctively turns its mouth towards anything that brushes its cheek (the rooting reflex). Here the stimulus produces the response, without the need for either thought or motivation. The reaction is a complete pattern that encompasses both action and the setting of a goal, both of which are built into the reaction. Cognition and motivation are scarcely separated at all. If there is a separate role for motivation, it is to encourage or discourage the instinctive reaction as a whole. Cognition and motivation remain closely tied in associative learning. Finally, in natural thought we find that the stimulus is more clearly separated from response and cognition from motivation. In one of Kohler's (1917) experiments with apes, fruit is placed out of reach, outside their cage, and a stick is placed inside the cage. Their problem is to attain the fruit. The only workable solution is to pick up the stick and use it to drag in the fruit. To do this they must envisage the goal first and then consider what means could attain it. Thus there is motivation to reach a clearly envisaged goal, which has not occurred in earlier forms of behaviour.

The main driving force in development at the biological level is practical action, which is as yet unallied to language and only influenced by consciousness in a preliminary way (Vygotsky, 1930k, 1931b, pp. 28–30, 67–68).

Historical development

Vygotsky accepts Marx's claim that human capacities were developed historically, through the productive activity needed to produce those things, that human beings use and consume (Vygotsky, 1930h, 1930k, 1931b). For instance, production was originally carried out using mainly visual and other kinds of intuitive estimation to tell whether something was the right size, shape, weight and so forth. This meant that people needed the skills of visual and other, corresponding, forms of estimation, as a way of estimating amounts. To find out whether the handle of a tool would fit into its socket in the head, first of all the sizes of both would be estimated visually, then the fit would be assessed by trial and error. As production became more scientific, more precise methods of counting and measuring things were used for this purpose. The handle and the head would now be measured as they were made, to avoid work in adjusting them when they were put together. So people came to acquire these skills, as well as the concepts that go with them.

Map of historical development

Vygotsky also adopts Marx's analysis of the levels of activity involved in production, which we have already met: tool use; social relations used in work; consciousness and signs, including language; self-consciousness or consciousness of the self (Marx, 1846a, 1859, Appendix 2, 1867, Ch. 13).

In tribalism, we find the initial value of each of the four levels: tools modelled on the body using imagination; primitive cooperation; language operating with figurative and imaginative meanings; a self that has barely formed (Vygotsky, 1930k, 1931a, Ch. 6, 1931b). After this, each of the dimensions has three more steps to pass through, making four in all. However, to understand both Vygotsky and Marx, we must, as previously stressed, avoid thinking that at each stage in historical development, all dimensions move up one place. Sometimes they go up by more than one step, sometimes they go down.

When Vygotsky discusses history, he does not say much about Marx's complex patterns of advance and retreat, along the dimensions representing productive activity, although he makes it clear he accepts them (Vygotsky, 1930h). He concentrates, instead, on when the values along the dimensions were first reached.

Tool use

The central feature of both Vygotsky's and Marx's view of the development of tools is that it begins from the holistic use of tools, moves to analytic use and then to a more abstract and scientific use that synthesises the holistic and analytic uses (Vygotsky, 1930h, 1930k, 1931b). Tools begin as intuitive extensions of the body, belonging to such natural activities as hunting, fishing and gathering (Marx, 1846a, 1867, Chs 7, 13). A core example of this was what Marx called handicraft production, in which one person makes something by intuitive methods, as when they make a spear, a pot or spin and weave a length of cloth. The dominance of handicraft was followed by a long period in which the elements of the scientific production we see today were nurtured alongside the old methods. Two of these elements stand out. In both cases Vygotsky saw the replacement of automatic, unconscious ways of doing things by consciousness.

First, the production of any artificial object is now achieved by breaking down what was once a unified production process. Now one person may make the spear tip and another the shaft; one may take clay out of the ground, a second fashion the pot and a third decorate it; one spins the thread for the cloth and another weaves it. This occurs in two main ways: Manufactories and the market. In the former someone in authority, usually a slave owner or a capitalist, collects together a number of workers on one site; some of the work groups specialise in making one or a small number of the various components, while others assemble them. In the latter, the makers sell the components on the market, where the assemblers buy them. In both cases, at least some of the participants must engage in more conscious planning than someone who makes and assembles the components for themselves.

This is closely related to the other way in which production becomes more scientific, which is in the application of the principles and knowledge of science to production, which also involves the use of consciousness. At first we have the use of such things as counting, measuring and simple quantitative rules to plan and organise production. Eventually, such simple rules of thumb are superseded, particularly in the capitalism of the late eighteenth and nineteenth centuries, by machines designed using sophisticated scientific theories (Engels, 1878, Part 3, Ch. 13; Marx, 1867, Ch. 15; Vygotsky, 1930h). Marx (1867, Ch. 15) pointed out that the machines used by industrial capitalism would have been impossible without the mechanical theories of Galileo and Newton.

Although this general picture of the dialectic of holism and analysis in the development of tools and machines is largely common to both Marx and Vygotsky, they look at its dynamics differently, as we will see later. One aspect of the first movement, away from the holistic use of tools in tribalism, is *voluntary attention*, which both Marx and Vygotsky thought necessary for work and any use of tools involving a sustained effort (Marx, 1867, Chap. 7; Vygotsky, 1931b, pp. 20–22, 88). Voluntary attention is deliberate attention that has been directed to some chosen end. So a worker who works at a repetitive process, say weaving cloth or cleaning hides, has to decide to keep attending to what they are doing. They cannot, if production is to be efficient, give in to involuntary attention and look at everything that moves outside the window or look up at every sound of the wind on the roof.

Marx places the origin of voluntary attention in production at the start of his second stage, corresponding to state slavery, which is roughly with the rise of class societies and cities. It is needed when people start to do work they are not very interested in, and must attend for long periods to boring or distasteful work processes.

Vygotsky (1931b, pp. 20–22, 88) is rather evasive about the origin of work as an effort and voluntary attention, although he recognises their importance. He praises the French psychologist Ribot (1888, 1897), who, like Marx, placed this at the start of towns and cities, but he stops short of endorsing either Marx's or Ribot's ideas. It seems, however, likely that he actually agrees with Marx and Ribot on this topic, as this fits his theory.

Cooperation in production

The most important social relations binding together the process of production, for Vygotsky, are those involving cooperation, in the special sense that Marx used this term. These are explained in most detail in 'The socialist transformation of man' (Vygotsky, 1930h). Here, Vygotsky outlines the historical origins of his schema more explicitly than usual, by endorsing

Marx's idea that human beings are destined to pass through three stages in production. The reason that three stages are mentioned, rather than the four that Vygotsky usually refers to, is that Marx often coalesces his middle two stages in the development of cooperation and other aspects of production into one.

Thus, for Vygotsky, the shift from primitive cooperation to cooperation by command occurs with the rise of cities and thus with state slavery; the shift to commanding self-instructing slaves probably comes at the same time; the shift to rational cooperation based on science and contract gained a mass base only with modern capitalism, although its origins lay in ancient Greek society (Vygotsky, 1930h, 1931b, pp. 20–22, 60–63).

If there is one key process that is stressed in Vygotsky, but seldom is in Marx, it is the internalisation of social relations and language use. For Vygotsky, first the worker relates to and takes orders from someone who is separate from them; then they bring the outside person inside and the relationship is internalised; they begin to command themselves. Yet more than once Vygotsky recurs to a place in Marx where even this is prefigured. This is in Marx's *Theses on Feuerbach* (1846b). Marx says in one of these that human nature is nothing but the totality of social relations internalised. Vygotsky comments: 'We do not specifically want to say that this [Vygotsky's theory of internalisation – PEL] is specifically the meaning of the thesis of Marx, but we see in this thesis the most complete expression of everything to which our history of cultural development leads' (Vygotsky, 1931b, p. 106). This shows Vygotsky was closer to Marx on this issue than he appears.

Signs and consciousness

Signs here again means anything that can communicate meaning, such as gestures, speech or writing. The second step in the development of signs involves the gradually increasing use of commands, by authority, to instruct individuals to undertake work. This, according to Vygotsky, predominantly occurred during the shift to agricultural societies and cities in the Neolithic period (Vygotsky, 1931b, pp. 58–60), which is much the same as the transition to state slavery.

The third step in the development of signs involves their internalisation, when workers begin to give instructions to themselves in the course of their work. Vygotsky tells us this had occurred by the time of classical slavery, when he cites with approval the use by Roman writers of the idea that slaves had, by Roman times, become both talking tools and tools that controlled themselves by their own talk (Vygotsky, 1931b, p. 58). However, he implies that, in the earlier system of state slavery, slaves, as well as free individuals, were already capable, on a limited scale, of the more sophisticated abilities promoted by inner speech, such as mathematics and writing. This again has Vygotsky in agreement with Marx.

The fourth step in the use of speech is again similar to that of Marx. It is indicated by the appearance of more abstract science and mathematics, based on abstract concepts or meanings. Vygotsky does not comment explicitly on when this occurred, but it was assumed by Marx and Engels, and probably Vygotsky too, that this occurred in the West with the ancient Greeks (Engels, 1878, Part 3, Ch. 13; Marx, 1867, Ch. 15).

Moral reasoning

Vygotsky, at this time, as later, viewed the historical side of moral development as an aspect of the development of signs, following the same historical laws (Vygotsky, 1931b, p. 169). However, he only deals with the details of moral development in the child, which are covered in the next chapter. We can, however, infer, from what he says about children, that the pattern of moral development in history is that described by Engels (1878, Ch. 13).

Morality develops with increasing consciousness (Engels, 1878, Ch. 13). At least in the later stages of development, it is able to solve problems in the regulation of relations with others that have arisen from the historical process. Marx and Engels thought of morality chiefly as a form of enlightened class interest. Each class takes its own self-interest to be what is right and good for everyone and then invents reasons that explain away any inconsistencies this creates. To take an example from Engels (1878), in societies where the ruling class owns private property, it is usual to find that the moral sanctity of private property is proclaimed by that class. If it is asked why this should apply to the poor, in a society with great disparity between rich and poor, the wealthy will often argue that the poor, for various reasons, deserve their poverty. The reasons given might be that they are lazy, squander any money they get, have not been chosen by God and so forth. The desire to provide excuses of this kind shows that an idea of fairness in distributing the rewards of society has already taken root. One of the characteristics of progressive classes is that they are able to claim that when they rule this fairness will be greatly improved, if not perfect.

The nature of the first stage of historical morality is obscure, but we do know when it appeared: with tribalism. Morality based on external obedience to others, particularly through fear of punishment, represents the second stage in the historical growth of morality and appears with cities and the rise of state slavery. The internalisation of this authority is the third stage, which also appears with cities and state slavery (Vygotsky, 1931b, p. 169). Discussions about fairness among equals correspond to the fourth. Vygotsky seems to assume that Engels (1878, Ch. 13) is mainly talking about the fourth stage. Engels concentrates on morality in societies since classical Greece and Rome. So we can say that, like abstract concepts, this form of morality began to emerge with the classical slave states based on individual ownership of slaves. At first it existed in a distorted form, but emerged in a purer, although still often distorted, form in modern European societies.

The self

Vygotsky says little directly about the historical self. However, he discusses the self in the child at some length in this period, although his ideas here are more compatible with Hegel than they are with Marx. Vygotsky also gives Hegel as the source of his view (Vygotsky, 1931a, Ch. 6).

Hegel's (1807, 1831) self begins by being conscious of the environment, after which it becomes conscious of itself. Then it becomes conscious of what other self-conscious beings think of it and finally becomes self-conscious, in a second sense, as a result of internalising the other person. In addition, and contrary to Marx, the development of the self in this way drives forward all other aspects of the individual, both in history and in the child. This is thus a top-down, idealist, version of history, as opposed to Marx's bottom-up, materialist one.

Vygotsky certainly does not simply endorse the idea that the self is the main motive force in development, but when discussing it he talks as though the self were acting in a region of its own, relatively divorced from practice. His leading idea, as with Hegel, is that we are what others think of us and that we internalise this and gain control of it through self-consciousness. As a description of what happens in development this is close to Hegel, but not to Marx. However, he does not follow Hegel in arguing that the whole development of the human personality is driven by the development of the self. For the child and adolescent he claims that there are some upward and some downward influences on the self, without saying which predominate (Vygotsky, 1931a, pp. 172–181, 1931b, pp. 212–220). If we project the development we find in the child (Vygotsky, 1930f, 1931a, pp. 172–181, 1931b, pp. 212–219) onto history, we find a similar progression to that found for signs and morality. A self based directly on what external authority thinks people are, as well as of its internalised counterpart, appears with the rise of cities and state slavery. From the beginning of historical times and the classical civilisations, the self among the masses is formed to a greater extent by considerations of the general welfare and discussions among equals about the most desirable forms of the self.

Motivation

Vygotsky was particularly intrigued by Engels's comments on the connection between medieval and modern romantic love. According to both Engels and Vygotsky this is a different form of the same thing (Engels, 1878, Ch. 9; Vygotsky, 1931b, Ch. 3). It represents a different way of going through the same stage of motivational development. Nowadays this occurs in adolescence and youth, among all classes, whereas in medieval times it seems to have occurred mainly in youth (about 17–25 years) and adulthood (25 years on), among the ruling class. In ancient Greek and Roman society it occurred in different ways again, being manifested in the love affairs of courtesans, and in homosexual and extramarital affairs. Vygotsky is not explicit about the psychological mechanisms involved, other than to say that they are those involved in modern adolescence. He uses this contrast as an example of how the same developmental stage can be manifested in different ways in history and in the contemporary development of the individual.

Dynamics of development

Throughout his career Marx maintained that consciousness played only a subordinate role in the improvement of production until the rise of capitalism and the use of science to design machines and other productive forces. Up to that point, it is primarily the development of tools and technology, apparently largely by trial and error, that drives forward production; and production drives forward society, although he does allow for other influences (Marx, 1846a, 1859). Vygotsky differs from him in that, at least over the long historical period between tribalism and capitalism, the dynamism of consciousness, signs and self-consciousness are identified as the chief factors within the forces of production that drive them forward.

As already mentioned, for Vygotsky, the main dynamic feature up to the end of tribalism is tools and practice. After this we find a cycle of influences in the developing historical system: The social relations of work provide a basis for changes in consciousness, including that involved in signs; this influences self-consciousness; there is then downward influence via signs that moulds the use of tools; this in turn produces development that reacts back on the social relations of work, bringing them to a higher level (Vygotsky, 1930k, pp. 41, 67–68, 1931b, Ch. 7). The main dynamic phases in this cycle are signs and self-consciousness. Motivation also exerts a dynamic influence after the phase of social relations. This short-term cycle of influence is as yet fairly vague in its timing and nature, although its successor in the last period was to be specified much more precisely.

In this period, the way in which self-consciousness acts to spur development forward in its middle period is particularly unclear. He presents two models for this influence. One was that the main effect of self-consciousness is on particular functions, such as attention, memory and perception. He also has a model for the influence of self-consciousness on the whole personality, which is that it acts on all the individual's functions conceived as a system. However, he did not publish his first paper on this second idea in his lifetime (Vygotsky, 1930g); and the idea only appears in a tentative form in the later writings of his penultimate period (Vygotsky, 1931a, 1931b, Ch. 15). It comes into much greater prominence in his last period.

We can infer from what he says about children that in relatively recent times, dating probably from the time of the ancient Greeks, practice, language and full self-consciousness are united in advanced concepts, ending the divorce between language and practice (Vygotsky, 1931a, Ch. 3). Marx (1867, Ch. 13) also placed the origin of such concepts around that time. At this time, the dominance of signs and self-consciousness as dynamic factors gives way to the synthesis of practice and these two factors, all of which are found in advanced concepts.

A paradox of consciousness

Vygotsky (1927c, 1929f, 1930i) took the idea from Hegel and Marx that social consciousness is often backward looking (e.g. Hegel, 1838; Marx, 1846a, 1852). However, through a dialectical paradox, although looking backward it also succeeds in providing for the future. The French Revolution at the end of the eighteenth century, for instance, was promoted by philosophers and political activists who took the style, laws and customs of ancient Rome as their ideal. The buildings they and their admirers designed in Paris, such as the National Assembly, the Pantheon and the Arc de Triomphe, were all constructed on classical lines. In political life, republican Rome, with its ideal of self-sacrifice on behalf of the state and limited democracy, were held up as models. Yet, by breaking the power of the monarchy and aristocracy, the revolution ultimately paved the way for the further expansion of capitalism in France, which had never been an aim or ideal of ancient republican Rome.

Vygotsky took over this advance-by-retreat view of social consciousness in his ideas about the psychological functions of art, creativity and imagination in the present period (Vygotsky, 1930i). While he does not say explicitly that this applies to history, as Marx had said, it seems certain that he would have thought so.

Empirical evidence about the psychology of premodern people

This topic is of significance to Vygotsky as it provides him with evidence about psychological development in societies at a very different historical and cultural level from his own, mainly in the area of cognition. In *History of the development of higher mental functions* (1931b, Ch. 3) he uses psychological fossils as a unit of analysis for this purpose. The fossils concerned are early forms of psychological activity, simple natural methods of communication or for making choices, such as carving notches on sticks or throwing bones to make decisions, that will later change to cultural forms through the process of cultural mediation. Although in history these things were originally living processes, they have become fossils by surviving until today, buried underneath or at the fringes of social activity. As these ways of doing things were natural, they should appear in social development even before the social use of speech.

He looks for the same psychological forms in tribal societies as he looks for today in psychological fossils: the use of external devices to make decisions, such as throwing bones; the use of external devices to direct attention, such as marking objects; the use of devices to aid memory, such as making notches in sticks. His use of authors on tribal culture, especially Levy-Bruhl (1922), is largely to confirm that the external use of such devices is more common in tribal cultures than in our own. However, this is only quite indirect evidence for his argument, as all such societies have long ago developed social speech, so we cannot directly observe a stage where natural methods predominated.

So far we can say that the use of anthropological information in Vygotsky (1931b) is unambitious but offers some support for his general position that there will be an initial phase of natural external control of psychological functions. But there is another more questionable side to Vygotsky's use of anthropological evidence (especially in Vygotsky, 1931b). This is his tendency, which was generally prevalent at the time, to underestimate the level of thinking and general functioning in tribal people. Perhaps the chief culprit in this regard was Levy-Bruhl, whose best known work on the subject, *The primitive mind* (1922), Vygotsky mentions quite frequently.

Levi-Strauss's influential book, *Primitive thought* (1956), is a sustained and effective demolition of Levy-Bruhl's viewpoint here (see also Van der Veer, 1994, 2003). Levi-Strauss shows that tribal peoples were considerably more sophisticated in their thinking than Levy-Bruhl had realised.

In the early 1930s, mostly in 1930 and 1931, Vygotsky and Luria worked on a joint project known as the Central Asia Project, whose main purpose was to assess the joint impact of the collectivisation of agriculture and the introduction of Western-style education on tribal peoples in the Soviet Union, often referred to as national minorities (Luria, 1976; Vygotsky & Luria, 1930). The design of the studies compared the performance of tribal peoples, who had not yet been influenced by these innovations, and that of those who had on various psychological tasks. These were mainly those that Vygotsky believed would assess the level of development of core psychological functions, such as attention and memory, which are described in the next chapter. Some reservations about these tasks are expressed there. It was predicted that the unmodernised individuals would, as Vygotsky's theory suggested, generally lack such things as voluntary memory and attention, while those who had experienced collectivisation and Western education would possess them.

As we will see, the main task used to assess voluntary attention certainly substantially underestimates this capacity, making results in this area hard to interpret (Zaporozhets & Elkonin, 1971). However, overall, the findings do provide qualified support for Vygotsky's view.

This interpretation of these findings has been subjected to an influential critique by Cole (1988, 1996), who believes that the findings offer Vygotsky little support. His arguments are covered in Chapter 11.

Conclusions

The development of the human species consisted of two parts: biological development, to produce the original human biological type through biological evolution; and cultural development, to transform early tribal society into modern industrial societies. The development of the human biological type took place through three stages: instinct; associative learning; and natural thought.

Vygotsky adopted Marx's idea that the historical development of human capacities takes place through the development of production. This occurs primarily through the interaction of four levels of activity with motivation. The four levels of activity are: direct practice and use of tools; social relations within production, especially cooperation; signs and consciousness; the self and self-consciousness. Each of these levels develops through four main steps or stages. His analysis of the self in this period is more Hegelian than Marxist. Changes in motivation also contribute to the development of the productive system.

His view of the forward dynamics of the productive system, after the second stage of development, differs from Marx. The cycle of influence is: Social relations of work provide a basis for a new form of consciousness, especially the social consciousness promoted by signs; this influences self-consciousness, which initiates a downward reaction, altering the use of tools. This produces development that reacts on the social relations of work, which are recast at a higher level. The main dynamic factors are signs and self-consciousness. Following the new form of social relations at the start of this cycle, a new form of motivation appears, which is also a significant dynamic factor.

4 The child, 1928–31

Outline of the underlying model

The map of development is the same as for biological and historical development. It continues to be organised around three main dimensions: Marx's four levels in the organisation of production, adapted for the child (Figure 4.1); motivation; relations between the inner world and the outer. Each of these dimensions has some impact on the others. For instance, a different form of motivation exists at all four steps in the levels.

Turning to the dynamics of development, Vygotsky stresses long-term shifts of emphasis between the levels. To begin with, development is driven forward by the use of tools and practice. After this initial period, which lasts until about $2\frac{1}{2}$ years, signs and self-consciousness take over as the dynamic forces in development (Vygotsky, 1930k, 1931b, pp. 23, 62–63). 'Signs' here is used in the broad sense of anything that can communicate meaning, such as gestures, speech or writing. Finally, in adolescence, tools, practice and signs are synthesised in advanced concepts, overcoming the divorce between signs and practice (Vygotsky, 1931a, Ch. 3). Now such concepts become the dynamic force in development.

There is also a rather vaguely specified short-term dynamic cycle, acting at roughly the level of one forward step in the levels for each cycle. Progress along the levels and in motivation are linked, in this, as for species development. Beginning from early childhood (1–3 years), the starting point in a cycle of development is a new form of social relations (Vygotsky, 1931b, Ch. 3). This results in changes in motivation, which lead to changes in signs, self-consciousness and then practice (Vygotsky, 1931a, Ch. 1). The involvement of motivation here is because the child needs to achieve motivational distance from situations in order to move up steps along the levels. An infant usually reacts to what is around it without thinking; an adult scientist needs to wait before trying to reach a goal, to allow time for thought.

Vygotsky's justification for this stress on the dynamic function of signs begins from the fact that this is required by the social nature of development (Vygotsky, 1930k, pp. 40–44, 1931b, pp. 60–63). He argues that fundamentally new psychological functions cannot emerge from natural, innate,

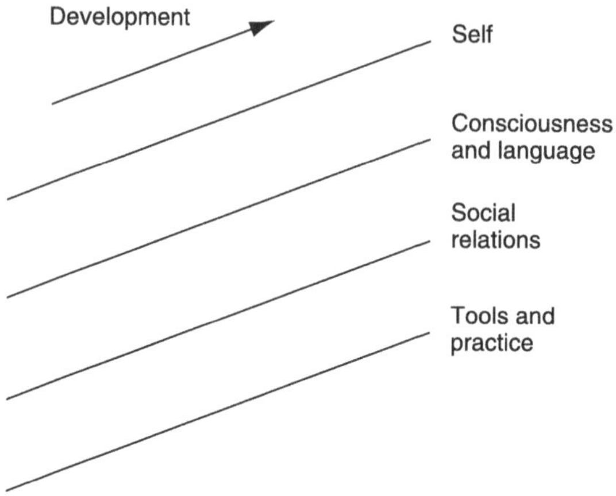

Figure 4.1 The four levels

functions after the first part of development, because it is only the first part that arose from biological evolution. To put this at its starkest, there are only two kinds of evolution: biological and social. Therefore, development after the initial period must be social.

However, Vygotsky (1930k, pp. 40–44, 1931b, Chs 1–3) is obliged to admit that in the child biological and social development overlap somewhat, with biological maturation continuing in the child up to adolescence, long after social development has begun. This is biological development that originally took place before the emergence of the first modern humans, but in the child it is telescoped together with social development. So he moderates his position to saying that social evolution is adapted to take account of the child's biological immaturity and, as a result, after early childhood, the two occur together, although social development predominates.

This adaptation in social development is not such as to alter the underlying nature of the steps in social development. When the child uses tools, for instance, to begin with it uses ones that are simplified and adapted to its lack of strength and dexterity, but are not different in their underlying nature from those that were used in historical development.

We next have to consider what can transmit social influence to the child. In Vygotsky we find only three main contenders: shaping, that is rewarding right actions and discouraging wrong ones; imitation of actions; meaning conveyed by signs. If we conceive that what the child is learning is just habits, then the first two will serve. However, if, as Vygotsky maintains, the child is to learn meanings and concepts, it cannot learn them by these mechanisms, as they are not designed to explain this kind of learning. So we must invoke the social transmission of meaning and thought by signs.

There is, however, as we have already seen, an alternative here that is not mentioned by Vygotsky. This is suggested in the later works of Marx and by

A. N. Leont'ev (1948, 1960, 1974). This is that the transmission of practical behaviour is effected by shaping and imitation and consciousness of what has been learned is then supplied by the child.

The reason that Vygotsky does not mention this argument may well have been that he and A. N. Leont'ev studiously avoided mutual criticism and, in fact, succeeded in maintaining quite cordial personal relations. Whatever the truth of this, Vygotsky did give prominence to a counterargument to it. This was that signs have acted in cultural evolution to improve human capacities in a way that neither pure practice nor conscious practice could have done. If we look at the action of certain kinds of sign we can see that this is so.

The role of speech in the second and third years of life is to take the child from having quite context-centred ways of conceiving the world to having more context-independent and social ways of doing so. Arithmetic provides another example. In Vygotsky (1930k, pp. 42–43) he spends more time on this, in discussing the present issue, than on any other particular aspect of the development of signs. This is probably because it is in some ways the clearest example of signs as cultural amplifiers, as Bruner (1990) was later to call them. Counting to establish what number of objects is in a collection enables the child to know things they could not possibly know without counting, in particular how many objects are in any collection containing more than about seven objects. We cannot count without using numbers, which are a kind of sign. Without this, the huge scope and significance of arithmetic in everyday life cannot be realised.

Another example is the role of writing in promoting meanings designed for a generalised audience. Here the case is slightly different, being that the child would otherwise not have the motivation to develop context-independent forms of communication. However, this still makes writing into an indispensable tool for the creation of abstract, context-independent meanings.

The result of this argument, about signs as amplifiers of our natural capacities, is to show that Leont'ev's approach through conscious practice cannot be sufficient. There is no plausible way in which consciousness could add to practice what signs do in these cases.

Differences between species and child development

We have already seen that in species development, once social development begins, biological evolution stops. In children, by contrast, the two kinds of development are somewhat telescoped together.

Another difference is that child development goes through the various steps, along the levels and other dimensions, in a more or less evenly spaced lockstep manner; whereas in history there had been relatively sudden surges forward, as well as large steps back.

In history, according to Marx, the dismembering of the process of production, through analysis into its component parts, was originally undertaken more by the market than by the kind of cooperation found in manufactories

(Marx, 1867, Chs 7, 13). That is to say, it was originally more common for the different parts of an object to be made for sale on the market. The assembler of the final object would then buy them and put them together. In manufactories, which became prominent in Europe in the seventeenth and eighteenth centuries, but had existed for a long time previously, the different parts of an object are all manufactured on the same site and assembled there. But in the child, for Vygotsky, the route via markets is absent and this step in the historical process must be undertaken through face-to-face cooperation, occurring through commands given in the style of the manufactory (Vygotsky, 1930h).

Map of development

The levels

Origin of the levels: Infancy

At the beginning of the child's development there is no separation between the levels, but after it commences they soon come into being. For Vygotsky (1929f, 1929h, 1930a, 1931b) they have all appeared by the end of infancy. The four levels are distilled from the undifferentiated state of the infant through two processes. First, the natural functions of the infant are detached from their setting and original organisation. Then, different combinations of these detached functions are reintegrated to form the levels. The levels are not functions that existed in the infant, but are compound functions formed by the reintegration of the infant's functions into new wholes. This is shown in schematic form in Figure 4.2. This also shows how, in adolescence, the four levels achieve at least a preliminary reintegration into a single whole.

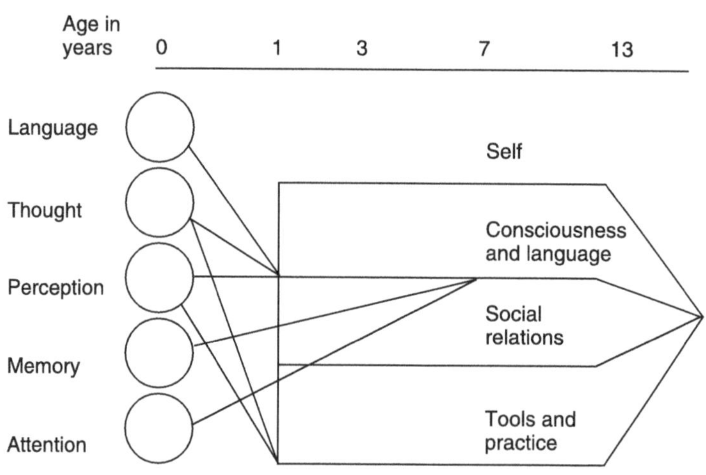

Figure 4.2 Formation of levels from functions, third period

In *History of the development of higher mental functions* (1931b), he takes over the position of Karl Buhler (1913, 1918), which was held by a number of other workers, that infancy should be divided into a substage of instinct, one of associative learning (i.e. conditioning) and one of naive thought. So the substages of infancy are largely a repetition of Buhler's analysis of biological evolution, which we met in the last chapter.

In Vygotsky (1931b), he describes early infancy as a period of natural behaviour (pp. 243–247). Such behaviour undergoes most of its qualitative development through maturation, that is, through the unfolding of preset genetic patterns. Natural behaviour particularly covers the kind of behaviour for which a special term was coined by Baldwin (1911–12) and popularised by Piaget (1926b, 1936). That term is 'circular reaction'. Here, the infant begins from reflex actions, such as the rooting reflex, that enables it to find the nipple by touch by turning towards it. Such reactions are circular, as the initial stimulation (the nipple brushing the cheek) leads to a reaction (turning towards the nipple). This often leads to an overshoot, with the nipple brushing the cheek on the other side and a second, more accurate, turning towards the nipple and so on, until the nipple is in the mouth. The reaction is circular, because each reaction produces the stimulus for a further reaction. When next the whole cycle of reactions is called out, it will have been modified in the light of previous experience.

Vygotsky also points out, largely following Jennings, that the concept of a reflex is not entirely suitable to describe these reactions, which contain extensively prewired patterns of movement, that can be modified in pre-established ways in response to the external situation (Vygotsky, 1931b, p. 244). Thus a small fish can do certain things with its fins, because it is biologically programmed to do so, while an infant can do quite different things with its arms, as they have also been programmed, but in a different way. The term reflex has the connotation of a fixed action called out by a fixed stimulus. Circular reactions are the product of organised functions that control the limbs and senses and they can only be modified as a whole, not as isolated reflex arcs.

There are four elements that Vygotsky says are the key to understanding the first phase of infancy: natural speech, natural memory, logical development of the dominant and assimilation of a pattern as a counterpart to concepts (ibid., p. 247). These are four aspects of circular reactions.

Natural speech includes such things as reflex cooing, that is the making of reflex language-like sounds in the first months of life, and is itself a form of primary circular reaction. *Natural memory* does not involve speech, in contrast to cultural memory. Vygotsky speculates that we do not recall events from the first year of life, because we later learn to link speech so firmly to memory that we cannot access memories that have no speech component linked with them. Natural memory is like the eidetic memory found in some older children and adults, often called 'photographic memory'. It consists, for visual memory, of a digested copy of what has been seen that is usually only weakly under voluntary control (ibid., pp. 194–197). A well-known characteristic of eidetics is that they often cannot get rid of visual images of scenes from the past, even when they want to (Luria, 1960).

The 'development of the *logic of the dominant*' refers to Bekhterev's (1904, 1921, 1926a, 1926b) theory of dominant reflexes in infancy. Bekhterev pointed out that only certain of the reflexes that humans and other young animals are born with can be the basis for conditioned reflexes. He thought that these are ones where attention can be transferred from the unconditioned stimulus to the conditioned stimulus. In one of Pavlov's experiments with dogs, salivation produced by eating food was transferred to sounds that preceded the arrival of food. To Bekhterev, this is because the dogs were able to transfer their attention from the food to the bell. This kind of conditioning of salivation can also be achieved with human infants making this a dominant reflex (Bekhterev, 1926a). The Moro reflex, by way of contrast, which is an innate reaction in the human infant of curling the foot to touching its underside, is difficult to transfer to other stimuli. This is typical of the class of nondominant reflexes.

Some aspects of Bekhterev's theory evidently impressed Vygotsky and he refers to his ideas here and elsewhere (Vygotsky, 1926d, 1931b). The logic of the dominant is to develop conditioned reflexes only from the few unconditioned reflexes that support them.

The *assimilation of a pattern* is significant, as the young infant takes in holistic perceptual impressions of the environment, rather than approaching it through meanings. Vygotsky says: 'For the infant, objects are divided into objects to recognise, to grasp, etc., that is they are distinguished according to different sensory patterns' (Vygotsky, 1931b, pp. 246–247). Thus the meaning of 'pattern' is 'action pattern', which is an aspect of circular reactions that governs the recognition of object uses and situation possibilities.

To reiterate, the four types of reaction found in the first phase of infancy are:

- natural language reactions
- memory
- dominant reflex reactions
- pattern recognition

At this stage cognition is closely bound up with action. However, it is also closely bound up with emotion, as it is of the nature of circular reactions to involve emotion. When the infant turns to the nipple, pleasure is involved, but it is attached in a diffuse way to the whole process of finding and enjoying the nipple, not just to the part where the goal is reached (Vygotsky, 1931b, pp. 243–247). Vygotsky also argues, largely following Piaget (1926b), that in the first phase of development the young infant suffers from an inability to tell the difference between the outside, objective world and the inside, subjective world (Vygotsky, 1931b, pp. 245–246).

In the second phase of infancy, that involving associative learning and conditioning, the four areas we met in the first phase develop further. From about 6 months, the child modifies its babbling in accordance with the sounds it hears from adults. In the area of memory, we find the beginnings of associative memory, an example of which is conditioned reflexes. As part of the same process, dominant reactions, in Bekhterev's sense, are elaborated into conditioned reflexes. Pattern recognition mechanisms are now able to learn new patterns, rather than just operating from innate patterns.

Karl Buhler's (1913, 1918) term for the third phase of infancy was the 'chimpanzee age', referring to the fact that the solution of practical problems using tools is now possible, on the model of the studies with apes by Kohler (1917). K. Buhler was the first investigator to show, using naturalistic observations, that it is approximately in the last three months of the first year of life that similar problems are solved by infants. The emergence of this chimpanzee thought was deemed by Vygotsky to mark the highest point of cognitive development reached by the infant without the assistance of language.

Vygotsky also adopts Kohler's term for the most fundamental aspect of this kind of thinking, namely naive physics. That is, in the fruit and stick problem, by realising such physical aspects of the situation as that the stick is rigid, how long it is, how strong it is, how far the fruit is and how heavy it is, the chimp solves the problem. In *History of the development of higher mental functions* (1931b), this thinking through naive physics is used as an early anchor point to show what the infant's cognition is like before it becomes synthesised with linguistic abilities. This is partly on the basis that chimps are prelinguistic, yet close to human mental capacities; thus they will be a model for the prelinguistic infant. Vygotsky also uses studies on human children attempting the fruit and stick and other Kohler problems to reinforce this point (Vygotsky, 1930c, 1931b, pp. 197–201).

In the first year of life, the practical strand of development dominates the linguistic. We might think that linguistic development is important because the infant obtains so many things by crying. However, crying is considered a nonlinguistic sound, both by Vygotsky and by most other investigators, because getting things by crying has little in common with the use of words to convey meaning, that begins in the second year of life. Linguistic development in infancy takes place through the use of the parts of language, particularly phonemes, in game-like explorations, but at this stage this is not used for obtaining anything. Rather it is experiment for its own sake. This is a sidestream of development in the first year of life.

The most prominent example of this kind of experimentation is babbling, in which the infant produces syllables, often repetitively, such as 'do-do' or 'ba-ba'. Until the end of the first year of life these are seldom used to mean anything, but seem to give the infant the pleasure of being in control of its sounds.

Although within each of the phases of infancy there is learning, and thus the infant profits from experience, the formation of the new functions that emerge as the phases unfold is natural and mainly due to maturation. That is to say, it is not produced by social mediation of the kind that appears around

1 year of age. At the end of infancy, that is around 1 year, functions begin to combine in a new way; this leads to the formation of the levels and their components. Most importantly, the babbling of infancy combines with naive thought to produce speech proper. Other aspects of the emergence of the levels are now examined.

Tools

There are four stages in the use of tools between the end of infancy, around 1 year and the end of adolescence around 17 years. The first involves a pictorial and holistic approach to objects that corresponds to Marx's first stage of tool use (Vygotsky, 1930k, 1931b, Ch. 3). We have already seen that one of K. Buhler's (1913) observations, showing tool use in the last quarter of the first year, was that if the infant drops a toy attached to a string, it will know how to pull it back with the string. This is the use of simple tools using natural intellect, as yet uninfluenced by interaction with signs or with more advanced tools or machines. Here the child is not just reorganising the visual field, but is thinking what would happen if certain things were done by using its knowledge of the physical properties of objects. So the thread might not be suitable to pull up a toy if it were too thin.

Although Vygotsky's approach to the naive representation of the world began from Kohler's idea of naive physics, he was critical of direct extensions of the idea to children much over 1 year of age (Vygotsky, 1931a, 1931b). One example of this was Kohler, who thought of naive physics as something arising from the interaction of heredity and direct experience of the physical environment and remaining relatively unchanged thereafter, even in humans. But, according to Vygotsky, after 18 months children's use of language interacts with their naive representations of the world, producing an altered representation of the world (Vygotsky, 1931a, Ch. 3).

The second stage in the use of tools involves a partial breakdown in the approach to objects and situations as wholes, precipitated by the analytic tendencies of language. Now objects are seen as things that can potentially be decomposed into their parts. In the third stage, the analytic tendencies of language dominate and objects are regarded as something to be decomposed into analytic parts that can then be used to reconstruct them, with increasing use of more precise methods. In the fourth stage, in adolescence, objects and their manufacture are regarded from a scientific point of view (Vygotsky, 1931a, Ch. 3).

Thought, in Vygotsky's special sense, is closely related to the use of tools. The sequence of events here is: Practice dominates in the holistic and practice-based thought of infancy and early childhood to about 2 years. In this period it is the chief means by which problems are represented. Speech then increases in influence until it dominates in problem solving from 7 to about 16 years, now becoming the primary form of representation. A holistic and more advanced derivative of the young child's practice-based thought reasserts itself, thereafter, as the primary means by which problems are represented (Vygotsky, 1931a, Ch. 3).

His ideas here suffer from the difficulty that studies of problem solving do not show a shift to analytic modes of operation in middle childhood. In his last period he modified them to remove this difficulty.

Social relations

The main form of social relation recognised in this period is cooperation in Marx's sense (Vygotsky, 1930h, 1931b), that is, cooperation in the process of production. Vygotsky assumes that the child's use of tools takes place within Marx's various forms of cooperation, but that these forms of cooperation also take on a life of their own and are used by the child in nonproductive as well as productive activities (Vygotsky, 1930b, 1931b). More than one form of cooperation may also exist side by side, as when command by adults exists side by side with collaborative cooperation with other children in the age of first school (7–13 years) (Vygotsky, 1931a, Ch. 3).

His sequence of types of cooperation is close to, although not identical with, that of Marx. Marx's sequence was: holistic cooperation; cooperation through command, the workers all doing the same thing; cooperation through command, the workers doing different things; advanced scientific cooperation, with machines, etc. Vygotsky also divides cooperation by command into an earlier period where the workers all do the same thing and a later one where they do different things; but Vygotsky thought this change was produced by the internalisation of the role of adult or supervisor, which is not mentioned in Marx (Vygotsky, 1930k, 1931b). On this point, Vygotsky thus adds something to what Marx said.

In the first period in which language appears in the child, about 1–3 years, we have primitive cooperation that uses signs, but in a natural way (Vygotsky, 1928h, 1930k, 1931b). Cooperation here is natural cooperation, in which the young child does one thing, such as waving an object, and the adult responds with the natural response of looking at the object. In his second stage of language (3–7 years), we focus on the child as receiver of orders and the way that this moulds its meanings and thought, so as to move them beyond what is purely natural.

In the third stage (7–11 years), commands are internalised and mental life is dominated by self-instruction (Vygotsky, 1930k, 1931b). Here the child can receive a command, or otherwise decide on a course of action, and then tell itself how to carry out the task in detail.

There is also a further kind of cooperation that begins beside rather than after the internalisation of speech in middle childhood. This is cooperation within children's groups, which possess simple forms of cooperation even before 7 years, but after that show a concrete form of the more advanced and rational cooperation of adolescence (Vygotsky, 1931a, 1931b, 1931c, pp. 199–202).

Finally, we meet self-conscious cooperation based on freely entered into agreements, designed to ensure the satisfaction of mutual interests, which appears in adolescence (Vygotsky, 1930d, 1931a, Ch. 6, 1931b).

Signs and consciousness

Problems of definition. The term 'signs' is used in two senses. Sometimes, it means anything that means something. So gestures, symbols and signs with an arbitrary meaning are all signs in this wider sense. It can also mean just signs with an arbitrary meaning. Signs in this narrow sense are things that convey meaning in spite of having no inherent connection with what they mean. A sign in this sense is connected to its meaning by convention, not by similarity. So if two bank robbers agree that, when one has cut the alarm, he will blow a dog whistle, the whistle has no inherent connection with cutting the alarm; it has been attached to this idea arbitrarily. In this narrow sense signs means the most developed form of signs in general. In this book, I have used the term 'signs proper' to mean signs in this narrow sense, where what is meant is not obvious from the context.

The terms 'consciousness' and 'self-consciousness' are also potentially confusing. Consciousness is usually a broad term. In this guise it means being aware of something. The highest form of consciousness is self-consciousness, being aware of oneself. On occasion Vygotsky uses consciousness to mean self-consciousness, because this is the highest form of consciousness. I have avoided doing this, except where the context makes the meaning obvious. So consciousness of the self is called self-consciousness. Consciousness in my usage is usually awareness of the outside world.

In my terminology, partial consciousness and partial self-consciousness are consciousness of part of the outside world and consciousness of part of the self. Global consciousness is consciousness of the whole of the outside world and global self-consciousness implies consciousness of the whole of the self.

Problem solving and signs. Vygotsky's approach to the meaning of signs stressed, in this period, that this is formed within what would nowadays be called a problem-solving space (Vygotsky, 1930k, 1931b). This was an idea he took from the Würzburg school in general and Ach (1921) in particular. According to this, every problem we face presents us with certain possible routes for solving it, some of which will succeed and some of which will not. These routes have to be assembled in the mind of the solver like the segments of a road route. As we travel along each segment it will take us nearer to, or further from, the goal we seek. An example Vygotsky was fond of here was one we have already encountered, which is Kohler's (1917) problem of the fruit and stick (Vygotsky, 1929d, 1929e, 1931b).

This provides a very simple example of a problem with a goal (to get the fruit) and various routes that may or may not reach the goal. These routes are just the methods the child might try to solve the problem. When the problem is given to children, the child is usually separated from the fruit by a net rather than bars. So it might try reaching directly through the net (failure). It might try throwing anything it can lay its hands on at the net, a method very young children quite often adopt (failure). It might try pleading with the fruit (failure). It might try picking up the stick and using it to pull in the fruit (success). The second and fourth of these routes are composed of two parts that must be put together to make the complete route: picking up objects and then throwing them; picking up the stick and then using it to drag in the fruit.

Kohler (1917), and most other investigators using his problem, believed that the ape or child who correctly solved the problem was able to envisage, before acting, that picking up the stick would bring it closer to the goal of getting the fruit and that from this point it could proceed to the goal. So it was able to represent the correct solution route mentally. Kohler's main evidence for this was that apes typically do not pick up the stick and then wander around for a while thinking of what to do with it; they seem to have a sudden insight into the solution, pick up the stick and go directly to pull in the fruit. Children often behave similarly. The problem-solving space, for this problem, is just the sum of all the successful and unsuccessful routes as they are represented in the mind of the child.

Vygotsky's attitude to these routes in this period was ambiguous. At times he already sees them, as the Würzburg school had, as a series of judgements organised by the pursuit of a goal; at these times he is critical of any approach that views them just as sequences of behaviour, as a behaviourist or reflexologist might (Vygotsky, 1931b, pp. 35–37, 72–77). However, in dealing with the role that meaning plays in cooperation, as well as its connection to social relations, he still often considers meaning as a form of behaviour (see Chapter 6).

As children get older, they solve the fruit and stick problem more quickly and they also go through a period when they will talk to themselves out loud about how to solve the problem, particularly if with other children (Vygotsky, 1928h, 1929e, 1929h, 1930k, 1931b). So, on the occasion they think of the correct solution, they may pick up the stick while saying to themselves 'Use the stick' or 'Pull it in'. This first occurs during problem solution at about 4 to 5 years of age. According to Vygotsky, this self-instruction is a result of the child using on itself methods that others had previously used on it. So if a parent had seen the child in this situation and noticed the child was stuck, they might have said 'Use the stick', as an instruction about how to solve the problem. This kind of instruction from someone else would later be internalised and become first a spoken or whispered instruction, by the child to itself, and then an inner instruction that the child said to itself silently. These last two processes begin about 6 or 7 years.

In this period Vygotsky thinks that words are, from about 3 years, introduced to the child as an instruction about how to proceed within a problem-solving situation. This does not usually happen in the stick problem when given as a test, as no instructions are given to the child in the experimental situation as to how to succeed. However, it is assumed that this will occur in other situations and this will transfer to the fruit and stick problem and other situations where no actual instructions are given.

This provides a wide-ranging model of what happens in development, as it also covers motivation in the form of the goal to be reached. This will be set by motivational processes. It covers will and voluntary action, as these are needed to enable the child to pause and think about how to solve the problem, rather than just acting without thought in the most obvious and immediate way. It even covers consciousness. This appears in childhood when the child is partially self-conscious in its use of language to solve problems. It is also involved when, in adolescence, the adolescent becomes fully self-conscious about his or her approach to problem solving, enabling them to review both meanings and problem-solving methods self-consciously (Vygotsky, 1931a, Ch. 1).

There are three strands of signs: speech, writing and arithmetic. These are now reviewed in turn.

Speech. Different kinds of meaning are thought to belong to different periods of speech development. The main sequence is: At first, meaning is based almost entirely on perception (up to about 2 years); then it passes through various kinds of complex and pseudoconcept, which are a first step in the formation of true concepts (2–7 years); then preconcepts appear, as a further step on the road to true concepts (7–13); and finally concepts proper (13–17 years) (Vygotsky, 1931a, Ch. 2, 1931b, pp. 198–215).

These stages were derived from studies conducted under Vygotsky's direction and published as Sakharov (1930). The following is a slightly simplified version of his task. The subject is given an array of blocks of differing shapes and colours and told that some have a certain nonsense word on the reverse and there is a rule connecting the word to the blocks. So, it might mean red ones or red and square ones. The subject is shown one example of, say, 'zop' and asked to put to one side all the blocks they think also have this word on them. If they are wrong, they are shown what is on the underside of one of their chosen items that should not have been chosen. This goes on until they give up or the right meaning is given.

In the first stage of the development of speech, beginning at about 1 year, the child understands that speech is a rule-governed system, but thinks that words mean what they mean because of some inherent connection between the word and what it indicates (Vygotsky, 1931a, Ch. 2, 1931b, pp. 203–205). The most obvious example of this is the onomatopoeia found in such childish words as 'chu-chu' (steam train), 'woof-woof' (dog), 'tick-tock' (clock) and 'baa-lamb' (lamb). Here the word makes the sound that the thing it represents makes.

Another property of early speech is the tendency for early words to have made-up meanings, rather than those found in adult speech. Vygotsky argues that a large proportion of these are suggested to the child by some resemblance it has noticed between the thing and the word that is not obvious to others, but that, to the child, justifies the association. This means that only those who are familiar with the child's personal meanings can converse with them easily at this stage.

Vygotsky agrees with general experience and later studies that the period of preliminary speech just described is over, on average, by 2 years, although it goes on much longer in some children.

Complexes arise after the age of 2 years, because the child leaves the stage of using perception to form meanings and begins to make judgements, but at first it cannot control these (Vygotsky, 1930k, 1931a, Ch. 2, 1931b, pp. 203–205). Complexes are poorly controlled sequences of judgements. A chain complex, for instance, might involve a child saying that first a coin, then a round dog tag and then a dog are called 'enny'. They have judged that the coin and the dog tag are similar, because they are round; and that the dog tag and the dog are similar, because they are connected to dogs; but they have not coordinated these two judgements into a consistent meaning for the word.

As well as the use of complexes we also find a continuing tendency for the child to connect picture-like meanings with words whose form is picture like. Such words, or indeed any kind of sign that is like this, are called *symbols*. It was debated in Vygotsky's day whether the child's speech in the period 2–13 years consists mainly of signs proper, that is arbitrary signs, or mainly of symbols. Vygotsky, following particularly Potebnya (1864, 1894), thought that it consisted mainly of symbols. The majority of everyday words are like what they mean. Nowadays Vygotsky's view here is a minority one. It is now conventional to think that words like 'woman', 'house', 'bird' and so on have no inherent connection with what they mean; they neither look nor sound like the things they mean, any more than the French words 'femme', 'maison' and 'oiseau'. It is also thought that most words are like this. This contrasts with a minority of words that are symbolic in being like what they mean. So, onomatopoeic words sound like what they mean, words like 'hiss', 'tinkle', 'boom' and 'crash'. A few words also convey symbolic meaning using the order of the sounds, as in 'topsy-turvy', 'higgledy-piggledy' and 'zig-zag'.

Vygotsky assumes that, although we are usually aware of a small number of words that sound like or otherwise resemble what they mean, making them obviously symbolic, we are not normally aware of the hidden symbolic similarities between the majority of words and their meanings. These are revealed by etymology and Vygotsky appeals to Potebnya's (1864, 1894) work on this. So, for instance, the Russian word for ink is 'chernila', which is derived from the root 'cherno-' meaning black, as originally most ink was black (Vygotsky, 1931b, Ch. 6). However, the symbolic connection here is between the meanings of 'chernila' (ink) and 'cherno-' (black). Originally they were thought to be similar because both were black. There is no such connection between the root 'cherno-' (black) and the meaning black; 'cherno-' no more resembles black than 'schwarz' (in German), 'noir' (in French) or 'black' (in English). So, even if we admit that such secondary symbolic connections are common, we are still obliged to conclude that they usually begin from primary connections, such as that between the root 'cherno-' and the meaning black, that are not symbolic but arbitrary. As the young child's language must contain many such primary connections, which are not symbolic, it must have the ability to make nonsymbolic meanings, which Vygotsky does not allow for.

Furthermore, neither this example, nor the others Vygotsky offers, show that children actually realise the existence of the symbolic connections between words established by etymology. Children in Vygotsky's time did not see mainly black ink, in fact they probably saw mainly blue ink. There is little reason to think that most children would realise that there once was a world where ink was mainly black and this explains the connection between 'cherno-' and 'chernila'. This suggests that many of the secondary connections Vygotsky points to are also experienced as arbitrary.

The supposed symbolic nature of words in the child's early language sits uneasily with the claim that at this time the child's language is dominated by complexes. The two things predict quite different kinds of meaning. Symbols should give fairly consistent, albeit somewhat vague, meanings, while the meanings given by complexes will be, as we have already seen, quite unstable, oscillating between quite different meanings as the basis for comparison changes.

Vygotsky (1931b, Ch. 6) offers at least a partial explanation for this apparent contradiction. This comes from studies of eidetic imagery, mainly by Jaensch (1920, 1925, 1927a, 1927b), which he claims show that perception and memory can enable the young child to form quite sophisticated meanings naturally, without the process being mediated by social influence. In this guise, natural perception and memory can combine representations with one another to form early meanings.

Vygotsky thought eidetic imagery was a process representative of normal visual imagery. If one shows an eidetic, say, a series of pictures of dogs, then they will end the session with an image of a kind of ideal dog that combines the various breeds shown. This must be an active process since, were we just to project the different dog images on top of one another, using a slide projector, we would see a brown blob. The mind of the eidetic organises this composite image not by adding up the components, but by extracting an idealised mean.

So symbolic communication in speech is a natural form of communication based on natural eidetic abilities. It exists alongside socialised and mediated forms of meaning that produce complexes. Vygotsky also says he is uncertain how much later than this natural eidetic communication lasts (Vygotsky, 1931b, pp. 198–199). If it lasts for much of the next stage, the preschool age

(3–7 years), we can say that in that stage there are two parallel forms of communication: natural and symbolic and complex like. This removes some of the problems that arise if we assume that meanings in this stage are mainly complex like, although it still does not explain why natural meanings were not detected in Sakharov's (1930) studies in this age range.

Next, from around 6 or 7 years, we find self-instruction by internal monologue or inner speech (Vygotsky, 1929h, 1930k, 1931a, Ch. 6, 1931b, Ch. 6). In the previous period other people instructed the child or it instructed others. Now this process is internalised. In this period, the main function of speech is self-instruction and the child uses inner speech to guide its own actions. Although he does not advance as much evidence for this as he was to do later (Vygotsky, 1934c), the evidence in the present period is suggestive and the later evidence for the role of inner speech in self-direction quite convincing.

The form of meaning produced by the internalisation of speech is the preconcept. Preconcepts isolate single attributes and dimensions. So, in the dog tag example given earlier, a child using a preconcept could have selected the attribute 'round' to define 'enny' and then have applied this only to things that are round. Although this appears to be a coordinated series of judgements, rather than a complex, Vygotsky argues that it retains elements of perceptual thinking that make it a preconcept, rather than a concept proper.

Finally, in concepts proper, which appear around the age of 13 years, several attributes can be coordinated in defining a concept; these can be abstract rather than just concrete; and the adolescent can make systematic tests of hypotheses about such concepts (Vygotsky, 1931a, Ch. 2).

Vygotsky (1931a, Ch. 6, 1931b, Ch. 3) deals with two further issues. First, we learn that the meanings of words are the content of the development of meaning and cognition, while judgements and logical inference are its form. We also learn that the development of the content of meanings drives forward that of form. He continued to advance this suggestion during his last period (Vygotsky, 1934c, Ch. 6).

What he has in mind is that the way we make judgements and inferences changes, as the kinds of meaning we use change. The clearest contrast here is between the nonanalytic meanings that come before adolescence and the analytic conceptual meanings of adolescence. Consider this syllogistic inference: 'All dogs have tails; Fred is a dog; therefore Fred has a tail.' A child with nonanalytic meanings cannot satisfactorily grasp the initial judgement 'All dogs have tails'. They cannot realise that a tail is a separate part of a dog and all dogs have one. Their idea of a dog probably includes the idea of a tail, but it is too much part of the overall image of a dog to be separated.

Without grasping the analytic meaning of the judgement 'All dogs have tails' we cannot begin to understand the syllogism. According to Vygotsky, we learn to make this judgement by learning to grasp the analytic concepts 'dogs' and 'tails'. So the status of our concepts underlies the status of our judgements and inferences and, as our concepts develop, this drives forward the development of judgements and inferences.

At times he presents a different picture of these connections. This is that in the period 2–17 years the ability to control judgements determines the kinds of meaning the child can form. From this point of view, it is judgements that produce meaning, rather than the other way round (Vygotsky, 1931a, Ch. 6). Based on this, he claims that if we take meanings and judgements as the content of development they drive inference as a form.

These two views are not resolved in the present period. In his last period the first view continues to be dominant, but the second still plays some role.

Two aspects of Vygotsky's scheme for the development of meaning are, in the light of subsequent research, obviously wrong. It is worth mentioning them now to forestall the confusion they are bound to evoke in anyone aware of more recent research. These are that Vygotsky claimed that complexes are common in the speech of children in the period 2–7 years and preconcepts (one-dimensional meanings) in the period 7–13 years. Later research, including that of Piaget, has found that he greatly underestimated the sophistication of the meanings of the child in both age ranges (see Chapter 12).

Writing. Vygotsky's first phase in the chain of development for written language is gesture. This is not writing as such, as it does not use visual signs to denote verbal signs, as when the written word 'snake' denotes the spoken word 'snake' (Vygotsky, 1931b, Ch. 8). Next come play and drawing.

Drawing is a visual sign, but again it is not yet writing, as it does not denote verbal signs or at least not obviously. Vygotsky claims that the signs used in dramatic play are closer to writing, as they usually use a visual sign to denote a meaning, as when a box is used to represent a car in play. This represents the car because the child has decided that it will (Vygotsky, 1928a, 1930i, 1931b). This kind of representation is also like speech at the same age; the connection between the thing that represents and the thing represented is like the relation between a word and its symbolic meaning. In the case of the box and the car, the two have the similarity that you can get inside both. Such elements of symbolism are typical of dramatic play objects.

In addition, in play, the sign (such as the box) means a word as well as an object. This is because, usually, the child will give play objects labels. When the child says to itself or others 'This is a car', indicating the box, the box comes to stand for a car partly because the word 'car' stands for a car. So there is a further rationale for including play in the line of development of writing. The written word 'car' stands for the spoken word 'car', which stands for a car; so in play the spoken word 'car' stands for the box, which stands for a car. Moreover, the connection, in play, between the spoken word and the box is on the way to attaining one of the main characteristics of written language: That it involves a sign proper, that is a sign with an arbitrary connection to its meaning. This is because the connection between the spoken word and the box is only partly due to the fact that in some ways the box looks like and can function as a car. On other days the child might say 'Let's pretend this is a car' about a range of other objects: an old oil drum, a wooden crate, a scooter or a tricycle. The other part of the meaning of the object in all cases is not given by the way they resemble cars, but by the fact that the child has decided to say that they are cars. This part of the decision matches the word 'car' arbitrarily with the object chosen. It is this that prepares the child to pair the written form of a word with its spoken form.

Vygotsky thought that similar arguments could be extended backwards in the chain, of precursors to writing, showing that gesture and drawing should be included too, although they are not superficially related to writing. Once again he argues that the way that meanings are designated is semi-arbitrary. In gestures we decide at the time we use it what a certain gesture, like beckoning, will mean. It has an element of set, symbolic, meaning, but this is interpreted depending on the situation.

Once drawing reaches a certain level of development it becomes largely symbolic, but early in its development the connection between what the child draws and what is represented is often quite vague and general and children decide what a drawing represents after they have done it. So the decision to say what the drawing is like again plays a large role and again prepares the child for the arbitrary pairings found in writing.

The pictographic writing of the young child is also related to drawing. Here words are represented by shapes. Again the onus is on the child's decision to connect the words to the shapes, as there is usually only a vague connection or, indeed, there may be none at all. Children will often read their pictograms as meaning one thing on one occasion and another on another.

Vygotsky's arguments about the role of written language proper (i.e. reading and writing) are among his most influential. From key texts in the present period (Vygotsky, 1931a, 1931b), until his last writings (Vygotsky, 1934c, 1934e, 1935a), he consistently claims that written language necessarily involves the use of concepts proper and, furthermore, it plays a leading role in forming them. His argument (Vygotsky, 1931a, 1931b) is that writing in languages using alphabets involves the use of signs proper, that is signs with an arbitrary connection to what they mean. In learning to write we learn to use signs as arbitrary designations and this then spreads to other areas, such as speech. The arbitrary designation of meaning by alphabetic systems takes place in two phases. The first is when a written word designates a spoken word; for instance, the written word 'pig' means the spoken word 'pig'. Here our adult perception of both the written and the spoken word is that it is composed of three units in order, in the one case letters and in the other case sounds or phonemes. These three letters represent these three phonemes. For the sake of argument, we can imagine a written language in which we can generalise this and say that a definite sequence of letters always means a definite sequence of phonemes, which is called a language with phonetic spelling. In general, languages whose spelling was, at some time in their development, codified by official bodies on a rational basis, approach this ideal more closely than languages such as English, whose spelling evolved from the eccentricities of particular authors. As Russian has a relatively regular spelling system, Vygotsky probably overestimates the existence of regular spelling in comparison to languages like English.

To understand the connection between letters and the sounds of words, the learner must reduce both written and spoken words to an analysis that differs from the global perception of the spoken word found in spoken speech. So, the word 'pig' must be changed from a single unit, heard as a whole, to the three separate units comprising its three sounds. This then leads to a connection between written and spoken words that is based on the arbitrary connections between the letters of the language and phonemes. The letter 'p' does not represent the phoneme 'p' because it looks like it or sounds like it. In fact, in Greek and Russian our letter 'p' stands for a phoneme close to what we call 'r'.

Under the influence of writing, the child in the period of first school (7–13 years) moves away from words with a symbol-like connection with their meaning. The role of the alphabet and of breaking down words to spell them is to replace this with more strictly sign-like connections between meanings and words. At the start of the period of first school, a word like 'tinkle' means the sound it represents because when we pay attention to the sound of the word as a whole, it sounds like the sound of tinkling. At the end of the period, this has been replaced by attention to the phonemes making up the word, which have no particular connection to the sound it represents. If we sound out the word 'tinkle' as a primary student might, we say 't-i-n-k-l'; this no longer sounds like a tinkling sound. The process of analysis has destroyed the symbolic linkage and the word now means the sound of tinkling because that has been assigned as its meaning. Of course, this is only an approximation, as in many languages, particularly English, the connection between letters and sounds is often irregular.

Vygotsky then argues, following Delacroix (1924a, 1924b, 1926), that, once written signs have come to signify spoken signs, the spoken signs begin to drop out, leaving just the connection between written signs and meanings. This is the second phase in the appearance of signs. It begins when the child can read silently without saying the words to itself as inner speech. The child's meanings are then further transformed by the process of becoming directly attached to written signs. One additional reason for this is that the learner has now come to understand what a system of analytic meanings, found in the letters that mean sounds, is like and thus begins to reconstruct its system of word meanings on this model. It is in this second phase, shortly before the onset of adolescence, that concepts proper are formed (Vygotsky, 1931a, Ch. 8). However, in his most central piece of writing on adolescence, in this period, he insists that concepts proper do not form until mid-adolescence (Vygotsky, 1931a, Ch. 3). What he probably means is that the capacity to form concepts proper begins before adolescence, but is not fully formed until mid-adolescence.

The consciously analytic attitude to written language needed at the word level is also needed to cope with the grammar and semantic structure of written language, greatly intensifying the pressure to adopt an analytic attitude to all aspects of language (Vygotsky, 1931b, Ch. 7). In the case of semantic structure, this is particularly strong. Previously, the child's way of putting words together to make phrases and sentences was global and pictorial or at best based on preconcepts. Now, the use of words as precise names for meanings means they must be put together in an analytic way, that is according to precise rules. This means that if the meanings of some words were to remain global, pictorial and somewhat vague, they would act like grit in the semantic machine, when the words are put together in a precise way. It is as if someone were to build a wall with precise rules as to how to lay the bricks, stating how high each row of bricks must be and how many bricks there are in it, but the brick manufacturer forgot to standardise the size of the bricks. The wall builder would phone the brick manufacturer and complain.

The development of writing from middle childhood to adolescence also produces pressure to communicate more explicitly. When we talk to someone they are often in the same room and share the same concrete context. Children begin writing to particular people, but they do not know where the recipients will be when they read their notes and letters; later on they write for an abstract audience and in this mode they do not even know who they are writing to. They can no longer say things like 'Mummy I want it' or 'Look'; they must now write things like: 'Once upon a time, there were three bears. A daddy bear, a mummy bear and a baby bear. They all lived in a house in the wood.' This makes clear the context of the following story, which is needed, as the three bears and their house are not immediately present. The child is obliged to develop the abstract and disembedded meanings underlying written language by this pressure to be systematic and explicit.

Vygotsky says the motive provided by communication pressure leads to disembedded meanings (Vygotsky, 1931b, Ch. 7). Communication pressure is, in turn, produced by developmental changes in social relations. So it is the shift in the child's social relations, from face-to-face groups, to the larger groups that make up society, that lies behind the rise of the motivation for decontextualised communication.

Arithmetic. The sources of Vygotsky's information on the development of arithmetic are general familiarity with the process and observations by Stern (1922, 1927) and Piaget (1926a). I will concentrate on Vygotsky's stages in counting, as the local stages found in this area are extended to other aspects of the topic.

Vygotsky (1931a, Ch. 2, 1931b) argues that direct perceptual assessment of how many objects are in a collection constitutes the first stage of development, which is established by 3 years. Such assessment without counting is nowadays often known as subitising and more recent research confirms that it is found in a majority of children as early as 3 years (e.g. Gelman & Gallistel,

1978; Klahr & Wallace, 1975). Such judgements enable the child to say whether a collection of objects is larger than another or the same in number just by looking at them; but this method cannot usually succeed with more than five or six objects. Here the 'arithmetical' signs involved are the words 'same', 'more', 'less' and the like. The child has learned to use these signs, but by using a purely natural method of assessing number.

Then comes the stage of external counting. No ages are given for this, but general knowledge and more recent literature suggest $4\frac{1}{2}$ years as the age for successful external counting (Gelman & Galistel, 1978; Klahr & Wallace, 1975; Langford, 1987a, Ch. 6). Vygotsky also includes in this stage a preliminary period, in which external counting is attempted but is not successful, which would take it down to around $3\frac{1}{2}$ years.

Vygotsky (1931a, Ch. 2) reports with approval Piaget's (1926a) argument that until the age of about 7 years children do not understand the result of external counting. From $4\frac{1}{2}$ years they can arrive at a correct result, but when asked what the result means they cannot explain. So in this period, counting is successful but not understood. However, this conclusion is apparently at variance with the account of preschool arithmetic given in *History of the development of higher mental functions* (1931b), which is that the child begins to understand arithmetic at this point, but does so in a pictorial or figurative way. What is probably intended in Vygotsky (1931a) is that at this stage arithmetic is not fully understood, rather than that it is not understood at all.

Finally, from 7 years on, counting can be performed internally, rather than by counting out loud and the results are understood.

The development of arithmetic thus approximately follows that of the other two strands, in that we find an initial use of signs accompanied by natural psychological mechanisms ($1–3\frac{1}{2}$ years); then the external use of signs, with a change in meanings produced by the pressure involved in communicating with adults ($3\frac{1}{2}–7$ years); finally the internal use of signs from about 7 years. A difficulty is that the external use of signs in arithmetic does not obviously involve command. However, we are probably expected to infer that guided counting, in which the child has to follow what the adult does, represents command in this context.

Moral development. Vygotsky, following Marx, regarded moral ideology as a kind of honorary member of the club of signs and made no provision to extend his general model to accommodate it, apparently happy that it was already accommodated. So, in the chapter of *Pedology of the adolescent* (1931a) devoted to 'Dynamics and structure of the adolescent's personality', he says the following:

> The personality is by nature social. This is why we were able to detect the decisive role that socialisation of external and internal speech plays in the process of development of children's thinking. As we have seen, the same

> process also leads to the development of children's ethics: the laws of construction here are identical to the development of children's logic.
> (Vygotsky, 1931a, pp. 169–70)

His account of moral development mainly follows Busemann (1925, 1926), of whom he approves in general, although not of certain aspects and details (Vygotsky, 1931a, pp. 172–81). In the preschool period (3–7 years), what is right is dictated by what adult authority says; from 7 years to about 15 years this adult authority is internalised; while in mid-adolescence it is replaced by the views of the peer group. Finally, at a time later that is not specified, the adolescent becomes self-conscious and able to rearrange and reorganise their views, through a process of reflecting on them (Vygotsky, 1930f, 1931a, pp. 172–81).

He also says that around 7 years children shift from external obedience to the rules of games, to the internalisation of the rules (Vygotsky, 1931a, p. 169, 1931b, p. 197), citing Piaget's work on this. He probably took this observation from Piaget (1930), although its more influential form was to be in Piaget (1931). At this date he only takes this particular idea from Piaget, to confirm Busemann's claim that internalisation occurs around 7 years; in his last period he was to embrace Piaget's ideas on the subject more generally.

At this point in Vygotsky's career, Busemann was attractive to Vygotsky, as he had the child internalising adult moral authority in the period 7–13 years, just as Vygotsky had the child in this period internalising adult authority in his theory of signs. In both, the child internalises adult commands, thus coming to command itself.

For Vygotsky, moral development is also closely bound up with the development of will, as it is the development of the will that allows the child to avoid impulsive actions and to stand back and reflect on the likely outcomes of its actions (Vygotsky, 1931b, Ch. 12). In going from the child to the adult, we go from short-term local goals to long-term global goals. He argues that the development of the will is not just a cognitive matter, but also a moral issue. As the child's moral outlook develops, it shifts from assessing the effects of its actions and those of others, on a short-term and local basis, to assessing them on a long-term and wider basis.

The self

The self for Vygotsky usually means a self that is in some degree self-conscious. He deals with two kinds of self-consciousness, partial and global. The former will more easily be dealt with in the next section, when we look at the mediation of elementary functions by signs, which in key instances involves partial self-consciousness. This section deals with the latter.

Vygotsky maintains that selves can be fully self-conscious or minimally self-conscious. In defining conscious and unconscious selves, he often adapts Freud's terminology (Vygotsky, 1930f, 1931a; Vygotsky & Luria,

1925). For Freud, any mental entity that can fairly easily become conscious is called conscious (Freud, 1900, 1915–16). That it is not conscious at any particular time is not relevant here, as this property is not distinctive. There are few mental entities of which we are conscious all the time. What interests Freud is the contrary phenomenon of things that never become conscious, which are what he calls unconscious mental processes: such things as repressed memories and complexes.

So selves can, as a first approximation, be partitioned into those that are self-conscious some of the time and those that are self-conscious none of the time. Vygotsky agrees with the first element of this partition. He thinks there are selves that are self-conscious some of the time and that access to them is at least partly under conscious control: such selves as those the young child enters in play or the adolescent in their more superficial fantasies (Vygotsky, 1930i, 1931a, Ch. 4). At the same time, there are selves that allow little conscious access, at least at certain times, such those that belong to dissociative states, such as paranoid and other dissociative forms of schizophrenia or fugue states (Vygotsky, 1931b). Here, one self can become conscious of another, but only with difficulty; when you think you are Peter the Great, Tsar of all the Russias, you may be peripherally aware that you are also Ivan Smolensky, asylum inmate; but you do not dwell on the fact.

These pathological selves find it difficult to communicate with the everyday self. However, the main counterpart of the everyday or outer self in the normal person is the inner self, which takes on something of the role of Freud's unconscious self, or id, but finds it easier to communicate with the outer self than Freud's id.

The main outline of the development of the self is as follows. The infant is unable to distinguish itself clearly from other people, showing a lack of separation of the self from other people (Vygotsky, 1931b, pp. 212–219). In the next period of early childhood (1–3 years), the self is separated from others, particularly because the young child learns it has a name (ibid.). During the preschool age (3–7 years), the self is a product of what adult authority says about the child. That is to say, the child thinks it is what the parents think of it. The views of adult authority are then internalised in the time of first school (7–13 years). In mid-adolescence this is replaced by the views of the peer group. The adolescent thinks they are what the peer group thinks of them. Finally, in late adolescence or thereafter, the adolescent becomes self-conscious and able to rearrange and reorganise their own personality, according to how they judge themselves (Vygotsky, 1930f, 1931a, pp. 172–181). For instance, if the adolescent adopts a certain political philosophy or a certain religion, they may systematically review all their beliefs and actions to make sure they fit in with this.

Although the self exists before adolescence, it does not play a very active role in development until then. Systematic reviews of the personality are based on the capacity of the self for synthesis, which first assumes a dominant role in adolescence (Vygotsky, 1931a, Ch. 6). This was then and is now a fairly common position and Vygotsky takes much of his stance here from Busemann (1925, 1926, 1927), although he mentions that Spranger (1925, 1928) had also adopted the same general idea, differing on how the child got there. More recent supporters of the idea have been Erikson (1960, 1968) and Kohlberg (1958, 1984; Colby & Kohlberg, 1987).

As well as reviewing broader aspects of the personality, the adolescent also acquires the ability to review purely cognitive abilities. A central result of this is the ability to coordinate and control the various moves in the game of using concepts. This is seen in the adolescent's ability to use information to find out what a certain word means, as in the studies of Sakharov (1930). In these, as described earlier, the child has to find out what a nonsense word means, based on certain information. Adolescents are able to use a conscious strategy to solve such problems, such as taking the first positive example as a whole as a hypothesis and then rejecting aspects as they are shown to be irrelevant. If the word means red and the first positive example is red and round, then the hypothesis is red and round; when a red and square example comes along that also has the word on it, the aspect round can be dropped, leaving red.

Self-conscious review of motivation includes the capacity to review interests and decide, using principled criteria, what to be interested in and what not. Influence is also exerted in the reverse direction. So the emergence of the self in adolescence is influenced by the development of cognition. One key cognitive achievement of adolescence that leads to changes in the self is the isolation of key traits or qualities that define a concept or meaning and their deliberate use as systematic criteria to identify instances. This is of significance for the self, as the adolescent's conception of the self is now determined by these operations of meaning formation, just as the nature of objects in the outside world is determined in this way (Vygotsky 1931a, pp. 56–58).

For instance, for the adolescent to know whether they are brave, clever, beautiful or religious, they now turn to abstract meanings denoting these things, rather than the picture or complex meanings of younger children. For instance, the younger child may think that being religious is determined by superficial images, such as wearing certain clothes, participating in ceremonies and kneeling to pray. The adolescent begins to think that there is a more abstract core to religion, for instance, believing in God and acting on certain abstract principles of the religion, such as helping others. The younger child believes it is religious if it has the concrete characteristics it understands belong to religion, but the adolescent comes to think that to be religious a person must have these more abstract and central characteristics.

Another aspect of the self in childhood and adolescence is to exert mastery over the personality, so that ultimately freedom becomes the knowledge of necessity (Vygotsky, 1931b, pp. 212–219). This mastery appears by degrees, first attaining a significant form in the internalisation of commands around 7 years, but not assuming anything like its full form until adolescence. Such self-mastery plays an important role in this period and we will meet it again, particularly in relation to the mediation of cognitive functions.

Motivation

The main developmental sequence for motivation is as follows. The will in infancy is merely a passive accompaniment of needs, which are inborn and natural. In childhood the child develops interests, such as stamp collecting or computer games, that are not biological but acquired (Vygotsky, 1931a, p. 15). Furthermore, they are acquired by development, through internalising the motives of others, not by mechanistic forms of learning.

The child develops interests, such as cars or films, as a specific form of mediated motivation that frees it from the most immediate dependence on the internal and external environment. It is a step towards independence and freedom, as now they can choose their interests, as well as when to take them up and when to put them down. Both aspects contrast with biological motivations, which are not chosen, emerge unbidden and often refuse to depart to order.

An argument against this is that children can develop obsessions with their interests that put them beyond the realm of the voluntary. One well-known example of such obsessions today is with computers, but they can also develop obsessions with collecting or whatever is the latest craze among children of their age. However, Vygotsky would regard these as pathological versions of normal interests and it is with normal interests he is most concerned.

In adolescence, the individual acquires self-conscious interests, that is to say interests for which they can give a conscious explanation and which they may review and reject if need be (Vygotsky, 1931a). An example here is that a conscious decision can be taken if two motives conflict with one another. In the chapter on interests in *Pedology of the Adolescent* (1931a) he says: 'In a higher form, becoming conscious and free, interest stands before us as a realised striving, as an attraction in and for itself, in contrast to instinctive impulse, which is an attraction in itself' (ibid., p. 12, my trans.).

For Hegelians between the in-itself and the in-and-for-itself comes the for-others. So we have biological impulses as the in-itself, motivations acquired from others as the for-others (interests), then self-conscious interests as the in-and-for-itself. We can equate these periods with infancy, childhood and adolescence.

Inner self and outer self

As the self becomes internalised around 7 years it splits into an outer and an inner self (Vygotsky, 1930g, 1931a, Ch. 6). Thereafter, in both later childhood and adolescence, the dialectic of the inner and outer selves becomes an important motor of development.

The inner self, beginning from the age of first school, plays a somewhat similar role to Freud's unconscious self or id. However, in contrast to Freud, this inner self neither suffers from a full-blown dissociation from the rest of the personality nor is it an entirely hidden and unconscious self, although it is normal for it to be somewhat dissociated from the external self, as well as from other, less central, selves. The main role of the inner self, which retains a large element of picture-like thinking, is to keep the personality in touch with the concrete realities of life.

Dynamics of development

There are dynamic forces driving the development of the whole personality forward associated with each of the three main developmental dimensions: the levels, motivation and the inner and the outer. These are the most important aspects of dynamics, as they operate over a wide field.

Vygotsky also has a further theme in dealing with dynamics, which is the development of the parts of the personality dealing with speech. This involves the levels, but only as they influence the development of speech.

The levels

The most important and complicated influences come from this source. As for history, he stresses long-term shifts of emphasis between the levels. In infancy and the first part of early childhood, development is driven forward by practice and the use of tools. From around 2 years, signs and self-consciousness take over as the dynamic forces in development (Vygotsky, 1930k, 1931b, pp. 23, 62–63). Signs in this case has the meaning of anything that can communicate meaning, such as gestures, speech or writing. In adolescence, tools, practice and language are synthesised in advanced concepts, overcoming the divorce between language and practice (Vygotsky, 1931a, Ch. 3). Now such concepts provide the dynamic force for development.

Particular examples of these general categories of function are influential at particular times. These are: practice (infancy); speech (the later part of early childhood); play (preschool); writing (first school); concepts (adolescence) (Vygotsky, 1930h, 1930m, 1931b).

In addition to this long-term dynamics, there are also influences operating over the shorter periods he calls infancy, early childhood, preschool, first school and adolescence. After infancy, each of these is governed by a short-term cycle. This is not described as clearly or used as consistently as the long-term dynamics, although it laid the basis for the more rigorous treatment of this area in his last period.

In each of these shorter periods we begin from certain social relations; on this basis certain forms of consciousness, especially those involving signs, are erected, which influence self-consciousness. Signs here is again used in the broad sense to mean anything that can communicate meaning, such as gestures, speech or writing. This leads to improvements in the nature of tools and practice, which then produces a changed form of social relations (Vygotsky, 1930k, pp. 41, 68, 1931b, Ch. 7). Within this cycle, it is signs and partial self-consciousness that give the system its greatest forward impulse, at least from $2\frac{1}{2}$ to 13 years. After that it is advanced concepts and global self-consciousness.

Motivation

Vygotsky points out that there can be no cognition without motivation. This justifies putting motivation on the same level as cognition. However, Vygotsky puts it in front: Motivation leads much of development, not cognition. The development of motivation pulls that of cognition along behind it (Vygotsky, 1931a, p. 3). He also says that changes in motivation lead other changes that occur within psychological systems (ibid.). This is again salutary, as we are tempted to think of psychological systems as purely cognitive systems, on the pattern of Piaget's cognitive structures. But, by contrast, Vygotsky's systems also include motivation, not just as one element, but as a leading element.

The main reason, that the right kind of motivation is needed for cognition, is that there needs to be the right kind and amount of separation between the means to get something (cognition) and the end sought (motivation). The connection between motivation and cognition is a close one and Vygotsky takes seriously the idea that means and end are inextricably linked (Vygotsky, 1930k, 1931a, 1931b). In infancy, as a result of the predominance of schemes of action, there is at first no psychological separation of means and end, as the end is not represented prior to action, which is triggered by events in the immediate environment. So if the infant's cheek is brushed by the nipple, it turns towards it by a circular reaction, without entertaining the goal of feeding. However, by the end of infancy, the infant has come to separate means from end and cognition takes up the role of means, while motivation takes on that of determining ends (Vygotsky, 1928g, 1929b, 1931b). For instance, at the end of infancy, if the infant sees food and is hungry, it will look on the food as an end or goal to be achieved and then start to think of how to get it. So it might think of asking for the food, ways to steal it and so forth, all of which involve representing the goal of the activity as being distinct from the action itself.

The developmental level of motivation is linked to the developmental level of cognitive systems. The motivational level and inclinations of the child determine the form of the systems of meaning they will construct. This is most easily seen in the transition to adolescence, which involves a further distancing of cognition from motivation. Only at this point can the adolescent accept concepts that are defined in the spirit of pure supposition, with immediate motivational payoff put into the background. The paradigm for such concepts for Vygotsky is the scientific concept. In science and mathematics we are often asked to accept concepts that defy everyday experience on the understanding that, in the long run, that is once the concepts are attached to theory, we will understand everyday experience and be able to benefit from this. An example is an algebraic equation such as '$x + y = 0$'. This tends to confuse younger children, as there is no one right answer, but as adolescence approaches they understand that a great range of pairs of values fit the equation, such as (1, -1), (2, -2), (3, -3), etc. (Collis, 1975, 1989). The pairs of values produce, for instance, a straight line when interpreted in geometrical terms, with x the distance of a point along the x (horizontal) axis and y the distance along the y (vertical) axis. This is often indirectly useful, even though there is no one correct result for the initial equation.

Such removal from immediate results, according to Vygotsky, can only be justified by its ultimate result: The theories that can be built on such concepts then enable us to understand and control the world in ways we otherwise would not. To be willing to do this, we must also be willing to entertain the general motive of understanding and controlling certain wide-ranging aspects of the world. A young child, whose motives are direct and limited, will not be able to acquire systems of concepts of this kind.

A number of further reasons for thinking that motivation is required for cognition are also discussed. Motivation is the driving force in the formation of higher cognitions, not only because it is necessary, but also because where it appears it directs their content, structure, system and use. The example of content is most obvious. If a child or adult is interested in a topic, and is motivated to pursue it, they will know a lot about it; if they are not, they will not. It also determines the content of vocabulary within the child's language. This can be seen from the facts, often pointed to in discussions of the relation between thought and language, that the Inuit have more words for snow than most other peoples, as they use snow for more uses, while Indonesian languages have more words for rice, as they have more uses for rice. So do their children. The interests and motives of particular individuals will also determine the precision of their semantic systems in different areas. The child who is interested in planes may be able to name several dozen types of plane; one who is not may just name them as jumbos, bombers, fighters and biplanes, inaccurately cramming the rest into these categories or into 'not sure'. Vygotsky (1931b, pp. 213–215) also says that motives direct the use of cognitive means. He expresses this by saying that motives combine with cognition to make a determining tendency or set. Such sets were, by Vygotsky's time, well known from studies of perception, attention, problem solving and other areas, undertaken by the Würzburg school, the Gestalt school and others (e.g. Ach, 1921; K. Buhler, 1922; Kohler, 1917, 1929, 1932; Wertheimer, 1922, 1925).

Set predisposes the person to rely on a particular method or on particular information in solving a problem in a certain situation. The effect of motivation on set had been widely studied in perception (K. Buhler, 1922; Wertheimer, 1925). In a study described by Wertheimer (1925), people were briefly shown words with some letters blanked out. In one condition the words could relate to food. Thus the reduced word M E – – could be seen as MEAN or MERE; but it was found that a hungry person will tend to see it as

MEAT or MEAL. Postman and Crutchfield (1952) found in a large replication study that they could only get this effect by complicating the procedure; however, their findings with the revised procedure still illustrate Vygotsky's point.

Vygotsky also claims that when a particular motivation predominates, particular parts of a person's meaning systems relevant to the motive will be potentiated. They will then, for instance, be more likely to be used in solving problems relevant to the motive than others. Motivation encourages a set to use certain meanings in solving a problem.

Vygotsky also mentions the effect of previous experience in establishing set, which is not so clearly related to motivation, but is worth including. The most famous of all the Gestalt studies to show the effects of set are on this topic. These were published by Luchins (1942), but first undertaken in the 1930s, in which subjects are asked to measure out amounts of water using a set of measuring jars of various sizes. It is appropriate to mention these, as, unlike some other early studies in this area, discussed by Vygotsky, they have been found to be extremely robust (Luchins & Luchins, 1994a, 1994b).

For one group of subjects a series of problems soluble by one method is given first, followed by one that needs a different method. For a second group, the last problem is given alone or following neutral problems. In the first group, the use of the first method creates a set to use it in the final problem that interferes with use of the correct method. The second group finds the final problem easier. Vygotsky contends that just as repetition can produce a set, so can solving problems under the influence of a particular motive. When we switch to another motive, this original set may not be aroused and the person is then unable to solve the problem given.

Inner self and outer self

The dynamic role of the inner and the outer is that while the inner is, in some respects, more infantile than the outer, the inner is also more in touch with concrete reality and so development depends on both. The contrast between the inner and the outer relates to two main areas: the self and speech. It also applies in a lesser way to some other areas, such as subjective versus objective motivation. This section will deal only with its application to the self, as its application to speech has already been covered.

The most significant appearance of the inner and outer selves, in this period, comes in relation to imagination and creativity. The role of imagination and creativity, in mediating between the inner world and the outer, is not explained as explicitly in this period as it is in the next. However, we already see clear signs of their assuming this role (Vygotsky, 1930i, 1930l, 1931a, pp. 138–140).

Imagination and fantasy are closely linked to the development of the self, by providing a connecting route between the inner self and the outer. Their role in development is to perform the work of steering and coordinating development that earlier in human evolution was performed by everyday thinking (Vygotsky, 1930i, 1930l, 1931a, pp. 138–140). In other words, at that time there was a substantial component of imagination and fantasy in everyday thinking. When we enter these, we enter states that were common in the past but no longer are. This view is also applied to dreams.

At first this seems baffling, as, if our modern methods of thinking are superior to older ones, which Vygotsky thinks in many ways they are, why should we regress to earlier forms? The answer to this is that for some aspects of our problems we need the older methods as the new ones are, in these respects, inadequate. This is because the imagination, at all its levels of development, is able to be creative from the ground up, as it is more closely in touch with the vast amount of concrete experience that each of us has than is verbal thought (Vygotsky, 1930i, pp. 17–20). If we are to change ourselves, it is often more fruitful to do this while staying in touch with reality through the imagination, rather than remaining on a purely verbal or conceptual level, where we might stray from reality in using only the knowledge that is encoded in words.

So, an adolescent might adopt the methods of the outer self and abstract reason and assume that there are various factors involved in choosing a career, such as the money, the satisfaction, the human contact and the stress involved. They could think of each in quantitative terms, on a scale of 1 to 5, from a little satisfaction to a lot. They could weigh each in terms of its importance to them, add up the weighted scores and hence arrive at a level of preference for each profession. However, Vygotsky argues, imagining life in each profession will give a more useful indication of what it actually feels like for all these factors to be brought to life in the work of the profession.

To support his argument that creative imagination can often do better than rational thought, he mentions two of the standard examples of insight in adults, achieved through imagination, after years of assembling knowledge and experience of a topic. These are Newton's (supposed) sudden realisation of the law of gravity by having an apple fall on his head and Hamilton's stroke of insight when he invented quaternions, a new kind of number invented in the nineteenth century (Vygotsky, 1930i, pp. 17, 18). Although the story of the apple's falling on Newton's head is no doubt apocryphal, had it happened it would be quite typical of the way in which concrete leaps of imagination spark discoveries.

The direct precursor for this argument about creativity and imagination was the work of the French psychologist Ribot (1900, 1906), although interestingly Vygotsky also points out that his approach to dreams, another branch of the imagination, is similar to Jung's problem-solving theory of dreams (Vygotsky, 1930i, passim; 1931a, pp. 138, 154, 162). According to Jung (1939, 1945, 1955–56), the main function of dreams is to solve problems that have arisen in our lives, suggesting solutions in the form of imaginative images.

Speech

The dynamics we have looked at so far have acted on the personality as a whole; the dynamics of speech are secondary to this. They reflect the dynamics of the whole personality and, in the process of conveying these to speech, they also contribute to the forward motion of speech, in an independent way.

He thinks that the meaning we give to speech needs to be supported by three key psychological functions: perception, memory and attention. However, in their natural form, as they emerge from infancy, these cannot support sophisticated forms of meaning. For development to occur, from early childhood to first school, these functions must become more sophisticated. This occurs as they are used in conjunction with signs, particularly speech, in these periods. In other words from the collision between signs and these functions we get something that is more than either the signs or the natural functions that went into the collision: It is what Vygotsky calls mediated functions; functions that have been mediated by signs. These mediated functions are then integrated with meaning and it is this newly improved or activated meaning that takes on the role of a dynamic factor in development. Speech is, among other things, rendered dynamic by the process of mediation, especially in the period from about 1–7 years. This is not the only source of its dynamism, but it is an important one.

This is a problem to which Vygotsky gives much attention in this period (Vygotsky, 1928a, 1928h, 1929a, 1929c, 1929h, 1930e, 1930g, 1930j, 1930k, 1931a, Ch. 5, 1931b, Ch. 3). Mediated perception, memory and attention are functions that are required by the three lines of development of signs (Figure 4.2). The interaction of these functions with signs is mainly illustrated with examples from the development of speech, although we should assume that similar interactions occur for writing and arithmetic. Mediated functions are combined to form the various kinds of meaning that develop in childhood; meaning in this sense is a compound function.

There are three key questions we can ask about the mediation of functions:

1 Are cognitive functions mediated by signs?
2 If so, do the mediated cognitive functions thus produced result in changed varieties of meaning by alterations in the mechanics of meaning formation?
3 Or do they result in changed varieties of meaning by changing the mechanisms governing meaning use?

It is important to separate these issues, as, in his most extended discussion (Vygotsky, 1931b), he concentrates mainly on the first, which is really a preliminary to the more specific issues raised in 2 and 3, which he does also discuss, but more briefly. He sometimes gives the impression that an affirmative reply to the first question will amount to an affirmative reply to the other two, which of course it will not. However, the first question is significant, as, if the answer to it is negative, the other two are redundant.

Are functions mediated by signs?

Vygotsky (1931b) begins his survey of empirical evidence on childhood cognitive functions with a short encapsulation of findings from a range of experimental tasks and sources of observation. The topics covered are:

- remembering with the aid of signs
- the selection reaction (a task involving choice)
- development of attention
- mediated perception

His object is to show that, in each case, there are three stages of development. The first, at least in the strict interpretation of the theory, involves the naive or magical use of signs; the second the external use of signs to control the behaviour of the child in a more rational and less naive way; the third, the internalised use of signs so that the child controls its own behaviour. These are thus similar to the three stages in the mediation of signs we have already encountered and correspond to early childhood, preschool and first school. There is, however, persistent ambiguity as to whether the first stage is the naive or magical use of signs or naive functioning without signs. While the first accords better with his overall theory, the second is sometimes introduced when the evidence will not support the first interpretation.

Vygotsky's studies of memory usually use some variation of one of the best known tasks in the study of human memory, which is now called serial recall of a word list. In the version used by Vygotsky and his co-workers, the experimenter reads out a list of words at a certain rate and the subject must repeat them at the end of the list, in the order in which they were given. To this, Vygotsky and his co-workers then added a second, less conventional, condition, which was that the child be given a pack of picture cards and told either, vaguely, 'Perhaps these cards will help you remember' or, more definitely, that it was advisable to connect each word to a card.

He claims that we find naive or natural memory in the 1–3-year period. Although children younger than 3 years were not tested, it is reasonable to assume they would find it hard to use the picture cards as an aid. However, they would probably use natural memory, without the use of signs, not the naive use of signs to assist memory.

We then move to a form of artificially assisted or mnemotechnical memory, as Vygotsky grandiloquently calls it, in the period 3–7 years. At preschool age (3–7 years), children can use the pictures to help recall the words. They usually do this by creating a story or visual scene or other meaningful idea that links the picture with the word. An example given is of connecting a picture of a camel with the word 'death'. The association is created by saying, 'A camel in the desert is a wanderer and dies of thirst.'

When he describes the child's use of the cards, Vygotsky seems torn between what his theory requires and what almost certainly happens. Thus, at the outset he says that, when the child uses the cards, the connections made without the cards are each replaced with two connections, one from a neighbouring word to the picture and the other from the picture to the current word (1931b, p. 181). This accords with the theory, at this date, which suggests that signs connect two original stimuli by replacing a single connection with two.

This is a possible strategy to adopt in the word list task, but it is probably not the most effective one and is not the one that subjects describe in the comments Vygotsky reports (1931b, pp. 181–182). This is to form a single connection between a picture and each word, as just described in the camel example.

There is no evidence given for the internalisation of assisted memory that should form the third stage in the development of memory. It is not obvious that it will be present in the form Vygotsky claims, which is as an internalised version of his version of the external use of the cards.

The lack of evidence about when and how the stimuli used in mediated memory are internalised is said to be remedied by another study, which compared the above serial recall task with cards to the same task without cards. This produced the parallelogram of memory development, a phenomenon first demonstrated using the experimental tasks just outlined by A. N. Leont'ev (1930) (Figure 4.3). In the natural memory task, that is without cards, from 3 to 6 years performance is fairly poor and improves little. At the same time, performance in the aided memory task improves rapidly. But from 7–13 years performance on the aided memory task reaches a plateau, improving only slowly, while that on the natural memory task begins to increase rapidly, reaching about the level of the aided task by the end of this period.

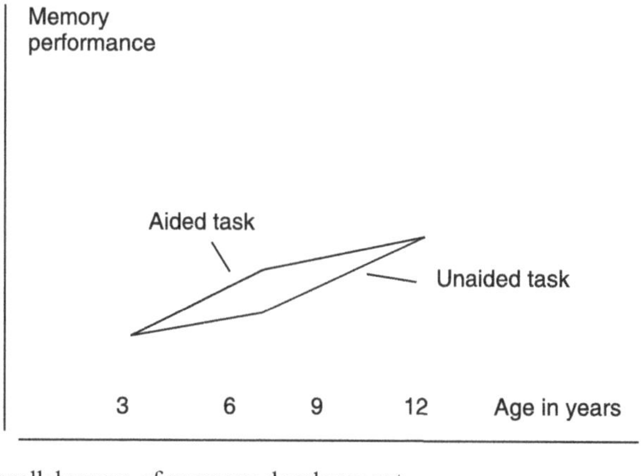

Figure 4.3 Parallelogram of memory development

It is inferred that the improvement in the aided memory task from 3 to 6 is due to increased use of the aids. It cannot be due to increased functioning of natural memory, as performance on the natural memory task remains roughly static. The plateau on the aided memory task, from 7–13 years, appears because the assistance that can be gained from the aids has now been almost fully taken up. The increase in the natural memory task in this period is because the child is now able to generate its own internal aids and increasingly benefits from these. So such children are able to realise for themselves that they should try to associate each item to be recalled with an internal stimulus.

Although this is ingenious, there is a problem. The use of internal memory aids does not provide automatic correct ordering, in the way that a pack of physical cards does, unless the individual does one of two things. The individual may be familiar with mnemonic methods such as the 'mental journey', in which the memoriser imagines that each thing to be memorised is left at a point along the route of a journey that has previously been memorised (Luria, 1960; Yates, 1964). However, this seems unlikely among a high proportion of 7–13 year olds and is not invoked by Vygotsky, who again refers to the example of the camel and death. It seems more likely that the internal strategy of most children will be to combine each word with the next using an image, although this is not an internalised version of the external strategy. This is still close to Vygotsky's theory, but it is not exactly what it requires.

The next topic covered is choice, for which he uses the selection reaction. In this, the child is asked to respond to a range of stimuli with a range of responses. The stimuli might, for example, be several coloured cards and the responses pressing a key with a particular finger for each colour. Children can usually master such a task unaided by age 6.

He uses two alternative conditions here. The first is when the stimuli are ordered or organised, as when they are shapes with increasing numbers of sides. Such figures can be placed in order next to the response keys. It is critical to the child's success in this condition that it is able to grasp the organisation found in the stimuli without assistance. When this occurs, the organisation in the figures helps the child to press the right key.

A second condition is when the nature of the organisation is not immediately apparent to the child, but instructions are given to help the subject to organise the stimuli. So if we use colours as stimuli, most children will not see any organisation in the colours. However, we can advise them to order the colours from left to right, according to how hot or cold they appear to be: red, orange, yellow, green, blue. Under these circumstances, most young children will be able to use the organisation in the colours and pair the colours with the keys.

The inference that Vygotsky draws from this experiment is that there are again three stages in the psychological processes involved in the selection reaction: The connections between the keys and the cards are remembered by natural memory; they are remembered by means of active and organised processes, when the stimuli suggest such activity and organisation or when it is pointed out; they are recalled by self-generated, active strategies. In contrast to the pure memory studies, the first stage here involves natural memory processes applied to external cultural devices, which is what the theory requires. It is reasonable to think that such application will predate the use of organisation in the stimuli, although this particular study does not show this. However, once again it is neither obvious nor shown by the study that the use of external memory aids always predates that of internal memory strategies. Vygotsky only claims that the latter is somewhat more difficult than the former, while the theory makes a stronger claim than this. It is, however, true that most children were found able to use external memory aids at the age of 6 (the youngest age studied), which fits the theory. Overall, this task supports the theory, as applied to choice reactions, somewhat better than the memory tasks.

Next, we come to the development of attention, where Vygotsky relies on studies by A. N. Leont'ev (1931). The first involves two experimental conditions, both involving a game of questions and answers. A simplified version is this. The child is asked a succession of questions, to some of which the natural answer is a colour (e.g. What colour is grass?) and to some of which it is not (e.g. Do you go to school?). The child is told that it must not mention the forbidden colours black or white or say any of the nonforbidden colours, for instance, green, more than once. So if the question is 'What colour is snow?' the child must avoid answering 'White'. If the child has already said 'Green' to the question about the colour of grass and the question is asked 'What colour are pine trees?', the child must avoid answering 'Green' again. Given that the rules of the actual game were even more complicated than this, it is not surprising that even 9 year olds were found to have difficulty in playing the game correctly.

A second condition was introduced in which there was the opportunity to use external devices to focus attention on the requirements of the task. These devices were a set of coloured cards, which included black, white and then various other colours, such as cream and red. Vygotsky does not actually tell us how subjects used these cards, but we can surmise one way of using them, which would be to separate the black and white cards from the others at the start, placing them somewhere prominent, so as to be reminded that these are danger colours. Then, as other colours are given in answers, we could add them to the prominent group, as they have now also become dangerous.

The explanation given for performance is essentially the same as for the memory parallelogram (Figure 4.3). At the start of the preschool age there was little difference between mediated and unmediated conditions, presumably because subjects could not take advantage of the mediating materials. During the preschool period (3–7 years), performance on the mediated condition improved rapidly, while that on the unmediated condition did not. This presumably showed that the preschoolers were increasingly able to take advantage of the mediating materials, that is the coloured cards. During the period of first school (7–13 years), this improvement in the mediated condition levelled out and it is claimed that this is because the use of external devices has now been fully taken up. But, at the same time, performance in the unmediated condition improved quite rapidly because, it is claimed, the children are now able to generate their own mediating processes, such as internal representations for the colours. By the time adulthood is reached, the two conditions are once again similar in performance terms, although both were much improved from their preschool level.

Once again, these findings do not demonstrate Vygotsky's theory in its entirety in the form proposed. There is no demonstration that attention is directed by the natural use of external devices in the initial period. Also, preschool children are not shown to be under the control of others, but under their own control, through their own external actions and use of materials.

Vygotsky does not report any studies by his own school on mediated perception. However, because at that time it was thought that perceptual constancies appear around 1 year of age, he is able to suggest that this appearance is due to the influence of the infant's first speech on perception (Vygotsky, 1929d, 1931a). Two examples of perceptual constancies are these. First, the ability of the child to realise that, when it moves away from or towards objects, although they appear to get smaller and larger, they do not do so in reality (*size constancy*). Second, when an object rotates in front of an older child or adult, although it seems to change shape, the viewer realises it does not do so in reality (*shape constancy*). The appearance of constancies in infancy, itself due to speech, is said to later react back on speech in the child's early language, especially as it stabilises perceptually based meanings (Vygotsky, 1929d, 1931a).

As today we know that some perceptual constancies appear in the first half of the first year of life and probably as early as 2–4 months this argument could not be accepted today (see Chapter 12).

Vygotsky also considers object permanence as a form of perception and makes a similar argument in relation to this (Vygotsky, 1931a). Object permanence is the child's belief that even though objects often go out of sight, they usually continue to exist and move about in unseen space. In this case, probably following Piaget (1926b), he puts the achievement of object permanence around 8 months. This leads him to think that it emerges from the child's practical uses of objects. Later studies have again shown that this emerges earlier, casting doubt on this suggestion (see Chapter 12).

The idea that as meaning develops it has mediating influences on perception is also canvassed (Vygotsky, 1931a). So the ability to name objects that comes with language has the effect of encouraging perception to become more analytic and breaks the world up into separate objects.

We have seen in this section that there is at least promising evidence in key areas, in the age range 1–13 years, from studies by Vygotsky's own school, that signs can mediate certain cognitive functions, although there are some problems in confirming that this takes the specific form that Vygotsky suggests. He also uses evidence from the general literature on early perceptual constancies and the permanent object concept to throw light on development in the first year of life. At the time he was writing, this seemed reasonable, but later work has shown that these abilities appear earlier, meaning that his ideas here need some rethinking (Chapter 12).

It is also worth noting that, in Vygotsky's main example of internalisation, which is speech, the internalised cognitive aid, words, could not exist in an internal form had it not first existed in an external form. For one thing, we have inner speech in a particular language, such as Russian or English, which we must have learned from those around us. This is not true of many examples of the internal stimuli we use to direct memory, attention and choice. For instance, the images we use to help in memory, leaving aside packs of cards, could probably be formed without any previous exposure to pictures. So the inherent plausibility of the internalisation explanation that exists in the case of speech is lacking in some of these other cases.

Do mediated functions support meaning formation?

Vygotsky suggests two processes are involved here: Contact with language breaks down holistic perception into components; and voluntary memory and attention enable the child, from about 7 years, to exploit systematic strategies to use these. Some of these strategies will be used to form new meanings. He mainly relies on the argument that, because certain kinds of meaning appear at the same time as do voluntary memory and attention, the appearance of these functions causes the appearance of the new kinds of meaning (Vygotsky, 1931b, Chs 9, 10). His arguments about this have been invalidated by subsequent research, which has altered the timing of both the meanings and the functions. Consideration of this is therefore postponed until Chapter 12.

Do mediated functions support meaning use?

He applies the same kind of argument here as for meaning formation. Changes in the nature of signs are predicted to take place at the same time as changes in meaning use. This gives his claims the same weaknesses as those relating to meaning formation.

Conclusions

In this period, the development of the child is pictured as the development of three dimensions of psychological activity: the levels, motivation and the inner and the outer. The levels are: tools and practice; the social relations within which practice occurs; signs, including language, and consciousness; the self. Except for some writings that are atypical of the period but point towards his last period (Vygotsky, 1930g, 1931b, Ch. 15), he avoids saying that the levels develop through general stages. Rather, the different levels and different strands develop through their own particular stages. However, given that signs are already seen as exerting a controlling influence on many other processes and that a series of similar local stages applies to three of the main kinds of sign, we are already on the threshold of general or global stages.

The development of the personality up to about 2 years is mainly driven forward by practice. After this, it is driven by speech, play, writing and concepts, in successive periods. This means that there is a long-term shift from practice to signs and then to a synthesis of the two (advanced concepts). In the middle part of development we find the following cycle, although as yet not used rigorously: First comes social relations, these are the basis for certain forms of consciousness, especially those involving signs, and then for self-consciousness; this leads to improvements in the nature of tools and practice; which then produces a changed form of social relations. The main drive forward in this cycle comes from signs and partial self-consciousness. In adolescence the synthesis of practice and language in advanced concepts becomes the predominant driving force in development and this sequence of phases is less in evidence.

His series of local stages, in the development of spontaneous meanings, persisted almost unaltered into the final period. Spontaneous meanings are those formed from informal conversation, as opposed to formal education. This sequence is, roughly: perceptual meanings; complexes; preconcepts; concepts proper. Some problems with the second and third stages were mentioned.

Vygotsky tried to show that the natural functions of attention, memory and perception are mediated by the use of signs, thus becoming mediated functions that are able to further promote the development of signs and other compound functions. The evidence he cites for this is flawed and suggests at several points that development does not follow the series of local stages he suggests, namely the use of signs with functions in natural, external social control and internalised control modes. Some of these problems could be reduced with greater attention to the way in which tasks do (or do not) involve the processes he is seeking to study.

Motivation has a dynamic effect on the formation of cognitions not only because it is necessary, but also because it directs the content, structure, system and use of such cognitions. For instance, if a child or adult is interested in a topic and is motivated to pursue it, they will know a lot about it; if they are not, they will not. The use of cognitions is also determined by the influence of motivation on set.

The role of the inner and the outer is not explained as clearly in this period as in the next, but the contrast is already present. It relates to two main areas: the self and speech. Imagination and creativity are used by the inner self to communicate with the rational, external self. The importance of the related contrast between inner and outer speech is also stressed, although this is not as clearly linked to that between the inner and outer self as it became in the following period.

5 Biological and historical development, 1932–34

The year 1932 is an arbitrary date at which to begin Vygotsky's last period. In reality he began to change his position in 1930 and was still changing when he died. However, by 1932 the new ideas had come to dominate.

These changes came partly from Vygotsky's desire to improve his dynamic model for his shorter periods, which he now called *stages*. He had advanced preliminary versions of this in 1928–31 and sketches of a complete model appeared in works of this period (Vygotsky, 1930g, 1931b, Ch. 15). However, he was evidently dissatisfied with that and produced a considerably revised version (Vygotsky, 1933i, 1934f). The changes of the last period were only partly due to this. They were also an effort to use the ideas of Hegel and Spinoza more consistently. There was an attempt to carry through more thoroughly than he had done in the previous periods the programme of integrating the Marxist and Hegelian traditions; as well as to face the full implications of his own stress on signs. He had begun this in 1928 but had failed to carry it through to its conclusion. This was, for instance, seen in his revised approaches to meaning, motivation and the development of the self.

Underlying model

In one sense the underlying map changed greatly, because the content of some of the four levels and of motivation changed. However, if we look just at the general nature of the four levels, the general nature of motivation and the number of steps along which the child can advance on each, things remain much the same. The third main dimension in the map of development, the inner versus the outer, remains the same, even in content.

His new dynamic model is also an evolutionary rather than a revolutionary development. He implies that this model will apply broadly to history as well as the child (Vygotsky, 1933i, 1934f), although there are, once again, some differences. This model continues to have three main features: the succession of dominant dynamic functions, mostly connected with signs used in communication; the mediation of the functions of perception, memory and attention by signs; the mediation of thought by language.

Dominant dynamic functions are now called stable neoformations, which are functions that emerge during a stage, and whose maturation towards the end of the stage leads to a structural reorganisation of other functions; this then leads to an alteration in the child's general consciousness, particularly its self-consciousness (Vygotsky, 1933i, 1934f). These functions are mainly those previously considered as dynamic functions: for infancy, the maturation of biological functions (0–1 year); for early childhood, speech (1–3 years); for the preschool period, play (3–7 years); for the age of first school, writing (7–13 years); for adolescence, advanced concepts (13–17 years). On this level there is little change from the previous period, but this framework is now used more rigorously and comprehensively and is fleshed out with considerably more detail.

The new personality formed by the stable neoformation at each stage, through its action on the system of the child's functions and on its self-consciousness, then revolts against the social relations that originally brought it into being; these are then revolutionised in turn. After the first stage, these neoformations all involve signs used for communication.

The mediation of functions by signs occurs in a similar way to before, but the timing is different, with memory mediated earlier than before.

In dealing with the dialectic between thought and language, he continues to suggest that practical activity maintains its dominance in the advance of thought through most of early childhood. It is not until towards the end of this period that true speech, resulting from the synthesis of practical activity and language sounds, achieves a dominant form (Vygotsky, 1932d). The dominance of speech over thought continues until late adolescence, when practice and language are synthesised in advanced concepts (Vygotsky, 1933g). After early childhood, speech remains a kind of transmission belt communicating to thought more fundamental influences originating from the leading functions: play, writing and advanced concepts. However, thought now remains the primary vehicle for the representation of problems throughout development.

We can continue to think of Vygotsky's theory of how the child acquires knowledge as dialectical realism. That is to say that first practice, then speech used for communication and then their synthesis in advanced concepts take on the role of connecting the child and adolescent with reality.

He also alters his emphasis in approaching meaning. As he says little about this in dealing with species development, it will be more conveniently dealt with in the next chapter, on the child.

Biological development

Vygotsky's conception of biological evolution changed considerably in his last period, while his conception of historical development remained, in broad outline, a modified version of Marx, although now viewed in a different way. That he should change his ideas about biological development is not surprising, as his earlier ones had relied substantially on reflexology and he now rejects this.

The new ideas in this area are not stated directly, but we can infer them from what is said about children. The main influence of biology in the child is now to determine the organism's level of dependence or independence. Each stage of development is now said to begin with what he calls a social situation of development. This is produced by the organism's state of dependence or independence. So, infancy begins with a social situation of development involving minimal biological maturation and progresses to the point where the infant becomes somewhat conscious of itself and its world, enabling it to see the need to change these in order to achieve further development (Vygotsky, 1933i, 1934e, Lects 1, 2, 1934f). The minimal biological maturation of the newborn infant is responsible for its social situation of biological dependency. The biological maturation of the ability to walk is an important part of the social situation of development that begins the second stage of development, around the start of the second year of life. Later on, sexual maturation will be one of the keys to the social situation of development in adolescence (Vygotsky, 1933g).

There is, however, a substantial difficulty in understanding how this applies to biological evolution. The social situation of development that begins infancy is produced because the infant is helpless and depends on adults to look after it. This is a peculiarity of human biology and is not something that is found in all our ancestors. In fact, our more distant ancestors, such as reptiles, amphibians, fish and their invertebrate predecessors, are mostly born able to fend for themselves shortly after they hatch. Below the level of mammals and birds, parenting is the exception, not the rule. Most fish, amphibians and reptiles are able to swim or walk around and feed themselves shortly after hatching. Most are entirely deserted by the parents and have to fend for themselves (Greenberg & Haraway, 2002; Griffin, 2001; Hinde, 1966).

This seems to mean that, according to Vygotsky, such animals have managed to avoid the process of *becoming* independent as they are *born* independent. This seems to show that social development is optional. Vygotsky's theory seems to imply, if taken literally, not only that social development is compulsory, but that it is also required for cognitive development. On the last point, quite a number of species below the level of birds and mammals that begin life able to take care of themselves seem to have at least as much intelligence as others like them that rear their young socially, such as mouth breeder fish and some kinds of snake. The solution here may be that the 'infantile' development of animals that have little parenting does begin, but it is one sided. Various strands of development that belong in this stage, such as perception and visual thinking, proceed well, but because other strands, particularly the social, are weak or absent, such animals do not develop the consciousness that would allow them to synthesise the functions of the first stage and develop beyond it.

In principle, an animal with more rounded development, such as an ape, could achieve this. Vygotsky, taking his cue from Engels, claims that even insects have a very elementary form of consciousness (Engels, 1878, Ch. 7; Vygotsky, 1933i, 1934f). However, he was adamant that animals do not achieve the synthesis of vocal sounds and visual intelligence needed for human-like language; and human-like language is the gateway that takes humans from stage 1 to stage 2. So if we can assume that all animals below the humanoid level remain at stage 1 in their development, in the wild state, there will not be a problem.

However, studies of chimpanzees and gorillas since Vygotsky's time have shown that they are able to acquire human-like language in something like Vygotsky's sense from contact with people (Greenfield & Savage-Rumbhaugh, 1990; Premack, 1971; Savage-Rumbhaugh, McDonald, Sevcik, Hopkins, & Robert, 1986; Sternberg, 1995, pp. 210–11). The main thing they lack is phonemes, that is, discrete speech sounds that are combined together, but they have the other elements he mentions and it is not clear that this is central. As these animals show close bonds between the mother and infant and elaborate parenting, they are thus within the bounds of Vygotsky's theory. Those with this kind of human contact appear to have moved into his second stage.

Historical development

Although Vygotsky's view of historical development changed, it remained largely within the confines of the orthodox Marxist view of history, except for its stress on signs and self-consciousness. From 1928 he had been attempting to put flesh onto the bare bones of Marx's view of the historical development of human psychology. It was this flesh that he largely now removed, replacing it with a new version. This was particularly true in two areas: cognition and motivation. In cognition, he took more of his approach from Hegel and other writers who stressed the distinction between cognition and behaviour. In motivation, he stressed the desire to know more and biological motivation less.

These transformations are mainly seen in what he says about the child, which is covered in the next chapter. We are to understand that they will probably also apply to historical development.

Marx and historical development

We cannot be sure that Vygotsky retained everything from Marx's view of historical development, even outside the topics of signs and self-consciousness. However, in his general comments about Marx's view of history, as well as in those about some particular aspects of it, he continued to give assent to it in a general way.

A general comment comes in Vygotsky (1934c, p. 120), to the effect that his investigations of thinking and speech are carried out within the framework of historical materialism. This term was at that time, in most contexts, and certainly in this one, used as a synonym for Marx's theory of history. So it seems that it is the historical development of production, as conceived by Marx, that still underlies Vygotsky's historical analysis; although, as often with Vygotsky, there is an unstated fudge here, as he differs from Marx on the roles of signs and self-consciousness.

One problem here is that Vygotsky (1934c, Ch. 2) is a reworked version of an article originally published as Vygotsky (1929d), so it could contain material that does not reflect the postures of the last period. However, significant changes were made to reflect his change in views in the later text, so it is likely that had he no longer subscribed to this, it would have been changed.

Another general comment on historical development appears in Vygotsky (1932c), an article that was also included in *Thinking and speech* (1934c). Here, Vygotsky contrasts his own view of how people learned in history with Piaget's (1924) view. He says: 'According to Piaget, primitive man learns from experience only in isolated and specialised technical contexts' (Vygotsky, 1934c, p. 89). He then goes on to say that Piaget lists as such contexts agriculture, hunting and production; which could be shortened to just production. Vygotsky contrasts this 'little learning from production' view of Piaget with his own, which is that historically much was learned from production. He justifies this briefly by saying that production is the basis for primitive man's contact with reality and also the basis for his existence. He then says that, in historical development, learning from the practical activities of production was central to learning in general. This shows that, on this pivotal issue, Vygotsky had not changed his ideas from the last period.

Another change in Vygotsky's late theory suggests that a further shift away from Marx may have occurred. This is because his approach to social relations in the child no longer reflects Marx's social relations of production as closely as it had previously (see Chapter 6). In particular, he no longer argues that the child is subject to the same kind of subordination and command as were slaves. However, he could not have thought that slave production did not exist. So, it is likely that this was less a move away from the Marxist view of history than a move to make the connection of the historical social relations of production, to the child's social relations, more indirect. Marx had thought that the long-term trend of history was towards emancipation, but that the development of production had necessitated a detour in the middle part of history, towards relations involving domination, that would ultimately be reversed. It is as though Vygotsky now thought this detour would be ironed out in the child and development would be straightforwardly one towards emancipation. He could have justified this by pointing out that, according to Marx and Engels, one of the main reasons for repressive relations of production was to enable the accumulation of the means of production, which would otherwise be consumed (Engels, 1878, Part 2, Ch. 4; Marx & Engels, 1848).

There are two other places that strongly suggest his continuing commitment to aspects of Marxism. In Vygotsky (1934e, p. 80) he says that the highest form of society is based on a communist economy and that there is a series of stages in economic development that lead to this. In Vygotsky (1934a), he counterposes reactionary, ultimately fascist, and progressive, ultimately Marxist, psychology in terms that can only indicate his support for the latter.

In addition, Kolbanoskii, who was a Communist Party member assigned as Vygotsky's minder in 1930–34, was so positive about Vygotsky that he brought out *Thinking and speech* after the author's death. He is unlikely to have done this had he suspected he was not a Marxist in some fundamental sense.

Turning to more particular issues, in four places he talks about Marx's view of the four levels of activity with approval (Vygotsky, 1933i, 1934e, 1934f, 1935e). He also says that, in historical development, language is supported and its development driven by social relations of cooperation, which coincides with Marx (Vygotsky, 1933j, 1934c, pp. 48, 49, 259). In Vygotsky (1933i, 1933j, 1934e, 1934f) he repeatedly attributes his conception of consciousness to Marx, although here again, as we will see later, there is a certain amount of fudge involved. In the first chapter of *Thinking and speech* (1934c), probably written in 1933 or 1934, he says: 'Human speech, a system that emerged from the need to interact socially within the labour process, has been and will always be the prototype of this kind of means' (p. 48).

We can summarise this by saying that Vygotsky's statements about Marxism suggest he continued to regard his approach as Marxist and he could indeed assent to some of the most fundamental tenets of Marxism, particularly that the development of the forces of production drives forward that of the relations of production, that is the forms of ownership that apply to them. However, he continued to disagree with Marx that cognition and the forward movement of production arise directly from practice and the use of tools in the middle period of development. He continued to believe that signs must predominate in this period.

Historical pattern of development

Vygotsky now makes it clearer than in the previous period that the steps along the levels are tightly bound together and so an individual, historical or otherwise, must be almost entirely at step 1, 2, 3 or 4. This was one interpretation of his stance earlier, but now it is inescapable. We saw in Chapter 3 that this can be reconciled with Marx's view of the historical development of production as follows. In historical development there will be sudden advances and retreats in the underlying aspects of production, which will all advance and retreat together, as when the levels went up from 1 to 3 in moving from tribalism to state slavery and then down from 3 to 1 in moving from private slavery to feudalism. However, this does not mean that feudalism is the same as tribalism, as these will be accompanied by other kinds of alteration, in this case particularly in the legal relations between the participants in production.

The self

Here, Vygotsky rejects his earlier disguised Hegelianism. He had argued that we are what others think of us. While for Marx we can have direct consciousness of the practice involved in production, and the self is built on this, now that Vygotsky has shown this to be a fallacy, he must build the self on signs. The use of signs to know and act on the world is now the basis for the self and as the use of signs develops through stages, so does the self (Vygotsky, 1933i, 1934f).

He deliberately compares his view of the self with that of Marx by several times harping on a definition of consciousness adapted from Marx (Vygotsky, 1933i, 1933j, 1934f). This is that for both the human being in history and the child consciousness is 'his relation to his environment'. This is abbreviated from Marx: 'Consciousness is at first, of course, merely consciousness concerning the immediate sensuous environment and consciousness of the limited connection with other persons and things outside the individual who is growing self-conscious' (Marx, 1846a, Sect. 1a). Although the two say slightly different things, the only real difference in the definition of consciousness is that Vygotsky should have said 'his conscious relation to his environment', although this is implied.

This is, apparently, a curious definition of consciousness to take from Marx, as it is wider and more general than Marx's more usual idea that consciousness arises from production and the social relations and institutions growing from it. However, this atypical definition serves Vygotsky quite well. Marx no more endorsed the idea that the self arises primarily from signs than he did the idea that cognition arises primarily from signs. However, by choosing to cite this unusually wide definition from Marx, Vygotsky makes it appear that they are in agreement.

Dynamic interaction of levels

Vygotsky now stresses a process that is very prominent in Marx's theory of history. As the forces of production develop ahead of the relations of production this generates social consciousness of the need for a change, leading to social action to create change, often involving the revolutionary overthrow of the society supported by the old form of the relations of production. This consciousness is often imperfect and distorted. For instance, in the transition from feudalism to capitalism in Europe, the class consciousness of the feudal orders was represented by Catholicism, that of the rising bourgeoisie by Protestantism. The English Civil War of 1640–50 was triggered by underlying issues of power and taxation between these two loose coalitions, but, during the fighting, religious issues were uppermost in the minds of the participants (Engels, 1878, Chs 9, 10; Vygotsky, 1934c, Ch. 1, 1935e).

But its indirect connection to material interests notwithstanding, religion served as an effective means by which consciousness, including self-consciousness, could react back on the social base. Vygotsky also applies this idea of consciousness reacting back on the social base to the child, in an even more wide-ranging way than he had previously.

Conclusions

Vygotsky's view of biological development changes fundamentally in his last period. He now stresses the situation of biological immaturity in which lower organisms find themselves and the role of self-consciousness in leading out of this; although it is unlikely that anything more than a preliminary form of this self-consciousness exists in animals other than apes with human contact.

Vygotsky continued to endorse Marx's view that the historical development of fundamental human capacities is driven by the development of production, as well as other aspects of Marx's philosophy. However, he continues to stress the dynamic function of signs and a self-consciousness that is built on them, in a way that is contrary to Marx.

6 The child, 1932–34

Underlying model

This was outlined in the last chapter. The following is a summary and extension of what was said there.

In his last period, Vygotsky continued to focus on the three dimensions he used in the previous periods: levels of activity, motivation and the inner versus the outer. The least developed of these at the end of the previous period, the inner versus the outer, remained in much the same form as before. The other two were subjected to fundamental revision in their content, but their overall form changed little and the way they interacted in development only moderately. There continued to be four levels of activity, each with four developmental steps along it: practice and tools; social relations; signs; self-consciousness. Motivation continued to develop along five steps, one for infancy and four corresponding to the four steps in the levels. The inner and the outer developed along two steps only, as it was only formed at the start of the fourth stage of development, around 7 years.

The main emphasis in dynamics is on the short-term dynamics involved in stages. The model of long-term dynamics remained broadly the same, stressing practice at the start of development, until about $2\frac{1}{2}$ years; signs and self-consciousness in the middle period; and the synthesis of these two factors towards the end of adolescence.

The short-term dynamic model, operating within stages, is that dominant functions, or neoformations, mature towards the end of each stage. These are responsible for creating new steps in consciousness and self-consciousness, which react back on the rest of the personality, prompting an overall change both in the personality and in social relations. This cycle then repeats itself. The dominant functions for each stage are much the same as those suggested for the corresponding periods in 1928–31. The main difference is embodied in the change from describing such periods as infancy, early childhood and preschool as periods to describing them as stages. Periods are defined by loosely bound collections of functions; stages are tightly bound collections of functions, which are connected together into systems and subject to sudden, revolutionary, changes as one stage gives way to the next.

In the personality as a whole the leading functions are: practice (infancy); speech (early childhood); play (preschool); writing (first school); concepts (adolescence) (Vygotsky, 1933i, 1934f).

Another change in dynamics was in the differentiation and synthesis of psychological functions. The general picture of psychological functions, which differentiate in infancy and are later synthesised into a single stream, is retained in the last period, although there are some differences from the previous period (Figure 6.1).

The way in which the division of functions takes place is, however, quite different. Consciousness is now formed from the identification of patterns and order in the external or internal worlds, rather than from self-mastery. Internalisation still takes place through the regular way in which functions go from a phase of external social cooperation with others to an internalised version of the same form of cooperation, although now consciousness precedes rather than follows internalisation (Vygotsky, 1934c, Ch. 7). Following internalisation, the internalised function can then itself become conscious on a higher level. Although Vygotsky does not say this, it is as though the process of internalisation encourages the patterns and order in mental life to become more salient. Consciousness of the parallels between two or more functions, which is needed to produce synthesis, is now also formed on the same model. The merging of language and thought at the end of infancy is one of the most significant of such syntheses.

The main reasons for these changes to the theory were: efforts to cope with problems in the earlier version; willingness to accept the implications of empirical generalisations reached in the previous period; efforts to further extend and refine the use of Hegel and Spinoza in the theory. There may also have been some attempt to make his approach more politically acceptable, as alleged by Joravsky (1987, 1989) and Kozulin (1999), although this was

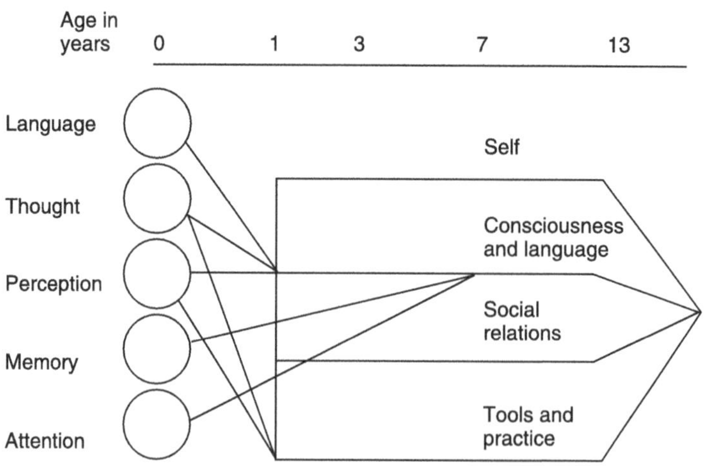

Figure 6.1 Formation of levels from functions, last period

probably not as significant as they think. Two areas where we are most inclined to see the influence of political pressure are as follows: in the shift to the Spinozan view of motivation; and in the shift in his educational views, to coincide with the overall change in official educational philosophy and policy that began to be implemented in 1930. This second shift made modified traditional education into the ideal of communist education. However, there were good reasons why he might have made these changes without political pressure.

The use of Spinoza is not surprising, as he was one of Marx's favourite philosophers. The shift to traditional education may have been because he, like those in authority, had become disillusioned with the failure of social progressivism, insofar as it had a foothold in the system prior to 1930, to challenge the average child. In addition, had Vygotsky been inclined to give in to pressure he would not have continued to maintain that educational potential is limited by inheritance after this view had been condemned (Vygotsky, 1934e, Lect. 3).

Differences between species and child development

As in the previous period, in species development, once social development begins, with the emergence of human beings, biological evolution stops. In children, by contrast, biological development stretches over development at least up to adolescence; long after social development has begun. Infancy and early childhood are still mainly occupied with attaining the results of biological evolution, while the balance of biological development occurs during later stages. Another continuing difference is that child development goes through the steps, along the levels and other dimensions, in a rather evenly spaced lockstep manner; whereas in history there were sudden surges forward as well as large steps back. Another important, and this time completely novel, difference is that, after the third stage of development, much of the child's learning now takes place through formal teaching in modern societies. This produces a kind of top-down learning that begins with instruction in general rules; this contrasts with the bottom-up learning found in historical development that begins with examples.

Map of development

The levels

Tools and practical activity

Vygotsky continues to argue that the nature of practical activity in each stage of development is considerably influenced by the kind of language and consciousness found in the stage. From the end of infancy, we have the separation of the means (e.g. the thread used to pull up a toy) from the end (e.g. the child gets the toy). At this point the infant acts individually, rather than socially. In the stage of early childhood (1–3 years), the child's problem solving begins to be influenced by suggestions from others, conveyed in gesture and speech. These are influential from about the middle of the stage of early childhood. He cites the shift from autonomous speech and the emergence of more cooperative and conventional speech around 2 years as evidence of this (Vygotsky, 1934b, 1935g).

The start of the preschool stage (3–7 years) is marked by the beginnings of an analytic approach to objects. This is reasonable, as children of this age are beginning to play with such things as construction toys and dressup dolls and to engage in construction and building with materials found to hand. A particular linguistic advance that helps to further practical problem solving within such activities in the second half of the stage continues to be egocentric self-instruction, found in the stick and fruit problem, as well as in many others (Vygotsky, 1934c, Ch. 7). Here, spoken language is used in self-instruction while solving a problem. The use of language to search for a solution to problems makes the search more fluid and more effective.

As development proceeds beyond the preschool age, the search for solutions to problems is removed, from the commonsense problem spaces of the young child, to the realm of more precise and semi-abstract meanings (Vygotsky, 1934c, Ch. 7, 1934e, Lect. 2). These enable the use of measurement and elaborate planning, both in schoolwork and in the hobbies and interests of the child in the age of first school (7–13 years): such things as constructing models, buying and selling, planning routes and designing clothes.

Sources on adolescence in this period are meagre, but he retains his emphasis on abstract concepts as the key to adolescent cognition (Vygotsky, 1933g). In view of this, he almost certainly continued to think that a new kind of more global consciousness in problem solving influences the adolescent from mid-adolescence (Vygotsky, 1931a, Chs 2, 3). This provides a new form of practical activity and problem solving to correspond to adolescence, with its new and more abstract interests in such things as economics, social philosophy, politics, psychology and literature.

Perception is also closely linked to practical activity. Vygotsky (1933i, pp. 274–281, 290–292, 1934f) first explains perceptual generalisation by saying that people generalise objects according to their social purpose. So if we see a collection of saucepans and frying pans, we can separate the two, as they have different purposes in our methods of cooking; but someone from a culture with no metal, who was unfamiliar with our uses for pans, would not realise this, dividing them according to some purpose with which they were familiar, perhaps their potential as weapons.

Three stages in the development of perception from 1 to 13 years are described. The first is the syncretic stage from 1–3 years, in which the holism of the child's perceptions also dominates the meanings it gives to words. From 3–7 years the child is able to form improved generalisations that enable objects to be seen as representatives of a type of object, that is, defined by attributes rather than the vague resemblances of the syncretic period. So, the child will learn that 'frying pan' is defined by the attribute that it is a pan and is used for frying, not by other accidental features, such as its size, the material of which it is made or the colour of its handle. This is the first stage in which there is an analytic approach to objects.

From 7–13 years, by way of contrast, we find that, among other things, perception expresses the child's growing self-awareness. It is now able to comment on its own internal states by saying 'I am sad', 'I am clever' and so forth. It appears that this applies to cognitive as well as emotional states, although no examples of the former are given.

The stages in perception are described as starting from the beginning of the main stages, rather than from the middle, as was the case with the influence of language on the practical use of objects. It is not clear why this is, as the mediation of cognitive functions by language is now, in general, claimed to begin in the middle of stages (Vygotsky, 1933i, 1934f, 1935e). For this reason, it is likely that the ages at which perceptual changes begin should be delayed, so they also begin in the middle of each stage.

Social relations

The social principle behind Vygotsky's whole late theory of development is that as the child develops it gains freedom and independence. Social relations are no longer constrained by being very similar to Marx's social relations within production, as they had been in the third period. Vygotsky (1933i, 1934e, 1934f) says that a certain form of activity corresponds to each stage, activity that takes place within a certain form of social relations. The main social relations typical of a stage are now usually depicted as all of a piece; but it seems likely that he thought that other kinds of social relations, not central to that particular stage, could also exist beside them, as had been the case earlier.

The way the child cooperates with the adult is now captured by the broader everyday sense of the word 'cooperation', rather than being confined, as previously, to its Marxist sense (e.g. Vygotsky, 1934c, Ch. 7). The everyday sense of cooperation is that the child and adult act together towards a common goal. These relations of cooperation range from the dependent relations of infancy and early childhood to the independent relations of adulthood.

His stress on the development of freedom must be understood within the Hegelian and Marxist context within which it is intended. Freedom and independence can only be fully realised in someone who understands the limitations under which they live. It is not real freedom to believe you can do anything you like. You might jump off a tall building believing you can fly and in one sense you are, of course, free to do so. But to be really free, you must understand the laws of the physical and social world and make them serve your will. So if you are at the top of a tall building and want to get to the ground, you will take the lift or the stairs. The sense in which you are free to jump is not true freedom. If you want to do things you must know how to make them happen. If you do not know this then you are not free and your actions will probably result in something entirely different from what you wanted. The infant begins not knowing how to do much at all. It does not know how to feed itself, how to change its nappy, how to walk, how to talk, how to pick things up and a host of other things. It does not know how to get the world or people to do what it wants. It can only tell people it wants something by crying. From here, it must acquire the knowledge that will enable it to get the world and people to do what it wants (Vygotsky, 1934c, Ch. 7).

It must also acquire self-control. The infant in its early stages does not think before it acts. It is very impulsive and if it sees something it wants, then it will try to get it immediately, without thinking of the consequences. Such impulsiveness is a continuing characteristic at least until the age of 7 years. Young children will run out onto roads after balls without thinking, cross roads without looking and eat unknown substances, with hardly a second thought. According to Vygotsky, getting control of oneself is not just something else you must do as well as learning to think about what you are doing: It is an important part of it.

As the child develops, it gradually masters the problem of becoming an independent actor in the world. This means that the action of the child's personality in the social situation around it is one of mastery. It not only masters the external environment through practice, but by internalising the environment it comes to master it, not in the trivial sense that an imaginary environment will do what it wants, but in the sense that it comes to understand the external environment through the internal, represented environment and is thus able to master the external environment.

In this period Vygotsky stresses that each stage begins from a social situation of development, which is a distinct kind of social relations that embody a certain level of dependence or independence for the child. The social situation of development for infancy is determined by the young infant's maximum dependency and minimum capacity for interaction with others (Vygotsky, 1932b, p. 217, 1934b). This situation arises from the loss of physiological support that occurs at birth, which means the infant needs to be fed and sheltered by the deliberate actions of those around it, rather than receiving these things automatically from the mother's body (Vygotsky, 1932d, p. 265).

With the start of walking and talking in early childhood, the child leaves its earlier state of biological dependence, as it can now begin to perform such biological necessities as feeding itself. While social relations in infancy were unconscious or barely conscious on the part of the infant, in early childhood there are real, conscious social relations to others. The partial independence achieved through walking and talking is the basis for the social relations that form the social situation of development at the start of early childhood, that is immediately after the age of 1 year on average (Vygotsky, 1932d).

The social situation of development at the start of the preschool age (3–7 years) focuses on relations of authority with the parents (Vygotsky, 1933f). The tendency for children at the end of the previous stage (2–3 years) to be difficult and uncooperative is well known and is mentioned. This leaves a residue of problems over authority that must be resolved in the social situation that begins the preschool stage (3–4 years).

Little is said directly about the social situations of development for first school and adolescence. However, one thing we do learn is that the achievement of sexual maturity is part of the social situation of development for adolescence (Vygotsky, 1934e, Lect. 5). The starting points for development in all stages involve shifts towards independence. Thus, sexual attraction encourages the adolescent to further loosen its ties with the parents and form strong emotional bonds with those of its own age, as part of the route towards independence.

Signs

Signs here means anything that can communicate meaning, such as gestures, speech or writing. His conception of signs and language, one of the centrepieces of the entire theory, underwent a shift of emphasis. He now left behind the reflexological view of language, elements of which had been retained in his previous approach. This had been particularly seen in his idea that meaning is an instruction to do something. Although he had already criticised this approach in Vygotsky (1931b, pp. 72–77), he tended to revert to it even in the same work when discussing the connection between meaning and cooperation. Instead, he now turned more consistently to traditional conceptions of language and meaning, particularly those of Aristotle and his followers.

The central part of this can best be expressed in our contemporary jargon by saying that meaning was now seen consistently as propositional content, rather than an instruction to do something (Vygotsky, 1932c, 1932e, 1934c, Ch. 6). The propositional content of a communicative act such as asking a question, giving a description or a command is the factual content of the act. So if I ask the question 'Where is Moscow?', the propositional content is 'Where Moscow is'. If I say 'Moscow is in Russia' the propositional content is 'Moscow is in Russia'.

The key difference between propositional content and meaning as an instruction to do something is that the former sees meaning as a store of information about the world that can be communicated to someone else; while meaning as an instruction sees meaning as a kind of order, rather than a store of information. Although Vygotsky in the present period regarded words and not propositions as the fundamental unit of language, if we express the same shift in relation to words, we have to say that the shift is to conceptual meaning or word meaning. Both can be confused with Vygotsky's earlier terminology. For this reason I have described the change as one to propositional content.

Along with the idea of propositional content, we also get that of word or conceptual meaning, in the sense of the cognitive meaning of the components of a proposition, such as the meanings of 'Russia', 'cold' and 'winter', in the sentence 'Russia is cold in winter' (Vygotsky, 1934c, Ch. 6). This was of key importance to Vygotsky in this period. He stresses that word meaning is a central unit, because it connects the opposites of thought and physical sound and mediates between them (Vygotsky, 1934c, Ch. 6).

The change from meaning as a command to meaning as propositional content also had an influence on the way that the transmission of change from one level in the child's activity to another took place. Previously this transmission, where it was psychological, had been achieved by very much the same means that enabled Thorndike's (1902, 1911) cats to escape from their puzzle box. The principle was that if an action leads to positive results keep doing it, if it doesn't stop doing it (Thorndike's law of effect). So if a new way of cooperating gets better results keep it; if a new way of talking within the new way of cooperating gets better results keep that. Vygotsky, like Bekhterev (1926a), had recognised that the reward for a social action may be experienced at first by the whole group, but the group will then be capable of rewarding its members in turn. Within the new view, by contrast, transfer of influence usually takes place because the child understands what is needed.

Among the three main lines in the development of signs, namely speech, writing and arithmetic, most attention continues to be given to the development of speech (Vygotsky, 1932b, 1932c, 1932d, 1932e, 1934c, Chs 5, 6). However, we are to understand that the new analysis also transfers to the other two strands. Only the spontaneous development of speech is dealt with in the sections immediately below; discussion of the development of taught meanings in speech appears later, in the section on the dynamics of development.

Spontaneous meaning of speech Spontaneous meanings are those that arise from informal conversation, as distinct from more or less formal teaching. The development of such spontaneous meaning changes in two ways from the earlier period. Previously, the stages in meaning were derived from Sakharov's (1930) experimental studies of concept attainment. The task used in these was described in Chapter 4. A short summary is as follows. The child is given an array of blocks of differing shapes and colours and told some have a certain nonsense word on the reverse and there is a rule connecting the word to the blocks. They must continually guess what the word means by saying which blocks it will be found on and, if they are wrong, they are shown what is actually on the underside of one of their chosen items. This goes on until they either give up or the right meaning is given.

These studies identified four main ways in which meanings can relate to objects, which are, in developmental order: syncretic, complexive, preconceptual and conceptual. Now, as a result of turning to studies of actual as opposed to artificial meanings, he adds to this substantially (Vygotsky, 1934c, pp. 228–30).

The development of meaning is now seen to proceed along two interlinked but distinct axes: structural generalisation, which is similar to the previous approach; and generality, which is a new vertical dimension, such that meanings higher in generality include those lower down, as 'bird' includes 'sparrow' and 'eagle'. As development takes place and each level of structural generalisation emerges, it makes possible a certain number and type of levels of generality.

Syncretic meaning has only one level of generality, as meanings that include others are not possible, because syncretic images stand in isolation and cannot include one another; for complexes there can be more than one level; for preconcepts more than two; and for concepts more than three (Vygotsky, 1934c, Ch. 6).

In spontaneous meanings we find that, as before, the child's ability to grasp a particular stage of meaning is closely related to the level of development of their cognitive functions, brought about through mediation by sign use. However, now the role of the functions and the means by which they experience social mediation is considerably altered.

Our main source for this is Chapter 5 of *Thinking and Speech*. We need to take some care in consulting this as it was probably written in 1931 and originally formed part of *Pedology of the Adolescent* (1931a) (Minick, 1987). For this reason it does not, strictly speaking, belong to the last period. However, the ideas it contains were among a number that Vygotsky had already developed by 1931 and were carried over into this period.

Vygotsky now says that each stage in the development of meaning involves the predominance of a certain function. In both spontaneous and taught concepts we find three main levels of function: perception; memory; and attention (ibid., p. 157). These are the dominant functions in causing changes in the child's meanings in early childhood (1–3 years), preschool (3–7 years) and first school (7–13 years), respectively (Figure 6.1). During these stages each function is subjected to social mediation and alters from a natural or unmediated form to a social or mediated form.

When a new structure of generalisation appears it does not, as he had previously thought, begin again with a fresh conceptualisation of all aspects of the relations of meanings to objects. Rather, it takes over the previous meanings and leaves much of their organisation and content in place, although at the same time it transforms these in line with their new place in the overall scheme of things. The main example of this given in Vygotsky (1934c, Ch. 5) relates to taught development, but the point applies to spontaneous meanings as well. When true concepts appear, arithmetic is already in place, conceptualised through preconcepts. Concepts proper make possible the addition of algebra to the adolescent's mathematical equipment, which includes arithmetical concepts, but also rises above them to include them. At the same time, the adolescent's previous understanding of arithmetic is transformed, with arithmetical concepts now seen as a special case of algebraic concepts. So arithmetical concepts are not invented again within the new algebraic level of thinking, but are taken over from the previous level of preconcepts and integrated into the algebraic level. While this transforms them and they are now seen in a new way, they are not reinvented again from scratch.

As previously, Vygotsky (1932d, 1934c, Ch. 7, 1934e, Ch. 3) maintains that the nature of speech and other signs changes from symbolic in the period up to 13 years to signs proper thereafter. However, Vygotsky nowhere explains why he thinks there is a close connection between communicating with symbols and figurative meaning, on the one hand, and communicating with signs and abstract meaning, on the other. Hegel (1831), from whom he probably took this view, does. The meaning of symbols, according to Hegel, is externalised because the person looks to the symbol to find out how to abstract a meaning from the object. A road sign for a crossroads usually shows two bold lines in the shape of a cross. This symbol tells us to pay attention to the fact that there are two roads crossing and to ignore other aspects of the situation. A sign proper, by contrast, cannot take its meaning from the sign, because by definition in this case its form has no connection to its meaning. So the meaning of the sign proper must carry its own method of deciding whether something is an apple or an orange or a planet.

At first, the method of deciding the meaning of a symbol is just an internal version of the external one. However, because the original symbol expresses a general idea, such as two roads crossing, this general idea gains in importance and the original symbol loses its importance, because it is now superfluous. The assumption behind this seems to be that the external symbol had been attached to an advantageous method of validation. The main reason for having the symbol was to convey social meanings to the learner, which was facilitated by the resemblance between the symbol and the idea it represented. Because the symbol has now come inside it is no longer needed as a teaching aid, so it falls away, leaving only its general idea behind.

Vygotsky probably reconciled this approach to meaning with the one that emerged from Sakharov's (1930) studies, stressing the coordination of judgements, as follows. For Hegel, there is no problem of the coordination of judgements, as the learner is able seamlessly to extract a general idea from the uses to which a symbol is put. Vygotsky assumes that this is not so and that during the preschool period the child tries to do this, but ends up with complexes, based on mismanaged judgements. This is followed by the emergence of inner speech in the period of first school, which, as in Hegel, results in symbols dropping out and the emergence of the first nonfigurative meanings and, shortly after, the first signs proper.

Inner speech The role of inner speech in cognition has a further function in the new framework. Previously, it was primarily a form of self-instruction, in line with the general approach that stressed that meaning was the internalisation of instructions. Now, it is the fact that the child communicates to itself that is important (Vygotsky, 1934c, Ch. 7). When the child is conversing with itself, we have a situation that encourages context-bound communication. Such communication flourishes when the speaker and the listener share a high proportion of their information, as when two people in a room talk to one another about things in the room. In inner speech the two people talking are the same person, so they will share most information.

On the surface, inner speech would seem to be a step backwards compared to external speech, as context-bound communication is typical of early childhood. Vygotsky, however, now argues that these characteristics serve to advance rather than retard the child's thinking, because of their role in its overall functioning. Inner speech promotes *sense* rather than meaning (ibid.). Sense, in his meaning of the term, is what we infer about the content of a message from the context, while meaning is what is actually said in the words. Vygotsky now stresses that this apparently less developed, context-bound, form of cognition is also essential to the further development of the whole cognitive apparatus.

This is because, in using language, the child over 7 years must first go through the plane of ordinary meaning, then that of inner speech, dominated by sense, then on to thought, which is the means by which problems are represented through naive physics and its descendants (Vygotsky, 1934c, Ch. 7). The role of sense is to translate the more analytic medium of ordinary meaning into the holistic forms of thought and, if necessary, back again. It is able to do this because it is partly analytic, like meaning, but also partly holistic, like thought.

Speech and thought In Vygotsky (1934c, Ch. 4), the early part of the development of thought remains much as in the previous period. In infancy, thought is connected to practical problem solving and is holistic and embodies a form of naive physics. At the end of infancy it interacts with speech and, through a series of steps, the two are fused. However, the nature of this fusion, whose initial phase is complete by around 7 years, is now described in quite different terms from those used previously.

Then, speech came to replace thought as the primary means by which problems are represented and solved. Now, he claims that thought continues to be the primary medium for directing problem solving in the age of first school (7–13 years) (Vygotsky, 1933k, 1934c, Chs 1, 7, 1934d, 1935e). Inner speech and sense take on the role of communicating between analytic meaning, which is attached to outer speech, and thought. This is needed, because analytic meaning breaks the world down into components, while thought remains holistic. Without sense and inner speech as intermediaries, the two would not be able to communicate. It is implied, but not stated, that thought and outer speech remain in the same general relation in adolescence as they had in the age of first school. This retains the picture of adolescence that had existed previously. Thought in adolescence remains strongly spatial, but now takes the form of abstract spatial schemata, such as Venn diagrams or the diagrams used in science (Vygotsky, 1931a, Ch. 3). In addition, it seems that thought remains dominant in the representation of problems.

This raises an apparent paradox, as for Vygotsky all thought remains spatial, or image like, during adolescence, rather than becoming entirely abstract. This claim seems paradoxical, because adolescent cognition is often thought to involve the liberation of cognition from its dependence on spatial imagination. This does not mean that thought loses all contact with perception and imagination. These are still needed for the starting points and results of cognition to make contact with the world of reality. Thus rocket scientists may use abstract physics and mathematics to calculate the trajectory of a rocket to go to Mars. But they still need to make measurements of the weight and thrust of the rocket to make their predictions and then to perceive which path the rocket actually takes to assess them, even if only on a screen.

What occurs in adolescence is, according to this picture, that the abstract representations involved in the path, from contemplation to practice, become progressively more removed from spatial imagination and progressively more dependent on meanings, many of which in fact defy spatial imagination. There are many examples of this in the concepts of mathematics and physics, in particular. In geometry we are asked to believe in points with zero size and lines with zero width, neither of which could exist in the physical world.

Vygotsky, however, gives a continuing dominant role for spatial thought in adolescence. He maintains there are abstract, but still spatial, schemata, that act to guide the use of abstract meanings. The idea of such schemata was well known to Gestalt theorists in Vygotsky's day, such as Wertheimer (1922, 1925) and Bartlett (1932). They were usually assumed to have a substantial picture-like and thus spatial component. An example is the Venn diagram, often used to picture problems in logic (Figure 6.2). This pictures two sets that have common members as two intersecting circles. It thus transforms the

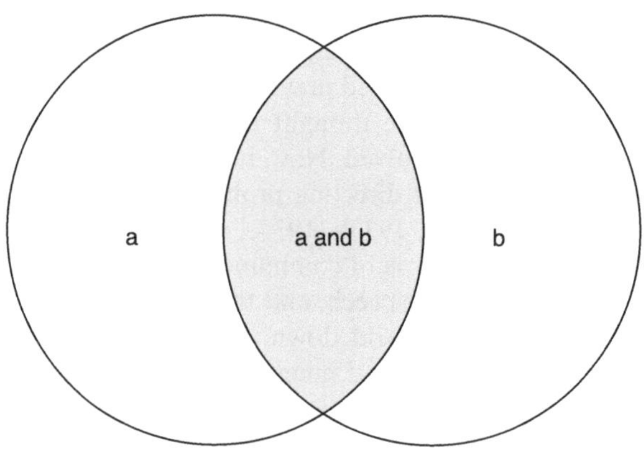

Figure 6.2 Venn diagram for intersecting sets a and b

logical situation into a spatial one, making it easier to think about. This is a good illustration of how schemata can become abstract, while remaining spatial. The schema, in this case, abstracts even from particular objects that it might apply to, as no objects are pictured inside the circles. It pictures only the logical relations between the objects. Many of the diagrams used in secondary school mathematics, physics and chemistry are also abstract schemata in this sense.

We can therefore say that, although we need to free ourselves from spatial intuition to form abstract meanings, we need to reconvert these into a spatial form in order to work with them. Thought, for Vygotsky, always had the primary connotation of using representations to solve problems.

Why did Vygotsky make these changes? One reason was a serious problem in his earlier view. His previous stance claimed that the main representation in problem solving is primarily nonlinguistic up to 7 years, then for a brief interlude, until 13 years, it becomes linguistic and then after this it becomes nonlinguistic again. Because linguistic representations are primarily analytic and nonlinguistic ones are holistic, this suggests that problem solving in the period 7–13 years will be analytic and outside it mixed or holistic. However, studies of the fruit and stick problem do not suggest any change in style for children in that period compared to younger ones (Vygotsky, 1931b, Chs 3, 11). Although he does not mention studies of other problems, in this connection, we do not see this effect there either.

A second reason is probably that his last position coincided, in an important respect, with the views of the Gestalt psychologists, especially Kohler and Wertheimer, as well as that of Charlotte Buhler (1928). This was that thought remains the dominant means by which problems are represented and solved throughout development. Vygotsky had always owed a substantial part of his theory of cognition to these sources (see, especially, Vygotsky, 1934i).

A development during the period His main analysis of the development of meaning, developed in 1931 and 1932, was retained throughout the period (Vygotsky, 1933b, 1934d, 1934e, Lect. 4, 1934h). However, he also gives indications that he was unhappy with the analysis of the stages of structural generalisation, that is the most fundamental kind of meaning, given in *Thinking and speech* (Chs 5, 6). In Vygotsky (1933b, 1934e, Lect. 4), his earlier claim that meaning in early childhood is dominated by unstable complexes is significantly scaled back. This was probably wise, as naturalistic studies of children available to Vygotsky and performed since have suggested that complex-type meanings tend to fade in the second half of the second year of life, being replaced by at least apparently componential meanings that are refined in a more orderly way than complexes (Bloom, 1970, 1984; Frawley, 1992, 1997; Lewis, 1957; Wells, 1974, 1983, 1987). His conclusions, in *Thinking and speech*, Chapters 5 and 6, had been largely based on his own and others' experimental studies on artificial tasks. However, he remained confused on the issue and allowed results from the experimental tasks to continue to dominate.

Moral development He continued to see morality as an aspect of signs. Vygotsky's ideas in this area came to rely more on Piaget (1930, 1931) and less on Busemann (1925, 1926) (Vygotsky, 1933k, 1934e, 1934h, 1935b, 1935f). The reason for this was probably that Busemann's idea that the child's morality, like its social relations in general, are dominated by parental authority from 3–13 years, fitted in perfectly with the theory of his third period. The theory of the present period abandoned this and stressed cooperation, in the everyday sense, rather than authority, as the key relation between parent and child. So Piaget's view was now more congenial as, although it retained authority as the key relation for the preschool stage (3–7 years), it saw cooperation with the peer group as more central in the period 7–15 years. In addition, Piaget also thought that the internalisation of moral rules began at 7 years, which still suited Vygotsky's new theory.

We saw in Chapter 4 that the development of the will is important for moral development. The main change here is that his view of the formation of will changes, from the achievement of mastery through the internalisation of the wills of others, to the mastery over one's own behaviour achieved as a result of consciousness (Vygotsky, 1934c, Ch. 7, 1935c, 1935d, 1935e). Consciousness arises from the existence of system in the external social world and the presence in the child of enough maturity to benefit from it.

The self

Vygotsky now left behind his previously rather Hegelian view of the self, moving towards something closer to, but still different from, Marx. The new view was designed to take seriously the leading role that Vygotsky gave to signs, as well to act on his conviction that development is not just a matter of an inner unfolding, but involves the interaction of the child with the environment.

Self-consciousness remains, as before, consciousness of the entire personality. This now arises at a definite point in each stage as a result of the coming to fruition of the leading function of the stage. This leading function acts to reorganise other functions according to its own predominant way of acting, even before it becomes conscious (Vygotsky, 1933i, 1934f). The leading function then becomes conscious and it extends this consciousness more generally over the system of functions. Once the new form of consciousness has grasped the totality of functions, it further perfects their reorganisation in accord with the needs of the new dominant function. Self-consciousness in the strict sense is what we get once consciousness has grasped the totality of functions.

While these central features of the self are reasonably clear, we need to fill this picture out to fully appreciate what Vygotsky means. A first point is that when he talks about consciousness in relation to these issues he means both consciousness of the external world and self-consciousness (Vygotsky, 1933i, p. 199, 1934f, p. 243). It seems that consciousness of the external world is the leading aspect of this process, with self-consciousness following behind. We can infer this because the development of leading functions involves interaction with the outside world, so this makes the process depend on this interaction. Were self-consciousness to lead the process, this would be another version of Hegel's self, which acts as a self-developing entity, something Vygotsky sets himself against (Vygotsky, 1933i, 1934c, Ch. 1, 1934f).

Vygotsky's view gives signs a major role in the formation of the self, as the leading functions for the three middle stages are all signs and that for adolescence is strongly influenced by signs. This is in itself neither surprising nor novel: Peirce (1868, 1892, 1923) and Baldwin (1911–12) had suggested it before Vygotsky; and Lacan (1966) and Nelson (1997, 2000, 2001), among others, were to do so after. However, they came close to identifying the self-conscious use of signs with the self. Vygotsky's idea is wider than this, as for him it is consciousness of the personality as a whole as structured by signs that forms the self.

Turning to developmental aspects of the self, the main function of the self, in this period, is to assist the child to complete the inner dialectic of its development, in particular to complete the incipient organisation of functions that is achieved in the middle of stages (Vygotsky, 1933i, 1934e, 1934f). From the middle of each stage, this forms part of the general process of becoming conscious that dominates the second part of the stable period of the stage. The self does this because it arises on the basis of the social situation of development with which the stage began.

Vygotsky does not say what it is about the social situation of development that can give an impulse to the self that later works its way around the sequence of phases to become new forms of language and practice. However, the logic of the situation suggests that it is the relative independence, or dependence, of the initial social relations that is involved. There are two reasons for saying this. First, this is the most prominent feature of these relations. Second, independent relations will generate an increasingly independent self that will be consistent with increasingly context-independent language, in the form first of speech and later of writing. We can reconstruct the nature of the self, at the different stages, as follows (Vygotsky, 1932b, 1933g, 1933j, 1934b, 1934d):

1 *Infancy*: Here there is only the forerunner of the self proper. This is called the 'Original we', meaning that at this point the infant has not yet distinguished itself from other people.
2 *Early childhood*: The I as a distinct entity emerges as someone who bargains with those around it, rather than automatically acquiescing or automatically resisting. This is based on the greater abilities of the child to walk, talk and do things generally, which lead to initial forms of

independence. In assigning speech as the leading function, providing the form of the self in this period, Vygotsky, as usual, has in mind the effects of speech on the personality as a whole, including such things as its effect on cognition.

3 *Preschool*: Instability of the self, shown in the ability to switch between one fantasy self and another in play. This also shows greater control over the selves once they have been entered, alongside the instability about which will predominate at a given time. This further enhances the child's independence.
4 *School age*: Division between the inner and outer selves. The outer self is more able to do things and communicate its wishes than previously, resulting in greater independence. The inner self assists the child's development by keeping it in touch with concrete reality.
5 *Adolescence*: Greater control over the worlds of the inner and outer selves. The outer self is once again more able to do things and communicate its wishes than previously, giving the adolescent greater independence. The inner self assists development by keeping the personality in touch with concrete reality. This is more necessary than ever, as the adolescent must negotiate more difficult and complex problems than ever before.

Motivation

There was now a more active and more intellectualised model of the child's motivation (Bozhovich, 1968). As Vygotsky notes in *Thinking and speech* (1934c, Ch. 1), the previous approach tended to focus on outside social influences, particularly that of signs. It also had strong overtones of the idea that the natural inclinations of the child need to be curbed by adult authority, to produce a cultured individual, which in its more militant form is typical of Augustine, Protestantism, Nietzsche and Freud. Now he turned to the optimistic and intellectualistic view of child nature taken by Aristotle, scholasticism, Spinoza and Feuerbach. The child is by nature inclined to desire knowledge, this desire dominates its motivation and provides much of the impetus for its development. It is also the active author of its own destiny.

The conservative model of human nature had from the outset of Soviet power been viewed askance and the unwholesome interest that Luria and Vygotsky showed in Freud, one of its exponents, was tolerated rather than encouraged in the 1920s (Joravsky, 1989; Luria, 1925; Vygotsky, 1926c; Vygotsky & Luria, 1925). With the advent of the ultra-left period after 1929, this turned to dangerous hostility. At that time there was overwhelming pressure for psychology to turn to doing something practical for the regime or risk being abolished altogether (Joravsky, 1989). Its political masters certainly did not want to hear about the limitations that human nature places on the perfectibility of man. They wanted to hear how the new socialist man could be created overnight.

It may not be accidental that Vygotsky's main theoretical rivals, A. N. Leont'ev (1930, 1931, 1948, 1998) and Rubinshtein (1934, 1935), also adopted the desired stance, although whether they too changed their views, as Vygotsky did, is less clear, as their earlier publications said little on the topic. As mentioned earlier, we do not know that Vygotsky changed his mind for opportunist reasons, as Spinoza and Feuerbach were two of Marx's favourite philosophers and he may have been influenced by this or other factors. However, it is certainly possible.

Vygotsky was particularly interested in Spinoza's view of motivation and emotion, which was the subject of one of the main works of the late period, *Teachings on the emotions* (1933l). The aim of the text as a whole is to criticise the James-Lange theory of emotions and put in its place Spinoza's theory of emotions, rightly understood. This seems paradoxical, as many psychologists in Vygotsky's time, and still today, thought and think that the latter was very similar to the former. Vygotsky's argument, presented at considerable length, is that the two are similar in their description of the different types of emotion, which they both inherited from Descartes (1637). But their explanation for what happens in emotional reactions is quite different.

In James-Lange, emotional states are held to be the conscious perception of the bodily changes that accompany emotion. If we feel, say, increased heartbeat and sweating, then we will perceive that as arising from an emotion. We can tell which emotion, as each emotion involves a different pattern of bodily changes and we recognise these. In this schematic form, neither James nor Lange actually held the theory, but to contrast its fundamentals with Vygotsky's version of Spinoza this is close enough.

As it stands, this theory is obviously inadequate, as it does not say how the body is influenced to set off the pattern of bodily reaction that we perceive as a particular emotion. However, it is not difficult to add that there is some process, conscious or unconscious, that does this. Thus, to give an example from James (1902), if a bear chases us we feel fear. Somehow, we perceive the situation as one in which we should be afraid and this sets off the bodily reactions.

Early in his manuscript Vygotsky tells us that, among contemporary theories of emotion, he would much prefer the ideas of the noted American physiologist James Cannon (1927a, 1927b, 1929) to the James-Lange theory. Cannon in turn inherited some of his ideas from Sherrington. According to Cannon, emotional experiences do not originate from the perception of peripheral changes in the body, they come from the thalamus, which is linked to the hypothalamus and limbic system. The thalamus triggers them quite readily when faced by biological threats like the bear, or by biological pluses, like food when hungry. Normally the cortex acts to damp down these reactions and bring them under cortical control, in which case we experience ourselves as reacting rationally to the emotion; but when cortical control is lifted they break through into irrational emotion. The peripheral accompaniments of emotion, such as heart rate and sweating, are a byproduct of this process and are not required in order to feel emotion.

Cannon also had the idea, which Vygotsky adopts, that the cortex represents the mastery of the objective aspect of the person over the subjective emotions of the thalamus (see also Vygotsky, 1934g). But, according to Vygotsky, for the person to develop, the restraints of the objective personality need to weaken, so that the forces bound up with subjective emotions can break through into the objective side of the person to form the marriage of objectivity and subjectivity needed for overall self-consciousness to be achieved. This is a further expression of his general beliefs about the roles of the inner, emotional, and outer, rational selves in development.

Vygotsky goes beyond Cannon when he also adopts Spinoza's conception that development is itself motivational. In Section 19 of Spinoza's *Ethics* (1688) it is said that the self is what urges us to greater knowledge and power and this is an instinct. Vygotsky (1933l, p. 220) commends this view. Thus, we have a kind of instinctive drive to seek greater knowledge and power by developing ourselves.

Feuerbach was a Left Hegelian who also exerted considerable influence on Vygotsky in his last period. Although he is less explicit in linking Feuerbach with his new view of motivation than Spinoza, this aspect of Feuerbach would obviously have appealed to him. In his best known work, *The essence of Christianity* (1840), Feuerbach argued that Christianity was a projection of ideal human nature and activities onto a realm beyond this world, due to their frustration in this world. While something similar had been suggested previously by philosophers such as Anaxagoras and Spinoza, Feuerbach was distinguished by the explicit way in which he outlined the features of human nature and the detail in which he compared this to Christianity.

He gives a thumbnail sketch of human nature as follows:

> Reason, love, and willpower make us perfect; they are our highest powers, our absolute essence, in so far as we are human, the purpose of our existence . . . Only things that exist for their own sakes are true, perfect, and divine. But love, reason, and will all exist for their own sakes . . . When, impelled by love, a man gladly sacrifices his life for his beloved; is it his own strength that makes him overcome his fear of death, or is it rather the power of love? Who has not experienced the silent power of thought, given that he has truly experienced thinking?
>
> (Feuerbach, 1840, Ch. 1, my trans.)

Once again the stress is on motivation produced by the intellect and the will. In Feuerbach's case, the emotion of love is added as a more emotional dimension, but the overall effect continues to be one of reason married to naturally benign and social emotions. Everything is undertaken for its own sake at the instigation of a power larger than the individual. So his view of love is romantic. His view of learning and knowledge is similar to certain kinds of education that encourage learning for its own sake and contend that this is something greater and larger than utilitarian education.

Inner self and outer self

The splitting of the self occurs around 7 years. This enables the inner self to retain its holistic and integrated character in the face of the specialisation and atomisation characteristic of the outer self, produced by its necessary engagement with the outer world. The inner self is able to impart an element of this holism to the personality in general and to its approach to developmental tasks in particular. An interesting discussion of the formation of the two selves appears in Vygotsky (1933g, pp. 242 ff.). One point of reference is the notion of a complex put forward by Freud and Jung. In Freud's version, which Vygotsky prefers, part of the personality belonging to an earlier stage is pushed into the unconscious, because it is not compatible with the consciousness of a later stage. The most prominent example is the Oedipus Complex, which for Freud is a conscious conflict prominent in the period about $1\frac{1}{2}$ years to $2\frac{1}{2}$ years, that is then repressed. At no stage in life are you allowed to kill your father and marry your mother (or vice versa in the case of the girl).

However, Vygotsky rejects such extreme splitting, in which the two halves of the personality cannot communicate with one another, as the key to development (p. 253). Instead, he invokes the Hegelian principle that development cannot advance to a higher level, unless the original wholeness of the person is split up and these splits are then periodically healed in a higher synthesis. For this, the opposites that have split apart must, periodically, come into contact with one another, unlike Freud's inner and outer selves, that remain for long periods out of contact with one another. In the development of the self and its consciousness, in the period from 7 years up to the end of adolescence, splitting predominates.

Vygotsky often talks about this split as involving dissociation (e.g. Vygotsky, 1932a, 1933g, 1933m, 1934j, 1934k). This is primarily the process by which parts of the personality or different selves divide from one another and thus are not conscious of one another. Vygotsky, following Kretschmer (1926, 1928), and by contrast to Freud, has the conscious external self as primary and the inner self as later and secondary. The partition between the two selves is also more porous in Vygotsky than it is in Freud. In Freud, the two selves try not to think about one another because they are in a real sense at war and if they become aware of one another they may destroy the person. In Vygotsky, they have mainly lost contact with one another because they reside in different psychological spaces: inside and outside. The inner self is given to fantasies about how it would like itself and the world to be. The outer self tries to deal with what is.

This situation is certainly the basis for incompatibility. After a car crash, for instance, the inner self may say that the crash was the other party's fault, as it rejects the idea of being careless or a poor driver. The outer self may reply that this is not in accord with the facts, which are that I was careless and a poor driver, on that occasion, and that I need to change what led to these things. However, the two selves will probably eventually be able to talk to one another about the situation.

Freud would probably have agreed with this analysis of this situation, but he would not have thought it typical of the relations between the conscious and the unconscious. Vygotsky thinks this kind of thing is typical of the relations between the inner and outer selves. The two selves will have a reasonable chance of eventually talking to one another and sorting things out. Freud focuses on cases where the emotional stakes are much higher and the chances of the two selves talking to one another without outside assistance, or even with such assistance, small. His central case is, of course, the incestuous sexual fantasies of the young child, which the child discovers are so unacceptable that they must be forever sealed into the capsule of the unconscious mind, never to be revealed to the ego or outer self.

In Vygotsky, the relatively easy communication between the outside and inner selves determines the nature of development: The major developmental crises after 7 years, at 13 and 17 years, are relatively short. In each crisis, the inner and outer selves are realigned in accordance with developmental needs and they are realigned quickly, because they are able to talk to one another. Their need to be realigned stems from the fact that, during the crisis at the end of each stage, the inner self leads in the opposition to the current state of affairs, harbouring fantasies of how things could be different, while the outer self remains more tied to the actual state of affairs in the outside world. As the crisis proceeds and the outside world changes, the outer self needs to change to catch up.

This contrasts with Freud. When the unconscious comes close to and needs to be realigned with the conscious ego, the result is liable to be a deeper and more long-lasting crisis, because, as soon as the two become aware of one another, they start a shooting war. His main example of this is adolescence, where the repressed material dealing with the incestuous sexuality of early childhood reappears, due to adolescent sexuality, and must be dealt with by the conscious mind. This takes much of adolescence because of the difficulties involved (A. Freud, 1958; S. Freud, 1920). In the neurotic personality, which for Freud means a high proportion of the adult population, it also drags on through adulthood.

Vygotsky introduces experience as a developmental unit that links the inner self to the outer. He gives the term unit a special significance, meaning a mediating subsystem that contains the essential features of the whole to which it belongs. The main units he identifies are, in the last period, word meaning and experience. He implies (Vygotsky, 1933k, 1934c, Ch. 1, 1934e, Lect. 4) that experience is in a loose sense superordinate to meaning, that is to say it is more general than it and includes it. The subjective inner world of the individual is formed by the internalisation of the functions of the outer self, during the age of first school (Vygotsky, 1933g, 1933j, 1933k). So the formative process of internalisation that occurs for meaning is at the same time duplicated in the division of the self. Meaning divides into that attached to outer speech and that attached to inner speech, which is called sense (Vygotsky, 1934c, Ch. 7, 1934e, Lect. 4). The self divides into the outer self, which first originated in early childhood (1–3 years), and the inner self.

Experience links the inner and the outer. To do so, it depends on the use of signs, particularly speech in the early stages (Vygotsky, 1933g, 1933j). We saw in a previous chapter how meanings can determine the way in which a child conceives itself. This applies not only to outer self-consciousness, constrained by the increasingly rational processes attached to signs. It also applies to the inner self, expressed in art and imagination. The child's early use of signs in art is closely linked to the use of imagination and the inner self (Vygotsky, 1934c, Ch. 7). Vygotsky's concept of experience is almost certainly connected with that of Hegel in the *Phenomenology of spirit* (Hegel, 1807, Preface), as he uses the same term and the two concepts play the same role. This does not mean that the two follow precisely the same developmental course, as on many occasions Vygotsky adapts the ideas he takes from Hegel. However, the two have broadly the same function.

Dynamic model

The personality as a whole

Vygotsky's earlier dynamic model underwent substantial change, although some of its most fundamental features remained (Vygotsky, 1933i, 1934f). Its novel aspects were particularly designed to explain the dynamics of his newly created stages.

The new version concentrates on the idea of a stable neoformation, which is a function that emerges during a stage and whose maturation towards the end of the stage leads to a structural reorganisation of other functions and thus to an alteration in the child's general consciousness, particularly its self-consciousness. This creates a new personality that then revolts against the social relations that originally brought it into being and these are revolutionised in turn. The neoformations, after infancy, are all connected with signs.

At every point in development, the available levels and functions interact together to produce the characteristic modes of functioning of that point in development. Their way of interacting at one time is called a system (Vygotsky, 1933i, 1934c, 1934e, Lect. 5). There is still no consistent attempt to say what in general characterises these systems, although in infancy the system is holistic and natural, while in later periods systems become mediated and differentiated (Vygotsky, 1934b, 1934c, 1934e, Lect. 3).

He also continues to hold that, in these systems, one strand or component dominates the others in each stage, giving the system its most characteristic features. These components are much the same as those that dominated the shorter periods before they became stages: in infancy, instinctive mental life; for early childhood, speech; for the preschool period, play; for first school, writing; for adolescence, concepts (Vygotsky, 1933b, 1933d, 1933g, 1933i, p. 197, 1934c, Ch. 6, 1934e, Lect. 2, 1934f, 1935a).

In all cases, it is the dynamism of the process mentioned we are to pay attention to. In particular, his use of the term instinctive mental life is intended to point to the dynamism of this aspect of mental life, which in infancy means the maturation of instincts. In the previous period he had given learning through practice as the dominant dynamic function in infancy. This shift was probably brought about by his move away from reflexology, which stressed learning from practice in infancy.

His general justification for thinking that signs are the main dynamic force in development in its middle period continues to be the one he used in the previous period: That human development past the stage of infancy is social; its crucial motor is consciousness; and that the social nature of development requires this to be social consciousness, which is associated with signs (Vygotsky, 1934c, pp. 45–50, 126–127; 1934e, Lect. 4). He also continues to rehearse some of his more particular arguments for this, based on the need for natural powers to be amplified by signs, if they are to tackle certain tasks. So he repeats those made about writing (Vygotsky, 1934c, Ch. 7, 1935a) and about arithmetic (Vygotsky, 1934d, 1935g).

The argument about arithmetic was detailed in Chapter 4. That on writing says that writing provides the child with a motive to communicate to a generalised audience that does not share their immediate context; and that this is one of the main pressures to develop the abstract meanings and communication strategies needed for such an audience. This shows that writing is in a strong position to encourage the child's transition from concrete to abstract thought at the start of adolescence. Although signs are dominant over practice in the dynamics of development in the middle period, they are not absolutely dominant; new practices precede the development of new signs, but theirs is a partial and halting development that needs to be taken up and brought to fruition by signs (Vygotsky, 1934c, pp. 47–51, 1935e).

The first two parts of his schema for the long-term dynamics of the child are now the natural, biological maturation of instinct, followed by the cultural dynamism of signs. If we follow the pattern of the previous period we would expect that adolescence would mark the synthesis of these two opposites. However, as far as we can gather from what little he says on the subject, the dynamic force in adolescence remains advanced concepts, which remain a synthesis of practice and signs (Vygotsky, 1933g, 1934c, Ch. 7). In this case, the nearest we can get to restoring the satisfying symmetry of the previous period is to say that practice appears in infancy under the guise of instinctive action, followed by signs, followed by the synthesis of practice, in the guise of learning, and signs.

He now describes the dynamic processes that occur within a stage in some detail. The underlying steps within each stage are: the initial social situation of development; the reaction to this by the personality, which includes the development of the particular functions, called neoformations, which have a key role in development. Once the leading neoformation reaches a certain point of dominance this alters the existing constellation of functions, producing a new form of generic consciousness and self-consciousness; this produces changes in the personality, which change and heighten the existing level of consciousness. There is then conflict between the personality and the social situation, because the two no longer match; a crisis ensues; this is followed by resolution of the crisis and by the formation of the new social situation of development for the next stage (Vygotsky, 1933i, 1934e, Lect. 2, 1934f). While affect and motivation are important in the first substage, in the later parts of the stage it is consciousness and intellect that dominate (Vygotsky, 1933i, 1934e, Lect. 2, 1934f).

One reason that self-consciousness is important in the middle part of the stage is that otherwise the dynamism and forward motion of the new dominant function, which are crucial in the first part, come to a halt and there is stagnation (Vygotsky, 1933i, 1934f). Self-consciousness reactivates the forward motion of the system and enables it to reach the crisis point at the end of the stage.

One of the main ways in which this occurs is through validity, which is a further aspect of self-consciousness. Through validity the child becomes aware of its own method of assessing the validity of propositions and other experiences (Vygotsky, 1933f, 1934h, 1934k). Furthermore, it is the development of validity that produces development in meaning and so in other parts of the child's cognitive system and thus in the rest of the personality. In a real sense everything else stands on the ground of validity.

Validity is similar to Hegel's 'idea', as well as to the suggestions of other philosophers, including the contemporary notion that meaning is established by truth conditions (largely due, in different forms, to Frege, 1888, and Tarski, 1944). The meaning of a proposition is the conditions under which it is true; the validity of the proposition is, for Vygotsky, the method by which we establish whether it is true. Obviously this must be connected to the meaning of the proposition. We can decide that 'Russia is cold in winter' means that in the capital, in nine out of ten years, there are more than 60 days when the temperature is below zero degrees centigrade. The validity of the proposition is the checking methods we would need to establish if this is true; such as the need to check weather records going back many years; the task of counting up how many days in each winter were below zero; as well as drawing up a precise definition of which days are in winter. An adolescent might do this, but a young child could not, which is the difference between validity in the young child and validity in the adolescent.

Vygotsky does not describe the nature of validity at each stage of development, but we can assume that it must be such as to support the kind of meaning that exists at each stage. He is more forthcoming about the influences that produce the development of validity. The most important of these is the development of the inner self at 7 years, which is associated with the internalisation of speech (Vygotsky, 1934d). This inner self is more capable of achieving self-consciousness about the bases of validity than the external self. With the onset of adolescence this tendency is still further increased.

At the start of each stage, a certain function is selected to play the role of the central neoformation of the stage. Although this may not even exist right at the start of the stage, it has already been preselected for prominence, through the nature of the social situation of development, which will in the future stimulate the personality to produce it. It is central to the theory that the right constellation of functions appears in each stage, as otherwise the stages would not fit together and would not lead anywhere.

In addition to stable neoformations, there are positive and negative unstable neoformations, found at the times of crisis (Vygotsky, 1932e, 1933e, 1933g, 1933i, 1933j, 1934e, 1934f). The unstable neoformations begin the process of dismantling surrounding social relations and building new ones.

One of the central features of the negative unstable neoformation is its high proportion of negative features. The child needs these to enforce change in those around it. This is balanced by the positive and constructive features of the positive unstable neoformations that look forward to the positive outcomes of the crisis. The unstable neoformations assess the conflict between the personality and its social relations and then resolve it by changing the child's social relations (Vygotsky, 1933e, p. 192–195, 1933i, 1934f). This is akin to one way in which Marx uses the term consciousness; a form of consciousness assesses social contradictions and then seeks to resolve them (Marx, 1852, 1876; Marx & Engels, 1848).

The content of this negative activity at each crisis is:

1 *At 1 year*: If the child is refused something this may lead to crying, sulking, tantrums or regressive behaviour, such as refusal to walk (Vygotsky, 1933a, pp. 243–244).
2 *At 3 years*: The chief characteristics are obstinacy, stubbornness, negativism, capriciousness and self-will. In all cases the main aim is not so much for the child to do what it wants, as not to do what the parent or caregiver asks (Vygotsky, 1933f, pp. 192–193).
3 *At 7 years*: The disruption of equilibrium and instability of will and mood are the chief characteristics (Vygotsky, 1933j, pp. 289–295).
4 *At 13 years*: Behaviour shows a negative and protesting character, with overall negativity tending to reach a high level (Vygotsky, 1933g).

A problem arises here, as the crisis at age 1 does not seem to fit the general spirit of negative unstable neoformations. Rather than being an attempt to dismantle the previous stage, this seems to be an effort to cling to it. Correspondingly, rather than being a bid for independence it seems to be one for dependence. The crisis at the end of infancy is a particularly significant one, because it marks such a significant turning point in development. It appears that it is, for this reason, an exception to the general rule of crises and that at this point the magnitude of the changes involved causes the child, at first, to long to return to its previously dependent state.

We now turn to the positive aspects of unstable neoformations. In the crisis of the newborn, which is the first of all the crises, the positive unstable neoformation comprises all positive aspects of growth, such as the successful use of feeding reflexes. In the crisis at age 1 we find standing and learning to speak as positive developments of the crisis that will lead on to the developments of the next stage (Vygotsky, 1933a). In the crisis at age 3 we find moves to gain further independence from the caregivers (Vygotsky, 1933f). In the crisis at 7, independence increases further and relations with other children change, so that each child retains a greater sense of separateness and individuation in the process of forming such relations (Vygotsky, 1933j).

In the crisis at 13, there is a change from interest in what is obvious and on the surface to efforts to gain understanding and use deduction to penetrate beneath the surface of things. So the younger child reacts to manufactured objects such as the crockery, cutlery and cooking utensils found in the home, mainly in terms of their immediate use and the techniques used to make them. The adolescent also looks at the economic and social conditions surrounding the acquisition of their raw materials and manufacture (Vygotsky, 1933g). Although Vygotsky does not mention greater independence and emancipation as an aspect of this positive neoformation, it is likely that they are also included.

Dynamics of speech

The process of social mediation that brings about much of the development of meaning involves the imposition of adult meanings on the child. So the child might be inclined to call a cat, then a dog and then a small horse 'kitty', but the adult will tend to call only the cat 'kitty' and correct the child for the other two uses. This may not occur immediately, as the adult may be too pleased the child is using words at all or too amused to correct it. However, sooner or later the adult will begin to correct the child or fail to understand what it says and this is the imposition of word uses that Vygotsky is thinking of.

The result of the child's being corrected in the way it uses words is not that it takes on the adult's meaning perfectly. It is rather that a conflict or contradiction appears between the child's meaning and that of the adult. The result is that the child moves towards the adult's uses, as best it can, by calling on its current level of functioning. If that is perceptual meanings, then the child will try to use words in the same way an adult does by using perceptual meanings. The result will be that in many cases the child now appears to use words in the same ways that an adult does, but the meanings they attach to the words are quite different. They both say 'kitty' when a cat is present and not when one is not, but to the child 'kitty' is something with the perceptual appearance of a cat, something that looks like and moves like a cat. The adult is probably able to place the cat in a wider and more abstract categorisation of animals, knowing that it is part of the cat family, which belongs in the family of mammals.

Within each stage, the collision between the meanings of the child and the adult's uses occurs in three substages (Vygotsky, 1934c, Chs 5, 6). In the first substage, the child's meaning is as yet largely uninfluenced by that of the adult and is thus relatively natural; and so is described as 'in itself'. In the second substage, the meaning itself is not much changed, but the child realises that it should conform its uses to those of the adult or older children; it realises that it should not call horses 'kitty', but doesn't know why. This is described as 'for others'. Finally, it becomes conscious of the function it has been in the process of mastering (perception, memory, attention or concepts), so that it is able to have the same, or mostly the same, uses as the adult by modifying the type of meaning used. So if it has been functioning at the perceptual level, it will now move forward to reliance on the function of memory. This is 'in-itself-and-for-others' (often abbreviated to in-and-for-itself), that is, it is the synthesis of the original meaning and the demands of others.

Within the patterns of response found in the Sakharov concept attainment task, Vygotsky (1934c, Ch. 6) was able to identify these three substages within each of his main stages. For instance, for complexes, the kind of response associated with the preschool age (3–7 years), the first substage is represented by associative complexes, in which meanings depend on one thing being associated with another (ibid., p. 135 ff.). The second substage is represented by a range of complexes, in which the child shifts from relying on associations between objects to making comparisons using judgements; but these are not yet consistently coordinated, as in the chain complex, which we have already encountered. The third substage is the pseudoconcept, in which the child appears to have abstracted and used a single characteristic or dimension with which to define a meaning, but has not. Their behaviour thus mimics the use of simple concepts, but the underlying function is still complex like, rather than based on abstraction.

The types of meaning characteristic of a stage correspond to the function that is being mastered in that stage: perception, memory, attention or concepts. In the third substage of each stage, the child achieves consciousness of the function they have just been passing through. To be conscious of something means to attain a synoptic view of it and thus to be able to take in its pattern as a whole and then reorganise it.

This kind of consciousness results in the shifts from perception to memory, to attention, to concepts, as we move from the second to the fifth stages, as a result of self-conscious awareness of these functions at the end of each.

Why consciousness of the previous function should produce these particular changes is not made clear. We can, however, reconstruct the process with a reasonable degree of confidence. There is a movement from passivity to activity as we move between the functions. Also, the child steps outside each function to look at it as we go along. In perception the observer is not clearly separated from what is perceived; in memory we step outside perception to look at events and control them by bringing them back when we want to, but only after they have happened; in attention we stand outside perception and direct what we perceive, as it happens; with advanced concepts we control the process of forming and using such concepts in a broader and more strategic manner. The idea of introducing these functions one after another in this way was probably taken from Hegel (1831, Part 3).

Another important area of change was in the relation between speech and concrete experience. He now suggests that there is a fundamental difference between spontaneous and taught development, particularly as far as the development of meanings is concerned. The child's spontaneous level of meaning is what it achieves as a result of picking up meanings from informal conversations. When the child is taught meanings in a formal way, as happens at school, for instance when it learns the meaning of words like 'plus' and 'minus' in arithmetic, it can learn at a developmental level over a stage above its spontaneous level (Figure 6.3). As a result, developments from 7 to 17 years are earlier by a stage.

He now argues that Sakharov's (1930) studies had only captured the child's ability to form concepts or meanings unaided. This was plausible, as the child in Sakharov's tasks was asked to discover concepts unaided. But in real life, particularly after the child goes to school (7–13 years), the child learns some important meanings from teaching and is thus not unaided. In the light of this, Vygotsky reasons that the child in this age range should possess more sophisticated meanings than those suggested by the Sakharov tasks. This provides an explanation for a fact he had previously been at a loss to explain. This was that the child in this age range can, in real life, master meanings

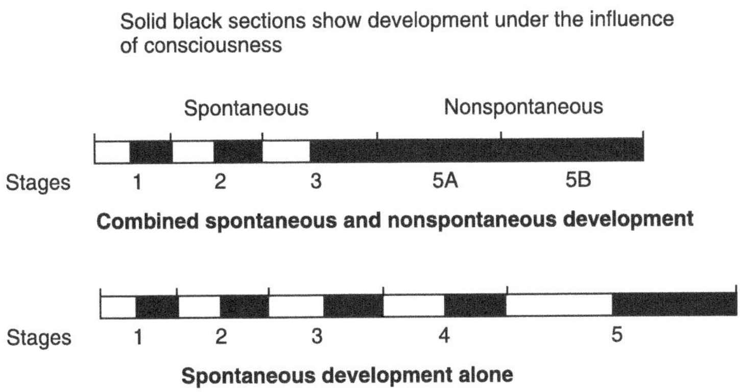

Figure 6.3 Spontaneous versus nonspontaneous development

involving the coordination of several dimensions, such as those involved in writing and arithmetical multiplication (Vygotsky, 1934c, Ch. 6).

Taught meanings are said to be learned in a top-down manner that is most influential after the start of first school, when top-down learning becomes easier; provided of course that the teacher is willing to engage in it. Here, the teacher gives general definitions of meanings rather than examples. So, for instance, we could consider the concepts 'prime number', 'mammal' and 'social revolution' (the last an example from Vygotsky, 1934c, Ch. 6). In the top-down approach the teacher would introduce these by their definitions: A prime is a whole number not divisible by another whole number; a mammal is a warm-blooded animal that suckles its young; a social revolution is one that changes the relations of production. A child could be allowed to discover these ideas by examples, but in top-down learning they are given the definition in the form of general rule first and then encouraged to explore examples later.

The issues involved here have been much debated in recent decades in the West. For example, there is much debate about the wisdom or not of giving rules of grammar, spelling or phonics before examples, during examples or not at all (on the second see Bryant & Bradley, 1985; Ehri, Nunes, Stahl, & Willows, 2001; Graves, 1991; Harris & Sipay, 1990; on the third see Goodman, 1967, 1985; Graves, 1983; Meyer, 2002). Majority opinion is probably ideally to give them during examples, that is after a certain number of examples have alerted children to the problem, but not waiting to see if they can solve the problem by coming up with a general rule, as in many cases this takes a long time. Similar debates have also occurred in mathematics teaching (see Chapter 12).

Introducing explicit generalisations, after some examples have been encountered, coincides in a general sense with Vygotsky's conception of top-down learning, although in some cases he seems to want to bring the explicit teaching of rules and definitions even before this (Vygotsky, 1934c, Ch. 6).

The consciousness of the general rules and principles that are taught chiefly comes from outside, so it is sometimes referred to by commentators as external consciousness (Bozhovich, 1977; Cole, 1988). The process of learning from rules and definitions brings the child into contact with the more organised meanings of the adult, leading to consciousness of the organisation found within them (for recent applications see Brown, 2002; Brown, Thomas, & Tolias, 2002). For spontaneous meanings, this organisation only appears at the end of each stage and is responsible for the child's ability to change their meanings and take them to a higher level of functioning. The teaching of meanings is able to achieve this earlier, as it points up the organisation within meanings more forcefully and immediately than learning by examples. However, there is a limit to bringing spontaneous meanings forward in this way, which is just over a single stage. This is because, while teaching can promote learning, it needs a functional soil that is ready for its crop before it can succeed.

Everyday and scientific learning differ in another way. Everyday meanings develop from the bottom up, emerging from repeated concrete experiences, and advance from an unorganised to an organised system. Scientific meanings begin with system and organisation that is provided by the definitions and explanations used and then acquire concrete reality through experience.

It is worth noting that while this kind of teaching is top down in the sense that it begins with the definitions of concepts and then goes on to concrete examples, it differs from the kind of top-down learning suggested by Piaget. For Piaget, during most of his career, the linkages between the elements within a logical structure are the primary source of development, particularly those produced by logical operations. We can describe these linkages as logical forms. These then lead to the learning of the elements in the structure, that is, concepts. So Vygotsky's move to emphasise top-down learning is not a move to the kind of formalism espoused by Piaget, which Vygotsky always opposed.

There remains a significant problem. If arithmetic is taught in primary school while logic is not, at least not with anything like the same intensity, then why, in broad terms, do they both appear in this period? Vygotsky's answer to this is that the experience of learning scientific concepts, such as arithmetic, generalises to spontaneous meanings and they too assume many of the characteristics of instructed meanings (Vygotsky, 1934c, Ch. 6). However, while spontaneous concepts are brought some way up to the level of taught concepts, they do not come entirely up to their level. In addition, they continue to retain many of the qualitative features of spontaneous concepts, namely that they are less developed in form and as a result less precise and scientific.

We now turn to the effect of the social situation of development on the child's meanings. Vygotsky (1933a, 1933b, 1933f, 1933h) claims that in each stage the social situation of development at the start of each stage leads on to the intellectual development found later.

Dependent social relations encourage an inexplicit communicative situation. In infancy the adult usually knows all about the child and its likely wishes and their communication takes place within an immediate situation that tells the adult much of what the child wants, without having to rely on its gestures or sounds. The autonomous speech of early childhood also fits into this mould, although the child's communication is already somewhat less dependent on the context than that of the infant. In these stages the child's meanings remain pictorial and figurative and dependent on the context of the communication. Contrariwise, as the adolescent becomes increasingly independent and self-sufficient, they are asked to communicate with people they have only just met and even, in writing, with people they will never meet. Adolescent communication often has for its context not the here and now but the world of ideas. This requires more abstract meanings that do not depend on context. The preschool and first school-age child are in intermediate states, between the extremes of early childhood and adolescence.

Because social relations are the basis for the development of meaning, in this conception, it is easy to think that they must therefore play a part in driving development forward. However, it appears that what Vygotsky means here is that social relations are a kind of intervening link. They result from the changes in signs and self-consciousness in the previous stage and provide a soil from which the new kind of signs will grow, although they themselves do not impart an independent dynamism to this process.

Dynamics of thinking and speech

The dynamics of thought and speech continue to feed off the dynamics of the whole personality. The long-term dynamics are: Practical thought predominates to about $2\frac{1}{2}$ years; speech then dominates, in an immediate sense, to about 16 years; both these things are dominant thereafter, as they are combined in advanced concepts. After the end of early childhood, speech is only a secondary source of dynamism, which gets its primary impetus from the dynamic forces found in the personality as a whole. In this larger sphere, the leading forms of signs after early childhood are, as we have already seen: play (preschool); writing (first school); and concepts (adolescence) (Vygotsky, 1933i, 1934c, Ch. 6, 1934e, Lect. 4, 1934f).

The direction of psychological influence that language exerts on the practical use of tools has scarcely changed from the previous period. We have the same picture of the dominance of tools and practice until late in early childhood, the increase in the importance of language in the preschool period and thereafter, followed by, in late adolescence, the synthesis of practice and language in advanced concepts. However, the way in which the relation between practice and signs is realised in the last period is different from the way it was realised in the previous period. There, consciousness came into the linguistic system as a result, primarily, of the social mediation of perception, memory and attention, which acted to make meanings conscious. Now, this is still a contributor, but after 7 years it comes in mainly through the influence of teaching.

Steering

Why does development progress in a regular way through regular stages, with the levels and functions organised in the appropriate way in each, and not just end up in a muddle? We have already seen the role self-consciousness plays in this, but there are also a number of other mechanisms involved. In his third period he had mentioned: self-consciousness (Vygotsky, 1930g, 1931b, Ch. 15); the role of creativity and imagination (Vygotsky, 1930i); Levy-Bruhl's social symbols for the connections between functions (Vygotsky, 1931b, p. 46); the motive to master and control (Vygotsky, 1930k, p. 67, 1931b, Ch. 12). In the present period he is more explicit on these topics and gives more recognition to Spinoza's view of motivation as the motive to master and control (see, respectively, Vygotsky, 1933i, 1934e, Lect. 4, 1934f, 1935e; and 1933d, 1933g, 1933i, 1933i, 1935e, 1933i; and 1933l, 1934f, 1935e).

Levy-Bruhl's (1910, 1922, 1927) theory of social symbols played a role in the previous period, but is more prominent in the present one. Vygotsky (1931b, p. 46) uses, as an example, a story from Levy-Bruhl (1922) about a chief of the Kafir tribe in South Africa, who was asked whether he approved of a plan concocted by the missionaries for his son to attend boarding school. He replied that he would dream on the question. This meant that he would wait to see what his dreams told him about it. This is not a reply that Western or Soviet leaders would have given in Vygotsky's day, or in our own. They would say, 'I'll think about it'. For the Kafir chief, dreams are part of the loop of decision-making functions; for Westerners, and for most Soviet citizens, they were not.

Although this is a modern story about contact with the West, we can assume that there were traditional Kafir stories in which this message, about how to use dreams, was transmitted. In fact, in the Western Judaeo-Christian religious tradition and in the Koran we find the same kind of story. One of the most famous tells how an Egyptian pharaoh had a dream that seven fat cows were eaten up by seven thin ones. Joseph, who was working in Egypt, was asked to interpret it and said it predicted seven years of plenty followed by seven of famine. On this basis, the pharaoh stored up food in the seven years of plenty and so was able to feed his people in the seven years of famine.

Levy-Bruhl believed there were also less obvious external symbols of integrated functions, particularly religious and artistic symbols. For instance, Morpheus, the Roman god of sleep and dreams, was often in the past thought of as a kind of personification of the inspiration we can receive through dreams. Vygotsky does not comment on this kind of symbolism, but it provides a further application of the general principle found in the story of the Kafir chief.

Conclusions

The changes in Vygotsky's map of development mainly concerned the content of the four levels and of the motivational dimension. The development of meaning is now divided into spontaneous and taught meanings. The development of both kinds of meaning is divided into two strands: structural generalisation and generality. Structural generalisation is similar to meaning in the previous period, except that new levels of generalisation develop on top of old ones, rather than replacing them. Generality is the ability to conceive conceptual hierarchies, whose extent will depend on the level of development of structural generalisation.

His previous frequent use of the conception of meaning as an instruction to do something is eliminated and he now relies entirely on one based on propositional content. The self arises mainly from functions involving signs.

His ideas about the self are now closer to Marx, through they stress signs more than he did.

There was also a change to a more active and intellectualised model of the child's motivation. He turned to the optimistic and intellectualistic view of child nature taken by Aristotle, scholasticism, Spinoza and Feuerbach. The child is by nature inclined to desire knowledge and this desire provides much of the impetus for its development.

The inner and outer selves appear in middle childhood and play a substantial role in development. He contrasts his view with that of Freud. He argues that the autistic functions of the inner self that achieve imaginary gratification by nonrational means, such as dreams and fantasies, appear later than those of the rational outer self, following the onset of inner speech. Freud had things the other way round. For Vygotsky, the differentiation of these two selves and their self-consciousness is essential to the development of a more complex personality.

Although there were changes in the model of the child's dynamics, the fundamental shape of the model remained. He now assumes that the child's development passes through a series of global stages. Each stage involves a leading function, or neoformation, and a particular way of organising functions. Around the midpoint of the stable part of the stage, the development of this organisation reaches a point where it results in self-consciousness, in which the self becomes conscious of itself and begins to perfect its most central feature, which is this system of organisation. This leads the personality to develop beyond the possibilities of the current social relations and thus to come into conflict with them, precipitating a crisis, out of which the next stage emerges. The most dynamic phases in this cycle are still signs, that is, things used to communicate meaning, and self-consciousness.

The development of signs is, to a greater extent than before, powered by the move from context-dependent to context-independent use of language as the child gets older. This, in turn, is driven by underlying changes in the child's social relations, from dependence to independence, although these changes, as before, react to earlier dynamic changes in the cycle, rather than being themselves dynamic.

After about 7 years of age the child is able to learn consciously, by first being taught meanings and principles and then applying them to make them more concrete. This inaugurates the taught strand of development. This enables the child to tap into the dynamism of the conscious use of language and signs earlier than would have otherwise been possible. In taught development, meanings can be learned a little over a full stage earlier than in the spontaneous strand.

Part II

Application and interpretation

7 Vygotsky and education

Vygotsky's views on education are supposed, at least by some commentators, to have even greater influence in our own day than his psychological views. As late as the early 1990s many in the Soviet Union and the CIS attributed the entire ethos of their education system to the ideas of his last two periods (Bernstein, 1993; Daniels, 1993, D. B. Elkonin, 1984). Informed commentators claim that his ideas about the psychology of learning are now more influential in Western education than those of Piaget (Cole, 1996; Tomlinson, 1999).

However, inspiring as they are, and true as they are in a way, the second and third statements can be misleading. The structure and ethos of the later Soviet education system stemmed from plans for reform that were already formed and began to be implemented in 1930 at a time when Vygotsky's educational philosophy ran counter to them (Joravsky, 1989; Price, 1977). It is true to say that Vygotsky's late ideas provided one of the most important rationales for the Soviet education system once they had appeared, but that is not quite the same thing. However, this is certainly influence on a massive scale.

The third statement is also potentially misleading, as it includes not only the influence of Vygotsky's own ideas about education, but also that of the widespread Western misconceptions about Vygotsky's educational psychology.

His influence on education in the West was ambiguous for two main reasons. Some of his ideas have been misunderstood. In addition, he espoused three very different views of education in his career, yet this point is often ignored. He maximised his opportunity for influence by spreading his imprimatur so widely. Of course, at the time he wrote he was not thinking of this, but this is the final result. Widespread influence is slightly less impressive when we know that it has been achieved in this way.

I begin with Vygotsky's own views and ask two questions of each of his three positions in turn. First, what was it and when did he hold it? Second, does it have anything to offer today? His last two positions are dealt with first, as they have been more influential. The same questions are then asked about dialogism, which is a loosely connected web of educational ideas currently popular in the West that often claims to be Vygotskyan, although it is not entirely so.

Social progressivism, 1928–31

This predominated in the third period. The main sources are *Imagination and creativity in the school years* (1930i), *History of the development of higher mental functions* (1931b) and *Pedology of the adolescent* (1931a) (see also Vygotsky, 1930l, 1931c, 1931d, 1931f).

Social progressivists, of whom the best known today are Dewey (1897, 1916) and Vygotsky, assert that education should be based on the principles that the child is part of society and that its learning is social. The school should encourage what is social within the child to blossom on an individual basis. What is relevant to social needs and issues determines the curriculum, preferably in such a way that the child sees social needs as its needs. The teacher often turns to the child's interests for information about what the child needs to know, because the child is a social animal and exists as part of society. The child's needs are imbued with the social needs of the society around it and in turning to them we find the best way to make the child's education relevant to the society around it, as well as to the child.

Vygotsky contributes little new in relation to this general approach, as the fundamentals had already been described, by, among others, Bogdanov (1920), Dewey (1897, 1915, 1916), Lunacharsky (1919) and Russell (1926a, 1926b). This is a point Vygotsky readily acknowledged (Vygotsky, 1931a, Ch. 6). However, he had more to offer than other advocates of this philosophy in the greater precision of his view of development.

It is usually an assumption of this approach that society is a self-organising system, at least as far as the child is concerned. This means the child will acquire its needs and interests from society and that pursuing them will have a beneficial influence on the child and on society. Among the more prominent social theorists who suggested this was Hegel and it is not surprising to find that both Dewey and Vygotsky were strongly influenced by him.

The Hegel connection here is particularly seen in the way in which both men emphasised the idea of automatic development. Hegel himself sometimes used the expression 'the cunning of reason' to express the idea that, however senseless development may seem on the surface, spirit has an underlying plan that it is working towards. Nothing happens that is without some essential contribution to the overall progress of development, whether of society or of the child. This idea is something that Hegel toyed with at certain times in his development, rather than one that is inherent in his philosophy as a whole, but it has always had great appeal to those who think that history will inevitably unfold in a certain direction. On the side of liberalism Potebnya (1864), Green (1885–88) and Fukuyama (1989, 1992) are examples of this tendency; on the left, Lenin (1925) and Lukacs (1923, 1967) sometimes lean towards it.

If we took this to its logical conclusion, then we could safely leave the child to its own devices and things would be bound to turn out right. However, most advocates of the approach want to intervene, so as to at least channel preexisting tendencies, and Vygotsky was increasingly counted in their number.

The methods associated with this kind of education are, above all, those that allow the child to express its underlying needs and interests. Examples of this are self-chosen project work, free choice of essay topics, free choice of books to read, choice between modules within a course and choice between subjects. Project work, for instance, will be on a topic chosen by the student or a small group of students working together. The choice of topic will, in theory, reflect their understanding of what is socially relevant to them.

Suppose the general area is set as the study of the environment, and students choose a topic within that area. One group might choose the pollution of a local river and its effect on things that live in the river. Assistance will come both from the input of other members of the group and from the teacher. The input of the teacher should come at the points where the group is stuck about how to find out about a particular topic or needs certain facts that are difficult to access.

There are obvious practical problems in this kind of teaching, which include the high workload it imposes on the teacher if they must discover and make available resources relevant to each project chosen by the class, which may all be different from the ones chosen in the previous year. There is also the problem in the present case that there may be no written information on the river and thus, to truly conform to the spirit of social progressivism, the students should go down to the river and take samples and analyse them. However, this would mean leaving either the rest of the class unsupervised or the river group unsupervised, which for good reason is forbidden by most education systems, as it could contribute to an accident or adversely influence the learning of the unsupervised group.

There are, however, ways round these difficulties to make social progressivism into a viable educational practice. These are considered later.

In pure social progressivism it is often thought that the child's development, as part of society, will always be a perfectly self-guiding process. This is typical of the phase of development in which Vygotsky wrote *Imagination and creativity in the school years* (1930i). By the time we come to *Pedology of the adolescent* (1931a) and *History of the development of higher mental functions* (1931b) he already stresses the kinds of problem with the approach mentioned above; the one he spends most time on is the need to guide rather than accept the child's interests. This edging away from the automatic development view of education is quite consistent with Vygotsky's Marxism. For Marxists, the child, in both class society and the proto-socialist society of the Soviet Union, was considered to be subject to many contradictory influences. There is a tendency for capitalist society to turn the child into a well-functioning cog in its machine. Marxists will think this is something to be struggled against rather than encouraged. In the nascent socialist society of the 1920s and early 1930s, there remained many social forces in the Soviet Union needing to be combated, particularly those emanating from the small capitalists and rich peasants created by the limited return to capitalism of the New Economic Policy.

During the publication year of 1931, this led to a transitional position. In *Pedology of the adolescent* (1931a, pp. 24–5), Vygotsky points to the key importance of interests in secondary education, but he implies the child's interests are not necessarily appropriate for the educator. He is quite interventionist, advocating the creation of new interests if they are needed for the child's education and are not already present. At one point he even seems to endorse Thorndike's (1913) suggestion that avoiding punishment creates its own kind of interest: one in avoiding punishment! Furthermore, he implies this may on occasion be a justifiable way of creating interests. If the student is not interested in mathematics, then they can acquire an interest, by being punished for not doing their maths homework and so forth. This is in contrast to the belief of pure social progressives that the child's interests are a uniquely valuable achievement of the child's own development and must be the basis for its education in their original form.

It is not clear how far Vygotsky means to take this. It is quite common for educationalists to argue that school students should be pushed to at least begin subjects and topics they are not initially interested in, as they may become interested in them once they find out what they are. Despite Vygotsky's desire to mould students, he remained keen, from what he says elsewhere, that students should as much as possible work from their own interests (Vygotsky, 1931a, Ch. 1).

Vygotsky's comments here find an echo in our contemporary concern that many of the interests of today's child have been formed by advertising, the media and computer games and thus are neither necessarily social nor necessarily good. *Pedology of the adolescent* (1931a) is in some ways a transitional work. Its stress on the alteration of interests seems to point forward to the attitudes of the last period, in which the stand against the spontaneous interests of the child becomes even stronger.

Turning to how students are to learn, his preferred form of learning for the younger child, up to 7 years, is discovery learning (Vygotsky, 1930l, 1931b). His suggestions that the child be allowed to discover how to paint and draw could have come from Piaget himself (Piaget, 1948; Piaget & Inhelder, 1956). Although he says less about the older age groups, it follows from his idea that the student should be allowed to choose what they want to study that most of the learning will come from the students; the teacher will be unable to engage in whole class teaching when the students are all studying different things. His comments suggest, however, that he does not advocate such an extreme reliance on discovery learning as at the younger age groups and that the teacher should scaffold the learning of individual students by offering individual comments to help their progress.

By scaffolding he means that the teacher offers individual assistance when the student needs it during their ascent of the wall of knowledge, which would otherwise be sheer. Although this is a Vygotskyan term that was popularised in the West by Bruner (1981a, 1984a, 1984b; see also Wood, 1998) and became closely associated with the idea of Vygotskyan education, it is not very prominent in Vygotsky's own writings. This was probably because no sooner had he coined it than he hurtled into his last period of educational thinking, in which it was effectively frowned on, as an embodiment of the illusions of social progressivism. His treatment of the development of writing (Vygotsky, 1931b, pp. 148–152) also shows his attachment to discovery learning for younger children. He says that the child, given the necessary materials, will gradually pass through the various stages in the development of writing, spontaneously making scribbles, then organised drawings, depicting objects with pictograms, using letter-like shapes to denote words and then words with invented spelling.

As a chapter in the history of ideas this is surprising, as this short précis describes precisely the research findings and educational prescriptions for teaching writing of the American educationalist Donald Graves, as they existed in his first period of influence around 1980 (Graves, 1983). Graves based his views on what he thought and what were generally taken to be the novel findings of his own research, although Vygotsky (1931b, pp. 148–152, 1935a) had described the same observations decades earlier, taking most of them from Delacroix (1924a, 1924b, 1926, 1930).

It is interesting that Graves, unlike Vygotsky, had the opportunity to see the widespread implementation of this method and later decided that most children could not discover all the essentials of writing for themselves and needed to be given teaching in such things as the phonic correspondence between letters and sounds. So Graves drew back from a radical version of discovery learning in this area (Graves, 1991). Although Vygotsky did not react in this way in his suggestions for younger children, he did so for older children, in a much more radical fashion.

It may help to fill out this rather sparse picture of the modified social progressivist method of teaching with some examples of it that are not mentioned by Vygotsky, but are often associated with it. They usually involve some compromise with the principles of the theory to make it practicable. For instance, instead of offering an open choice of project, teachers will make up a list for which they have already assembled the materials and that do not involve outside trips. Students then choose which of the offered topics to work on. Alternatively, teachers may take students on a visit to something of interest chosen by the teacher, such as a river, a factory or a museum and then have the students devise projects based on the trip. Neither of these methods precisely taps matters of most social relevance to the learner, but both do so approximately and both can be made more practicable than the pure model.

It is worth also mentioning some of the arguments that have led to scepticism about discovery learning since Vygotsky wrote even for young children. Taking, for a minute, the pure discovery learning that Vygotsky envisages in the early years, if the student is rapidly able to discover what there is to discover about the topic they are studying, few would argue against the idea that discovery learning is the best form of learning. However, the problem is that in many cases students do not discover what they could, or if they do, they take so long to do so that the total number of topics they can cover is severely limited. A classic exposition of this view is by Ausubel, Novak, and Hanesian (1978).

A further problem with discovery learning is that it has been shown, since Vygotsky wrote, that the idea that young children usually discover painting and drawing for themselves, at least in the early stages, is probably something of an illusion (Booth, 1975, 1982, 1984; Richardson, 1992; Van Sommers, 1984). Studies have shown that young children actually draw what someone has shown them how to draw and they draw it in the way they have been shown. Because many preschools and primary schools ban showing children how to draw things, teachers gain the impression they are discovering this for themselves, when in fact they are copying methods learned outside the classroom or from other children in the classroom. Other more subtle examples of how adults are deceived into thinking children invent methods of drawing are given in Freeman (1980) and Van Sommers (1984).

The case of scaffolding has been less intensively researched. It will obviously suffer less from the difficulties of pure discovery learning, as it contains an element of teaching. However, we could anticipate that, compared to teaching whole classes, or groups, who attend to and are ready to absorb what is offered, there will still be a substantial advantage for the latter. Wood and O'Malley (1996) found the empirical evidence on this inconclusive, although there were indications in this direction. The problem in contemporary Western education systems is to realise these conditions, which were almost certainly closer to being achieved in the Soviet system after 1930 than they are in many Western schools today. The reasons for this are discussed later.

In this period, Vygotsky also thought that the teacher should provide various kinds of personal guidance, beyond the fostering of students' interests (Vygotsky, 1931a, 1931e, pp. 260–261). He thinks that we need to build a realistic level of self-assessment for the child, at the same time as building up its competence, so it has a fairly accurate idea of how it is doing (Vygotsky, 1931e, pp. 260–261).

We should also, where necessary, devalue the child's fantasies of omnipotent competence, building its actual competence up and the omnipotence down until they meet and are thus at a realistic level in relation to one another. However, he recognises that this is a particularly delicate process in children with a defect, who often develop an overestimation of their capacities as a form of overcompensation for the defect, which for many provides a valuable way of coping with its social consequences (Vygotsky, 1927b, 1931e, pp. 260–261). At the same time, where such a child's self-evaluation is too low, it needs to be built up.

Vygotsky was particularly close to Alfred Adler on issues related to self-esteem and the assessment of schoolwork (Adler, 1907, 1927, 1930a, 1930b; Adler & Furtmuller, 1914). He agreed with Adler that it was important to bolster the self-confidence of children who suffer from a sense of inferiority, by encouraging them to engage in tasks at which they can succeed (Vygotsky, 1931b, Ch. 6). Vygotsky's followers have followed up the implications of his ideas about self-confidence, which are essentially the same as those deduced by the Adlerians. Thus a number of writers have argued convincingly from a Vygotskyan point of view for the use of cross-age tutoring for the development of self-confidence (Bountrogianni and Pratt, 1990; De Guerrero & Villamil, 1994, 2000; Wood & O'Malley, 1996). This is the practice of having older children teach younger ones to improve the confidence of the older children.

Vygotsky says less about discipline, but the Adlerian view of this is also in accord with his principles and can be mentioned. In the hands of Adler and his immediate disciples, the important thing with discipline was that the rules imposed should be necessary and not arbitrary and they should be seen as being like laws of nature, not as a trial of wills. As much use as possible should also be made of natural consequences, rather than imposed consequences, to deter the child from doing wrong. So, if a child runs in a school corridor, bangs into another child and hurts themselves, this is a natural consequence of breaking the rule not to run in the corridor. Among Adler and his earlier followers, there was a realisation of the limits of natural consequences, both because it is often not the child breaking the rule alone who is hurt and also because with other rules, such as 'Do not go onto the road', the consequences may be terminal.

Some later disciples of Adler, such as Glasser (1974), who are more familiar today, tended to lose sight of this balance in Adler's own views and advocated a more exclusive reliance on natural consequences.

Vygotsky also says that, if the student gives evidence in their work of large-scale social or family problems, the teacher should counsel them as to how to resolve these (Vygotsky, 1931a, Ch. 4). He says that such personality problems as hypobulia (weakness of the will), schizoid tendencies and even outright schizophrenia can be helped by either a combination of therapy and education or a specially devised educational programme alone (Vygotsky, 1931e, pp. 261–266). However, when advocating therapies here he does not go into details.

An institutional way of acting on the child's social development is to organise mixed ability classes, as these make for better social relations between children and thus a better collective, with better all-round development (Vygotsky, 1931e). This is also the kind of group that children left to their own devices will organise. Cooperation with the more able child will enable the less able to rise to a higher level.

Return to traditional education, 1932–34

Vygotsky's approach to education changed as dramatically between 1930 and 1934 as his psychological views. What is to be learned changes from the topics dictated by the child's interests to an externally set curriculum. The learner learning is now, for students over 7 years, replaced by the teacher teaching. The learner is now, primarily, motivated by the desire to learn what gives them the power to take a constructive part in society, in the present and the future, but this desire is to be aroused primarily by the central set curriculum. Knowing the central curriculum will give them this power. This is a shift from social progressivism to a modified traditionalism.

Vygotsky's late view of education appears in a clearly defined form in 1932, only two years after the great changes in the Soviet education system that began in 1930. This new centralised and traditional model of education is sometimes called the command-administration model (Daniels, 1993; Price, 1977). This dominated Soviet education from 1930 until the fall of the Soviet Union. In this, the curriculum is centralised and taught in a traditional manner. This took away the progressive aspects of the system that grew up in the 1920s and replaced them with command administration. Vygotsky did not resist these new teacher-centred methods when they became mandatory, but tried to make them work better and to justify them. At the same time his principle that in child development the form and content of learning are reversed, compared to historical development, also led, as we have seen in the previous chapter, to the conclusion that traditional methods of teaching were indeed superior. That this principle, like those that lay behind his previous social progressivism, also came from Hegel is surprising, but not incomprehensible. There were many sides to Hegel's thought and earlier Vygotsky had stressed one, where now he stressed another.

In the West, traditionalism has tended to focus on the end product of education and to think the most important thing is for the student to take a constructive part in society, when they finish their education. It was often divided about what this part was. For some, usually with a more aristocratic ideal, it was the scholar gentleman or accomplished gentlewoman (e.g. Arnold, 1869); for others it was the efficient professional with a broad outlook (e.g. Herbart, 1808). However, any lack of interest or engagement in the long years needed to achieve these ideals was usually replaced with compulsion.

A striking example of this in some European countries until well after the Second World War was the teaching of Latin. On the one hand, a good grasp of this was essential for the scholar. But, on the other, it was claimed, following Herbart, that the formal discipline obtained from learning Latin could assist the formation of the efficient professional. However, most students found it difficult and pointless and had to be pressed into its study by compulsion.

Vygotsky's desired final outcome was, of course, various types of Soviet citizen. But an equally fundamental difference was that he thought the curriculum could be formed so as to engage the student's interest at every level, ensuring a minimum of compulsion along the way to achieving this goal. This aim has also been adopted in many curricula in the West in recent years, such as the National Curriculum in the UK. Whatever doubts there may be about the success of these curricula in this regard, they are certainly much more attractive for the student than those that predominated in the West in Vygotsky's day.

From 1932 Vygotsky embraced the new national Soviet curriculum and philosophy of education that had begun implementation in 1930 (D. B. Elkonin, 1984; Joravsky, 1989; Vygotsky, 1934c, Ch. 6; 1935g). This involved a transition from a mixed and somewhat deregulated system, in which progressives were free to experiment, to one that was uniform, based on the traditionalist model and centrally controlled. We can look at this change from two points of view: That of those who opposed it; and that of those who supported it.

The rationale for social progressivism given by Vygotsky had been that it was better than education by compulsion and rote learning. Its products would be active and involved members of the new socialist society, rather than just passive factory fodder. This was the standard justification for this style of teaching in East and West, although in the West the word 'socialist' would be removed by liberals and replaced with 'democratic'.

The best known advocates of social progressivism in Soviet education in the 1920s had been Lunacharsky (Minister of Culture, 1923–27), Bogdanov (friend and later philosophical adversary of Lenin, disgraced leader of Protekult after 1925), Krupskaya (prominent educational activist and Lenin's widow), and Vygotsky (the greatest star among the younger Soviet psychologists). However, the fame of its advocates had only given this approach a foothold in the system, partly because the first two were notorious for their deviations from orthodox Marxism and their sponsorship did more to repel than attract the authorities. Many had long argued against social progressivism in Soviet education and undoubtedly welcomed the changes of 1930, even if, in the case of Trotsky and some others, it was from the perspective of exile (see Trotsky, 1924). Their view of social progressivism was startlingly similar to the complaints often heard against progressive education in general in the West in more recent times: Students were not learning, they were not challenged and when allowed to learn just what interested them, tended to learn what was eccentric, unbalanced or trivial (Carr & Davies, 1969–78, Vol. 2; Joravsky, 1989; Price, 1977).

An interesting question here is whether Vygotsky changed sides in the debate through conviction or through opportunism. Any complete reply to this is probably impossible. To Joravsky (1989), it is obvious that the shift was due to opportunism. However, the reasons given for deserting social progressivism by its opponents are far from absurd and are also widespread in the West. So we must plead to keep the case open.

This shift also had an indirect justification at the level of theory. Vygotsky had been converted by general theoretical reasons to the idea that the teacher should have maximum impact on the students, rather than letting the students do all the learning; so he had to adopt the idea of a centralised curriculum, as this is the only way to ensure that the teacher can engage in predominantly whole-class teaching and thus have this impact. Two more direct justifications for the centralised curriculum are that, if framed well: It will be able to engage the interests of students; and it will have a more worthwhile content than that generated by student interests. On this second point, we have seen that Vygotsky already harboured doubts about the natural constructiveness of student interests in his previous period.

Vygotsky (1934c, Ch. 6; 1935g) tells us that the teacher should teach and the overall impression is of a fairly teacher-centred model (see also Karpov and Bransford, 1995; Vygotsky, 1933c, 1933h). In Vygotsky (1935a), on the other hand, we are told that the child should be allowed to discover, rather than the teacher teach. However, most of this discrepancy is due to the ages at which the remarks are aimed. In the former, he is talking mainly about children 7 years of age and over, in the latter about the under-7s. Although the contrast is drawn more sharply than usual, an alteration of this kind is built into most parts of the Western education system and, whether it is desirable or not, it is certainly not an unusual view.

One of the central examples of good practice given for the teacher of 7–13 year olds is the teaching of foreign languages. A fairly full description of this is given in Vygotsky (1933h, 1934c, Ch. 6), and it turns out to be nothing more or less than the grammar translation method, usually considered a rather teacher-centred method. In this, students learn a language by being taught the grammar and lists of vocabulary items and then practise using these by translating passages of written prose or poetry. For living languages, they will also have conversation practice. This does not mean a rote learning view of teaching. Vygotsky agreed with Tolstoy that the teacher should not just drill the students in concepts and meanings, resulting in merely rote learning, rather than understanding (Vygotsky, 1934c, Ch. 6).

We can call this an instruction practice model of teaching. The teacher gives formal instruction in the principles to be applied and then the students undertake activities that enable them to apply the principles. This is in accord with Vygotsky's leading theoretical idea about education in this period, namely that students need: first, to be exposed to general principles, presented in a deliberate and conscious manner; and, then, activities that will enable them to test their understanding of these and ground them in concrete reality.

The main further requirement for successful teaching is the need for students to be roughly homogeneous in regard to intellectual maturity, in the subject studied; thus, in Vygotsky's terms, having their zones of proximal development (ZPDs) aligned with one another. Otherwise, students who are significantly behind or ahead of the group will suffer, as whole-class teaching will have to be directed at the mean level.

This general style of teaching could be implemented in three ways: through streaming, so each student is permanently assigned to a stream depending on their average level of development; through sets, that is, streaming specific to particular subjects, so the whole class will be, more precisely than for streaming, at the same level in each subject; by having groups within a less homogeneous class, of about the same developmental level, periodically taken aside and given instruction (Vygotsky, 1935b, 1935d, pp. 394–398, 406–408, 1934c, Ch. 6). As he refers to 'groups', rather than 'classes', in this context, he probably countenanced some use of the latter. However, there is also clear evidence from these sources that he had no problem with streaming based on ability as such and the reason for the term 'groups' was probably to suggest that the principle could be applied to classes or groups within classes, as circumstances dictated (Vygotsky, 1935b, 1935d, pp. 394–398, 406–408). Furthermore, the use of streaming and sets is more in accord with Vygotsky's late philosophy, as he wants as much well-targeted teaching by the teacher as possible and, when the teacher is occupied in teaching a subgroup of the class, the rest are not being taught. Also, the Soviet system, which in general he endorsed, at that time moved to reliance on streaming. In short, Vygotsky probably wanted mainly streaming or sets, with only minor use of teaching subgroups.

We must now consider how students are to be assigned to streams, sets or groups. The usual way would be to look at students' performance in recent assessments, undertaken as a normal part of the educational programme. However, Vygotsky wanted to use novel forms of psychological testing to achieve improved placements. Vygotsky (1934c, Ch. 6, 1934e) argues that teaching needs to be delivered in the ZPD for every child, to be maximally effective. At this point, the child is most able to profit from teaching. This cannot be achieved, for most of the child's teaching, except by having stream-like or set-like classes, based on novel forms of psychological testing, that test what the child can do with assistance, rather than without.

In his last period, Vygotsky put considerable effort into how to assess students, so we can know what their developmental potential is and what their ZPD might be. This is then to be used to organise streams or sets (Vygotsky, 1935b, 1935d, pp. 394–398, 406–408). The method of assessment is to give students problems to solve that are slightly above their current level of achievement and then give them assistance. The students' capacity to profit from this assistance, in solving the problem, is the index of their ZPD. A large amount of subsequent research shows that this method achieves a better prediction of future achievement than standard testing methods (see Chapter 11).

One perplexing feature of Vygotsky's own work here is that he uses only a single measure to assess the ZPD, which can thus only be used to form streams and not sets. But in a class based on the streaming principle, students will be quite disparate for any particular subject. He could have achieved a better result, in terms of his own principles, by using separate assessments in each subject area and then assigning students to sets. It seems likely that he chose a single measure of development because the Soviet system had gone towards streaming and more specific assessments would not have found much use.

He also says that each stage of development has its own teaching method (Vygotsky, 1934c, Ch. 6). We have already seen that this certainly applies to the preschool period (3–7 years), where discovery learning predominates, compared to the period after 7 years, where formal instruction predominates. It seems that what changes most, between the period of first school (7–13 years) and adolescence (13–17 years), is the nature of the principles that are taught and the degree of consciousness the learner attains about them. In teaching reading, writing and arithmetic in the years 7–13, we teach rules based on concrete experience. The rule that '4 + 2 = 6' is directly based on examples, such as that these four buttons added to these two buttons make six buttons.

In adolescence, we have the appearance of the ability to conceive algebra. An algebraic equivalent of the above rule is 'x + y = z'. This equation is satisfied by the values given above, but also by a vast number of others, such as 3 + 1 = 4, 9 + 2 = 11, and so on. The equation makes no direct reference to anything like buttons, blocks and coins or, indeed, to anything that exists as an object in the real world. It only refers to numbers, which are abstract properties of collections of objects; so it refers to something (numbers) that refers to the real world. Algebra climbs on the back of numbers to tell us what numbers are like, just as numbers climb on the back of collections of actual objects to tell us what they are like. Algebra is a second-order reflection on the world, numbers are a first-order reflection.

One example he gives of the role of consciousness in learning through teaching involves number systems (Vygotsky, 1934c, Ch. 6, 1934d, 1934h). The child in first school (7–13 years) is taught the decimal system, without being aware of what it is or why the rules for using it are as they are. (This may not be true today, but usually was then.) The secondary school child, who learns about alternatives to the base ten system of numbers, comes to conscious awareness that there are indefinitely many systems of numbers, with different bases, and the decimal system is just one of these. So a second aspect of changes in teaching methods is that adolescents are taught to be aware that many systems of rules are arbitrary and can be changed purely by the decision of the rule maker. The child in the age range 7–13 years learns to be conscious of the rules, but not that they can be changed. To teach an adolescent means to teach the changeability of rules, while to teach a child in the earlier period means to teach only consciousness of what the rules are.

Some more recent research on this issue seems to create problems for Vygotsky. This is that Dienes (1960, 1966) claimed that primary age children can be successfully taught to understand the arbitrary nature of number systems, using Dienes blocks and others forms of apparatus. However, there has also been considerable scepticism about what it is that primary children learn from these realisations (e.g. Freudenthal, 1974; Langford, 1988). This is mainly for two reasons. The first is that primary children show they can operate within a number of different systems, but this does not show that they understand the relations between them or that they are arbitrary; the second is that learning multiple systems does not appear, as hoped, to improve their operation of the standard base ten decimal system. For these reasons, claims about primary age children's capacity to use multiple number systems are not as problematic for Vygotsky as might appear.

So far, we have considered students who are in the normal developmental range. For Vygotsky, those who are sufficiently retarded to be labelled as such need to be considered separately, as do those suffering from other serious handicaps or abnormalities. Examples he gives include the blind and deaf, as well as the then common thyroid disorder of goitre, Pick's syndrome and schizophrenia (Vygotsky, 1933e, 1935e, 1935g). Among the retarded, he distinguishes those who are retarded from the effects of an impoverished or abusive social environment and those who are so for organic reasons of whatever kind. Again, each is to have their own kind of education. The socially retarded are to be given enriching education that will take them from their current level to the level they would otherwise have attained. The organically retarded, contrariwise, are to have education in special schools that concentrates on teacher-centred instruction, even for the young ones, because this is what those with this kind of organic problem benefit from most. The instruction will not only be teacher centred, but also will concentrate on explicit teaching using rote learning and drills, if necessary, in the details of how to do things. In learning to spell, for instance, the normal child will pick up a great deal about how to spell words from their reading. The organically retarded child, by way of contrast, finds it hard to learn incidentally in this way and needs direct instruction in how to spell words, with learning spelling lists by rote as part of their programme (Vygotsky, 1935e).

Special schools were as much part of the Soviet education system as they were for most of that same time in the West. Part of Vygotsky's educational philosophy was that for most handicaps there is a route to achievement that can avoid the handicap and enable the child to achieve what the normal child can. The role of special schools is to provide this alternative route to learning. This applied, for example, to such major groups as the retarded, the blind and the deaf. In most cases it does not result in short-term normalisation, that is return to the environment and school of the normal child, during the usual period of education. However, especially in the case of sensory and motor handicaps, he thinks this will be usual at the end of formal education.

This attitude was widespread in the West at the time, although it was often also tinged with a sense of defeatism about the problem. The special school would try its best to achieve this result, but it would probably fall short of complete success. Vygotsky was by nature an optimist and he was very confident they would achieve success, at least in the great majority of cases.

Finally, two additional topics: his objections to Piaget on education and his advocacy of imitation as a learning mechanism.

In Vygotsky (1934c, Ch. 6) he deals with Piaget, who had from early on assumed the mantle of a leading proponent, in many eyes *the* leading proponent, of individual progressivism in education. Individual progressivism is the belief that in real education the child discovers everything practicable for itself, spurred on by its own interests and curiosity. It can be divided into three components: knowing what is to be taught; arranging that the learner learns it; motivating the learner. In its most usual form, it argues that the content of the curriculum is not particularly important, as the object of education is to teach the generalised skills of literacy, mathematics and thinking and it does not matter what the child or adolescent studies to acquire these skills, as long as they acquire them (Bliss, 1987, 1996; Elkind, 1991, 2000; Piaget, 1970).

In its extreme form individual progressivism also teaches that it is of overwhelming importance for the child to learn and of little importance, or positively undesirable, for the teacher to teach. The reason for this is that the child cannot understand what it learns unless it discovers it. Things said or otherwise imparted by the teacher or educational media are hardly ever properly understood. Its leading principle here is 'Do not teach, let the child discover.'

The individual progressivist view of motivation is, at bottom, that it is like the content of the curriculum: irrelevant as long as it's there. As long as the student is interested in something that gives them a basis for work to acquire generalised abilities, all will be well. What kind of interest it is does not matter, as long as it comes from the student and is not imposed by the teacher.

Vygotsky (1934c, Ch. 6) challenges the assumptions behind this, particularly that what is learned through teaching has no connection with what develops and is furthermore of little real significance for the child. His own approach to the theory of teaching rests, he claims, on the empirical material and theory he reported in *History of the development of higher mental functions* (1931b). However, as so often, this genealogy is not entirely accurate. Not only has his view of the development of functions changed since then, but in what is perhaps the focal topic, his approach to consciousness, there has been, as we have already seen, a sea change compared to the earlier texts. There is, in fact, little empirical evidence to back the shift; its origin appears primarily theoretical or ideological.

We can divide this issue into two. First, the amount of development due to teaching is almost certainly exaggerated in Vygotsky's account (Chapter 12). However, that considerable development can be achieved by teaching is supported by more recent evidence.

Furthermore, the link between development and teaching is now presented as the fundamental thesis of Vygotsky's new approach to education and, in particular, the learning of nonspontaneous, taught, concepts (Vygotsky, 1934c, p. 191). Teaching, for Vygotsky, does not, as Piaget would have it, just go past the child without affecting its development. Rather, for the modern child, teaching and learning from teaching are part of the normal route of development. Without them the child will learn more slowly, as it has to return to the historical method of learning by experience. In view of our conclusion about the first point, we cannot agree that teaching contributes as much to development as Vygotsky thinks; however, we can agree that it contributes more than Piaget thinks.

In Vygotsky's last period, the mechanism for learning in school is imitation of the teacher, although understood in an unusual way. This is designed to fit in with his stress on teacher-centred learning. His understanding of what it means to teach by imitation contrasts with a group of common ways of understanding this. According to these, learning by imitation gives rise to habits. In imitating someone's method of doing something, whether it be tying a shoelace, lighting a match or reorganising an equation, we mindlessly copy what they do and the result is a habitual way of acting.

The later paradigm for this way of looking at imitation in psychology was the social learning theory of Bandura (1991) and Bandura and Walters (1964), which arose as an offshoot of American behaviourism in the 1950s and 1960s. Social learning theorists looked at imitation as the method of social learning par excellence and attributed most of what could not be explained in human behaviour by standard conditioning mechanisms to it.

Vygotsky's ideas about imitation are, by contrast, based on Kohler's (1917, 1920) work with apes (Vygotsky, 1934c, pp. 100–105, 210, 222). For Kohler, as a leading member of the Gestalt school, imitation often leads on to understanding and insight.

Imitative learning is one of the chief methods of learning within the zone of proximal development. Vygotsky says in *Thinking and Speech* (1934c, p. 222):

> This form of explanation [the ZPD – PEL] is based on the notion that analogous systems in higher and lower domains develop in contrasting directions. This is the law of the interconnection between higher and lower systems in development. This law was discovered and has been supported through our studies of the development of spontaneous and scientific concepts, native and foreign languages, and verbal and written speech.

He had, in preceding passages, already claimed to show that these last three dichotomies involve, on the one hand (the first, spontaneous element), the ascent in development from the concrete to the abstract, while, on the other (the second, nonspontaneous element), the descent from the abstract to the concrete. The 'law of the interconnection between lower and higher systems in development' means that, in development, these systems, of spontaneous and scientific concepts, do not usually stay apart. Usually, the second grows on top of the first, as when, in learning a second language at school, the child uses the grammar and semantics of its first language as a springboard for the second language.

So, before the child is ready to fully understand the higher system (the second language) and has already grasped the lower (the first language), that is, before it is ready for a full integration between the two, it is able to grasp the higher by means of a preliminary integration of the two. Furthermore, imitation provides one way of establishing this preliminary link between the higher and the lower system. So imitation is not a process that forms habits, but one that leads to a preliminary kind of understanding.

An illustration is as follows. Say a foreign language teacher reads a list of German words with their translations and after every pair the class has to copy, or imitate, what she says. So she says: 'Hund–dog; Frau–woman; Kopf–head.' We might think that this is just learning a habit, but research on learning foreign languages suggests that it is not. The German words are initially assimilated to the semantic system of English that the student already knows. For instance, 'Kopf' can mean the crown of a hat in German, but the learner will not realise this, as this is not one of the meanings of 'head' in English. The German words are also initially assimilated to the syntactic structure of English when the learner wants to say something. So they might say: 'Der Frau hat verloren sein Wollmütze' for 'the woman has lost her woolly hat', which uses the English word order and fails to make the article 'der' and the possessive pronoun 'sein' agree with their nouns in gender. The correct German is: 'Die Frau hat ihre Wollmütze verloren.' So, although the students are imitating the teacher, they are not only forming habits, they are also assimilating new knowledge into existing systems.

The role of imitation is not to provide a permanent form of compromise knowledge. It is to prepare for understanding such things as the generally accepted meanings of words, generally accepted mathematical concepts and other kinds of agreed meaning.

Advocate of conditioning, 1918–21

In 1926 Vygotsky published a substantial book titled *Pedagogical psychology* (1926c), based on the ideas of reflexology or exclusive reliance on conditioning, which had been mainly written in the period 1918–21. The idea that rote learning and conditioning play some role in education has been widely accepted in most areas of education, although sometimes advocates of discovery learning have insisted that only principles that are discovered have any educational value, while what is learned by rote is so damaging to the child that it must be ruled completely out of court. However, to the consistent advocate of reflexology that Vygotsky was around 1918–21 when the book was written, as to most behaviourists and to some connectionists of our own day, learning can only consist of rote-learned associations. Thus, to ask that some other kind of learning, involving insight and understanding, take its place is nonsensical. There is no such thing.

This stance can be difficult to understand today, as there are few educationalists or educational psychologists who advocate it. However, the movement Bernstein (1993) called the corporate trainers, whose original home is in-house or outsourced corporate training, have often campaigned to move education as training into the mainstream. As Bernstein points out, they have also often used the magic of Vygotsky's name to promote their ideas. Although Bernstein is somewhat surprised at this appeal, insofar as it is made to Vygotsky's (1926c) book, it has some validity. However, the idea that there is no such thing as insight and understanding, that there is no such thing as grasping general principles to simplify what has to be learned in a subject area, these notions, once so popular, have relatively little hold within mainstream education today.

Vygotsky's early view, like most approaches of its kind, stresses the idea that the teacher will teach and the learner will learn under the control of the teacher. This comes from the metaphor of animal training that constantly underlies his rhetoric. So, to train a dog to come to heel we say 'heel' and when the dog comes to heel it is rewarded, usually with praise and stroking. The dog's behaviour is increasingly under the control of the trainer, as the training proceeds.

However, this stress on teacher control is not the only or the most distinctive feature of Vygotsky's view at this time. Traditional education also advocates teacher control, as when the teacher stands up in front of a class or a lecture group and gives a talk on the American Civil War or differential calculus. The most distinctive feature of Vygotsky's view at this time is the idea that teaching and learning are part of the process of conditioning. That is to say, that the student learns that things go together because they have occurred together in the past. For instance, in spelling we learn that the sequence of letters 'hymn' is associated with the sound of the word 'hymn' and the sequence of letters 'pineapple' is associated with the word 'pineapple'. We learn key dates in history, paired with what happened on that date. We learn how to add up large numbers on paper by following the sequence of steps: First, add up the right column, write down the units, carry the tens, move one column to the left and repeat.

The idea that this model of associations can be extended to everything that education tries to teach was an act of faith when Vygotsky wrote about it and it largely remains such. It is hard to explain insight into mathematical propositions, into the underlying processes of history or works of literature in this way. It was the inability of this model to bridge this gap that led Vygotsky to abandon it and that, by the 1950s, led to the decline in its popularity in both Western and Soviet psychology.

Although Vygotsky is sometimes used to justify the notion of education as training today, there is usually a significant difference in what is being advocated. Vygotsky wrote at a time when reflexologists believed that their approach could eventually be applied to the teaching of general principles and understanding. The subsequent history of attempts to do this is largely one of failure. However, the modern corporate trainer does not aspire to offer general education or understanding, but rather instruction in specific skills, such as using a particular computer program or how to service an engine. For Vygotsky this failure would have been disastrous, while for the corporate trainer it is not, as they have concluded that there is no such thing as general education.

Insofar as this kind of instruction is aimed at limited areas of this kind, it will often be quite appropriate. The concern that many educationalists have about this approach arises from attempts to transplant it into the education system at large. The problem here is that students will emerge from their education with a kit of skills, but no general understanding or development. This is problematic from several points of view. Such students will not be capable of informed participation in society, neither will they have had opportunities for personal development offered by their schooling. Furthermore, this new system will not even ensure that they have work-related skills, as there are so many kinds of work-related skill in society now that the chance of a student's arriving at their place of employment with the right specific skills, having gained them at school, is generally small. The main exceptions to this are driving and typing, but this has been recognised for a long time and does not require the kind of mass upheaval envisaged by some who want education turned over to training in skills.

I began by saying that the appeal of the corporate trainers to Vygotsky has some validity, insofar as it is an appeal to his reflexological period. Its validity is, however, limited. Vygotsky was not using reflexology to undermine general education: They often are.

Dialogism

A popular view of Vygotsky, among present-day Vygotskyans in the West, is that he advocated a narrower form of the social progressivism of Vygotsky's third period, often called *dialogism* (e.g. Daniels, 2001; Forman & Cazden, 1994; Wells, 1996, 1999, 2002; Wells & Claxton, 2002). In its pure form, this is based on the slogan that education is dialogue. We can get a rough idea of the relation of this approach to Vygotsky by saying that it adopts parts of Vygotsky's social progressivism and leaves others. There are both broader and narrower versions of it. I begin by looking at the narrower version that stresses external dialogue with the teacher, to the exclusion of almost anything else.

The main idea behind dialogism, in this narrow sense, comes from studies of the child's learning of a first language. This is both largely painless and highly successful. If we look at how comparable subjects, such as foreign languages, are learned in school, the process is painful and in most cases the result is failure. Why not start to teach foreign languages and other school subjects in the same way that the young child learns its native language: through dialogue?

In fact, this argument as a whole does not appear in Vygotsky. However, given that he advocates learning through scaffolding (Vygotsky, 1931b, Chs 3, 7), and learning through dialogue is a form of scaffolding, he advocates it indirectly. It seems curious that Vygotsky is invoked as the patron saint of a movement whose main tenets he only hints at. However, this is not as curious as it appears. First, Vygotsky's status as a psychological theorist encourages people to cite him in support of things he only hints at. Second, as he coined the term scaffolding, this provides at least half a reason to cast him in this role.

If Vygotsky did not originate this argument who did and would Vygotsky have approved of it? On the first point, the argument certainly originated earlier and was associated particularly with advocacy of the direct method of language teaching. This is the teaching of a second or foreign language in that language mainly as a spoken language. Thus the method makes foreign language teaching into something that is close to the way children learn their native language. A number of influential experts in the practical aspects of language teaching advocated this in the period from about 1880 to 1930 (Rulcker, 1969; Stern, 1983, pp. 456–460). It was also enunciated by a number of influential academic experts in this period, especially Gouin (1880), Jespersen (1904) and Palmer (1921). This movement was the basis for the Berlitz language schools, which popularised the idea by example, the first of which was opened as early as 1878 (Stern, 1983, p. 98).

It is unlikely that Vygotsky would have approved this argument at any point in his career as a central basis for education. We have already seen that in none of his three periods of educational thought does he rely solely on the dialogic principle. It is compatible with and could be considered as a subordinate principle within his social progressivist period, but it is never one of the main principles.

A further concern about dialogism is that, if narrowly interpreted, it could mean that education is just the actual dialogue between student and teacher. If the teacher has 30 students in the class this will mean each will get only one thirtieth of the teacher's attention, reducing the teacher's impact considerably. It is true that educational methods stressing dialogue often have the students talk to one another. This is a standard element in direct and immersion methods of language teaching and student discussion groups are, of course, a part of many methods of teaching other subjects. So, having students experience some dialogue is not difficult. However, for the sceptic, the problem is that if the whole programme is turned over to dialogue, the student is still largely deprived of the teacher's more expert input. Were dialogue a teaching method with a proven track record this would not be so problematic, but research in our own time suggests it is, at best, an unproven teaching method.

This problem has been highlighted by Wood and O'Malley (1996), who review studies of collaborative learning by small groups of young people, both in experimental situations and in schools (see also O'Connor, 1996). They point out that there is no single overwhelming question about the success or otherwise of such groups, as they undertake different kinds of task and do so under different conditions. Under some of these, collaborative learning may be successful, under others not. Two differences between tasks that are likely to be important are familiarity and level of difficulty.

The group is more likely to be successful, if left to its own devices, when tackling familiar and easy tasks than when tackling difficult and unfamiliar ones, where more teacher assistance is likely to be required (Rogoff, 1986).

When cognitive skills, such as ability to summarise issues or explain things, are weak in a substantial proportion of participants, this presents a more challenging situation compared to one where all are fluent in these abilities. It could be that, while the weaker members will hold the group back, at least to begin with, the experience of the group may ultimately help them to gain these skills. If the teacher intervenes to scaffold or teach these skills, then the possible outcomes could be even more various.

Wood and O'Malley (1996) find that the literature has unduly neglected these issues. They are nevertheless able to conclude that experimental studies of collaborative learning produce learning. They are unable to show that it produces faster or better learning than other methods when applied in experimental studies. At the same time, they find that there is no real evidence that collaborative learning in the classroom produces faster or better learning than other methods and there are concerns in the literature that it sometimes creates problems and some suggestions that it can actually slow learning compared to other methods.

Their suggested solution for this is that more attention should be given to the differences just alluded to, when collaborative learning is implemented, rather than just implementing a single fixed method. One method they are particularly keen to see trialled is computer-assisted collaborative learning, in which students are first computer matched for ability in the area to be discussed and then provided with software that gives scaffolding-style help in the course of the group's activities (see also Bruner, 1983, 1990, 1996). The advantage of this last method is that it overcomes a serious objection to group discussion methods, as well as methods based on scaffolding, mentioned above. This is that they reduce the impact of the expert, who is the teacher, on the students, as the role of expert is now taken by the computer.

In summary, the value of group discussion as a teaching method is still largely unproven. Few would doubt its value as part of an educational programme, but to turn the whole programme over to it is still to a large extent a leap of faith. A further problem Vygotsky would have had with dialogism is that it adopts a narrow way of looking at both psychology and education, that is at variance with his outlook in both his last two periods. In both periods, he realised that there is more to education than just face-to-face dialogue. A far more important principle for him is that education is education of the whole personality. In his third period, when he comes closest to the dialogical model of education, we can see this from three of the typical educational tactics of the social progressivist teacher mentioned above: individual or group choice of projects, individual free choice of essays and individual free choice of books to read. None of these activities necessarily involves dialogue, except when there is group work on projects. All of them connect with the whole personality of the learner.

It is this broad range of activities that Vygotsky advocates. Were this not so, his stress on developing student's interests would make little sense, as in a face-to-face dialogue we develop a joint interest not a personal one. His stance here is also thoroughly in accord with his emphasis on the importance of the internalisation of social relations and on inner speech. For him it would be naive to think that because a student works on his own he is asocial. For Vygotsky the personal is always the social and students working on their own or listening to a talk are, in an extended sense, cooperating with the teacher (Vygotsky, 1934c, Ch. 6).

Many Western Vygotskyans also think that he advocates individualised scaffolding by the teacher in the context of an immediate problem throughout the child's school career (e.g. Forman & Cazden, 1994; Wells, 1999, 2002). One origin of this idea is that that he does suggest this for the preschool period. For the reasons just reviewed, this is certainly part of his penultimate approach to education, but it is just as certainly not the whole of it.

A further misconception of this kind recognises that the teacher is supposed to give the student detailed assistance in the form of teaching, but neglects the accompanying idea, present in his third period, that the teacher should also give strategic advice (Vygotsky, 1930i, 1930l).

Next, it is worth mentioning some later general criticisms of the dialogic argument, which are often ignored by those who claim to follow dialogism, whether based on Vygotsky or not. They are not conclusive, but they show that the dialogic argument is far from being as convincing as it appears.

The total time available to a young child to learn its native language is, say, eight hours a day, seven days a week for four years, that is, about 12,000 hours. During these hours the child is mainly taught by personal tutors, namely its conversational partners. The child is also highly motivated. This contrasts with the child in school, who, say, spends eight hours a week, 36 weeks of the year for eight years learning, say, French or Italian, a total of less than 3,000 hours. During these hours it is taught in a class of 30 or so others, seldom receiving the individual attention of the teacher and is often poorly motivated. When we turn to research studies of language teaching, we find that if we equalise the amount of time spent learning a foreign language by 'direct' methods in the classroom, where the teacher and the students talk in the language and by formal grammar translation methods, we find no consensus as to which is superior (Littlewood, 1984, 1992; Stern, 1983, pp. 152–156, 1992). This is admittedly in part due to the inability of researchers to agree on and adequately assess what is meant by the rather nebulous terms 'direct' and 'grammar translation'.

It is true that language teaching by immersion is considerably superior to most classroom teaching methods (Hakuta, 1999; Perez, 2004; Stern, 1983, pp. 152–156, 1992). This is one form of direct teaching where the whole of schooling is conducted in the target language. However, as immersion usually involves much longer exposure to the language than classroom teaching methods, the comparison does not settle the issue of which learning style is most productive. In summary, it could well be that it is not dialogue but other factors that produce the difference between learning a native language and learning a foreign language in school.

Next, we can turn briefly to two examples of recent Western authors who interpret the idea of dialogism more widely than those just discussed and are closer to the social progressivism of Vygotsky's third period. Shotter (1995, 1998) has taken dialogism to include internal as well as external dialogue and includes practice as a key element in learning. However, he does not place as much stress on the role of the whole personality in learning as Vygotsky. To be fair to this approach, its author does not claim that it is entirely Vygotskyan, but it is worth noting this difference, as it is sometimes taken to be so.

Wertsch (1985, 1990, 1998; Wertsch & Sohmer, 1995; Wertsch & Toma, 1995) has also adopted the slogan of dialogism in education. However, he usually interprets this in a broad sense, identifying it with the social progressivism of Vygotsky's third period. But he sometimes throws in nonVygotskyan ideas that resemble the narrow version of dialogism outlined above. He also has a tendency, on the theoretical level, to swing between two extremes. Sometimes, he exaggerates the role of practice in Vygotsky, for whom language and consciousness were primary. However, on other occasions he emphasises dialogue outside the context of practice, particularly when he is considering Vygotsky's contemporary Bakhtin (Bakhtin, 1981; Wertsch, 1985, 1990).

One of the most common educational slogans raised by Western Vygotskyans who favour dialogism is 'social constructivism' (e.g. Forman & Cazden, 1994; Newman, 2000; Newman & Holzman, 1993, 1996). This is often intended to contrast with Piaget's 'individual constructivism'. At the centre of this is the idea that the teacher negotiates a common set of meanings and view of the world with the student, which is purely a social invention and has no connection to reality. It is claimed that only dialogue can produce this kind of construction.

This is certainly not Vygotskyan, as Vygotsky was not a constructivist, neither did he claim that dialogue is an exclusive route to understanding the world. The most unVygotskyan advocates of the linking of dialogism and social constructivism are Newman (2000) and Newman and Holzman (1993, 1996). For Vygotsky in his last two periods education is induction into a large scale intellectual culture, into large views of the world. Newman and Holzman, by means of very forced arguments, have him as a postmodernist, that is as someone who thinks there can be no large-scale intellectual culture and no broad understanding of anything, as there is no underlying reality. Vygotsky would certainly have been horrified to find his name used to justify a view so at variance with his own.

Vygotsky's educational stances: an evaluation

The most attractive options for would-be Vygotskyans in education are the social progressivism of the third period and the modified traditionalism of the last two. This is a more difficult choice to make than the committed partisans of the two sides are sometimes willing to admit.

We can ask, to begin with, how we could know which is better. This is immediately difficult to answer, as the two methods aim to produce different things. Social progressivism aims to produce someone who is an independent thinker, capable of both raising significant questions and answering them. Traditionalism, by contrast, aims at mastery of a set curriculum. This contrast is, of course, not absolute and each will try to reach some of the goals of the other, but it expresses what each leans towards. However, most evaluations of learning lean towards assessing mastery of a set curriculum, thus disadvantaging socially progressive education. So we must bear this in mind.

We can begin with general evaluations of national educational systems using standardised tests of educational attainment. The Soviet education system after 1930 was the envy of many, if not most, Western countries and its students continually outperformed those of Western countries (Daniels, 1993; Price, 1977). There is also evidence that the Soviet system achieved a more equal outcome than Western education systems, as well as a better one (Daniels, 1993). This is not to say that it achieved a completely equal outcome; it certainly did not intend to. International comparison tables show that, in recent years, Finland has taken over this role of having both better and less variable results than other countries (OECD, 2003a, 2003b). It too tends to use modified traditional methods, although it departs from the old Soviet Union in that streaming is discouraged. It is also true to say that the high regard in which education and teachers are held in Finland undoubtedly contributes greatly to its results, making it hard to know just what produces the success (Crace, 2003). However, the combination of essential elements is disconcertingly similar to that found in the old Soviet Union. These findings are interesting, but they do not give us a definitive answer about the role of teaching methods in education as there are many other factors that can influence results. To mention only a few, better relations between parents and schools, better discipline and less truancy all apparently characterised the Soviet Union and could all have a considerable direct or indirect influence on students' learning.

Within Western countries, there have been a number of studies that have tried to control for other factors. These have also tended to show that students undergoing traditional education tend to perform better than those undergoing progressive education (Bennett, 1976; Bennett, Wood & Rogers, 1984; Bourke, 1989; Good & Brophy, 1996).

Traditional education may do better than socially progressive education, assessed by results on standardised tests of academic achievement, but this is not completely convincing for two reasons: Performance on standardised tests is not everything; the difference is not large, compared to other factors. In relation to the first point, there is a plausible school of thought that argues that although traditional schooling scores well on immediate academic success, it may not do so well in terms of encouraging lifelong learning (deCharms, 1984; McMeniman, 1989). In addition, schoolchildren who have had a more progressive education can be shown to do better in tertiary education than those with traditional education, matched for marks in a school-leaving exam (Cummin, 1999).

However, this latter effect could be explained away. The latter students have probably had their academic potential realised to a greater degree than the former, as this is what traditional teaching does. The result is that the underlying academic potential of the latter group is less than that of the former group, to which they are matched. So when they get to university and are exposed to the same environment, the former do better.

One further problem is that there is good evidence to show that the effectiveness of teaching methods interacts with other factors in the education system (Bourke, 1989; Good & Brophy, 1985, 1996; Langford, 1989). For instance, students from lower socioeconomic status backgrounds tend to do better in school with more traditional methods, while those from higher socioeconomic backgrounds will do about equally well under either. This means that there is an overall advantage for traditional education, but this is due to an advantage for one group, rather than for the population as a whole.

Another example of this principle is that the child who is more able in and has greater previous knowledge of the subject being taught will discover more (Good & Brophy, 1996; Langford, 1989).

This aspect of the problem was neglected by Vygotsky, who first assumed that social progressivism would always be best and then changed to assuming that traditionalism would always be best, at least for children in the normal range. However, Vygotsky was not entirely an absolutist; under some circumstances he looks at how the influence of context and the qualities of the individual mediate the effects of teaching methods and style of education. We can see this particularly from his ideas about the exceptional child. For the child with organically based learning difficulties he recommends a structured programme (Vygotsky 1927b, 1931c, 1935e); for the child with socially based learning difficulties he recommends a programme of cultural enrichment (Vygotsky, 1931c, 1935e); while for the normal child he recommends whatever is his current recommendation for normal children (social progressivism or traditionalism). The problem with Vygotsky is that he does not apply the context principle within the range of the normal child.

As if the choice here were not difficult enough already, there are also significant philosophical and political issues involved. Perhaps the most important is whether we live in a society that we trust to set the national curriculum, or at least centralised exam syllabi, as in Vygotsky's modified traditional education this is what will happen. Do we want our children to learn Stalin's (or Mrs Thatcher's) version of history? The other side of this issue is: Do we trust teachers to guide our children or would we rather have teachers restrained by an external curriculum?

A last issue is that for many who might be inclined to the social progressivist view of education, the greatest setback of recent years has been the shift to vocationalism in the systems of most Western countries, which means a shift away from social engagement and understanding. In this connection, it might be the very compulsoriness of core subjects, encouraging social and other kinds of general understanding, rather than the way an external curriculum is taught, that is more important. Such observers might be inclined to shift to Vygotsky's modified traditionalism for this reason.

So, we should not ask whether Vygotsky's social progressivism or his modified traditionalism is best, but what the purposes and context of the education we are thinking of are. This applies both to national education systems as a whole and to local decisions about how to teach in particular schools and classes. Although Vygotsky was a pioneer in using this principle as it applies to handicapped children, he did not apply it to the normal child, which is a limitation in his approach to education.

Conclusions

During the period 1918–21 Vygotsky adopted the reflexological view of education, in which it is assumed that learning is in accordance with the laws of conditioned reflexes. In this period he wrote a substantial book on educational psychology. By 1928 he had become an advocate of social progressivism. Social progressivists, of whom the best known are Dewey and Vygotsky, assert that education should be based on the following principles: That the child is part of society; and that its learning is social. The school should encourage what is social within the child to blossom on an individual basis. The teacher often turns to the child's interests for information about what the child needs to know, because the child is a social animal and exists as part of society.

Vygotsky's approach to education changed again in 1932. What is to be learned switches from the topics dictated by the child's interests to an externally set curriculum. The learner learning is, for students over 7 years of age, now replaced by the teacher teaching. The learner is motivated by the desire to learn what gives them the power to take a constructive part in society in the present and the future. This desire is to be aroused primarily by the central set curriculum. Knowing the content of the central curriculum will give them this power. This is a shift from social progressivism to a modified traditionalism.

The cluster of views called dialogism in recent educational literature is outlined. It is argued that the kind of education designated by the core uses of this term are not fully Vygotskyan, although they are often claimed to be. They can best be described as an incomplete version of Vygotsky's social progressivism of the third period.

It is argued that the context principle in education suggests that whether Vygotsky's social progressivism or his modified traditionalism is best depends on the particular purposes and context of the education being considered.

8 Interpretations

Understanding of Vygotsky is still generally poor. We can tell this because there are so many interpretations of him and they cannot all be right. There are six main reasons for this: his difficult style; the suppression of his work under Stalin; the rapid changes in his views; the unfinished nature of many of his writings; the distortions of his work by A. N. Leont'ev; the ready availability in the West of writings on him by those who have not studied him closely.

Two aspects of his style that render it difficult are that it is both allusive and evasive. He alludes to things he expects us to know, but we may miss if we do not share his background knowledge, which is both enormous and not of our time. He is also evasive because he is trying to pretend that he is an orthodox Marxist, when he is actually trying to replace some of its fundamentals. His suppression by Stalin naturally delayed an appreciation of Vygotsky, but that is now long in the past. Inaccurate popularisations are probably inseparable from having a great name, but in most cases we would expect them to be balanced by more scholarly assessments. The reason that scholarly assessments of Vygotsky have also mainly been wide of the mark can be put down to the confluence of the remaining three factors.

They became closely entwined in an interpretation by A. N. Leont'ev (1982) of the rapid changes in Vygotsky's views. Because this was apparently the work of a friendly critic who was also one of the Soviet Union's most famous psychologists, who had worked with Vygotsky, it was a natural place to turn for enlightenment about the difficult issues raised by Vygotsky's writings. It was also printed near the front of the first volume of Vygotsky's *Collected works*, in both the Russian and English editions. The result was that its ideas became the foundation for much of later Vygotsky scholarship, both in Russia and in the West.

A. N. Leont'ev

A. N. Leont'ev was one of Vygotsky's earliest and most important collaborators, who broke with Vygotsky in 1928 mainly over the issue of whether signs and language are more important in the child's development than social practice, that is the combination of tools, practice and social relations. This was essentially a controversy over whether to adhere to the view of Marx, that social practice predominated (Leont'ev) or to break away from Marx (Vygotsky). This was always a difficult contrast for Vygotsky to manage, because rejecting any part of Marx was liable to be labelled anti-Marxist, which had the connotation of veiled hostility to the whole of Marx's theory. Marx tended to be regarded by Marxists of Vygotsky's generation as the author of a seamless output of works of unique insight. The problem was not much eased by the fact that some of the reasons for rejecting Marx's stance had only emerged clearly since Marx's death. At the same time the purely ideological opponents of Marx had been saying that new realities had appeared to disprove Marx's ideas, ever since the appearance of the *Communist manifesto* in 1848; and Marxists tended to think all criticism belonged in this category.

Once Vygotsky's writings were suppressed in the 1930s, Leont'ev saw little reason to do other than contribute to the conversion of Vygotsky into a harmless but misguided icon (Leont'ev, 1948). The controversy had been closed by authority in Leont'ev's favour and it was enough occasionally to celebrate the wisdom of authority. However, the rehabilitation of Vygotsky after the death of Stalin in 1953 changed all this, because it soon made his works available; the two most important collections of articles from the last period both became available in Russian by 1960 (Vygotsky, 1934c, 1960).

In the late 1950s and 1960s A. N. Leont'ev was widely considered as the dominant power in Soviet psychology, wielding great influence from his chair at Moscow State University. As yet he felt no reason for intellectual defences against Vygotsky. However, by the 1970s things began to change. S. L. Rubinshtein began to usurp his position as top dog in Soviet psychology; and people began to take notice of both Vygotsky's followers, especially Lydia Bozovich and Daniel Elkonin, and his writings.

So Leont'ev decided that he would no longer avoid Vygotsky, but engage him (Minick, 1987). The result was his sponsorship of Vygotsky's *Collected writings* (1982–84), which took about a decade to prepare, due to disputes about what to include. One of the main aims was evidently to convince waverers that Leont'ev was Vygotsky's true heir. On the surface this had little chance of success, as the six volumes of Vygotsky had to be weighed against only one introductory article by Leont'ev, interpreting Vygotsky as his precursor. However, as it turned out, the plan was a great success, due to three factors. First, Leont'ev's article is a masterpiece of tendentious interpretation; next, the presence of his article in the volumes seemed to testify to his positive attitude to his subject; finally, Vygotsky's writings were, as already stressed, extremely difficult to make sense of. The result was that many of the most significant interpreters since that time have adopted either all or key parts of Leont'ev's mythology about Vygotsky. Among Soviet interpreters this was undoubtedly helped by the still relatively strong political position of Leont'ev and his followers, compared to the weak position of Vygotsky's followers. More surprisingly, some of the most significant American interpreters, through their contacts with the followers of Leont'ev in Russia and Europe, also succumbed.

According to Leont'ev (1982, 1983), Yaroshevsky (1985/1989, 1998) and Yaroshevsky and Gorsnedze (1982), for Vygotsky, in the human race in history and in the child, the psychological process of gaining knowledge takes place within a social system. Although tools and practice are only prominent in driving the development of this system at the start and end of the five stages, they remain, as we have already seen, involved in the cycle of development in a passive role during its middle period. This is held to show that tools and practice continue to validate knowledge because they are an interface between the system and the world. Vygotsky's argument, in their view, as applied to historical development, is that it is not just one part of the system that is in contact with reality, but the whole thing, through the medium of tools and practice. If the system were not in contact with reality, then production would not be able to act on the world to produce things that are useful.

There are, however, two fatal objections to this ingenious argument. The first is that, in Vygotsky's scheme for the middle period of development, signs, especially language, produce tools and practice. This means that in historical development signs will have to be devised to enable improved production, when they are applied, before we know whether this will work or not. Second, Vygotsky does not say what they have him say. He does, by contrast, stress the dialectic of practice and signs on several occasions (Vygotsky, 1930k, pp. 23, 65–66, 1931b, Ch. 3, 1934c, Ch. 6, 1935e).

Another influential argument used by this group originated in Leont'ev (1982) and was widely taken up by Soviet and Russian commentators, as well as some in the West (e.g. Bruner, 1987; Minick, 1987). This is that while the above system model applied to the period in Vygotsky's work up to the start of 1933, in the last 18 months of his life he broke with this. In this last period he was, however, inconsistent, not to say somewhat disoriented. In Vygotsky (1933i), which became the first chapter of *Problems of child development* (1960), he talked as though practice and tool use now have little influence. However, he later saw the error of this (Vygotsky, 1935e) and again made practice central to development throughout its course, so bringing him closer to the earlier system posture, with its emphasis on practice and tools.

Ingenious as this is, again it cannot survive scrutiny. A talk, that later became Vygotsky (1934f) in his bibliography, covers almost exactly the same ground as Vygotsky (1933i), but was given in the last four months of his life and has almost exactly the same message. So there was no last-minute switch in his views. In fact, the idea that Vygotsky (1933i) represents a radical change in Vygotsky's views about dynamics is wrong. The shift that Leont'ev detects is almost entirely one of terminology. Instead of talking about practice, tools and signs as the sources of dynamism in development, Vygotsky now talks mainly about neoformations, which is his new term for dynamic functions. However, when we look at the sequence of neoformations, they are very much what they have always been: instinctive behaviour, speech, play, writing, advanced concepts. Their mode of action is also similar, shifting from action, to signs, to the synthesis of the two. It is made clear that, as before, the use of signs is not disconnected from tools and practice, in fact in the middle period the development of signs drives that of tools and practice.

In addition, practice does not predominate throughout development (Vygotsky, 1935e). This article is largely about mental retardation and most of the children he is talking about are developmentally just before or just after the onset of speech. He had always maintained that in such children, retarded or not, practice would predominate.

The idea that the late Vygotsky stressed practice over signs was also taken over by several of the most prominent and expert American commentators (Cole, 1988, 1996; Cole & Wertsch, 1996; Minick, 1987; Ratner, 1998, 2000; Wertsch, 1994a, 1994b, 1998, 2000). However, in their case the idea that practice dominated signs was sometimes allied to the notion that practice precedes signs or that the use of signs is built on practice (Cole, 1996; Wertsch, 1994a). This, as we have seen, is something that late Vygotsky did say, but it should not be confused with the idea that practice has greater or equal dynamism compared to signs in the middle period of development. Vygotsky's idea is that in these stages practice comes first and has only limited dynamism that soon runs out. Later in the stage it experiences a second and more fundamental period of development, courtesy of the derived dynamism imparted to it by signs.

Vygotsky and Western constructivism

Expert Western commentators have in large part seen Vygotsky as someone else wanted them to, namely A. N. Leont'ev. There has also been much comment on Vygotsky in the West from those who have not specialised in interpreting him. Given the difficulty of understanding him, this has opened the way for widespread comment that moulds what Vygotsky said closer to the views of the interpreter. Just as a physicist might be delighted to find that Einstein agreed with his or her views, a biologist might like to say that Darwin agreed with him or an Egyptologist might advertise the fact that Flinders Petrie was on her side, so contemporary psychologists are often keen to broadcast the idea that one of the most celebrated founders of the modern discipline, Vygotsky, agrees with them. In many cases they are quite justified in doing so. However, in others, the combination of their poor grasp of Vygotsky's texts and their desire to have him support their ideas, when he really does not, results in falsification of his ideas. There are two common versions of this mistake. Both originated in the West and make him into a constructivist. 'Constructivism' is a term that contrasts with realism and means that gaining knowledge is not a process of getting to know about an objective world, but one in which the world is invented. This may or may not be found alongside the belief that there is a real world, but, if this is thought to exist, it is claimed that it can never be known. Vygotsky, as previously stressed, was a moderate realist who thought that children come to have an approximate understanding of the world as it really is. There are numerous passages where he says this and none where he says he is a constructivist (Vygotsky, 1925a, Ch. 1, 1927d, Chs 1, 4, 1930a, 1930b, 1930h, 1931b, Chs 1, 2, 1931d, 1932c, 1934c, Ch. 2). However, the popularity of constructivism among Western developmental psychologists has made this seem a tempting conclusion.

A constructivist view stressing language is among the most popular in the West. The central point of this interpretation is that the child learns a socially transmitted conception of the world through language. This world is, at bottom, a socially transmitted illusion. In this view, language plays the dominant role in shaping the child's view of the world. It finds its greatest support among those who use Vygotsky's ideas in their work, without being Vygotsky interpreters, who have spent a great deal of time with his texts. Notable examples of this approach are Brown and Reeve (1987), Brown, Campione, Reeve, Ferrara, and Palincsar (1991), Daniels (2001) and Wells (1999, 2002).

The linguistic-constructivist thesis is wrong, simply because Vygotsky was not, as we have seen, at any time a constructivist. Also, given the concentration of this school on *Thinking and speech*, it is particularly surprising that they claim Vygotsky as a constructivist, as in Chapter 2 he severely criticises the constructivism inherent in Piaget's viewpoint.

There is also a constructivist view that stresses practice. It is claimed that, for Vygotsky, the child does not learn to understand an objective world, but learns a socially transmitted picture of the world primarily through practice, that is, through acting on the world. It is the peculiar nature of the practices of the culture, in which the child finds itself, that transmits a particular conception of the world to the child. As with constructivism based on language, the child does not learn to know about a real world, but about a constructed one.

Again, it is hard to sustain this as Vygotsky's view. The notion that practice is always primary in the direct acquisition of knowledge is contrary to Vygotsky. This school also ignores the numerous occasions on which Vygotsky commits himself to the moderate realist view of the child's knowledge of the world that he inherited from Marx.

It is true that one specialist Vygotsky interpreter has incautiously espoused this view (Valsiner, 1999). However, others who have advanced this idea are not specialists. Several have been Piagetians. They reason that if Vygotsky stressed practice and constructivism, then he is similar to Piaget, who, in fact, did. At a time when Vygotsky is becoming more popular and Piaget less so, this stance has obvious appeal for Piagetians (e.g. Cornejo, 2001; Shayer, 2003; Tryphon & Voneche, 1996). These authors make little attempt to argue their point in detail, and those just cited undermine their arguments with numerous factual mistakes in dealing with Vygotsky's texts.

Methodological view

Although not as popular as the other two groups of views about Vygotsky, this view has some standing among expert interpreters. In fact, it is harder to rebut than any of the previous views, although its advocates have, in my view, advanced it in an exaggerated form. This says that Vygotsky's actual theory was, for some reason, usually its incompleteness and his capitulation to political pressure, so unsatisfactory that we should virtually ignore it. We should concentrate instead on his real achievement, which is his methodology (Joravsky, 1987, 1989; Kozulin, 1999). It is probably significant that the main proponents of this view are both Russian émigrés, disillusioned with communism. The fact that Marxism is such an integral part of Vygotsky's theory has probably not endeared it to them, although had they reflected on the possibility of disengaging the theory, at least from some aspects of Vygotsky's Marxism, this might not have weighed so heavily.

The methodological view is not so much about what Vygotsky said, as about what its value is. This book can, in this sense, be read to see whether what Vygotsky said about developmental psychology is as worthless as they say. I hope you will be persuaded that it is not.

However, the advocates of this view are right about two things: Vygotsky's work was incomplete and it was probably influenced by political pressure. The issue here is how far the impact of these factors negated the value of his work, especially in his last period.

Other views

Other views of Vygotsky have been suggested without having wide currency. Among the most interesting are those of Holzkamp (1984, 1993), Papadopoulos (1996, 1999) and Tolman (2001).

Conclusions

Interpretations of Vygotsky by A. N. Leont'ev, Western constructivists and those who stress his method are reviewed. It is argued that both Leont'ev and Western constructivists have altered Vygotsky's ideas to be more in accord with their own. Vygotsky was both a moderate realist and an advocate of the dominance of signs in the key middle period of development. His dialectical view of development saw practice and signs as dominant at different periods, with the two ultimately synthesised towards the end of the period of development he analysed.

The methodological view of Vygotsky is based on an assessment of the worth of his writings, rather than on claims about what he said. It was suggested that this view is too extreme in its rejection of the value of Vygotsky's late theory.

Part III

Origins

9 Vygotsky's sources

A considerable amount has already been said about Vygotsky's debt to his sources, particularly Marx, Hegel and Spinoza. The object of this chapter is to cover several aspects of his relation to his sources not mentioned previously. This has three purposes. First, to set the scene for the next chapter on method, by further emphasising Vygotsky's debt to his predecessors. This is necessary because Vygotsky himself often gives the impression that he began his investigations with just empirical data and a method, when in fact he clearly began with theoretical preconceptions, derived from his predecessors, and a method. Second, to explain in more detail how Vygotsky could claim to follow Marx's historical materialism, when in some respects he clearly opposed aspects of it. Third, to consider some rival views of Vygotsky's background.

Vygotsky's debt to his predecessors

Marx

Dynamics of production

This section deals with two points, both dealing with the main difference between Marx and Vygotsky, which is in relation to the forward dynamics of production. First, Marx himself had gone through two periods in his attitude to this. In his early period, he took over Feuerbach's concept of man as a species being (Marx, 1844, 1846a; Marx & Engels, 1845). This species being was already endowed with all the capacities needed for advanced civilisation, but they needed to be awoken by the stimulus of sophisticated needs, which were in turn produced by economic development. He sometimes called them 'slumbering powers', a term he continued to use, albeit once only, in *Capital* (1867, Ch. 7). Consciousness was in most cases something that arose after developments had occurred, calling to mind Hegel's saying: 'The owl of Minerva flies after dark', by which he meant that after things have been done in the day, the owl of wisdom, or consciousness, reflects on them after dark.

Marx later seems to have realised that this did not explain where the sophisticated capacities needed for production had originated. At least by the time of Marx (1870), he was leaning towards Lamarck's theory of the inheritance of acquired characteristics. Marx was still not willing to accept that cultural evolution sustained by language and signs could be responsible; and he had for some time maintained that they were gradually learned by trial and error, up to the point where sophisticated science was applied to production (Marx, 1859, 1867, Ch. 15). By 1870 he concluded that the inheritance of the acquired characteristics, learned in this process of trial and error, was probably responsible for the ability of the child to gain these skills and abilities so quickly in its development. Engels (1878, Ch. 7, 1896) was later to support the Lamarckian view in a more unequivocal way, resulting in its being seen by many later Marxists as an integral part of Marxism.

The result of this was that Marx and Engels were not obliged to appeal to the cultural or linguistic transmission of the abilities needed in production because they could appeal to the inheritance of acquired characteristics. This Lamarckian view seemed quite viable, because some respectable scientists supported it, because there was no definite evidence against it and because the nature and origin of genetic variation within its rivals was still obscure.

Another feature of debate about this during the lifetimes of Marx and Engels was that the perceived timescale for biological evolution at that time was short. Engels (1896), citing a current expert of the topic, thought the earth was not much more than one hundred million years old, only about one fortieth of the figure given today. This also favoured the Lamarckian view, as it showed how biological evolution could happen relatively quickly.

Doubt about the nature of biological evolution persisted among experts in most Western countries until at least the 1930s. However, by the mid-1920s two things had begun to tip the scales in favour of the idea that acquired characteristics cannot be inherited. First, there was no positive evidence in its favour, despite numerous attempts to demonstrate it by giving animals and plants acquired characteristics and then looking at their offspring. Second, there was the announcement in 1927 of Muller's success in producing artificial mutations. This was seen as support for the Darwinian notion that alterations to heredity can occur by spontaneous or induced mutations and then be either selected or not.

Vygotsky held an ambiguous position on the issue of the inheritance of acquired characteristics. On the one hand, he hoped that there might be an intermediate position between the two views (Vygotsky, 1931a, 1931b, Ch. 3). On the other, he firmly maintained that the biological constitution of the first humans was the same as ours (Vygotsky, 1931b, Ch. 1). This second position seems to preclude Lamarckianism. In view of this, the hand held out to the Lamarckians was probably more political than scientific.

In the mid-1920s the situation in the Soviet Union was similar to that in other countries: The Lamarckians and their opponents were about equally matched. But the former had, by 1930, already succeeded in making Lamarckianism the party line in evolutionary biology (Sheehan, 1993, Ch. 4).

Vygotsky's claim that the first humans are biologically the same as we are provided the first step in his argument in favour of the dynamic role of signs in development. If our previous cultural achievements cannot be handed on to us by inheritance and they are in large part cognitive achievements, then they must be handed on by signs: Shaping and imitation cannot transfer cognitive achievements. It was partly because Vygotsky regarded Marx's ideas about the inheritance of acquired characteristics as having been disproved that he sought an alternative in signs.

There was also another problem in Marx that probably influenced Vygotsky's turn to signs. This was that while Marx often claimed that changes in production in general occur by trial and error, at the same time he recognised that nineteenth-century capitalism depended heavily on the use of the scientific theory of mechanics in the design of machines, such as the steam engine and iron bridges and ships (Marx, 1867, Ch. 15). The use of scientific theory to be able to predict what would and would not work could hardly be considered trial and error. This showed there was a need for a more cognitive approach to at least some kinds of production. This paved the way for Vygotsky to argue that there had been a more or less continual increase in the use of proto-scientific methods, such as counting and measuring, from very early in the history of production. It was hard to see how such methods could be transmitted to the younger generation other than by signs, which carried meaning rather than just instructions about what to do.

Historical materialism in general

According to Marx, as the forces of production develop, in history, they carry forward the relations of production, as advanced forces of production cannot operate within social relations of work that are appropriate for the forces of production at an earlier stage. If we break down the forces and relations of production further and only focus on the psychological aspects, the psychological aspects of production involve a series of levels, roughly organised from most fundamental to least. These are: the ability to use tools; the social relations of work; language and consciousness; the self and self-consciousness (see especially Marx, 1846a).

It is generally accepted that by the forces of production Marx meant the degree to which tools and technology have advanced and the skills and other psychological characteristics of the labour force that are applied to them (Marx, 1859, Appendix 2). A similar formula applies to the relations of production. In other words, the top two levels, of consciousness and the self, will bear on both the bottom levels and their relation. This means that the forces of production comprise the actual tools and hardware of production, with the psychological aspects of tool use and relevant aspects of consciousness and the self.

This produces one key result. One of Vygotsky's central claims is that in the middle period of development signs and self-consciousness dominate the psychological aspects of the use of tools and produce much of their development. 'Signs', in this context, means things that communicate meaning, such as gestures, speech or writing. This can be included within Marx's historical materialism, as we can say that consciousness and language, as applied to tools and practice, are part of Marx's forces of production, as previously defined. Vygotsky tended to stress this point, while sweeping under the carpet that his stress on the dynamic power of signs over that of tools is not found in Marx (Vygotsky, 1930h, 1934c, p. 120).

Hegel

Hegel's *Lectures on the philosophy of history* (1837) provide a useful introduction to his conception of history. His idea is that human beings are destined to pass through three main periods. In the first, they begin limited but whole. This corresponds to tribal society, especially in its early stages (which Hegel misleadingly calls African society). In the second period, the division of labour and other social and psychological divisions make humanity a stranger to itself and it loses its true identity by being divided into various conflicting tendencies. The first phase of this coincides roughly with the history of civilisation to the fall of the Roman Empire, particularly including class societies based on slavery (which he calls Asiatic and Slave societies). The prominent role given to the division of labour here is more in accord with Marx's materialist theory of history than with idealism, but it is typical of Hegel that he tacks between the two, with the overall emphasis on the latter.

In the second phase of the second period, represented particularly by Christianity, after the fall of Rome until about the end of the first millennium, the rifts that opened up in the previous stage reach the point of awareness, particularly as we come to feudal society. This is an unhappy period that Hegel calls 'the unhappy consciousness', because, while the problems of the self being divided against itself have become conscious, they cannot yet be cured.

In the third and final period, from the later middle ages to the present, we find two distinctive features. First, there are continual replays of the problems of the unhappy consciousness, but in a different form. Thus Hegel saw both the Reformation of the sixteenth and the Enlightenment of the eighteenth centuries as movements of this kind. Second, the rifts opened up earlier by the course of civilisation begin to be resolved, particularly through the achievement of self-conscious reflection. He sometimes implies that the leading European countries had achieved the synthesis of these opposites in his own day, at other times that they soon would. Even such an apparently disastrous and atavistic series of events as Napoleon's European wars was held by Hegel, particularly when he was younger, to show the imminence of a final solution to civilisation's discontents, through Napoleon's spread of the Enlightenment outlook.

In the third period, people will eventually become whole again, but on a higher level than at the first stage. At the first stage they were not conscious of and did not truly understand their life and world; at the third stage they will achieve this understanding.

Vygotsky's overall picture of development depended heavily on this Hegelian picture. The developmental course of cognitive functions, of the relation between motivation and cognition, of the levels of consciousness and other key aspects of the personality, all follow the Hegelian path. This is from whole but limited to fragmentation with one-sided development, back to being whole, having overcome earlier limitations by synthesising the fragmented parts (see especially Erdmann, 1902; Exner, Rosenkranz, & Erdmann, 1842; Rosenkranz, 1840, 1870).

Other details of Vygotsky's view were taken from Hegel (1831), particularly in the area of cognition. Vygotsky took two ideas from Hegel in this area and changed them so they accorded with his own materialist outlook. First, according to Hegel (1831), in the development of cognition we start off with elementary functions such as sensation and perception and move on to compound functions such as thought and the use of advanced concepts. This process is assisted by the social mediation of functions. Language, for instance, is at first a natural and innate function in the infant, but after infancy it is mediated by the language of others, because the infant has to adapt to others in order to communicate.

On this point Vygotsky held very similar views to Hegel. They also both thought that the interaction between language and meaning went through four phases, although Vygotsky reverses the order of two, compared to the order found in Hegel. They held similar ideas about the kinds of meanings found in the various parts of this development. Gesture, for Hegel, involves an early form of figurative meaning, in which the gesture is like what it means. The imaginative inner speech of the young child in Hegel's second phase also uses figurative meanings, that is, the words are like what they mean. The baby words 'moo-cow' and 'baa-lamb' sound like the noises made by these animals. This kind of meaning continues in the third phase. In Hegel's fourth phase we find signs proper, in which there is no such connection between a word and what it means. The words 'fig' and 'three', for instance, as understood by adults, have no particular connection with what they mean. As Hegel (1831) put it, the sign proper is like a pyramid into which a foreign soul has been conveyed.

In the second and third phases of symbolic meanings, the picture-like nature of the meanings tends to restrict communication to an immediate context, as when two children talk about what is with them in a room. The result of the shift to signs proper in the fourth phase is to make communication independent of context. We come to understand the words 'fig' and 'three' as abstract meanings, without relying on either an outside scene to make sense of them or an inside one. Vygotsky eventually took over all these ideas, although the order of the second and third phases was reversed, as Vygotsky thought that it was Hegel's idealism that inspired the idea of an inner, mental, form of communication, before an outer one in the real world.

Further issues about Vygotsky's intellectual background

The above way of looking at Vygotsky's intellectual background differs from the view of some Western commentators that while Hegel and Marx had considerable influence on Vygotsky, he was just as much influenced by an array of those who were either contemporaries of Marx or closer to Vygotsky's own time (e.g. Kozulin, 1999; Ratner, 1991, 1997, 1998; Van der Veer, 1996, 2001; Van der Veer & Valsiner, 1991; Wertsch, 1985, 1998).

The main figures in this list of alternative sources include the French writers Durkheim (sociologist), Levy-Bruhl (anthropologist) and Janet (psychologist); the Russian writers Potebnya and Bakhtin (linguists) and Russian formalism in linguistics and literary criticism more generally; the German philosopher Ludwig Feuerbach. Piaget has not been used in this way by specialist commentators, as Vygotsky is clear that his main aim was always to use Piaget's data, while rejecting his theoretical explanations and epistemological views (Vygotsky, 1931b, 1934c, Ch. 2).

These influences can be divided into four categories: those that belong within the Hegel–Marx sphere of ideas and thus accord with my approach; those that Vygotsky used as sources of empirical evidence, but not as a source of ideas; those whose authority he used, because they advocated particular ideas that Vygotsky had taken from the Hegel–Marx tradition; those that he didn't use significantly at all.

In the first category belongs Potebnya, a nineteenth-century Ukrainian linguist, whose work was much influenced by the idea of finding a materialist version of Hegel's philosophy of language. Feuerbach also belongs here, as he had long been seen as part of the Marxist tradition when Vygotsky wrote. Feuerbach was the link between Hegel and Marx in the German philosophical tradition; he attempted to produce a materialist version of Hegel, although in Marx's view he did not go far enough.

Levy-Bruhl belongs mainly to the second group and his chief importance was that he gave Vygotsky an apparently authoritative, although actually very misleading, source of information about thought in primitive societies (Van der Veer, 1994, 2003). Levy-Bruhl was widely considered at that time the leading authority on this topic. Vygotsky also inherited from Levy-Bruhl the idea that social symbols could stand for the organisation of elementary psychological functions into compound functions. In development, such symbols could thereby assist the child to know how to carry out this process of compounding functions, thus acting as a form of external symbolic consciousness. However, to jump from this to the conclusion that Vygotsky therefore subscribed to the overall views of Levy-Bruhl, and his mentor Durkheim, is far too great a leap (as suggested by Van der Veer, 1996; Van der Veer & Valsiner, 1991). As a Marxist, even though of a slightly novel kind, Vygotsky could not and did not show sympathy with Durkheim's overall view of society, even while using his argument about the dominating power of signs. Durkheim's overall view was based on the vague assumption that society is like a living organism and has always been derided by Marxists as inferior to their more detailed analyses of the mechanisms of economic and political life (e.g. Althusser, 1970, Ch. 1; Hirst, 1968; Lenin, 1929; Lukes, 1973, 1983; Plekhanov, 1897).

Janet falls into the third category. The famous French psychologist subscribed to the idea, that, in childhood, directions to the child from others are later internalised as self-direction (Janet, 1930). Vygotsky found this in Hegel and Marx, but Janet's prestige and observations provided a more recent confirmation that was too appealing to ignore.

It is implausible to claim that Bakhtin and Russian formalism were a significant influence on Vygotsky in his last two periods (as claimed by A. A. Leont'ev, 1995 and Wertsch, 1985, 1998). First, Vygotsky never mentions Bakhtin and but rarely mentions the formalists; second, his outlook was very different from theirs, as they stressed the outer manifestations of language, while he stressed its inner meaning.

Conclusions

Vygotsky took over Marx's idea of the levels of production and his description of four historical steps in the levels of activity contributing to production. However, by Vygotsky's time the demise of the Lamarckian view of biological evolution, based on the inheritance of acquired characteristics, and other developments had opened up a crisis in Marxist ideas about how production developed and how the abilities it needed were transmitted to the younger generation. This paved the way for Vygotsky's stress on signs. He also found in Hegel a number of ideas that helped to flesh out his picture and to apply it to the development of the individual. Vygotsky was able to argue that he was operating within Marx's historical materialism because, although he disagreed with Marx in some respects, he retained Marx's idea that the development of production is the main motive force in history. It is when we look at what happens within production to produce its development that Vygotsky diverges from Marx.

It was argued that the influence of a number of other thinkers on Vygotsky, such as Feuerbach and Potebnya, can be placed within this general context, as they belonged to the traditions of Marxist and Hegelian thought. It is argued that some other suggested influences are either not central or not influential at all.

10 Method

Analytic method in general

Vygotsky's method did not change in its fundamentals from the time he wrote *The psychology of art* (1925a) until his death. Yet over this period, as we have seen, his theory changed three times. This can be explained as due to two influences. First, the method, like most methods, cannot be expected to come up with the right answer immediately; its results need to be recycled several times, to improve them in the light of empirical facts, ironing out errors on the part of the user and so forth. In addition, in the years before 1928 Vygotsky was trying to apply the method under the serious handicap of thinking that he could not use concepts and suggestions drawn from idealist philosophers. In theory, he could have reinvented all the wheels that had already been invented by such philosophers, but applying the method in this way was bound to slow him further.

Vygotsky usually calls his method the 'analytic method' (e.g. Vygotsky, 1925a, 1926a, 1930m, 1934c). Taken on its own, this just means that the method will stress the analysis of concepts and principles. However, he means something more specific than this, which is the analysis of concepts and principles with a view to showing how the development of systems can be understood as a rational process. The kind of rationality he has in mind is that suggested by Hegel and Marx in their dialectical approach to development.

One of the main kinds of rational connection sought in the analytic method was first stressed by Hegel. It is that within each stage of development there will be a dominant conflict of opposites, that will assume something like the following pattern. An initial principle appears that is typical of the stage. This generates a counterprinciple or opposite. At first these coexist and they do not interact. Once they begin to interact, their inherent antagonism manifests itself and a period of conflict begins. This is followed by the emergence of a third principle, which is the synthesis of the two previous conflicting principles. One illustration of this in Marx (1867) is the sequence: emergence of the petit bourgeois, or self-employed business owner; the petit bourgeois grows to the point at which they employ workers, creating a true bourgeoisie, employing workers who to begin with coexist with their employers; the conflicting interests of the two become apparent after a while and a struggle between them begins; this struggle is resolved by socialism that absorbs both bourgeois and worker and creates a new kind of socialist citizen who is the basis for further development. The point about this is not whether it is true, but that it provides a simple, central, example of the analytic approach to development.

We have already met an example of this kind of analysis in Vygotsky's late period. The underlying processes within each stage are said to be: the initial social situation of development (first principle); the reaction to this by the personality, which includes the development of the dominant functions, called the neoformation (second principle), which at first coexists with the first principle; as the neoformation grows it alters the existing constellation of functions, producing a new form of generic consciousness and self-consciousness. As these solidify, conflict between the personality and the social situation breaks out, creating a crisis; this is resolved by the formation of the new social situation of development for the next stage, constituting the synthesis of the original opposites (Vygotsky, 1933i, 1934e, Lect. 2, 1934f, 1934k).

The analysis of dominant contradictions of this sort does not finish this kind of analysis. Were it to do so, Vygotsky could have left his analysis of stages at this general level. However, like Hegel and Marx, he saw the need to include other subordinate contradictions in his analysis, greatly increasing its complexity.

His method has two variants. Vygotsky is explicit that both are taken directly from Marx's method, especially as practised in *Capital* (Marx, 1867, 1872, Afterword; Vygotsky, 1931b, 1934c). In the first, the forward method, we isolate the fundamental kernel of whatever we are investigating in its most elementary form. In biology this might be a single-celled organism; in Marxist social history it might be the exchange of commodities; for Vygotsky, in psychological development one such kernel is word meanings, another is experience as a means of mediating the outer and inner selves. The forward analytic method says that merely from forming an accurate understanding of the structure and dynamics of these initial kernels we can acquire a good idea of how development will then proceed. However, to check our understanding, we should then look at how development actually does proceed and adjust the purely analytic analysis accordingly.

In the backward method, which Vygotsky used in *The psychology of art* (1925a), but not much thereafter, the investigator, instead of starting at the beginning of the developmental process, starts at the end, with the most fully developed state. They then take the end product to pieces by analysis and by stripping off one developmental layer after another reach the start. This is harder to apply than the forward method, as the end state will be more complex than the start and correspondingly harder to analyse.

These are two tendencies rather than two absolutely distinct methods. Both Marx and Vygotsky stressed that in an actual investigation the investigator will usually work in both directions, depending on the circumstances (Marx, 1872, Afterword; Vygotsky, 1931b).

There are also other dimensions that influence the application of the objective-analytic method. One is the type of observations drawn on, which may be naturalistic or experimental.

In naturalistic studies the observations used are taken in the wild state, as when psychologists observe children playing where they normally play. Vygotsky predominantly used a variant of such observations in *The psychology of art* (1925a) and this is also the predominant mode in Hegel and Marx. In neither of these last two cases was the observation usually at first hand. Instead, the historical, economic and other observations of others are drawn on. Vygotsky often uses other people's observations in this way (e.g. Vygotsky, 1931b, Ch. 7).

In experimental observations, which Vygotsky primarily uses, for instance, in *History of the development of higher mental functions* (1931b) and *Thinking and speech* (1934c), the observations are the outcome of experimental procedures.

In addition, the purpose of empirical studies can be at least twofold. Such studies may aim to test theories in the orthodox manner, but studies using this method can also produce theory. Marx, Engels and Vygotsky were at pains to point out that this second function, like the first, is also typical of orthodox natural science (Engels, 1879, passim; Marx, 1872, Afterword; Vygotsky, 1931b).

Thus, in the method applied in this second way, we can take one empirical example and analyse it to find out what makes it tick. We then try to assess how many other examples of the same kind of thing will tick in the same way. An example given by Engels (1879), cited by Vygotsky (1931b, 1934c, Ch. 5), is Carnot's heat cycle, which analyses how energy is transferred from state to state in one particular steam engine and then infers that it will be transferred in a similar way in all steam engines. This analysis played a central role in nineteenth-century physics and was a precursor to the principle of the conservation of energy.

Given this classification, we could conclude that the studies of Hegel and Marx applied the analytic method to naturalistic data to produce a theory that was then tested in Vygotsky's own experimental studies. This is quite close to the truth. However, the reality is more complex, as Hegel and Marx were already using the analyses, not just the data, of previous workers; and in order for Marx and Vygotsky to use Hegel, he had to be 'turned on his feet'. In addition, Vygotsky often used the studies of other workers to test his own ideas. These were often conducted using methods other than his own and the findings thus had to be adapted to be of use.

In short, while the objective-analytic method was of central importance to Vygotsky, his use of it was more many sided and complex than is generally realised or than his own comments on the subject often suggested.

This account of Vygotsky's use of his method is largely based on what he did, rather than how he said he used it. It explains how Vygotsky produced the theory he did and how his empirical studies and use of empirical evidence helped him to do so.

If we, rather, only pay attention to what he says about his method, this does not make sense. Thus he often promoted the idea that his own theory was produced directly from his own empirical analyses, particularly of studies by himself and his co-workers. We are often told that an investigation is to begin without taking account of any facts or ideas from the previous literature, usually when previous ideas are claimed so worthless as not to be of any use or not to exist (e.g. his key publications, Vygotsky, 1928h, 1931b, 1934c). The judgement that previous ideas are worthless is usually based on claims about the historical circumstances of the investigation, such as that it was inaugurating truly Marxist studies in the field. He must have known perfectly well that Marx himself never discounted valid previous work for this reason (Vygotsky, 1928h, 1931b, 1934c). Another common ploy is to say that the previous results were not part of psychology but belonged to philosophy or social theory, which offers a further set of ever-shifting goal posts (Vygotsky, 1927a, 1931b). Are Hegel, W. von Humboldt (1824) and Marx on psychology really psychology or are they philosophy or social theory? When we want to say their findings are irrelevant to a psychological investigation we can say that they were the latter, despite the fact that they wrote at a time when psychology was, perhaps wisely, less sharply delineated from neighbouring disciplines than it later became.

However, we know that Vygotsky was well aware of the fact that most of the ideas that he claimed to have discovered in his empirical studies actually came from Marx, Hegel and other previous authors. We know this because we often find from the same text, or from previous ones, that not only was there relevant material in previous literature, but also that Vygotsky knew this and endorsed these previous results that he later claims to have discovered afresh from empirical studies.

Put like this Vygotsky's reporting practices seem to border on fraud. However, before he is condemned too severely, we should realise that psychology has a long history of this approach to reporting findings, which was as prevalent in Vygotsky's time as in any other, with Piaget and Freud only the most distinguished of a long list of those adopting it. Freud's deliberately unacknowledged debt to Nietzsche has often been noted (e.g. Carrol, 1975, Langford, 1986, Reiff, 1959). Vygotsky himself justifiably accused Piaget (1923) of the unacknowledged use of previous results by philosophers; an ironical twist in view of his own extensive use of the same tactic (Vygotsky, 1932b).

There are other aspects of scientific reporting methods that Vygotsky was able to exploit to argue that he had come to his studies with a theoretical blank slate. The official view of the literature survey, then as now, is that it covers everything relevant to the study from previous literature. However, most real-world applications of this reduce its impact. They say that in some form or other the reader either does not need or does not want to know the justification for absolutely everything we say, so we can restrict references to previous literature to a reasonable minimum of what they need to, or want to or can cope with knowing. Vygotsky discusses this explicitly (Vygotsky, 1934c, Ch. 7). This ranges from the idea that the audience for certain kinds of publications is an expert one and so they only need to be told what they do not already know, through the idea that experts only need to be told enough to show them that the author grasps the background, to the idea, incidentally adopted by Marx in *Capital* (1872, Afterword), that too much intellectual baggage about the history of ideas will overwhelm the reader and so it should be trimmed to a minimum.

One illustration of how Vygotsky (1934c) uses these loopholes is that he presents the content of *Capital* as Marx's application of the method of objective analysis to the concept of the cell of commodity exchange (p. 320). So he says: 'Marx analyses the "cell" of bourgeois society – the value form of commodities – and shows that a cell can be more easily studied than a developed body.' This is thoroughly misleading. The analysis of the value form of commodities that Marx uses in *Capital* was not developed by Marx; neither did he claim it was. The analysis of the basic cell of commodity-producing societies – commodity exchange – was originally undertaken by the British economists who developed the labour theory of value, most notably Petty, Adam Smith and Ricardo. This theory says that the value of a commodity is proportional to the time it took to make it. Marx did not produce this style of analysis; neither did he produce its most fundamental findings in economics, a fact he nearly always recognises (Marx, 1849, 1859, 1867, 1886).

Turning to Vygotsky's motives, he undoubtedly wants to foster the impression that his own empirical studies were more important than the analyses of his predecessors, which had the additional advantage for him that it appealed to the prejudices of his audience, as it still appeals to the prejudices of many today. Then, as to a lesser extent now, the idea that psychology should clear away the rubbish of the past and build new theories based on empirical methods from scratch was encouraged by a desire to proclaim the profession independent from both philosophy and folk conceptions. This tendency was further magnified in Vygotsky's case by the desire to found a special Marxist psychology.

So, the combination of these motives with the ambiguity and flexibility of reporting methods led Vygotsky to produce ambiguous reports about how his conclusions were reached, in which the findings of his empirical studies, analysed by the objective analytic method, were foregrounded and the influence of his predecessors often placed in the background. The truth was rather the other way round in the period 1928–34, in that Vygotsky built on the two indirect uses of the analytic method outlined above: inheriting the results of others (Marx); adapting the results of others where the method had been incorrectly applied (Hegel).

If we become wedded to the picture of Vygotsky using mainly his empirical analyses to produce theory, we are liable to fall into three errors in reading his work. First, we look for his theory only after the empirical analyses, when it is often outlined outside them, particularly in writings that are not first and foremost empirical analyses (e.g. Vygotsky, 1930f, 1930g, 1930h). Second, within and outside his reports of empirical analyses, there is substantial reference to previous theories he has taken over or adapted, which we can miss. This may be overt or more subtle, particularly in the use of terminology that is distinctive to a previous writer. Third, Vygotsky relies to a considerable extent on the historical materialism of Marx and Engels and an adapted version of Hegel to provide the theoretical content of his theory. If we miss this then we miss valuable information and insight about what theory itself is like, not to speak of an indispensable source of understanding its significance.

In summary, Vygotsky had a strong motive for stressing his own empirical studies and downplaying the work of Hegel and Marx within the psychological profession, as this was in accord with professional prejudices, which were in favour of theories built on experimentation and empirical data, such as that of Pavlov. The example of Marx in *Capital* gave him further latitude to engage in this kind of presentation, as Marx had argued that too much concentration on the history of ideas would confuse the reader, though this attitude is also found in nonMarxist works in fields such as economics and mathematics. Closer to home, it can be found in the writings of Baldwin (1911–12), Freud (1915–16, 1923) and Piaget (1923, 1924), although their motive was often obfuscation, while Marx's was primarily ease of presentation.

Periods in the method's application

Vygotsky's four discernible attitudes to the application of his method were as follows. These are based on what he did, rather than what he said, although these coincided more precisely early in his career than later.

In *The psychology of art* (1925a), we find emphasis on the poverty of the available background information and theory and on the idea that Marxist psychology must begin more or less afresh to rebuild the subject.

Next, in *The historical meaning of the crisis in psychology* (1927d) considerable usable material from the past is identified, in the conceptions of materialist psychologists and philosophers who have advanced psychological ideas. Thus, Aristotle's and Bain's analyses of associations, Hobbes's and Spinoza's ideas about motivation and Ribot's work on attention are all commended, as well as, in their place, Pavlov's and Bekhterev's ideas about conditioning. However, compared to the richness that Vygotsky was to draw on after 1928, this represented rather slim pickings.

This enthusiasm for seeking background theory only in materialist authors played, as we have already seen, little role in the thinking of Marx, Engels or Lenin. It may have been the publication of the parts of Lenin's (1925) *Philosophical notebooks* dealing with Hegel that helped jog Vygotsky out of this simplistic approach to his background.

In the next period, from 1928, Vygotsky heeded the advice of classical Marxism and attempted to include, on top of the background he already had, the ideas of idealist philosophers, particularly Hegel, although now inverted to extract their materialist kernel. He also realised that his greatest resource was Marx himself and that among Marx's most significant ideas about psychology was that psychology is the subjective reflex of an objective social system of production. He had previously realised the potential of some of Marx's psychological ideas (Vygotsky, 1925a, 1925b, 1927c), but after 1928 he achieved a much more rounded appreciation of what Marx had to offer.

Finally, after 1932, he turned towards Hegel in a new way and back to the materialists Spinoza and Feuerbach, although this time using them in a more sophisticated way than previously. By now he had, of course, also his own earlier theory as one of his prime points of departure.

However, Vygotsky's progress through these postures is not a simple one. It describes his practice in general terms, but not his rhetoric. He is continually chopping and changing his story about where his ideas came from. So, for instance, he continually reverts from the last position given above to the early idea that he was beginning from scratch and there were no relevant previous ideas (Vygotsky, 1931b, Ch. 3, 1934b, Ch. 1, 1934e, Ch. 1). This vacillation, as already mentioned, seems to have been mainly because he was caught between the myth of the new empirical psychology, which was as tenacious in the Soviet Union at that time as anywhere, and his own awareness that he was building on the very philosophical materials that the new psychology thought it was rejecting.

Units of analysis

In *History of the development of higher mental functions* (1931b, Ch. 3), Vygotsky begins from psychological fossils as a unit of analysis, treating them to both backwards and forwards analysis. The fossils concerned are early forms of psychological activity, such as simple methods of communication or of making choices, that will later change from natural forms of behaviour to cultural forms through the process of cultural mediation. Such fossils do not differ in principle from the hypothetical original form of commodity exchange studied by Marx and other economists. Analysis of these roots reveals the later course of development. One of the main themes of *History* is that word meaning is explained by the coordination of functions. Further, although the method of objective analysis is applied to the problems of the development of thinking and speech in *History* and *Thinking and speech*, in the former the unit is psychological fossils, while in the latter it is word meaning.

What Vygotsky does in *History* is to study the same area as in *Thinking and speech*, that is the development of thinking and speech, but to look at it from a different point of view, that involves dividing the topic in a different way. If we think of the topic as a cake, then *History* divides it in half virtually at right angles to the way it was later divided in *Thinking and speech*. In the latter, the topic was divided primarily into form and content (the latter being word meaning); in *History* it is divided between cognitive functions in process of being mediated by signs and cognitive functions that have been mediated by signs, the latter being higher mental functions and the former being remnant psychological functions. So, in *Thinking and speech*, development is divided into an upper level (form) and a lower level (word meaning) which is a division that applies to every age level. In *History* the division is between the earlier and the later development of the mediation of functions by signs.

In the first chapter of *Thinking and speech* (1934c) the main focus is on method and how this can help to solve the problems of cognition. The method he recommends is one that analyses the complex whole by partitioning it into its units. A key feature of these units should be that they retain the characteristics of the whole, even if in altered form (p. 47). They should also not be capable of further decomposition. Such a unit is word meaning. The functions of word meaning are explained as generalisation and the coordination of functions. No justification for this assertion is given at this point, but we are told that it will be justified by its results in analysing the relation between thinking and speech (p. 48).

A second fundamental unit that appears in the last period is experience, which mediates between the inner and the outer (Vygotsky, 1932e, 1933e, 1933g). This unites and communicates between the fundamental opposites of the inner and outer selves.

If we think of Vygotsky's theory as having the three main dimensions we met in previous chapters, this means we have one mediated by the unit of experience (inner–outer), and one by meaning (consciousness and levels). It may not be too fanciful to see will as a candidate for a mediating unit for the dimension of motivation-cognition, although Vygotsky does not say this.

Conclusions

The analytic method as discussed by Vygotsky has two variants, both taken directly from Marx. In the first, the forward method, we isolate the fundamental kernel of whatever we are investigating in its most elementary form. Merely from forming an accurate understanding of the structure and dynamics of these initial kernels we can acquire a good idea of how development will then proceed, although this needs to be checked against the facts. In the backward method, which Vygotsky used in *The psychology of art*, but not much thereafter, the investigator, instead of starting at the beginning of the developmental process, starts at the end. They then take the end product to pieces by analysis and, by stripping off one developmental layer after another, reach the start. This is harder than the forward method, as the end state will be more complex than the start and, thus, correspondingly harder to analyse. Both Marx and Vygotsky stress that in an actual investigation the investigator will usually work in both directions, depending on the circumstances.

There is often a considerable gap between what Vygotsky says about his method and what he does with it. At times, he says he will apply it to the new empirical data that he and his colleagues have produced and from this his theory will emerge. However, at other times he advances the more conventional view that the method has been applied to psychological content in the past and he is reapplying it to his data to refine and test theory, including the ideas of the past. This second view is not only a more conventional view of method in general, but is also more conventional within the Marxist tradition, as both Hegel and Marx adopted it. Although Vygotsky plays down this second view of method, it is the one that governs his practice. To see this we need only note how much of Vygotsky's theories came from Spinoza, Hegel and Marx; and, usually when he is not reporting empirical studies, he admits this. The idea that he came to his empirical studies with a blank slate is not tenable; in fact he began with theoretical preconceptions.

Part IV

Prospects and problems

11 Supportive and neutral empirical findings

This chapter covers empirical findings supportive or neutral in relation to the theory of Vygotsky's last period, since his death. The following chapter covers areas where findings have contradicted aspects of that theory and suggests modifications to deal with this. The first two sections of this chapter deal with cognitive development and the role of practice in development; the third deals with some miscellaneous remaining topics.

Cognitive development

Inner speech

Two of Vygotsky's main contentions about the development of inner speech were: That children in the age range approximately 3–6 years are more likely to engage in egocentric speech, that is, speech directed at themselves, when other children are present than when they are not; and that, when children in this age range are engaged in tasks involving problem solving, they are more likely to show egocentric speech the more difficult the task. Reviews of empirical literature on these points have supported them (Berk, 1992; Berk & Winsler, 1999; Gaskill & Diaz, 1991; Kohlberg, Yaeger, & Hjertholm, 1968). Although some less central claims by Vygotsky in this area have been found wanting, slight modifications to the details of his approach can minimise the problems here (Berk, 1992).

Instruction more important than implied by Piaget

Vygotsky uses the terms 'meaning' and 'concepts' interchangeably, as he thinks the most important concepts are formed as meanings. In most of the book I have preferred 'meaning' where he uses these terms. However, the present section deals with authors who usually use the term 'concept' and do not use 'meaning', so I have preferred 'concept'.

The impression has sometimes been generated by Piaget's more enthusiastic followers that teaching concepts and intellectual skills is always counter-productive or at least pointless (Bliss, 1987, 1996; Bliss & Ogborn, 1989;

Elkind, 1991, 1999, 2000). Piaget himself was generally more circumspect, arguing that such teaching can have some impact on the child, although it is generally not great (Piaget, 1970, 1972, 1974). On this point there is less difference between Piaget and Vygotsky than sometimes thought, because, as we have already seen, Vygotsky placed considerably less emphasis on instruction in the period up to 7 years than thereafter and was prepared to countenance a fairly discovery-oriented mode of development in this period, in some areas, for instance for painting and drawing.

When we come to the period after 7 years of age, the messages from the two thinkers diverge considerably. Vygotsky's claims in his last period conform more precisely to the widespread conception that Vygotsky stressed teaching more than Piaget. However, how much further development is Vygotsky expecting as a result of teaching?

We can propose two replies to this.

1 More than Piaget.
2 At least a whole stage, as suggested in Chapter 6 of *Thinking and speech* (1934c).

Only the first, less ambitious view is dealt with in this section. Findings related to the second, more ambitious claim are treated in the next chapter.

During the period from the 1960s on much material has accumulated to show the following: Some abilities often credited with spontaneous appearance are not usually found in Western children unless they have been taught; cross-cultural studies show that children do not readily fill in substantial gaps in their culture; most teaching studies show an improvement of a third of a stage or less. These points are now dealt with in turn.

Spontaneous appearance of abilities

An outstanding example of the first principle is painting and drawing, where it has been shown that children generally need instruction in how to draw such things as a man or a house, in order to be able to do so (Booth, 1982, 1984; Freeman, 1980; Van Sommers, 1984). The culturally specific nature of early painting and drawing also points in the same direction (Freeman, 1980; Van Sommers, 1984; Richardson, 1992).

Although this example does not favour Vygotsky as much as we might imagine, as he held a fairly discovery-oriented view of children's painting and drawing, he remained agnostic as to the age at which teaching first becomes important and would probably not have been surprised to find that the effects of teaching found in the over-7s can also be found in the under-7s.

Cross-cultural studies

Cross-cultural studies have shown, in areas such as counting and conservation, that, if a culture lacks a concept, children brought up in it will not know that concept. In other words, they do not fill in substantial gaps in the culture for themselves. An example is children brought up in cultures with few counting words. They generally do not invent methods of going beyond the counting words that are available and do not conserve (Cole, 1971, 1988; Dasen, 1973; Kelly, 1971; Segall, Dasen, Berry, & Poortinga, 1999).

This kind of evidence is again only indirectly favourable to Vygotsky, as he thought that children would fill in gaps in knowledge because knowledge is a system (Vygotsky, 1934c, Ch. 6). But again, this finding is more in accord with his cultural approach to learning than with that of Piaget.

Teaching concepts

Our third principle comes from studies of teaching concepts. Piagetian theory can also explain the findings of these studies, but as Vygotsky can too they belong in this chapter. Since Vygotsky's time, there has been a virtual deluge of work on how to and how successfully we can teach concepts to children. Studies of this kind can be divided into two kinds: small-scale experimental studies in which the kind of teaching given is tightly controlled, but each child does not usually receive more than about ten hours of teaching, often spread out over a period of several weeks or months; studies of teaching programmes in schools. The great majority of the small-scale studies have failed to advance understanding of the concepts taught by more than 18 months, many less, particularly in the earlier part of childhood (Flavell, 1985, 1992, 1996; Inhelder, Sinclair, & Bovet, 1974; Langford, 1987a; Modgil & Modgil, 1976, Vol. 5). Things are scarcely any better in adolescence (Flavell, 1985, 1992, 1996; Langford, 1987b; Modgil & Modgil, 1976; Shayer, 1980, 1998; Shayer & Adey, 1993; Smith, 1994).

The teaching studies just discussed, typically, do not use the long periods of time devoted to teaching in school; and it was above all teaching in school that Vygotsky had in mind. This leads us to consider the second type of study, which is of teaching programmes in preschools or schools. Here we find considerably less control over the actions of the teacher, who is no longer teaching to a tightly defined script, but to the general orientation of a programme. However, this situation is of interest either if the child spends all her time in a particular subject, being taught by a particular method and philosophy; or, in some cases, we find that the child's entire school programme is run according to a particular approach. In these cases, we may find a total exposure in excess of 1,500 hours in one subject for a two-year programme. However, in some of the most interesting cases of programme evaluation, which come from preschool, we are dealing with rather fewer, because of the shorter length of the preschool day.

In such cases, we usually find that the overall cognitive development of the preschooler still does not advance more than about 18 months and often less. Even the Montessori method, which involves intensive and targeted instruction, achieved only moderate results of this kind in the large-scale studies stemming from the American Headstart Programme in the 1960s (Bloom, 1970; Toomey, 1976, 1989).

Despite this, both the experimental and the school-based findings on children over the age of about 7 years could be consistent with Vygotsky's view that teaching can advance concepts by over a stage, beginning from the age of first school (7–13 years). These studies are acting on a situation where, according to his hypothesis, even spontaneous concepts have already experienced considerable advance, due to the upward pull of taught concepts. For the preschool period (3–7 years), Vygotsky suggests there will be less effect from teaching, which is generally seen.

Conclusions

In conclusion, taking in all three of our principles, the effectiveness of teaching, both formal and informal, in promoting cognitive development is greater in some key areas than we might expect from Piaget alone. As Vygotsky predicts this, it has become one of the standard reasons given for preferring his view over that of Piaget.

In general the literature has neglected to stress that, as well as predicting that teaching will have more influence than Piaget thought, Vygotsky also thinks that in older children it will have more influence than it really does (exceptions being Bruner, 1984a; Van der Veer, 1994, 1998; Van der Veer & Van Ijzendoorn, 1985).

This is considered in more detail in the next chapter.

Other cross-cultural topics

The period from 1950 to the present has seen enormous interest in cross-cultural studies conducted within the framework of Piagetian theory, the theory used being mainly that of his middle period, as his early period ended in the late 1930s and the late period is still not very well known. This is significant for Vygotsky, as the views of his last two periods were devised to incorporate information from Piaget's first period, so while cross-cultural Piagetian studies are potentially relevant to him, this difference needs to be taken into account.

Piagetian cross-cultural studies have had three main aims. First, to confirm that in all societies the sequence of achievements in cognitive development, suggested by Piaget, is the same. Second, he predicts that in less 'advanced' societies, especially tribal societies, children pass through these sequences more slowly and stop at an earlier point. Third, studies have also examined which factors in a society are most responsible for determining how far the children of the society advance along the sequence, although Piaget's theory does not make any definite predictions here.

By and large, research has confirmed Piaget's first and second suggestions (Berry, Poortinga, Segall, & Dasen, 1992; Dasen, 1973, 1988, 1993, 1998; Seagrim, 1980; Segall et al., 1999). The most significant result in relation to the third issue is that the divide between rural and urban societies appears to correspond to that between Piaget's preoperational and concrete operational substages (Dasen, 1973, 1988, 1998).

The first finding translates into support for Vygotsky's last period view of cognitive development, because the two differences between Vygotsky and Piaget mentioned above act only to slightly weaken the support for Vygotsky's sequence, not to remove it. In Chapter 12, I suggest modifications to Vygotsky's theory that remove this weakening altogether.

For similar reasons, the second point also supports Vygotsky. Turning to the third point, as already mentioned the most significant indicator of whether or not a culture will show evidence of Piaget's concrete operations thinking is whether it is urban or rural (Cole, 1971, 1988; Dasen, 1973, 1988, 1998). To explain this, Piagetians such as Dasen have fallen back on the idea that urbanisation gives a general impulse to the level of activity of a society and this encourages the individual to improve their construction of knowledge. This is an explanation, but it is largely ad hoc. Vygotsky, contrariwise, makes a more definite prediction, which is that the transition to cities will correspond to this transformation in the child's thinking.

The validity of Vygotsky's view of these issues has been criticised by Cole (1988, 1996), who bases himself largely on a critique of Vygotsky's own cross-cultural research and that in the Vygotskyan tradition, although his arguments are also relevant to Piagetian research in this area. He has three main arguments. First, the poor performance of tribal peoples on some of the tasks used here, such as tests of voluntary memory, voluntary attention, sorting of shapes and so forth, can be explained as follows. It is due to the unfamiliarity of the materials and task situation, rather than because those tested do not possess the concepts and cognitive processes being tested. Second, assessment tasks should be based on everyday activities of the society concerned. The third is less an argument, more an assumption. This is that it is demeaning to tribal peoples, and others, as well as contrary to firsthand knowledge of them, to be told that they are less sophisticated than Westerners. Hence the research that shows this must be wrong. None of these points seems ultimately very telling. First of all, the use of unfamiliar content in the studies of Luria (1976) and Vygotsky and Luria (1930), which is one of Cole's starting points, is far more of a problem than it is in most of the more recent Piagetian studies, which have often gone to great lengths to ensure that the content of tasks is familiar.

Second, Cole suggests that no test should be based on activities not present in the society in question. This is misleading, because it rules out testing any ability based on an activity that is more advanced or developed than those possessed by the society in question. In a nonnumerate society, for instance, there will be no complex activities based on numbers, so there can be no tests of numerical thinking, so it cannot be verified that they are not present.

The main reason given for this second stance is that it takes us away from Vygotsky's mistake in this area, which was to use unfamiliar content to investigate the thinking of tribal societies. This is a good rationale, but it is applied in the wrong way. We can see this by comparing the way Cole uses his own and others' data and uses that have been made of ethnographic data by anthropologists. One of the outstanding exponents of ethnographic methods in the area of cognition has been Levi-Strauss (1955, 1956, 1964–71). He concluded that there was a great divide in style of thinking between tribal societies without cities and their accompanying numeracy and literacy and the emergence of societies with these attributes. He used ethnographic studies of tribal societies and general historical knowledge of societies with cities to show this historical change. His comparative method is quite different from the inward-looking method of Cole and others, which avoids comparing societies with one another in case it may be found that one is more sophisticated than another. So the distinctive side of Cole's method is not that it is ethnographic and committed to looking at a culture in its own terms, rather that it is committed to avoiding comparisons between cultures.

Because Levi-Strauss provides a factual ordering of societies in relation to their intellectual level, this does not lead him to the idea that those placed later are better. Levi-Strauss thought that, on balance, civilised societies had probably lost more than they gained through their break with tribalism.

Cole feels it is undesirable to say that societies are ordered in their intellectual achievements. However, to say that such an order exists is not a value judgement, but a factual claim, so to try to rule this out as an unthinkable thought is to say that there are some facts and some theories that science must not discover.

The point here is not whether Cole's fears about how such dangerous facts may be used are substantial. In fact, there is no doubt they are very substantial, as the history of imperialism through the ages shows. Imperialists have, when convenient, very often claimed that they have invaded foreign peoples because they are at a lower level of intellectual and general culture and thus require assistance in the form of subjugation. The ancient Greeks called everyone who was not a Greek a barbarian to assist in this process. European nations invaded and colonised North and South America, Africa and the Middle East from the sixteenth century, partly under the pretext that they were bringing a superior form of religion, but also claiming that they were assuming the 'white man's burden', as the British called it, of bringing proper government to and raising the intellectual level of the natives. It is also true to say that two of Hitler's worst actions, to attempt the invasion of Russia and the extermination of the Jews, were justified by and caused by his fanatical attachment to ideas about the cultural and racial inferiority of both Slavs and Jews.

However, these actions, and many others committed in the name of cultural superiority, are not based on the claim that societies are ordered in their intellectual achievements. This is a factual claim. They are based on the idea that societies later in the order are better and have the unpalatable duty to use force and attempted or actual genocide to drag the others up to their level or at least put them out of their misery. There is a considerable jump from one point to the other. We can see this by looking at other kinds of reaction to thinking that intellectual achievements in societies are ordered. Western liberals have often thought that this is true and that the higher levels are more desirable, without recommending invasion or genocide as a solution (Croce, 1906; Green, 1885–88; Mill, 1846; y Gasset, 1933).

Finally, Cole's objection to the idea of a sequence of intellectual achievements is also based on his, as he himself calls it, peculiarly American attachment to the idea that no one should be insulted by being told they are less intellectually or in any other way developed than anyone else. My concern with this is that while the idea he is rejecting is certainly a dangerous one in the wrong hands, Cole's contention also has dangerous implications to which he appears oblivious.

The dangerous implication here is one that Western societies, led by the United States, have begun to explore in recent decades. It is that once no one is more or less clever, deluded or aware than anyone else, the result will be that there will be an all round 'dumbing down', leading to an uneducated, unthinking society manipulated by the media, politicians and others in a position to do so. This situation, was, for instance, denounced by Marcuse in *One dimensional man* (1960) and Bloom in *The closing of the American mind* (1987). This is not just an educational or cultural crisis, but also a wider crisis, if the point is reached that the population can be so easily brainwashed by its political leaders and their use of the media that states begin to act recklessly without any restraint from public opinion. My point is not whether this situation has been reached, but that we must be nervous that it is approaching, when there is so much allegation among Western intellectuals that it is. It is not that the idea that all intellectual attainments are on the same level has been solely responsible for this situation, but there seems no doubt that it has helped shift Western societies in this direction.

Communication pressure and development

One paradigm in this area compares two groups of children, one of which is under more pressure to communicate explicitly and one of which is under less. The most common case in which this happens is when one group is cared for by their parents and family and the other is in daycare. In the family, the parents and others are likely to know what the child means without an explicit communication, as they know the child. In daycare, the staff and other children need the child to be more explicit, as they know it less well. One advantage of such studies is that it is possible to match the children in the two groups for things such as parents' social status and educational level.

Studies in this mould have shown that, in general, daycare groups are more explicit in their speech than groups cared for at home, from approximately 2 to 5 years (Cross, 1978a, 1978b; Nelson, 1974, 1990, 1999; Reynolds, 1988). A typical index of this is the proportion of pronouns to nouns in the child's speech. The use of a pronoun obliges the listener to fill in the content of the person or thing referred to. 'I want it' obliges the carer to divine what 'it' is. 'I want plate' does not.

However, this effect tends to wash out after about 18 months to two years' removal from the situation. So, if we took two groups of this kind and followed what happened to them when they all went to school and thus began to be treated on average the same, we would find that, after 18 months to two years at school, they would now speak with the same degree of explicitness (Cross, 1978a, 1978b; Nelson, 1974, 1996, 1999; Reynolds, 1988). This is not particularly troublesome for Vygotsky's theory, as this kind of washout effect tends to occur for a wide range of cognitive achievements, once children are removed from the original situations or educational programmes (Bloom, 1970; Elkind, 1991; Toomey, 1976, 1989).

In this kind of study, the differences between the two groups are usually taken to be in the communicative situation involved, showing that this influences style of communication in the way Vygotsky predicts. However, such studies can also be seen as involving contrasting kinds of social relations, as the children in daycare will usually have more independent relations to their caregivers than those at home have to their parents. Once again, this demonstration of such an influence on communication styles is in accordance with Vygotsky's predictions.

A second paradigm that has been widely used in this area correlates the explicitness of a child's communication with their academic attainment and cognitive development. Interest in these correlations originally stemmed mainly from the studies of Bernstein (1960, 1961). Bernstein took from Vygotsky the thesis that there is a causal link between social relations and explicitness (or as he called it *coding*), on the one hand, and academic attainment and cognitive development, on the other. His interest in social relations was almost entirely confined to social class, as opposed to developmental differences. For instance, in an early study he compared the communicative explicitness of a group of working-class boys from the East End of London with that of English public schoolboys (Bernstein, 1960, 1961). He argued that the working-class children came from families and neighbourhoods in which social relations were close and informal. This, he argued, was because of the influence of the work relations of their parents on the lives of their families and neighbourhoods. At work, talk would be about the immediate environment, because work was in the immediate environment; the workers would talk about what should be moved where, what fitted where, where the problem was in a particular machine and so forth. These social relations produced an inexplicit or 'restricted' form of communication. The public schoolboys, by contrast, came from social backgrounds in which social mobility was more common and the workplace and family relations of the parents were more formal. The doctor, lawyer and teacher use writing, the telephone and face-to-face speech to talk about environments that are not immediately present and so must be explained explicitly. So, the doctor writes notes on patients to be read by others who may never have seen the patient; the topic of a court case is usually something that happened away from the courtroom in the past; the teacher often talks to their class, after the beginning stages in education, about things far away in space and time or that involve the kind of abstract concepts we find in science and mathematics. As a result, the public schoolboys were used to an explicit or 'elaborated' form of communication. The predicted differences were found.

A large amount of later work has confirmed that there is at least a moderate correlation between social relations and explicitness (coding), on the one hand, and both academic attainment and cognitive development (Bernstein, 1994, 1995, 2001; Heriot, 1972; Poole, 1970, 1978, 1979a, 1979b; Toomey, 1976, 1989), on the other. However, it has been pointed out that the old adage that correlation does not prove causation must be applied in this case (Rosen, 1972; Toomey, 1976, 1989). One obvious possibility is that these links are actually the result of one or more additional variables that are their underlying causes. For instance, the general educational atmosphere of the home, as assessed by such things as the number of books there, could be responsible for both explicitness of communication and academic success. Such educational atmosphere is also likely to be related to the social relations and social class of the parents.

Vygotsky's theory in its original form requires that the connections discussed above be the direct ones originally suggested by Bernstein, rather than the indirect ones considered in the previous paragraph. Although the debate between the two has been long and tortuous, neither side has finally prevailed, because just as correlation does not prove direct causation, neither does it prove indirect causation. The correct perspective on the findings discussed so far is that they are in accord with Vygotsky's theory, although they may be susceptible to alternative explanations.

However, another old adage (this time mathematical) tells us that to find the proportion of one variable predicted by another we square the correlation between them. The correlation between language coding and cognitive development or academic success is generally less than 0.7. So, less than 49 percent of the variation in either of the last two is predicted by the first (explicitness). It will undoubtedly be true that none of the measures here will be thoroughly accurate, but measurement error is unlikely to explain the whole of this failure to predict. This suggests that trying to predict academic success from one underlying variable (linguistic coding) may be oversimplifying the problem. This is not contrary to Vygotsky's own ideas, as linguistic coding is one of the main features of a stage, not everything that occurs within it.

Findings in this area, therefore, are broadly consistent with Vygotsky's claims, even though reality may be somewhat more complex than he thought.

Mental models

The success of the mental models approach as a theory of reasoning in the past three decades provides evidence that is favourable to Vygotsky's claim that the primary medium for problem solving is thought in his sense. Thought in Vygotsky's sense means the rearrangement of image-like mental representations to solve problems, which is what occurs according to the mental models view of reasoning (Johnson-Laird, 1997; Johnson-Laird & Bara, 1984, Johnson-Laird & Byrne, 1990). As usually understood, Johnson-Laird's claim is that in order to solve problems from formal logic, not only children but also adolescents and adults translate the problems into picture-like models and manipulate these models to solve the problems. If this were all that he intended (and were it to be verified) it would provide a startling verification of Vygotsky's claims in this area. The general weight of evidence here does indeed seem to support Johnson-Laird's view. However, there are some qualifications. First, it is not the case that Johnson-Laird only envisages the use of concrete, scene-like models. To him, models can also be 'abstract' (Johnson-Laird, 1993). However, the main intention here seems to be to include abstract spatial models, such as the Venn diagram, which represents logical problems using intersecting circles (Johnson-Laird, 1970).

There is also the issue of whether the mental models theory has truly eclipsed its rivals in the psychology of reasoning, especially the rules theories of Inhelder and Piaget (1958), Piaget and Garcia (1991), Rips (1994) and others. Rules theories say that rather than manipulating spatial representations, people reason using rules, often ones that find verbal expression, such as the rule that 'All As are Bs' and 'All Bs are Cs' implies 'All As are Cs'. It would also be fair to say that while the models approach is currently in the ascendant among experimental psychologists, some informed commentators, such as Evans (2002) and Evans and Over (1997), do not regard the evidence as conclusive.

One problem is that the proponents of the two views tend to explain their data using highly elaborate versions of their own approach pitted against reduced versions of the opposition's view, giving their ideas an unfair advantage. In fact, it seems to be the case that in many of the standard tasks, for every models-based view of processing in a task, we can, if we are fair, construct a rules-based equivalent that predicts the same thing (Evans & Over, 1997; Langford, 2000). This does not remove all the advantage of the models-based view, but it restricts the evidence that favours it.

Thus far, I have posed the issue in terms of either models or rules, which is the standard way it is posed in the literature on the topic. However, Vygotsky saw the issue in less black and white terms. This is because he recognised that under different circumstances we may use *either* rules *or* models. The models view is intended to cover reasoning with understanding or what nowadays might be termed reasoning with deep processing. To a first approximation, we can say that this is likely to operate at the start of learning or with unfamiliar problems, as at these points the rules are not yet known. In both cases, children or adults will be obliged to resort to the deeper models level.

We should, by contrast, find the use of rules in two kinds of situation. The first is at the end of learning or with familiar problems, as here the child has learned the rules governing the situation. The second is when the rules have been taught in such a way as to bypass the use of models.

Because most of the literature on reasoning deals with tasks involving reasoning about logic, which is not much taught to most people in contemporary schools or universities, this explains why the models approach succeeds best in this area. As the reasoners are not all that expert in the forms of reasoning elicited, they often have no well-rehearsed rules to fall back on and so must tackle the deep structure of the problems as best they may.

By contrast, there is a widespread belief among those who study mathematical as opposed to logical reasoning in children and adults that the two levels of reasoning just discussed are often both involved from shortly after the start of schooling. This is natural, as the rules for making mathematical inferences are intensively taught in schools. For instance, number bonds, such as $2 + 3 = 5$, $3 \times 4 = 12$, are still widely taught, although not so widely as they once were. Many mathematics teachers, by the same token, believe that even if children cannot at first understand why they are doing something, they should be taught the rules of procedure in order to get the right answer. This has two advantages. It improves the child's confidence; and in many cases it will eventually lead to understanding.

So we have two kinds of development here (Brown, 2002; Brown, Thomas & Tolias, 2002; Freudenthal, 1974; Gelman, 1986, 2000; Langford, 1987a, Ch. 6; Resnick, 1987, 1992; Skemp, 1971). For the child with greater fluency in mathematical ideas, we begin with models-based thought involving understanding and then for routine problems shift to rules-based thinking, while unfamiliar problems still elicit models-based thought. The child with less fluency will begin by being a rules-based reasoner for familiar problems, but some of these will be able to switch to models-based thinking if necessary, as they become more familiar with a given topic.

Logicism

The aspect of logicism considered here is the idea that logic precedes mathematics in development, because the latter is built on the former. The best known advocate of this view in psychology was Piaget. According to Vygotsky, because mathematics is taught and logic not, at least not much, mathematical concepts will appear first.

If we adopt commonsense definitions of what it means to possess a logical, geometrical or arithmetical concept, then there is little doubt that more recent research shows that mathematical ideas appear before logical ideas in the child's development (Langford, 1981, 1987a, 1987b; Langford & Hunting, 1994). However, things are not so simple, as Piaget and his followers long ago began to argue that we should not use assessments of these mathematical concepts based on common sense, but rather on a special kind of assessment of whether or not the subject really understands the concepts. They set up two main criteria for real understanding. For geometrical concepts, it was that they had to be understood through systems of coordinates, similar to Cartesian systems (Piaget, Inhelder, & Szeminska, 1948). For arithmetic and logic it was that that the child had to be able to explain the arithmetical concept verbally (Inhelder & Piaget 1964; Piaget, 1926a, 1941). The first tactic is unsatisfactory, as it arbitrarily makes something that is clearly not needed to understand a geometrical concept into a criterion for such a concept. The second is also problematic, because relatively few children are ever able to give an adequate definition of concepts or an explanation for why they have given a correct answer in any of the common tasks used to assess concepts (Flavell, 1985, 1992; Langford, 1987a). Piaget and others persisted in arguing that while the various explanations that even older children give are not adequate or logical, a large proportion of those given by older children are in accord with child logic and thus satisfactory. However, these explanations not only have a peculiar kind of internal logic; they also fail to justify their replies or tell us how to use the concepts involved.

If a child knows the right occasion on which to give the right reply, it must possess some mental process that enables it to do this. If its explanation does not tell it when to give the right reply, yet the child *knows* when to give it, the role of the explanation must be suspect. The child is operating using methods that are not open to verbal expression and what it says is not connected to those methods.

These points do not settle the issue of how to assess real understanding. However, they do suggest that, at present, methods based on common sense are the most plausible. These tell us that mathematics develops before logic, thus favouring Vygotsky.

Aspects of the zone of proximal development (ZPD)

[The term 'concept' is again preferred to 'meaning' in this section, for the same reasons as previously.]

There is a large literature on the concept of the ZPD, much of which sets out to test the concept. However, the literature defines the idea in a wide variety of ways. The concept as used by Vygotsky is multifaceted, but many investigators have focused on only one aspect of his idea. I will assume that it contains three main aspects. These are: That a concept or meaning can be successfully taught somewhat more than a full stage before its spontaneous appearance; that assessment of what the child can do with help is more predictive of future success than assessment of what it can do without help; there are qualitative differences between taught and spontaneous concepts. Consideration of the first of these is delayed until the next chapter, as the evidence is not favourable to it.

There is good evidence that assessment using tasks where the child is assisted by the tester is, as predicted by the concept of the ZPD, more predictive of future success than so-called static assessment, where no assistance is given (Brown & Reeve, 1987; Brown, Campione, Reeve, Ferrara, & Palincsar, 1991; Fabio, 2005; Guthke & Stein, 1996; Kozulin & Garb, 2004; Tzuriel, 2001).

The ZPD includes not only a quantitative but also a qualitative side. There are predicted to be qualitative differences between concepts, because taught concepts are learned top down, spontaneous ones are learned bottom up. Spontaneous concepts are more easily applied, are less sharply or consistently defined and are generally less scientific.

Tulviste (1989, 1991, 1992) examined differences between adults who had and had not been to school in studies involving use of concepts, such as giving definitions, finding similarities, classification and discriminating between a concept and the things it subsumes. Most differences corresponded to those between everyday and scientific concepts as described by Vygotsky. However, not all the suggested differences were found. Those without schooling sometimes showed patterns of thought that Vygotsky claimed only appear during the course of acquiring scientific knowledge in school.

There is also evidence that taught concepts, such as those of arithmetic, are more sharply defined than those of spontaneously acquired concepts, such as those of logic (Langford, 1993, 2000; Langford & Hunting, 1994). This explains why inferences in arithmetic are usually of a standard variety, while the considerable range of interpretation of the premises found in logic results in a great range of conclusions (Evans, 2002; Evans, Newstead, & Byrne, 1993; Johnson-Laird, 1997; Johnson-Laird & Byrne, 1990; Langford, 2000; Langford & Hunting, 1994).

Before concluding, an example from a number of studies wrongly claiming that there is solid support for the notion of the ZPD in its original form. This illustrates some of the typical difficulties of such studies, particularly that a standard definition of the concept is not used and that support for peripheral aspects of the concept is taken as support for the idea as a whole.

Weil-Barais (1994) found it possible in ten teaching sessions to scaffold the learning of students of 14–15 years so that they comprehended an informal precursor to the concept of force used in physics. The details of how this was done were novel and interesting. However, this was claimed to provide support for the ZPD because: 'Acting on the zone of proximal development means taking advantage of what Ss already know to help them construct precursory concepts in preparation for new conceptual propositions.' However, that there can be such action and promotion is not part of the central concept of the ZPD for a good reason: It is not peculiar to Vygotsky's conception of cognitive development. It is part of almost any reasonable theory of cognitive development and has, for instance, been extensively researched by Piagetians and neoPiagetians. The claim is also confusing, as the learning was not undertaken in the ZPD for the concept concerned, but in its zone of actual development.

In summary, the child's taught concepts differ qualitatively from spontaneous concepts, in many of the ways Vygotsky suggested. Also, testing, while receiving assistance from the tester, is more predictive than the more usual assessment without such assistance.

Role of practice versus signs in development

This section first deals with three sources of evidence that might suggest that practice plays a greater role than signs in the development of the child's cognition, from about 3 to 11 years; this is contrary to what Vygotsky suggests. This evidence has long been used by Piaget and his followers to show that practice has the leading role in this period (Flavell, 1985, 1996; Furth, 1966; Inhelder & Piaget, 1964; Piaget, 1963). If valid, it would also support Leont'ev's (1960, 1974) claim that this is so. This section will argue that it can also be explained by Vygotsky.

Nonverbal tests of children's thinking

In this area, research since Vygotsky's death has not added to principles established in his lifetime. However, work done since then, particularly by Piaget and his school, has confirmed and made more certain the findings available then. In Piaget's work after 1940 he came to use what was called the revised clinical method. In this, instead of answering questions posed mainly in words, the child was given a concrete situation or a model of one and asked to make judgements or draw conclusions about it, often during or after doing something with the materials (Piaget, 1941; Piaget & Inhelder, 1941). It was found that this kind of task elicited more advanced thinking than those posed mainly in words. This became one of the bases for Piaget's contention that the child begins to think through actions and only later attaches these to words. Inhelder and Piaget, in their book *The early growth of logic in the child* (1964), marshalled particularly detailed evidence for this contention in relation to logical thinking.

While, in relation to logic, Vygotsky had relied mainly on Sakharov's (1930) studies of concept attainment, involving nonsense words, Inhelder and Piaget particularly stressed tasks in which the child is invited to sort concrete materials, such as blocks or shapes, into different categories. Such tasks had a history stretching back before the time of either Piaget or Vygotsky. Inhelder and Piaget (1964) found that the child's logical abilities in such tasks are significantly in advance of those in tasks requiring more verbal involvement, such as Sakharov's tasks or those presented mainly in words. Furthermore, the implied use of logical concepts in sorting tasks is more adult like in its form and more precise than in those needing verbal involvement. Piaget's claims here have been supported by later research (Flavell, 1985, 1992; Modgil & Modgil, 1976).

However, Vygotsky (1934c, pp. 87–91, 183–194) breaks from his previous indifference to such evidence and says that action can precede language in the child's learning of logic. He also says that here, as elsewhere, while Piaget's theory was wrong, his empirical findings were largely correct.

Although Piaget had not by that time shifted to the revised clinical method or gathered some of the other information he was to use later, he had already reached the conclusion that the child begins from a logic of action and then becomes more aware of this through the means of language. Vygotsky accepts this formulation, which implies that he viewed the logic of action as both precise and conforming to standard logic. His quarrel with Piaget was not over this but over the reasons that conscious awareness of the processes of logic arose. Vygotsky saw it as resulting from changes in the nature and system of psychological functions, particularly the role of signs, as well as from teaching. For Piaget, it arose primarily from the reflection of the child on its own actions and only secondarily from socially transmitted meanings.

So Vygotsky has an explanation for the priority of practice in the period $2\frac{1}{2}$–$6\frac{1}{2}$ years (in the revised timescale suggested later) and he accepts that there is a logic of action that is precise and similar to verbal logic. However, unlike Piaget, he thinks such logic is rigid and uncreative and that fluidity and creativity have to be added to it by the influence of language and signs. The child cannot move to the next stage until this occurs.

The weakness of Vygotsky's reply here is that Piaget had already pointed out that when logic moves from the plane of action to that of language it becomes less like standard logic in its concepts and methods of inference and reverts to many of the errors of the 4 year old. Vygotsky accepts this (Vygotsky, 1931a, Ch. 3, 1934c, pp. 47–51). However, it does not sit well with the idea that language brings to fruition what is dormant in the logic of action.

Another possible explanation is that sorting tasks tend to involve only a narrow range of logical concepts, most of which have been taught by both natural and social shaping. If we think of sorting shapes just by colour, with the colours being red, green and blue, then the only concepts needed are 'all the red ones', 'all the green ones' and 'all the blue ones' and the concept of colour as a dimension. There is a natural tendency for infants as young as 1 to gather together all the objects in a collection that are similar (Nelson, 1973; Ricciuti, 1965). They will not proceed to do this with more than one kind of object, but it provides an initial basis for this. The appearance of a collection that has been wrongly sorted or adult intervention will give clues when something has gone wrong. In addition, sorting and other purely practical tasks do not involve the logical relation that causes the most confusion for children and adolescents when stated in words, which is 'All the As are Bs'.

According to this view, it will be mainly the further extension and flexibility of logic that are achieved by the use of language. While the language of scientific concepts may encourage additional precision in their case, this will not apply to logical concepts, which in our culture are mainly spontaneous.

This provides a more convincing Vygotskyan explanation for the role of action in middle childhood than the one he gave, although the one given by Piaget remains equally so.

Language and the division of the world

The general literature on thinking and language has concentrated on the problem of how the individual learns to divide up the world. One aspect of this is that different languages and cultures usually have more words for things they are interested in and use. The languages of desert peoples have more words for different kinds of sand; many of the languages of Aboriginal Australians have many words for sticks, because different kinds of stick provided many of their tools. The debated issue is whether this finely divided canvas of distinctions arises primarily from the uses to which these things are put and is then transmitted in a secondary way by language; overwhelmingly from practice; or mainly from learning language, as a writer such as Whorf (1956) would claim.

This issue is not on the main line of march of most theories of cognitive development, including those of Vygotsky and Piaget, as they are more concerned with how divisions are made in the world than with where they are made or how many of them there are. However, both Vygotsky and Piaget have expressed views on the subject.

Piaget argues that distinctions will usually be produced either by practice alone or by practice with the assistance of language (Dasen, 1973, 1998; Inhelder & Piaget, 1964; Piaget, 1977). Thus, Inhelder and Piaget (1964) and Piaget (1977) admit that language has a secondary effect on cognition, particularly in transmitting the distinctions that have proved useful in the past to the younger generation; the primary origin of such distinctions is through the child's practice. Vygotsky also belongs in this category. Language transmits distinctions that have proved useful in past practice; he agreed with Piaget that there is a logic of action in middle childhood; this shows that distinctions can arise based on practice alone (Vygotsky, 1934c, Ch. 6). However, there is some difference of emphasis in regard to the child, with Piaget placing more emphasis on practice and Vygotsky on language.

We know that practice alone can determine this kind of division making. There have been a number of formal and informal studies showing that those working in specialist practical fields make distinctions between things and processes based on their practical use, rather than on those made by the language in cases where they differ (Pinker, 1994).

We also commonly find divisions made in accord with language and practice (Pinker, 1994; Sternberg, 1999). Some studies in this area have used perceptual tasks, which would not be relevant to Vygotsky's or Piaget's suggestions. However, there have been enough using sorting tasks and naturalistic observations of conceptual abilities to show that this also applies to concepts (Clark & Clark, 1977; Pinker, 1994; Sternberg, 1999).

These findings are therefore consistent with both Vygotsky and Piaget.

Blind and deaf children

Several studies up to the mid-1970s indicate that there is a considerable contrast between the development of the blind child and that of the deaf child, the second often assumed largely to lack language (Furth, 1966; Vurpillot, 1976). For example, the blind child tends to show considerable delays in cognitive development in infancy, compared to the sighted child. The deaf child, by contrast, shows little such delay (Furth, 1966; Modgil & Modgil, 1976, Vol. 5). This seems to show that in this period lack of vision disrupts practice, but lack of hearing does not.

However, since that time it has been realised that, after infancy, blind children catch up with sighted children in many key areas (Landau, 1991; Millar, 1994; Preisler, 1995). Vurpillot (1976) had already appreciated this and argued that the Piagetian view of cognitive development depends on the child having sensory input, obtained in conjunction with practice, to organise. It does not depend on what kinds of sensory information it has available. So, the blind child can substitute touch, hearing and other nonvisual forms of perception for vision. Following this general line of thinking, there has been much interest in how the blind child becomes aware of and represents space, using nonvisual sensory modalities (Mullet & Miroux, 1996; Nielsen, 1991).

The new observations are also in accord with Vygotsky. Up until the child was about $2\frac{1}{2}$ years, Vygotsky thought, practice was primary. He was also a pioneer of the idea that the child with a handicap will find alternative developmental routes (Vygotsky, 1927b, 1928b, 1928c, 1928d, 1928e, 1928f, 1929g, 1930p, 1931c, 1931e, 1933e, 1935e). So the blind child will use touch and hearing as substitutes for visual perception. After the age of 3 years, Vygotsky's blind child will continue relatively unhandicapped, as it will not lack the stimulation of language.

Turning to the deaf child, Vygotsky suggests that in the normal child language, language-like signs and self-consciousness are the primary motors of development from about $2\frac{1}{2}$ to 16 years. So the deaf child who 'lacks language' should be significantly handicapped in cognitive development. However, a complication here is that, both in the past and to an increasing extent today, many deaf children have learnt an elaborate sign language, such as American or Australian sign language, which is not obviously different in its power to express concepts from spoken languages (Fromkin, Rodman, & Hyams, 2003, Ch. 11). This has usually occurred because the parents know the language already, because they have learned it for the benefit of the child or because it is taught at school. However, it is also true that, historically, especially during the early period when studies of this issue began, many deaf children, whose parents did not know such a language, were not taught one at school. They thus relied on informal signing with a considerably reduced vocabulary and grammar compared to those of official sign languages or spoken languages.

Furth (1966) was particularly alive to this issue and went out of his way to look at deaf children with the informal, minimal form of signing and to compare them with children without a handicap. He still found that there was remarkably little difference in cognitive development between such children and those without a handicap. This has been replicated in other studies (Millar, 1994). This suggests two possibilities. Either Vygotsky was wrong about the significance of language in cognitive development; or deaf children who learn informal signing still learn enough from this, as well as from the little writing they are able to acquire, to develop in the same way as the child without a handicap.

Two points suggest that deaf children may indeed learn enough from signing to rescue Vygotsky's argument. The first is that hearing children have been found to need a relatively small amount of sophisticated speech to support relatively sophisticated language development. There is evidence that even a little spoken language learning can have a disproportionate effect. This has been observed in hearing children who have suffered reduced exposure to speech in their early language development. The most extreme examples here are wild and cupboard children, brought up by animals or locked in cupboards, who have had no exposure to human speech to speak of. Generally, such children do not develop language while they remain in these circumstances (Candland, 1993; Clark & Clark, 1977; Comrie, 2000; Tartter, 1986, pp. 378–384). However, once we move from such extreme cases to children who have had just a little exposure to speech, such children are little affected in their speech development by their reduced opportunities for learning.

This can also be observed in studies of children in a more normal range of circumstances, particularly those found in daycare and families. Some receive rather little speech, because the parents are not very communicative or the daycare centre focuses on physical care routines, but it is hard to find children who receive little enough for their language development to be discernibly affected. This has suggested that a rather low minimum threshold of exposure to language is needed for normal language development (Cross, 1978a; Hampson & Nelson, 1993; Parmenter, 1976; Reynolds, 1988).

One further interesting point about the cognitive development of the deaf child, which extends the parallels between their use of signing and the hearing child's use of speech, is that in the age range 4–7 years they too develop the preliminaries to inner signing and thus presumably, later, actual inner signing. This corresponds to the hearing child's inner speech (Jamieson, 1994, 1995).

A problem this explanation faces is that informal sign language is often thought of as predominantly symbolic. How can children learn concepts in middle childhood that should require sign-like communication when they are exposed to a symbolic language? Although this is not a problem for Vygotsky's theory in its original form, it becomes one once we remove one of the main problems of his theory, which is its underestimation of the rate at which the child acquires more sophisticated meanings (see next chapter).

However, such children may, in fact, use sign language as signs proper, that is, as signs that have an arbitrary relation to what they mean, at least after a certain age. This is because there is nothing to stop a nonfigurative meaning being attached to a figurative symbol in an arbitrary way. We are inclined to think that a circular hand gesture meaning a circle is attached to a naive and pictorial idea of circle, but to a mathematician it might well signify 'All points on a plane equidistant from a given point', with the plane and the points considered as mathematical abstractions. At some point between the young child and the mathematician we must have the power to transfer from one to the other.

Suppose a 6-year-old deaf child, with only informal signing, is given the conservation of correspondence problem discussed earlier (Piaget, 1941). First a line of wooden eggs is paired with the same number of wooden eggcups. Then the pairing is broken and the eggs are spaced out in a longer line, while the eggcups are bunched together. The question asked, when instructions are given in speech, is something like 'Are there the same amount of eggs as eggcups, more eggs than eggcups or fewer eggs than eggcups?' Suppose the signing version of this question involves two fists placed together for 'the same' and cupping the hands for 'amount'. These gestures for 'same' and 'amount' are undoubtedly figurative in their surface expression, but the 6-year-old deaf child who uses these may not be paying attention to this pictorial aspect, but may use them as signs, with an arbitrary connection to what they mean.

As far as Vygotsky is concerned, such a transfer of figurative movements to use as signs proper is certainly possible, as it has an exact parallel with the process he assumed occurred when, in adolescence, the child stops attending to the figurative aspect of speech and begins to view words as signs, in the strict sense, particularly under the influence of learning to spell. For him, words have not stopped having figurative aspects; it is just that the adolescent has stopped attending to them. Not only may such children use informal signing in this way, but we can show that they do. They can understand the instructions in the tasks, given to assess cognitive development in middle childhood and later. These instructions must contain the concepts being tested, which are, at least in their essentials, of the kind that, in hearing children, result from the use of language as a sign, with arbitrary connection between expression and meaning. So, within Vygotskyan theory, there is a plausible explanation for the relatively normal cognitive development of the deaf child.

Positive arguments

The studies reviewed in the previous sections have left us with some uncertainty about the true role of signs in development. We have countered some arguments against Vygotsky's approach, but have not garnered much in the way of positive evidence. This section reviews some more positive evidence on the subject.

The nature of culture

The most significant argument here is one that we have met several times already. It is that after the age of about $2\frac{1}{2}$ years the main forces acting on the child must be cultural, due to the way in which the human species developed. What the child learns is not primarily habits or associations, but thought, meaning and cognition. There is no other cultural means by which it could learn these things, except through signs, especially language.

There are also a number of other points in favour of the fundamental role of signs.

The hurdle argument

This argues that some kinds of sign are logically necessary for the child to progress from an earlier to a later point in development. We can begin with the signs that he thinks dominate during the various stages. The time at which Vygotsky thinks speech has the greatest influence is in early childhood (1–3 years). There is good evidence that in this period the child's meanings shift from being more unstable and bound to the context to being more stable, conforming to a greater extent with adult usage and less bound to context. This fits well with Vygotsky's idea that natural thought is by its nature like the former, while speech naturally exerts a pressure towards the latter.

The evidence that writing is significant is also convincing. It is hard to see what other motive could encourage such a decided shift away from context-based to context-free communication. That it plays the role of a motive suggests that there are also more cognitive factors involved that enable the goals of this motive to be reached; this is also Vygotsky's assumption.

The role of concepts proper in permitting abstract thought is plausible rather than certain. If we accept that learning depends on bottom-up processes, concepts proper will lead on to higher forms of inference and other aspects of abstract thought and the use of abstract meanings. This assumption is difficult to prove definitively, but it is plausible.

For the fourth dominant kind of sign, namely the symbols used in play, there is no support from the hurdle argument.

Turning to other signs, the most significant for the hurdle argument are arithmetical signs and counting. Here, it is hard to see how the child could progress from a perceptual approach to the topic to a conceptual one without such sign-based operations as counting, as the number of objects in a large collection can only be known from counting.

An example in this area, which has received considerable attention in the literature, is what I will call the linguistic mediation view of conservation. Although it is not usually called this, this view of conservation is very well entrenched in the more recent literature.

To succeed in conservation problems, the child must learn what constitutes adding or taking away an amount. The linguistic mediation argument says that the child knows what constitutes adding or taking something away in situations of this kind by using counting or measuring (e.g. Galperin & Georgiev, 1969; Gelman & Gallistel, 1978; Klahr & Wallace, 1975; Lifschitz & Langford, 1977; Peill, 1975). So, in the eggcups situation, the child learns to shift from relying on visual estimation of amounts to relying on counting. It does not actually count in the test situation, but in everyday life it learns to use counting to find out when something has been added and when something has been taken away. From this it learns the rule that merely rearranging objects in space does not add or take away anything.

We can explain the developmental course of conservation learning in Vygotskyan terms by assuming it follows the same course as arithmetic and counting. In early childhood (1–2½ years, in the new nomenclature suggested later), it involves natural mechanisms of perceiving quantity attached to the use of words; in the preschool stage (2½–6½ years), this is followed by the use of external counting and measurement to establish quantity in particular situations; in the age of first school (6½–12 years), we find the internalisation of the rules of conservation, learned by the use of counting and measurement, so as to solve conservation problems without having to count and measure.

Conservations are primarily invariants with respect to spatial displacement and deformation. That is to say, in the case of the eggs and eggcups, the problem is to judge what happens when these objects undergo spatial displacement by being spaced out or bunched up. Is their amount invariant or unvarying with respect to this displacement or not? For other conservations, the transformations involve spatial deformation, as when the child is asked to say if an amount of water that was in a tall thin glass is altered when poured into a wide squat one.

Given this point, we could expect the spatial alterations to be represented primarily in the system of thought rather than in that of linguistic meaning. They are alterations to the representation of space and that is the business, in Vygotsky's terms, of thought.

In addition, conservations involve rules, such as 'Moving objects around does not alter their amount'. We know that in the period 6½–12 years the child needs a combination of spatial representations and rules because even adults cannot solve conservation problems just by forming a spatial picture of them. An adult cannot know, just from such a picture, that the two amounts remain the same. It is only by appealing to the rule that this is understood. The exact nature of these rules is not known, but this is not essential from the present point of view.

The main reservation about this argument is that there is an alternative, suggested by E. J. Gibson (1969), which, unlike that of Piaget, is at least conceivable. Take the eggs and eggcups problem. There are only three eggs and three eggcups. The child can see from the fact that they are paired up, that there is the same number of each. This initial knowledge arises from perception, not from a systematic checking process. When the two kinds of object are moved for the next part of the problem, one row is squashed and the other elongated. At the start of this process, it is still possible to see from perception that the same number of each remains.

From this initial small movement, the child can gather that small movements do not alter amount. They can extrapolate from this that larger movements will not either. However, this view has been much less popular than the linguistic mediation view, probably because it assumes that cognition remains based on perception throughout development, while most investigators think that qualitative changes arise in development.

In summary, arithmetic and the conservations provide a good example of the argument that, without the intervention of signs, cognitive development in some key areas would be impossible.

Play

The role Vygotsky gives to play is perhaps the most surprising of all the roles he allocates to signs, as he claims that play is the main dynamic force in the child's personality in the period 3–7 years, when we might think it is more likely to be speech. Since his time, considerable interest has been generated by the demonstration that children who do not engage in dramatic play and are given the opportunity to do so show cognitive improvements (Peterson, 1996; Redgrave, 1987). Pellegrini (1984) also showed that children who engage in different kinds of dramatic play show predictable improvements in their use of language and other areas related to the kinds of play they engage in. This does not show that play has the all-consuming influence on subsequent development that Vygotsky thinks, but it does provide some support for his position.

Conclusions

The studies reviewed in the first three parts of this section left some uncertainty about the role of signs in development. We succeeded in countering some arguments against Vygotsky, but found little in the way of definitive supporting evidence. The following sections reviewed more positive evidence on the subject and reached the following conclusions. There is a strong argument from the role of intellectual culture in human development that signs are the origin of higher mental functions. More contentious issues are which signs are responsible and to what extent each operates. There is quite good evidence that speech and writing have the important roles he gives them, in early childhood, and the period of first school. There is more evidence for giving a central role to arithmetical and other mathematical signs in the period 3–6½ years than for giving this role to play, as the former play a hurdle role, while this is hard to demonstrate in the latter. It is reasonable to think that advanced concepts are part of a gateway to the world of abstract thought processes in adolescence, but this has not been shown conclusively.

Other topics

Crises

The ages given by contemporary Western research for the main emotional crises in development are not greatly different from those used by Vygotsky. This is not surprising, as the original basis for these ages in Vygotsky's writings was chiefly the conclusions of two Western researchers of his own day: Gesell (1930, 1933) and Goodenough (1931). These have stood the test of time and continue to be the starting point for most Western discussions on the subject (e.g. Ausubel, Sullivan, & Ives, 1980; Peterson, 1996). The ages usually used in Western literature are for crises at, on average, 2½, 6½, 12 and 17 years; those used by Vygotsky are 1, 3, 7, 13 and 17 years (Vygotsky, 1933a, 1933b, 1933f, 1933g, 1933i, 1934e). Vygotsky (1933i, 1934f) interprets these figures to mean that the crisis will start, on average, about six months before the age given and end six months after. Western literature is usually slightly more flexible in its interpretation.

The discrepancy in the age at which the crisis of puberty occurs is probably mainly due to the fact that age of puberty onset, in the West, has lowered by around one year between the early decades of the twentieth century and today, mainly due to improvements in diet and living conditions. The discrepancies at 3 and 7 years may also have been influenced by the tendency for physiological maturation to occur more quickly now, as well as by the Western tendency to treat children as more adult like than previously.

The most significant difference between Vygotsky and later Western orthodoxy is his suggestion of a crisis at 1 year; this is not included in most recent general texts. One reason is that the resistance to parental wishes that begins in many children around 1 year is looked on as the first tremors of the crisis around 2½ years (Ausubel et al., 1980; Erikson, 1960; Peterson, 1996). According to Vygotsky (1933i, 1934e, 1934f, 1934k), the typical crisis lasts from half a year before its maximum to half a year after. So, if there is a crisis at 1 year, this means it will not be over until 1½ years and another one will start at 2 years. This is an idealised picture and individual children will vary considerably around these ages; so only longitudinal studies that look at the progress of each individual child will be likely to pick up the dip between the two crises. Despite these problems, the few such studies that have been undertaken suggest that it does (A. F. Lieberman, 1993; Sander, 1969).

In addition, Vygotsky's description of the crisis at 1 year is less couched in terms of conflicts with caregivers than his other crises (Vygotsky, 1933a, 1934e). Its main characteristic is that it involves a transition from not having relationships with give and take and limits to having them. This has been confirmed by more recent observational studies of infancy (A. F. Lieberman, 1993; Sander, 1969).

It is a general assumption of most Western students of crises that they, at least in part, reflect the child's awareness of a need for developmental change in the social relations between itself and adults (Ausubel et al., 1980; Erikson, 1960; Peterson, 1996). This supports Vygotsky's idea that they are provoked by an alteration in consciousness. However, the significance of some of the crisis ages is construed in a way that is different from that suggested by Vygotsky.

The dominant view of the functions of crises is neoFreudian, and is that the crisis at age 2–3 years marks what Ausubel et al. (1980) called a crisis of ego devaluation, in which the infant's sense of omnipotent control of its parents and belief that the parents will always do what it wants and allow it to do what it wants are devalued. The child comes into opposition with its parents and their desire that it respect the restraints of culture. The usual outcome of the conflict is that the parents win and the child identifies with them, in order to experience a sense of derived power and importance in the world, although there may be other outcomes. We then have a child who is subservient to adults, but who, during subsequent crises, gradually rebels against this subservience and by the end of adolescence has once again achieved independence. These later crises are independence-seeking crises, largely on Vygotsky's model.

The main difference between the neoFreudian and Vygotskyan views is in relation to the early crises, before 6 or 7 years. For Freudians, the crisis at 2–3 years involves curbing the child's egoistic and antisocial desires. For Vygotsky, the first two crises are, like those that come after, crises of independence, in which the child gains independence rather than loses it.

It is possible to argue against the neoFreudian consensus on Vygotsky's behalf, as follows. The key characteristic of all the crises, except the first, is mainly of stubborn opposition to the parents or other caregivers, of not wanting to do things, just because the parents or caregivers have requested them. Now Freudians can agree that this represents a striving towards independence at the later crises, so it could do so in the earlier crises too. This would make all the crises after the first into crises of independence, as Vygotsky claims. The first crisis, at 1 year, has the character of mutual adaptation to the child's growing abilities and so has the obvious form of a crisis of independence.

However, there is still an apparent problem with Vygotsky's argument. Studies of emotional crises have confirmed what common observation has long seen: A significant proportion of children do not go through crises, even at $2\frac{1}{2}$ and 12 years, which are the most widely experienced and severe (Ausubel et al., 1980; Peterson, 1996). Some go through one and not the other, while some go through neither. Yet such children, so far as we can judge, are not unusual in their cognitive development, which is supposed to be linked to passage through the crises.

Although this is certainly a problem for the theory, it was one that was known to Vygotsky and for which he suggested a solution. This was that, for some children, the crisis is not visible, but remains internalised and hence does not result in the kind of overtly oppositional behaviour usually assessed in studies of childhood crises (Vygotsky, 1933i, 1934f). Although this raises the objection that it is erecting an untestable theory, it also has some psychological plausibility. In addition, while studies to date have usually used the child's overt behaviour as their measure of crises, it may be possible to devise an assessment for internal crises.

In conclusion, most aspects of crises have been found to be in accord with Vygotsky's claims, although most occur slightly earlier nowadays in Western countries than he suggests. Although the significance of the early crises tends to be seen differently nowadays from the way he saw it there is no bar to interpreting modern information on the crises in the way he did.

The early appearance of self-consciousness

First, the issue of how to diagnose self-consciousness. This is significant, as some methods of diagnosing this indicate an early onset of self-consciousness, while others indicate a later onset. Vygotsky's late stance was that global self-consciousness, consciousness of the whole personality, emerges at the end of infancy. This is in stark contrast to his earlier belief that such consciousness begins around 7 years. It seems likely that much of the reason for this shift lay in his shift from reliance on one method of diagnosing self-consciousness to another, although this was, in turn, probably linked to his theoretical shift.

There are two widely used methods here. One is based on the belief that if the child has a self or ego, then it is conscious of it. The other tactic uses a more specific criterion, usually the ability to explain aspects of the self in words.

The first approach once again goes back to German classical philosophy. According to Hegel (1807, 1831), it is the dialectic of self-consciousness that forms the self or ego. In other words, to have a self must imply consciousness of it. The idea behind this ultimately derives from Kant (1781, 1787, 1790) and is that the self is an inherently unifying entity and in order to be able to unify the personality, it must know the personality as a whole. The only way it can do this is through global self-consciousness.

This approach, in the hands of psychologists, usually leads to the conclusion that the child has a self from quite early in life, around the end of infancy. This is because it is thought that at this age the child is able to balance the achievement of one goal against another, negotiate its own interests against those of another person and so forth. This indicates it has a self.

As it is assumed that all selves are conscious, it follows that the child is self-conscious at the end of infancy. Three classic expositions of this position are Baldwin (1911–12), Erikson (1960) and Freud (1923).

This depends on knowing when the executive self has appeared. That it does so around 1 year has been accepted by many Freudians, neoFreudians and others, mainly on the basis of clinical observations, showing that the child is now able to balance motives and negotiate its interests with others (e.g. Ausubel et al., 1980; Bowlby, 1984; Erikson, 1960; A. F. Lieberman, 1993; Spitz, 1960, 1961). A substantial number of more formal observational studies have also shown that the period around 1 year is a time in which the infant begins to bargain about their place in the world as a novice personality or self (A. F. Lieberman, 1993; Sander, 1969). As the main role of this kind of self is to adjudicate the conflicting demands of elements within the personality, it is argued that it must be aware of the personality as a whole.

Another area that Freudians traditionally use to show the emergence of the self is attachment, on the basis that if the infant believes something like 'I am attached to X', then this shows the infant has an I (e.g. Bowlby, 1984; A. Freud, 1958; S. Freud, 1915–16, 1923; Spitz, 1960).

The alternative way of assessing global self-consciousness through verbal report has been pursued most consistently in questionnaire studies of Erikson's (1960) view of the development of the self (Marcia, 1966; Peterson, 1996; Rosenthal, Gurney, & Moore, 1981; Whitbourne & Tesch, 1985). However, as with most questionnaires, these are not generally suitable for children under about 6 years. That children under this age find it difficult to report on the self, either by questionnaire or interview, means that, if we adopt this method, we will conclude that the self does not appear much before this age.

There has been far more work on partial self-consciousness using this method, which has also arrived at much the same conclusion (e.g. Bryant, 2002; Bryant & Bradley, 1985; Bryant, Nunes, & Bindman, 2000; Clay & Cazden, 1992; Overton, 1990; Piaget, 1974; Pratt, 1993; Robinson & Mitchell, 1995). This is relevant to the question of self-consciousness, in the broader sense, as we would, if anything, expect partial self-consciousness to antedate global self-consciousness, as the latter is a more complex process (Vygotsky, 1931a, Ch. 6). So, once again verbal report provides a relatively late age for the appearance of the self.

Vygotsky's shift to regarding general self-consciousness as an early achievement, in his late period, seems to have come from a shift away from using verbal report, to using having a self, as a criterion of global self-consciousness. Even though he does not actually say this, he would have found it in Hegel, as well as Freud and Kretschmer, whom he does cite on the topic.

No doubt, this shift in method of assessing self-consciousness was also linked to the demands of his new theory, which since 1930 (Vygotsky, 1930g) had required that each new stage was prepared by change in the psychological system initiated by self-consciousness. This was held to apply to the early stages, as well as the later ones, requiring an early onset for self-consciousness.

Moral reasoning

This is an area where evidence is ambiguous, rather than definitely supportive, but as it does not signal any need for change in the theory, it is dealt with in this chapter, rather than the next.

As we saw in Chapter 6, Vygotsky derived his late view in this area fairly directly from Piaget. Piaget's stages are: respect for authority with little understanding of moral rules (2–4 years); respect for authority with initial understanding of moral rules (4–7 years); further improvement in the understanding of rules, which are respected if they are based on personal reciprocity, in which exchanges with other people are mutually beneficial (7–11 years); adult-like understanding of rules, justified by agreements within groups based on mutual benefit and respect (11 years on) (Piaget, 1930, 1931).

So the question of whether Vygotsky has been justified, by the later empirical literature on this topic, boils down to what it says about Piaget. The story of the reaction to Piaget has been approximately as follows. The two dominant theories in the period 1931–2004 have been those of Kohlberg and Piaget. Broadly speaking, we can detect the following trends in their reception. Until Kohlberg (1958), the field was dominated by Piaget. After this, Kohlberg's claim that he had improved on Piaget's theory through the use of new empirical methods and samples including a broader age range gained increasing acceptance and became the dominant view from about 1965 to 1990. After that there was some shift back to Piaget, based on the realisation that Kohlberg's new methods were flawed and his use of subjects with a wider age range, extending into adolescence and adulthood, may not have been as crucial as once thought (Langford, 1995, 1997; Peters, 1975; Trainer, 1982). So we can say that Piaget is once again respectable, but Kohlberg remains more popular. What is true for Piaget, on this topic, is also true for Vygotsky.

However, even those who base themselves on Piaget in broad outline have found one area where they are critical. So, according to Gibbs (1979), Gibbs, Basinger, and Fuller (1991) and Langford (1995, 1997), a viable contemporary version of Piaget on moral reasoning would need to include two further stages for adolescence and beyond, compared to Piaget's four stages. Our proposals here are somewhat different, although they could probably be reconciled. This is, in essence, a vindication of one of Kohlberg's criticisms of Piaget, namely that he did not interview any subjects over the age of 13 years. This suggests that a complete Vygotskyan account would need to include further stages for adolescence and adulthood.

Conclusions

Areas covered where the evidence is on balance supportive of Vygotsky or neutral were: a range of topics relating to cognitive development; the role of signs versus practice in development; crises; the early appearance of the self; the development of moral reasoning.

12 Empirical problems

Since Vygotsky's death in 1934, empirical work on child development has mushroomed and in some areas there have been enormous changes in generally accepted facts. The five sections of this chapter concentrate on the main areas in which this has produced problems for the theory and considers suggestions for overcoming them.

Cognitive development is too slow

Cognitive achievements placed too late

Infancy and early cognition

The realisation that such staples of infant cognition as the permanent object concept and the constancies can be shown to occur earlier than previously thought has constituted a revolution in thinking about this area since the time of Vygotsky (Baillargeon, 1998, 2002; Bower, 1974; Carey & Spelke, 1994, 1996; McKenzie, 1990; Spelke, 2000). Constancies are the ability to realise that sometimes the appearance of objects changes, even though the real characteristics of the object have not. This can be illustrated by shape constancy. This is the ability to realise that the shape of an object appears to change if our perspective on it changes but it does not really do so. The permanent object concept is the ability to realise that even when objects disappear from sight, they continue to exist. A problem arising from this is that Vygotsky (1931a, Ch. 3, 1934b, 1934e, Lect. 3) claimed that the constancies, which he thought appear around 1 year, are based on the beginnings of speech. However, if the constancies appear as early as 2–4 months, this cannot be so (Baillargeon, 1998, 2002; Carey & Spelke, 1994, 1996; Spelke, 2000).

The obvious response is to transfer perceptual constancies from the sphere of mediated abilities emerging after 1 year and place them, instead, among the innate abilities of early infancy, a suggestion that Vygotsky himself hints at (Vygotsky, 1934b, 1934e, Ch. 3).

Vygotsky had, by contrast, already realised that there must be a prelinguistic version of the permanent object concept, probably because Piaget (1926b) placed the origins of this around 8 months. The contemporary view that it begins in the age range 2–4 months does not challenge his position here. However, it does challenge his assumption that it first emerges from the child's use of objects as tools (Vygotsky, 1931a); the first occurrence of which would still today be placed where K. Buhler (1913) placed it, about 9 months.

This also puts in question one contemporary approach to this problem. Moro and Rodriguez (2000) and Rodriguez and Moro (1998) adopt Vygotsky's position and argue that the permanent object concept develops, first, through social interactions that use the object and this later leads to a more developed version of the concept, resulting from its mediation by signs, that is, things used to convey meaning. However, their evidence for this used tasks involving physical use of the object, rather than those that have shown the earliest appearance of the concept, which avoid such use; such as preferential looking at one scene as opposed to another or eye movements. Their method places a constraint on infants, who are generally not good at motor coordination. If we look at less constraining tasks, they show an initial permanent object concept as early as 2–4 months, which is younger than any of the versions of the concept used by Rodriguez and Moro. The obvious explanation is that the first manifestation of the permanent object concept belongs with the innate capacities of early infancy, rather than appearing as a result of practical activity (see also Subbotsky, 1996).

There has been considerable debate of a more general kind about how infants acquire abilities. This has involved two different versions of the infant mind: the modular mind of Carey and Spelke; and the learning mind of Baillargeon. In what follows, I use the term module as Carey and Spelke use it. In a module we have a cognitive domain or topic with three properties: The child has the abilities needed to recognise a set of entities in the world, say concrete objects and some relations between them; the child has the abilities needed for making inferences about these entities; both of these abilities are innate (Carey, 1995, 1996; Carey & Spelke, 1994, 1996; Spelke, 2000; Spelke & Hermer, 1996; Spelke & Newport, 1998). Some of the innate modules possessed by the infant are claimed to be for language, number, physics and the theory of other minds.

Their main arguments for innateness here are: first, the early appearance of the abilities, many of which have been shown to appear between 2½ and 4 months of age; and, second, learnability. The learnability argument says that what is being learned is too complex and relies too much on the detection of aspects of reality that are not obvious from appearances for learning to plausibly occur in the available time.

Two of Baillargeon's arguments against this are: That early achievements are patchy and inconsistent and require learning to become general and consistent; and that knowledge within parallel areas develops at different speeds (Baillargeon, 1998, 2002; Baillargeon & Wang, 2002). However, as these things are what we would expect under the modularists' scenario, it is not clear to what extent they, and other arguments advanced by Baillargeon, really undermine the modularists' perspective. Baillargeon (2002) seems close to admitting this, although Baillargeon and Wang (2002) take a step away from it.

One underlying problem here arises from our natural reactions to two statements: That innate modules exist; and that most of the infant's knowledge is learned. Superficially they are at variance, but properly understood they are not, because the innate modules contain knowledge that needs to be applied and the process of application will involve extensive learning. This application will proceed faster in some areas than in others. The infant also needs to learn how not to be misled by appearances. Although it is programmed to see past superficial appearances in some of its fundamental perceptions, situations can easily arise that exceed its initial capacities in this area.

As far as the evaluation of Vygotsky's theory is concerned, this debate does not seem to raise fundamental issues, as both sides assume there is a substantial basis in innate functions for the infant's achievements and this was the point he regarded as most crucial. Because it seems to accord better with the evidence, I will proceed as if modularism were true for infancy.

Preverbal communication and early speech

Subsequent Western research has moved the age at which infants are thought to communicate with adults somewhat earlier than was believed in the West in Vygotsky's time (Butterworth and Grover, 1988, 1989, 1990; Lamb & Campos, 1982; Trevarthen, 1993, 2003a, 2003b). However, as the Soviet research that Vygotsky relied on had already shown this in many areas, this Western shift has in many cases supported him.

Vygotsky's discussions of gesture are, however, an exception here. The gesture, for infants, usually communicates the wishes of the gesturer. Vygotsky tended to use gestures with the hands and arms as the index of gesture in infancy. However, one of the main principles of more recent research is that movements away from the head, and away from the midline of the infant's body, come under voluntary control later than movements connected with the head. This implies that turning or inclining the head would be easier for infants. Informal observations do indeed show that turning away from the nipple or teat when milk is not wanted occurs early in life and may quite rapidly become a gesture intended to communicate this. When one thing turns into the other is difficult to say, but it may occur as early as 4 months. So yet again we find a key achievement has moved earlier, although, in this case, it has no particular implications for the theory.

Investigations of turn taking in early infant 'conversation' have also changed the landscape in this area to a degree not suspected by Soviet investigators in Vygotsky's time (Trevarthen, 1988, 1993, 1999, 2003b; Trevarthen & Aitkin, 2001). Here, the adult and infant make eye contact and utter noises in a synchronised way. So, in an ideal 'conversation', the infant would make a noise and make eye contact and then stop, the adult would make a noise and make eye contact and then stop, the infant would make a noise and make eye contact and then stop and so on. Current observations show that infants can take turns in this way at 4 months and possibly earlier. This does not pose a problem of principle for Vygotsky, as turn taking can be viewed as another of those strands of prelinguistic infant development that come together in language proper, around the end of the first year of life, thus providing it with a place in Vygotskyan theory.

One of the most venerable debates in the area of early semantic development is between advocates of prototypes and advocates of components as bases for early semantics (Bloom, 1970; de Villiers & de Villiers, 1984, 1999; Gleason, 2001). It is significant that this struggle goes on in parallel within theories of early perception and within theories of early semantics. It is plausible to think, as Vygotsky did, that the very first meanings hardly differ at all from early perception, but later they become more conceptual in nature.

A perceptual prototype can, so far as visual perception is concerned, be likened to a picture of a typical example of the thing, action or quality. So, we might have the prototype of a parrot as a mental picture of a typical parrot. It has brightly coloured feathers, a certain shape, a broad curved beak and a harsh cry. This is used to recognise parrots by summoning it up and comparing it with the suspected parrot. If it has enough in common with the prototypical parrot then it will be judged a parrot, if not, not.

The componential approach to early perception, by contrast, says that the perceiver has a kind of mental entry for 'parrot' and this comprises a list of components. Among these might be having feathers, plus a long tail, bright colours and a strong beak. These are not what would identify a parrot to an ornithologist, but they are the kinds of thing that will tend to strike the child. What counts as a parrot might be something that has enough of these features. One reason that the conflict between these two views has been so protracted is that the advocates of the prototype view have often claimed that the prototype embodies a set of components, as did Vygotsky. So, the components just listed for the parrot could be turned into a prototype by making it have feathers, plus a long tail, bright colours and a strong beak. For this reason there has never been a satisfactory resolution of the issue.

Vygotsky's view was, following Jaensch (1925, 1930), that early perceptual or graphic meanings are formed from prototypes. However, their reliance on studies of eidetic imagery to support this view would be looked on askance today, if for no other reason than that eidetic imagery is not perception. But, this does not show that early perception does not involve prototypes.

Turning to the next stage in Vygotsky's scheme for the development of meanings, complexive meanings, we encounter more serious difficulties. The main problem is that Vygotsky argues that the functional capacity of the child using complexive meanings retreats compared to the previous stage of graphic meanings. This is part of a process of *reculer pour mieux sauter* (going back for a better leap). The transition to more conceptual thinking initially produces a retreat in functionality. Thus, the child using a prototype of a parrot will be able to successfully identify most parrots as such, but the child using complexive meanings will shift its criterion from one case to the next, moving, say, from a parrot to a coloured flag to a tablecloth. The coloured flag was like the parrot because it was brightly coloured, while the tablecloth was like the flag because it was rectangular. There is nothing implausible about this in general. The question, however, is when it occurs.

An indication of Vygotsky's problems here comes from his own writings. So, he several times cites the example of Darwin's observations of his grandson as showing complexive meaning (Vygotsky, 1931b, 1934c, Ch. 6). Here, a word that initially means 'duck on a pond' ends up meaning 'coin', as the meaning is transformed by the instability with which the user handles the components that go to make up the meaning (Darwin, 1881).

It is revealing that Darwin's grandson was only in the second half of the second year of life. Both common experience and more recent studies of young children's speech suggest that Vygotsky would have had difficulty in finding typical cases of this even a year later. By the time we reach 3 years, most children's meanings are much more consistent and we do not find dramatic alterations in meanings of this kind (Bloom, 1970, 1984; de Villiers & de Villiers, 1999; Gleason, 2001; Lewis, 1957). This is not to say that we do not find some dramatic alterations of meanings after this time, but they are usually alterations in the scope of meanings, rather than the alterations found in Darwin's grandson. The child may go from using the word 'parrot' for all birds, to using it for just parrots. This is an alteration of scope that can largely be explained by the addition of extra criteria to define parrot (Brown, 1958, 1973). We may, in other cases, find the removal of criteria to make a meaning broader, but in neither case are we dealing with chain complexes, the most common kind of complex, according to Vygotsky.

In the light of this, we have to reject the idea that meanings in the period 3 to 7 years are dominated by complexes, with chain complexes playing a major role. More recent studies show that complexive meanings are typical of the first part of the period Vygotsky calls early childhood (1–3 years), not of the period he calls the preschool age (3–7 years).

His main positive evidence for his claims about complexes come from Sakharov's (1930) meaning-attainment task and from Piaget. However, more recent research contradicts them. Sakharov (1930) undertook, at Vygotsky's instigation in the 1920s, studies on meaning formation (Vygotsky, 1928h, 1929g, 1929h, 1930k, 1931b, 1934c, Ch. 5, 1934e). Until about 1931 Vygotsky held that meaning-attainment tasks, such as that used by Sakharov, will show indirectly what kind of meanings a child can possess at any stage, by showing what kinds of meaning they can form. After all, it seems obvious that you cannot possess or use a meaning until you can form it. As Sakharov found that the meanings children could form in the period 3–7 years were predominantly complexes, this fitted in perfectly with the stance that complexes predominate in this age group.

While Sakharov's findings have been successfully replicated several times

(Krylov & Ostriakova, 1995), considerable doubts must remain about the validity of this task. The majority of studies using other tasks, of the concept-attainment variety, have concluded that stable one-dimensional meanings can be formed unaided by 4½ years (Ault, 1977; Sternberg, 1999). Two of his most illustrious predecessors, whom he generally relies on in other matters, also found this (Ach, 1921; Eliasberg, 1923, 1925). Furthermore, Vygotsky admits this, but glosses over it, by giving the impression that Sakharov has devised a better method of assessment, although he does not convincingly explain why it is better (Vygotsky, 1931b, p. 172).

One likely reason that most subsequent investigators have disagreed with Sakharov is that the kind of task he used seems unsuitable for the study of children. It has the same form as the concept-attainment tasks used by Piaget and others to study adolescence and adulthood, such as his pendulum and rods problems (Inhelder & Piaget, 1958), the game of 20 questions and the selection tasks used by Bruner, Goodnow, and Austin (1956). These tasks have two characteristics that make them more difficult for children: They ask the subject to seek information rather than just receive it; and they ask for comparison of single items of information with a hypothesis. The upshot of these characteristics is that success is usually only achieved by those who have a conscious strategy for discovering the meaning the experimenter has in mind that is implemented consistently. Effective conscious strategies are usually not found until adolescence. Children tend to become confused by such things as how to respond to successive items of information, often going back to hold hypotheses that have already been disproved by previous information. For instance, in 20 questions they might ask 'Is it an animal?' and be told 'No'; but later they might ask 'Is it a squirrel?' But if it is not an animal, it cannot be a squirrel and they have wasted a question.

Tasks that are more suitable for children tend to be modelled on the classic discrimination learning task, in widespread use by the 1920s (Ault, 1977; Gholson, 1980; Gholson & Rosenthal, 1984; Sternberg, 1999). These differ from tasks used for adolescents, in that they offer the subject no choice about what information they get and they present two examples at a time, choice of one being signalled as a correct choice that falls under the concept, choice of the other signalled as incorrect. This discourages use of sophisticated conscious strategies, as the subject has no control over what they see. There has been much ingenious argument about what strategy they do adopt. The following is an example of one such possible strategy, offered to illustrate the relative ease with which it can be used.

The cards presented are combinations of blue and red with triangle and square. The concept the experimenter has in mind is blue. The strategy is to begin by taking a positive instance and assume everything this example has, all its features, belong to the concept. In this case, if the first positive example is a blue triangle, then we assume that the concept is blue triangles. We then wait until another example of the concept comes along that falls outside our supposition and react by broadening it so that it is included. If a blue square comes along that is also an example of the concept, then the hypothesis should be widened to blue, not just blue triangles. It appears easier to react to what comes up rather than to choose what to know about by thinking about what it would tell us. In this latter situation, which is the one used by Sakharov (1930), younger children have a tendency to ask for what would confirm their hypothesis. By the time they have finished choosing all the items that could do that, they have become attached to their hypothesis, which has now been confirmed several times, so when a disconfirming example like the blue square appears they react to it poorly. This disadvantages them in this kind of task.

While we cannot be entirely sure which paradigm represents everyday learning of concepts better, the reception paradigm has the advantage that in everyday life most information about concepts appears to be presented to the child, rather than sought.

Piaget's early research also underestimated the sophistication of early meanings, because he asked mainly verbal questions, without providing the child with a concrete situation. When he adopted his revised clinical method after about 1940 he realised that this underestimation had occurred (Piaget, 1941; Piaget & Inhelder, 1941).

Meanings in the age of first school

In his last two periods, Vygotsky thought that only one-dimensional, fundamentally figurative meanings could be learned without teaching in this age. He called these *preconcepts*. So, for instance, the child could grasp the meaning 'red things', as this is based on only one attribute, red. It could not grasp the meaning 'large red things', as this is based on two attributes.

In this area he was misled by the same failings of the studies of Sakharov (1930) and the early studies of Piaget (1924, 1926a) covered in the last section. Piaget himself later came to realise his mistake and adopted the now general view that spontaneous concepts involving the coordination of two dimensions can be formed from 7 years. This also emerges from more recent studies of concept attainment. In his last period, Vygotsky also argued that teaching enables the child in this age range to grasp more sophisticated concepts and that even spontaneous concepts are pulled up, closer to the level of taught concepts, by the action of cognitive systems (Vygotsky, 1934e, 1934d, 1934h). Thus most concepts in the time of first school will be multidimensional, whether they are spontaneous or taught. Although this explains the observed level of both spontaneous and taught concepts, it does not explain the observed level of concepts that can be attained in a concept-attainment task, which is considerably greater than Vygotsky's argument requires.

Vygotsky overestimates amount of development due to teaching

This topic is connected to the previous one, because Vygotsky's treatment of teaching is designed to explain why the slow spontaneous development of meanings that he assumes does not lead to the level of immaturity predicted for the age of first school (7–13 years). Once we realise that spontaneous development is faster than he thought, we can conclude that the amount of development due to teaching required to close the gap between what should occur spontaneously and what does occur will also be reduced.

Vygotsky claimed that teaching pulls taught concepts up by over a stage in the stages of first school (7–13 years) and adolescence (13–17 years). But, as we have just seen, children can form multidimensional concepts unaided in the age range 7–13 years. If they can form them in the laboratory unaided, they will form them unaided, that is spontaneously, in everyday life.

So, spontaneous meanings in this age range are, without any influence from teaching, roughly at the level that we observe both spontaneous and taught concepts to be in this age range. There is no great gulf between them, as Vygotsky assumed, and that he tried to explain with his idea that teaching pulls meanings up by over a stage. Vygotsky's original rationale for saying that teaching can advance cognitive development by more than a stage has thus disappeared. There is no other positive evidence to support it. A hypothesis with no positive evidence supporting it and one good reason against it cannot be credited.

Suggested changes to the theory related to the above

1 That the spontaneous meanings and many of the child's other cognitive abilities, found in the period from birth to 13 years, are about a stage more advanced than those he suggested, which puts them in line with contemporary research. These changes were originally suggested by Donaldson (1978, 1993, 1996).
2 That there is only about one-third of a stage difference in level between spontaneous and taught meanings, although there are, in addition, some qualitative advantages for taught meanings. Similar suggestions have been made by Bruner (1984a), Van der Veer (1994, 1998) and Van der Veer and Van Ijzendoorn (1985).

Further discussion

Not only do these changes solve the problems created by more recent findings, but they also suggest an alternative explanation for a finding outlined in the previous chapter. It is probably no accident that the degree to which taught concepts are ahead of spontaneous ones, about one-third of a stage, is roughly the same as the amount by which teaching advances development, also about one-third of a stage. If taught concepts do not pull up spontaneous ones, this is just what we would expect.

Other aspects of development of signs

The nature of early language learning

Vygotsky assumes that the bases for language learning are acquired in the period of infancy, before 1 year, based on innate roots, and then come together in the second year of life. The first major component is the phonological expression of language, found in the babbling of the first year, but not yet attached to meanings. In the second year of life this interacts with thought, which is the basis for natural problem solving in the first year of life.

This may provide the kernel of early speech development, but more recent research on language development suggests that it does not explain how this kernel develops into the highly complex structures of language that soon emerge. This problem was originally highlighted in Chomsky's (1959, 1966, 1980a) arguments about language learning in the years 1 to 5 years, which introduced the learnability argument. To recap what was said earlier about this, the child would be unable to learn their native language, from the available information, in the available time, without even more extensive innate knowledge than writers like Vygotsky thought. Chomsky applied this to the learning of syntax especially. Up to that time, psychologists and the layperson generally had tended to vastly underestimate two properties of syntax in natural languages: That it is extremely complicated; and that it is composed of a two-layered system of rules, namely phrase structure (in Chomsky's early terminology) and transformations, whose composition is not at all obvious on the surface. These points are often difficult to appreciate, because most people either just use language without being aware of its complexity or they think that the syntax of their language is a few simple grammar rules, similar to those that they learned at school. Neither is true. All natural languages have a complex array of syntactic rules of which we are normally unaware, although we use them every day.

Chomsky's picture of syntax as two layered has sometimes been challenged, for instance by Pinker (1984). However, alternative proposals have not won widespread acceptance by linguists and have generally been open to the objection that they are not as parsimonious as the Chomskyan system and its close relatives.

Of more immediate concern to us is that Chomsky's learnability argument was widely challenged in the 1970s by researchers who queried his claim that the child hears language based on a highly complex system of rules, whose two-tiered structure is not obvious on the surface. Chomsky's model of the child's situation was, at bottom, that the child listens to adults having normal adult conversations. Yet it proved easy to show that this is not so. Two findings are particularly relevant here. First, adults typically simplify what they say to children, so that the length of their sentences is on average about 1.5 words longer than those of the child. So if the child is saying sentences one word long, they will hear sentences from adults about two and a half words long (Barnes et al., 1983; Brown, 1973; Cross, 1978b; Fraser & Roberts, 1975; Furrow & Nelson, 1984, 1986). Also, the child and the adult will usually be engaged in some joint activity, so that the child is given clues as to what the adult means.

Second, it is likely that what stands out for the child, in the simplified syntax it experiences, is the 'deeper' and simpler phrase structure (later called categorial) system of rules, rather than constructions from the transformational system. This is because when an adult speaks in sentences of mean length 2.0–3.5 words long, in response to the infant's sentences of mean length 1.0–2.0 words long, the transformations they can deploy are not likely to result in anything that is very salient to the infant (Fraser & Roberts, 1975; Slobin, 1973, 1982, 1997). Some kinds of transformation turn what is heard on the surface into a deeply scrambled version of what is meant underneath, such as those controlling passives and the embedding of one clause in another. However, adults avoid passive constructions with young children (Cross, 1978b; Reynolds, 1988), and it is hard to make sentences with more than one clause out of, say, four words, and, in any case, adults avoid them with young children. This provides an alternative explanation to that suggested by Chomsky for why, in the first phase of language learning, up to about $2\frac{1}{4}$ years, the child learns only phrase structure rules and not transformational ones (Gleason, 2001; McNeill, 1970).

The situation within which the child learns language is not that assumed by Chomsky. As a result, it can be said that Chomsky's argument is not as strong as he thinks; in particular the degree of innate knowledge needed is probably less than he assumes. However, it is still probably greater than Vygotsky thought (Slobin, 1973, 1982, 1997). This means that the truth probably lies somewhere between the quite Chomskyan approach taken by Carey and Spelke and that taken by authors such as Galperin (1959, 1968, 1969, 1978) and Vygotsky. Bozhovich (1997) has suggested altering Vygotsky somewhat to bring him into line with Chomsky here, which is not contrary to Vygotsky's historical arguments about the cultural nature of psychology, as core language abilities almost certainly appeared during biological evolution.

Emergence of signs proper

We saw in Chapter 4 that Vygotsky was probably wrong in thinking that speech takes the form of symbols in the period from $2\frac{1}{2}$ to 12 years. It is more plausible, and more in accord with contemporary thinking, to say that speech in this period is at least sign like. Most of the words used do not have figurative characteristics. Some precise use of words appears from about 3 years and by $4\frac{1}{2}$ years even relatively complex counting words are correctly applied (de Villiers & de Villiers, 1999; Gleason, 2001).

Vygotsky also seems to put too much stress on the emergence of signs proper in producing adult-like use of meanings. The development of the connection between something that represents and the meaning it is attached to is only one aspect of the development of meaning. To produce adult-like use of language the child must also develop meaning itself, making it both more consistent and more abstract. Vygotsky thought these two things are almost one and the same thing, but there is no logical necessity for this to be so. As the child apparently achieves signs proper long before it has fully developed its meanings, this shows that they are more independent of one another than he thought.

This issue will also colour how we view the child's main dynamic functions: instinct, speech, play, writing, advanced concepts. If speech involves signs from $2\frac{1}{2}$ years, then play is not a plausible successor, as play symbols are only partly sign like.

The early onset of signs proper also creates problems for another of Vygotsky's arguments about the development of speech. The idea that the internalisation of speech plays a major role in the production of signs proper is not compatible with these changes, as we have now moved the emergence of such signs back at least as far as the start of the preschool period, at $2\frac{1}{2}$ years. We cannot move inner speech back in a similar way, as the observations that suggest its existence do not do so much before 6 years. However, as suggested below, we can assign it a new kind of more advanced meaning to fit in with the new framework.

Mediation of functions by signs

A central contention of the late theory is that first perception (1–3 years), then memory (3–7 years) and then attention (7–13 years) are mediated by signs and this forms the meanings that predominate in the corresponding stages. The empirical evidence on the mediation of signs gathered in the third period and distilled in Vygotsky (1931b) is only relevant for attention where the support claimed is dubious. This is because the task used is quite unnecessarily difficult. In line with this, Zaporozhets and Elkonin (1971) report a study showing that, in a simplified task, mediated attention can be found as young as 4 years.

However, the theory is not in such dire straits as this suggests. A point that does support Vygotsky here has already been mentioned. This is that it is still widely believed that meanings in the period 1–2 years are closely related to perception. In addition, I have already suggested that the meanings belonging to his stage of first school ($6\frac{1}{2}$–12 years) need to be brought earlier, by as much as a stage. This means that they will appear in the stage $2\frac{1}{2}$–$6\frac{1}{2}$ years. The function that supports them is mediated attention, which we now know appears as early as 4 years. The synthesis of functions to form concepts in adolescence is more complex than any of the previous transitions. At previous transitions, single functions had become conscious, but now the formation of concepts itself becomes so, which involves several functions. This results in closer integration between the functions than previously. It has long been thought that the effect of consciousness in adolescence is to provide an overview and integration of cognitive processes and this is still the dominant view today (e.g. Busemann, 1925, 1926, 1927; Colby & Kohlberg, 1987; Gibbs, 1979; Inhelder & Piaget, 1958; Piaget, 1977; Spranger, 1925). This explains why adolescents form concepts using more integrated and holistic processes. This aspect of Vygotsky's predictions should, however, be tempered by the realisation that it is one of his least distinctive suggestions in this area, with some of the best known names in the study of cognitive development, both before and after him, pointing to this connection.

This leaves the stage of first school without a function corresponding to its meanings.

Suggested changes to the theory related to the above

1 As already suggested, the range of innate functions that contribute to early language development needs to be broadened.
2 The use of signs proper appears much younger than Vygotsky thought, probably around 2 years. This makes it unlikely that play is one of the five dynamic motors of development, as it would not be fulfilling a forward moving developmental function if this were the case. The use of precise and scientific speech could take its place for the period $2\frac{1}{2}$–$6\frac{1}{2}$ years.
3 The coming to maturity of internal attention in the period $6\frac{1}{2}$–12 years supports the forms of meaning found then. It plays the same role of splitting the internal representations of objects into their component qualities that external attention does for external objects in the previous stage. Improvements in attention enable the child to focus on individual aspects of objects and representations, rather than looking on them as undifferentiated wholes. It seems more likely that the sequence of mediated functions involved in the development of meaning in the period $2\frac{1}{2}$–12 years is perception–external attention–internal attention, rather than perception–memory–external attention, as suggested by Vygotsky.

Stages in the self

Valsiner and Van der Veer (1988) pointed out that empirical methods for studying the development of the self, from a Vygotskyan point of view, were at that time weak. There has been little improvement since. We can, however, make use of information gathered within other theoretical frameworks.

There have been a number of recent attempts to argue for a linguistic view of the development of the self, similar to that of Vygotsky. The conclusions of Nelson (1997, 2000, 2001) are based on a particularly detailed examination of the recent empirical literature on infancy and early childhood. She argues that self-consciousness goes through two main stages in these periods, the natural and prelinguistic stage of infancy, followed by the linguistic stage of early childhood. So far this is close to Vygotsky. However, her first, infantile, stage is more self-conscious and more complex than Vygotsky's. Yet her overall description of this stage is not outside the parameters he set.

Her second main stage in the self begins, as Vygotsky's did, around 2 years, that is in the middle of his second stage. However, Nelson's second self goes on developing until about 5 years, while Vygotsky's second stage lasts only until the end of early childhood, around 3 years, or even earlier at 2½ years, if we adopt the revised ages for stages suggested above.

It seems that what Nelson is describing in her second stage is two different stages, one for early childhood, and one for what Vygotsky calls the preschool age, which is 2½–6½, in the revised ages. In some ways these are similar to those of Vygotsky, while in others they suggest the need to revise what he says. We saw in Chapters 4 and 6 that Vygotsky thought the child was unable to stabilise its conception of itself until after 7 years, because its meanings are so unstable. This makes its attempts at self-description unstable. Nelson, by contrast, has the child begin stabilising the conception of itself that emerges from self-description and other language uses from 2 years. Her point here is to a large extent a corollary of changes in the assessment of child meanings that have occurred since Vygotsky's time. Now we understand that child meanings are more stable than he thought, we can also expect that children will be able to stabilise their self-conceptions earlier than he thought.

However, Vygotsky's idea that the preschool child has an unstable self exhibited in the many roles it adopts in dramatic play is plausible and this is indeed one of the later characteristics of Nelson's (1997, 2001) linguistic self. This kind of instability differs from the earlier one in that it involves switching from one stable self to another. This marks the onset of the third stage of the Vygotskyan self, around 3 years. The fact that the child can, with at least some success, shift from one self to another by a single act of will in play, gives quite convincing evidence that it has a number of internally coherent selves available.

We now turn to the most influential account of the development of the self in the Freudian tradition, that of Erikson (1960, 1968; see also Penuel & Wertsch, 1995). Erikson's stages have been operationalised in the form of questionnaires and other instruments and have been shown from empirical studies to form a stage-like sequence (Marcia, 1966; Peterson, 1996; Rosenthal, Gurney, & Moore, 1981; Whitbourne & Tesch, 1985). His stages are named after the main conflicts experienced by the self within each stage. These are, in the period to the end of adolescence: trust versus mistrust (0–1 years); autonomy versus shame and doubt (1–2½ years); initiative versus guilt (2½–6 years); industry versus inferiority (6–12 years); identity versus role confusion (12–21 years). I have already mentioned that Vygotsky's stages need slightly retiming to bring them into line with empirical studies of the crises. Once we do this, Erikson's stages fall almost perfectly on top of them.

There is also a general similarity in the content of the stages compared to those for the Vygotskyan self. Vygotsky has the self in charge of the overall mission of the personality, which is to obtain independent power and control over its world. This is achieved by cooperation with others in acting on the physical world, rather than simply by individualistic enterprise. For this reason, each of his stages of the self is a stage in the achievement of independent control over the physical and social worlds. Erikson, as a member of the neoFreudian school of ego psychology, adopts much the same view. The ego psychology view is that the self has a similar function to the one Vygotsky suggested; unlike Freud's own view that the self has little independent role and functions mainly to manage the conflict between the superego, or conscience, and the id, or instinctive demands for immediate pleasure. Erikson adopts the same posture as Vygotsky, stressing control over the world for some of his stages, namely initiative versus guilt ($2\frac{1}{2}$–6 years); industry versus inferiority (6–12 years); identity versus role confusion (12–21 years).

Erikson's first two stages are trust versus mistrust (0–1 years) and autonomy versus shame and doubt (1–$2\frac{1}{2}$ years). These are somewhat different, as they concentrate on relations with others by building trust and pride. They are, however, also quite similar to Vygotsky's first stages of the self, which also stress social relations. rather than the child's independent achievements; presumably, in both cases, because as yet the infant and young child are still so dependent on adults.

One point on which Vygotsky continues to differ from Erikson, however, is that the latter, as a follower of Freud, separates the inner and outer selves more sharply than he did.

All this suggests a serious problem with the timing of developments in the self. Vygotsky's own indicators for the emergence of the self in the ages of early childhood, preschool and first school are: the executive self; dramatic play; and the splitting of the self, respectively. He himself places these around 1, 3 and 7 years, respectively. Erikson's stages reinforce this. These times are close to the start of Vygotsky's stages, rather than halfway through the stable part of the stage, as his theory requires.

Although Nelson places the onset of the second stage around 2 years, she places more weight on the child's speech in this context than Vygotsky did. Nelson's placing of the start of the infant self around 2 months, however, does seem plausible in the light of contemporary understanding of the infant. This places the emergence of the first self right at the start of Vygotsky's first stage, not in the middle, as the theory requires.

Suggested changes to the theory related to the above

1 The problem is that new forms of the self appear at the start of the four stages from infancy through to the end of first school (0–12 years), when they should emerge in the middle of stages. The most obvious solution is to assume that the forms of the self observed originate in the last part of the previous stage, but are not readily visible, until they have assumed a dominant position following the crises separating stages. This emphasises

one of the weaknesses of Vygotsky's theory: That the bond between different strands of development is often poorly specified, making this kind of shift in identification possible.

Coordination between development of personality and cognition

The main problem here is that in the age range 0–12 years we have moved many central achievements, especially those connected with meaning, forward by about a stage. But we have not moved some other aspects of the child's development forward much, if at all, such as its social behaviour, the nature of the self, the nature of crises and so forth. The reason we cannot move them forward is that, broadly speaking, there is no reason to reinterpret the evidence that Vygotsky gave showing when they appear. So it seems that what has moved forward by a stage and what has stayed still will now be out of alignment, as each stage is supposed to form a coherent whole.

There are also more specific problems in this area. Vygotsky's general expectation was that the normal course of development leads to successive crises, each followed rapidly by a new stage of cognitive development, followed by another crisis. This sequence cannot be altered, although it seems that not every child reaches the end of development (Vygotsky, 1931a, 1933g). As some children stall part of the way through his sequence, we should find that the proportion of individuals reaching these milestones, that is the stages of cognitive development and crises, will fall off as we continue through the sequence. However, empirical studies show some variation from this orderly picture.

There are, it is true, no good studies of both social crises and periods in cognitive development in the same children. However, we can compare different samples. In the earlier stages there are some problems, but they turn out not to be acute. The 2–3 year crisis is found in about 70 percent of children between the ages of 2 and 4 years (Ausubel, Sullivan, & Ives, 1980), but over 90 percent pass from prespeech to speech proper in the period 1 year to 5 years (de Villiers & de Villiers, 1984; Gleason, 2001; Greene, 1987), which is held to be one of the outcomes of this crisis (Vygotsky, 1933f).

This raises two problems. First, both common experience and some suggestions from research studies indicate that there is a substantial number of children who pass to speech proper before they undergo the crisis at 2–3 years, when the theory suggests this should be the other way round. Second, by 5 years the proportion of children who have passed to speech proper is much higher than the proportion who have undergone the crisis.

However, in both cases, we can apply a familiar argument from the research literature on stage transitions. This is that to make a meaningful conclusion in cases of this kind we need to equalise the levels of measurement for both achievements. The social crisis literature usually uses fairly gross methods of assessing crises, such as whether parents report negative attitudes and behaviour, which probably fail to detect more subtle symptoms of crisis, thus underestimating the proportion of children passing through the crisis in a given period, as well as overestimating the age of onset. Tests of cognitive development tend to be more probing and pick up a greater proportion of those who have acquired the relevant cognitive achievement. This could explain away the two problems just noted. In fact, Vygotsky (1933g, 1933i) was certainly aware of our second problem and advanced a very similar solution: That in many children the crisis is not easily visible.

A more serious problem in matching the development of cognition with the crises comes at the other end of Vygotsky's span of interest. This is that a much higher proportion of individuals seem to go through the social crisis leading into youth (the crisis officially scheduled at 17 years) than complete the second phase of adolescent cognition (Ausubel et al., 1980; Peterson, 1996; Shayer, 1980, 1998; Shayer & Adey, 1993). Our previous argument, about the strictness with which the two things are assessed, still applies, but now it just makes things worse. Those experiencing the social crisis are, probably, even more numerous than they appear. Even on the raw figures, over 80 percent of Western adolescents will have entered the crisis by 20 years, but not more than 30 percent have completed the second phase of adolescent reasoning, as defined by Inhelder and Piaget (1958) (Shayer, 1980, 1998). Even if we adopt completion of the first phase of adolescent reasoning as the criterion for completing adolescent cognition (Piaget's formal operations IIIA), we are still looking at 80 percent and 50 percent, respectively (loci cit.).

Suggested changes to the theory related to the above

1. Only the central aspects of meaning (structures of generalisation) and aspects of cognition connected with meaning and thought move earlier. The social crises and other aspects of personality development are not well enough integrated with these aspects of cognition in the original theory for this to create a problem of mismatch between the two. Some other aspects of cognition, for which Vygotsky gave more reliable empirical evidence, remain where they are, such as play and inner speech.
2. More adolescents go through the social crisis at the end of adolescence than acquire adolescent reasoning. The easiest way to explain this is to assume that some pass through the crisis in a superficial manner, possibly due to outside pressure to do so. Many adolescents seem to experience the social transition to adulthood in a way that is imitated from others or due to outside pressure and not driven by underlying factors. This is probably connected to the fact that the social transition to life away from the parents is more compulsory than previous transitions.

Further discussion

There are areas where the original theory is less vague. One example is the link between inner speech and the creation of the inner self. Here, cognition and the development of the self are linked together in a definite way. First of all, we have the creation of inner speech at around 7 years, and the splitting of the self around the same time, creating the inner self. This is particularly significant for cognition, as it produces sense as opposed to meaning, which is an essential plane of representation, said to be needed for further advance.

However, this is not an insuperable problem, as we can suggest that inner speech and the splitting of the self are connected to a more advanced kind of meaning than Vygotsky thought. This moves the meanings associated with inner speech a stage earlier, as required by the new framework.

A second example of this kind is the instability of the self in the preschool age (3–7 years), which is linked to the capacity to redesignate objects in dramatic play. Without this capacity, the self would have no fantasy world to enter, to assume a new form. If a child can redesignate a box as 'racing car' and a circuit in the flat or garden as 'racetrack', then they can assume the persona of 'racing driver'. Otherwise, if they are still relatively bound to the outside world, they cannot. Again, this ability is closely linked to other aspects of the preschool period ($2\frac{1}{2}$–$6\frac{1}{2}$ years in the new version). So, once again, it should not be moved earlier with the basic forms of meaning.

To reiterate, the structures of generalisation and levels of generality that are closely attached to them should be moved forward by about a stage, but some other aspects of cognition stay where they are.

That most adolescents do in fact make the social transition at the end of adolescence, in the way suggested, was proposed by S. Freud (1915–16, 1923) and A. Freud (1958) as well as by Jung (1912) and they believed that such people often need to revisit the problems they sweep under the carpet in middle age, this being a component of the midlife crisis. A problem with this approach is that the two Freuds and Jung all thought that we could apply the same argument to earlier stage transitions, while Vygotsky tries to avoid this. Adoption of this last suggestion would not undermine the fundamentals of Vygotsky's theory, but it would make its surface manifestations more complex.

Conclusions

It has been shown that meanings and some other cognitive abilities appear much earlier in spontaneous development than Vygotsky suggests, in the years up to the end of childhood. Thus Vygotsky's assumptions here should be changed, although not all abilities should be moved forward in this way. His view of how much teaching can advance development should also be correspondingly moderated. It was argued that a middle way between Chomsky's (1980a, 1980b, 1995) modular approach to language development and

Vygotsky's original view is needed. Problems raised by the placement of play and inner speech in the new scheme were considered. Play may not be one of the dynamic motors of development (or neoformations) that Vygotsky suggested. It was tentatively suggested that precise speech might replace it in this role.

There is evidence that Vygotsky's order of development for mediated functions can fit into the revised framework, provided memory is removed, although this leaves a gap for the age of first school. It was suggested that the mediated function, responsible for the meanings characteristic of this age ($6\frac{1}{2}$ years–12 years), may be the voluntary direction of internal attention.

It was found that new versions of the self seem to appear at the wrong time for the theory. A suggestion was made to explain this. The problems involved in realigning cognitive abilities with other aspects of stages, given the decision to move the former considerably earlier, were considered. It was argued that these can be overcome.

13 Extensions and comparisons

Existing extensions to the theory

There have been a number of significant attempts to extend Vygotsky's theory. A problem with the suggested extensions is that they have all been framed within the original theory or at least within parts of it. However, they can all be made to fit within the altered version of the theory just outlined.

Bozhovich (1968) and Bozhovich and Slavina (1979) wanted to make the content of the child's personality development at each of Vygotsky's stages more concrete than he had been able to do. Their conclusions are based on extensive studies by Bozhovich and her colleagues, as well as considerable use of both Soviet and foreign literature. Her additions to Vygotsky's descriptions of the stages are as follows.

In infancy, she confirms Vygotsky's analysis, but does not go appreciably beyond it. In early childhood and the preschool period, the dependence of the child on adults is said to have a specific character, not mentioned by Vygotsky, which is that as yet the child is not expected to do any serious work, to maintain its relations with adults (Bozhovich, 1968, p. 287). Obviously this is culturally specific to both Soviet and Western cultures, as it is typical of tribal and semi-tribal societies that children from 5 or 6 years, and even younger, are asked to help with such things as gathering plant foods or tending flocks.

At the start of the school period, the child's interests are still dominated by the immediate situation, changing with whatever happens to be present at the time. If blocks are presented, then they will be interested in these, if tabletop puzzles, then in those. As the period of first school progresses, they become more stable and inner directed. At the same time, the child takes less notice of what teachers and other adults think of them or want and more of what other children think. The child is moving from an adult-centred approach to the world to a peer-centred view (Bozhovich, 1968, p. 289). Although these points are just routine as far as general child psychology is concerned, they are significant additions to Vygotsky's own analysis, which is thin at this point.

This movement away from adults is a movement in the child's social situation of development. It does not just move from adults to independence, as Vygotsky says, but from adults, to other children, to independence. The challenge to participate fully in the group is now one of the two most important factors in the child's development, the other one remaining, as for Vygotsky, its desire for knowledge and control of the environment. At the same time, the child also strives for self-esteem. As Vygotsky had suggested, at this age the child's relations to others have been internalised and so the child has added to seeking the approval of others seeking its own approval.

As puberty arrives, there is also another new desire, not stressed by Vygotsky: the desire to be grown up. This often adds to the typical conflicts of puberty, as it may conflict with both the desires of the peer group on some issues and with those of the parents on others. One of the most notorious manifestations of this desire today is smoking, which many adolescents in their early teens take up to appear grown up.

In adolescence, as Vygotsky had implied, the most powerful drive is towards a unified worldview and moral outlook. At this point, we see the full meaning of Bozhovich's earlier insistence that the main motor of development is the striving for wholeness. The drive for a unified view of the world and moral outlook is not just an internal striving, but is also one that will result in great changes in the adolescent's social relations. For instance, they may join religious or political groups in the service of this striving.

These points are also confirmed and elaborated in the sustained current of Soviet and Russian interest in these issues, including the work of B. D. Elkonin (1993, 1994, 1996), D. B. Elkonin (1971), D. B. Elkonin and Dragunova (1967), Ganzen and Golovei (1982) and Polivanova (1994).

McNeill's (1987, 1992, 2000) contribution is of a different kind. He attempts to bring Vygotsky up to date, particularly in relation to the greater degree of technical precision found in modern discussions of cognitive and linguistic development. Some of his suggestions are controversial and I will criticise one of them. However, it is important to confront the issues he raises, as they are significant.

The first issue is not technical, but it is perplexing. McNeill wants to know what Vygotsky thought that thought was like. He comes to the conclusion that Vygotsky believed that thought is image like, which is essentially the conclusion we reached in Chapter 6, in dealing with thought in Vygotsky's last period. McNeill (1983, 1987, 1992, 2000) reports a number of empirical studies that support this view. The weakness of his discussions is that he does not consider the reasons that many students of adolescent and adult cognition have the impression the shift in this period is away from spatial or imagery-based thought and towards abstract non-spatial meanings.

Inhelder & Piaget (1958), for instance, argue that one of the distinctive characteristics of adolescent ideas, in areas such as mathematics and physics, is their abstract character. I return to this problem below.

One of McNeill's other significant innovations has been to raise the question of which contemporary formal model of semantics would best go with Vygotsky's approach. This is particularly germane, as Vygotsky himself believed that formal models of psychological processes play a key role in psychological investigation (Vygotsky, 1934c, Ch. 6, 1934e). McNeill's (1987) answer to this is Montague 'grammar' (Montague, 1974). I believe this to be incorrect, but the question is certainly highly relevant. The term 'grammar' was adopted here because, at the time Montague was writing, following particularly Chomsky (1965), many linguists referred to all general theories of language as grammars. The most prominent feature of Montague's system is its semantics.

One aspect of Montague's proposal was that the meaning of adult language can be expressed by set theory. This is immediately controversial, as it is more common for contemporary theories of the semantics of natural language to represent meaning using the simpler model of first order predicate logic. However, in favour of set theory, there is the point that if we want to eventually couple meaning with adult conceptual abilities, as Vygotsky did, we will need a relatively powerful model of logic and this is provided by set theory, a point that one of Piaget's collaborators also acted on, although in a slightly different way (Grize, 1960). This is not to say that the child starts off with set theory, but that by adolescence it has acquired it.

However, the way Montague relates set theory to natural language syntax is more problematic. He claims that certain prominent grammatical units have a fixed connection to set theory concepts. Noun phrases, thus, always denote sets of sets, while verbs always denote sets. As a result, in 'Bill knows how to multiply', the noun phrase 'Bill' is held to mean 'the set of sets of which Bill is a member'. This is justified by saying that first there are the sets that include Bill, such things as his family, his sports teams and so forth. Bill can emerge from these if we say he is the common property of all these sets. This common property defines a set and that is Bill. In an apparently similar way, set theorists often define numbers as sets of sets. So they say the number three is the set of all sets having three members. However, in the second case it is reasonable to think that we have captured something about the fact that sets with three members are concrete, or at least particular, while the set of sets denoted by the number three is abstract. In the case of Bill, we seem to have succeeded in turning things upside down, by making the concrete individual Bill into something more abstract than the sets that contain him. This problem with Montague grammar is not a problem with set theory in general, as ordinary set theory contains a perfectly good way of expressing the meaning of Bill, which is that he is one of the primary objects being discussed.

Another interesting issue raised by McNeill (1987) is that most contemporary theories of semantics assume there is some systematic connection between the syntax and semantics of sentences. It has been well accepted since Chomsky (1959) that there are far too many grammatical forms needed for sentences of up to, say, 16 words long, for the meaning assigned to each one to be learned individually. There must be rule-governed connections between the two. However, as McNeill points out, if the sentences of adult language are signs proper, as Vygotsky and others such as Saussure (1916) claim, this means that there is an arbitrary connection between each sentence and its meaning. This would prohibit systematic, rule-governed connections and throw us back on having each syntactic structure arbitrarily paired with its meaning, which we have already seen is untenable.

It is in part for this reason that McNeill (1987, 1992) is attracted to Montague's (1974) solution, as it connects the meaning of a sentence with its syntax using a system of rules, to reduce the amount that has to be remembered. I have already raised doubts about this particular solution, but we will certainly need some solution to this problem.

A related course of action, which McNeill (1987) mentions as a possible interim measure, is to abandon Vygotsky's loose talk about sentences taking the form of signs and explicitly restrict the term signs (in the strict sense) to words and morphemes (the meaningful units of language). This seems an excellent suggestion.

Ratner (1989, 1991, 2000) has offered an extension to Vygotsky's theory of emotion. This again presents a valuable extension of Vygotsky and again in a different direction. However, there is a problem with his treatment, which is his description of Vygotsky's theory as a whole.

Ratner (2000) takes the questionable decision to ignore the huge changes that occurred in Vygotsky's outlook over his active life and to draw a picture of his view of psychological activity based on all periods from 1920 to 1934. The result is puzzling. He acknowledges that activities are bound together into systems and thus his view is correct for the last period, from an abstract point of view, although it is wrong for the period 1920–29. In addition, his actual discussions of such systems are drawn more from the historical and sociological domain than from Vygotsky's analysis of the child: He concentrates on such systems as capitalism and feudalism. Here he drifts into an ambiguous view of Vygotsky on historical systems by not stressing that it is the productive aspect of these that is central.

Ratner (2000) touches on three main areas in connection with emotion: the connection between emotion, cognition and the physiological reactions of the body; the way in which emotion is socialised by those who surround the child and the adult, based on their social relations and activities; and the way in which the child constructs its own emotions, on the basis of its social relations and activities. His approach to the first is essentially an updated version of Vygotsky's argument that, although emotions are determined, by both the way we understand situations, and our physiological reactions to them, understanding is dominant and determines which specific emotion we will feel. Physiology is a necessary component, but does not determine what we feel. For instance, if we are given adrenalin this will raise our heart rate and breathing, dilate the blood vessels and increase metabolic rate, but these bodily feelings alone will not lead to a specific emotion. If the situation suggests something to be angry about we will be angry, if it suggests something to be frightened of, we will be frightened (Schachter & Singer, 1963; Westen, 1994).

There are many ways in which emotions are socialised. The child's caretakers model expressions of emotion, they explain correct emotional reaction and they mould children's emotions by rewarding some, ignoring some and punishing some. So a mother may react to her child's fear of swimming using any of these reactions (Denham, 1998, Ch. 4). We see 'certain expressive patterns of toddlers and their mothers become more and more alike across time' (Denham, 1998, p. 110). What is socialised will depend on the cultural activities and concepts of the wider society in which the caregivers live. Some of Ratner's most interesting examples focus on attempts by social elites to influence childrearing in the population at large. Thus, after the First World War, Western women were encouraged to be envious and competitive, to stimulate the demand for consumer goods, and this influenced their childrearing attitudes.

He also gives equally relevant examples of childrearing being influenced by adults' desire for the child to develop the emotions and attitudes, needed for success in life. Through most of the history of modern capitalism it has been thought that boys, in particular, need to cultivate emotional control and a tough-minded, calculating attitude to life, so as to prosper in the harsh worlds of work and economic endeavour. They are also encouraged to show anger, but not hurt or sensitivity, for the same reason.

The novelty of the treatment here, compared to conventional psychological views of emotional socialisation, is that the wider social context of social influences on emotion is stressed, not just the child's face-to-face interactions. This context is also conceptualised more concretely than in the usual psychological concepts of 'social attitudes', 'childrearing attitudes' and so forth. This theme can be found in Vygotsky (1931b, Ch. 12), but Ratner's clearer and fuller presentation is very helpful. As Vygotsky was mainly interested in the form of the child's developing emotions, he neglected the problem of socialisation and Ratner's approach helps to correct this imbalance.

Finally, we come to the way in which the child forms its emotions, based on its social relations and activities. Here the approach is somewhat disappointing, as we get little more than several nods in the direction of this problem, acknowledging its existence; but he says little about how Vygotsky proposed to solve it. This is probably linked to his unwillingness to engage what is specific to the late Vygotsky, as it was in his late period that he made his most significant contributions in this area.

While Ratner mentions that, according to Vygotsky (1932e), the child's emotions result from its attempts to achieve its goals, he says little about the second fundamental source, which is its struggle to develop itself. In the first area, for instance, achievement of a goal by the child's own efforts will be accompanied by pride, while achievement of a goal through someone else's efforts may be accompanied by pleasure. He correctly points out that the nature of the child's emotions is produced by its stage of development, in relation to problem solving, while it is only secondarily related to adult socialisation.

A significant extension to Vygotsky's notion of scaffolding has been suggested by Bruner (1981a, 1981b, 1984a), Wood (1998) and Wood, Bruner, and Ross (1976). This brings together two of Vygotsky's themes. They begin from Vygotsky's idea of scaffolding, namely that someone more expert than the child can assist their progress by offering assistance targeted at their immediate problems. They then extend this using the idea of a discourse presupposition, sometimes called a discourse maxim, following Grice (1975).

Bruner and Wood point out that the child will need discourse presuppositions, in order to benefit from scaffolding assistance given by an adult, during a conversation. They concentrate, particularly, on such presuppositions within two functions: indicating and requesting. In order for the adult to indicate something to the child, the child needs presuppositions to interpret the adult's intention. If the adult points to something and the child has no such starting point, then the child may think the adult is making a meaningless movement, is reaching for the object indicated, is stretching and the like. For the child to interpret the pointing gesture as pointing at something, they must first come to the conclusion that the adult wants to indicate something. Then they must use the presuppositions of the indicating function to interpret what this is. In the case of pointing, they must also understand that the person doing the pointing points at what they want to indicate.

We can also indicate things to young children by waving at them, by standing behind the object and calling for the child's attention, by bringing the object close to the child, by bringing the child close to the object and by a number of other methods. If we think first of the pointing and waving methods, the common factor here is that, in each case, we indicate to the child that our attention is on the object. Thus the presupposition here is that, having entered the attention-directing game, the child should attend to what the adult attends to.

Bruner and Wood conclude that the child must possess this chief presupposition of attention directing, as well as other presuppositions, in order to even begin the main process of language learning. It also needs them to help in mastering the problem-solving strategies involved in learning later achievements through scaffolding, such as arithmetic and geometry. They also suggest that such central presuppositions would be too difficult for the child to learn in the time available, as they would probably be needed from around 1 year of age and, certainly, by 18 months. As a result, they suggest that there exists an innate system that is specially designed to ensure the learning of such presuppositions and other devices for discourse interpretation. Bruner (1981a, 1981b) calls this innate system the language assistance system (LAS), whose primary function is to ensure 'the ordered pattern of transfer of initiative in communication from the adult to the child' (Bruner, 1981b).

An example of this from the transfer of attention is that, to begin with, the adult signals to the child that this is an attention-directing situation and directs their attention to something. At first the child is not inclined to follow either of these moves in the game. However, the language assistance system then intervenes and tells the child to note that the cue for an attention-directing situation has occurred. This could be tapping the child on the shoulder, clearing the throat, making eye contact and the like. The child is able to do this because it has available the concept 'attention-directing situation', probably from general cognitive development.

The LAS then forms the rule that when someone else intentionally directs their attention, within an attention-directing situation, you should follow. The child has few indications from the adult that this is a rule and thus needs the help of the LAS to realise this. It now has available one of the main presuppositions for the direction of attention. Other such maxims are learned in a similar way.

Although this is an interesting extension of Vygotsky's ideas, it is doubtful that it is entirely Vygotskyan, in its approach to the learning of discourse capacities. While Bruner and Wood stress the child's ability to understand the adult, Vygotsky's (1931b, 1934c, Ch. 4) approach to the understanding of gesture stresses both this and the adult's ability to understand the child. He claims that, because the adult is able to come close to the child's understanding of the situation, the child is able to find out what the adult means, without such extensive assistance as that given by the LAS.

Vygotsky does not apply this to the learning of discourse presuppositions, but a direct extension of his approach to this area would say something like the following. He stresses the central nature of learning about requests, so we can focus on these. As we saw in Chapters 4 and 6, these begin with the child's own early gestures. These originate in attempts to reach things and other actions that are 'natural', rather than communicative. These are then seen by the adult who responds to them as gestures, even though they are not intended as such. Finally, the child realises that it can initiate communication by gesturing to something, for instance by pointing. The essential difference between this and the approach of Bruner and Wood is that in their view the child must find out what the adult is thinking. In the Vygotskyan approach the adult must first realise what the child is thinking and then the child must realise what the adult is thinking. This second approach seems more difficult when put into words, but Vygotsky's contention is that it is a help to the child, because it can more easily follow someone else's thoughts than have thoughts on its own. The former are supported by the adult's lead, while the latter are, in effect, unsupported.

One further extension

One of the greatest contrasts between Vygotsky's ideas and contemporary thinking is in the area of adolescent reasoning. The present suggestion is designed both to show why this is and that this view is at least as plausible as more conventional ideas, which stem mainly from Piaget. The main problem is that the two focus on quite different aspects of adolescent thinking because they regard these as fundamental. In Piaget's case this is propositional reasoning, in Vygotsky's it is algebra and set theory.

Propositional logic is based only on the truth or falsity of propositions, each one being considered as a whole. So, it is an inference from 'Proposition P implies proposition Q' and 'Proposition Q implies proposition R' that 'Proposition P implies proposition R'. This inference does not depend on the internal structure of the propositions, but, for instance, tells us that: If proposition P is true, then R is as well; while if P is false, R can be true or false. Young children are not very competent at this kind of thinking, which does not become at all fluent until adolescence. This shift is the one most emphasised by more recent research, particularly that inspired by the studies of Inhelder and Piaget (1958).

Vygotsky, by contrast, treats algebra and set theory as the fundamental aspects of adolescent reasoning (Vygotsky, 1931a, Ch. 3, 1934c, Ch. 6). Here, the stress is on what can be inferred from the internal structure of propositions. From the proposition $Y = X + 4$ we can infer that $X = Y - 4$ because of the internal structure of the original proposition. In propositional logic we centre on whether propositions are true, but in algebra and set theory we focus on what the proposition actually says.

Piaget and Vygotsky stressed these two different forms of logic because they suited their respective approaches. Piaget stresses the formal systems of relations found between propositions in propostitonal logic, because this accords with his idea that cognitive development is driven forward by top-down development in such formal systems. Vygotsky, by contrast, emphasises that such development is driven forward by the content of concepts and thinking, which corresponds to his stress on algebra and set theory. In adolescence these are no longer directly tied to concrete reality, but their development is driven from below by the concrete levels of thinking that lie beneath them.

Piaget agreed that there were these two paths, propositional logic and set theory, but thought that the first, propositional logic, was fundamental to adolescent thought, while the second was not (Grize, 1960; Piaget, 1963, 1967; Piaget & Garcia, 1991). It seems more in accord with Vygotsky's overall attitude towards these issues that things are really the other way round: The two paths both exist, but algebra and set theory are more fundamental, while propositional logic is secondary.

Because of the dominance of Piagetian theory, there have been no studies attempting to compare these two views. In the light of this and the inherent plausibility of the Vygotskyan view, it can be considered just as credible as that of Piaget.

Comparison with other theories

Having removed the most obvious problems of the theory and considered some extensions, we turn to a brief comparison of the revised theory with others. This begins with a reminder of the four main questions that Vygotsky thought should be asked of any theory if it is to qualify as a viable theory of the development of higher mental processes. Attention is then given to the approaches that remain. Issues that need investigation to adjudicate and improve theories of this type are discussed briefly.

Cognitive development

General defining issues

The first argument in favour of Vygotsky's view of learning is his contention that due to the nature of species development, the middle and later part of the child's cognitive development must be mainly driven by social and cultural learning and increasing degrees of consciousness. This is based on the argument that neither of these periods of development can be mainly based on biological evolution and that the only alternative is cultural learning of this kind. This shows that learning after the first period depends on social consciousness, which must be based on signs, as these are the way in which we share consciousness. More details of the argument on this point were given in Chapter 4.

Vygotsky's second argument is designed to deal with a serious objection to the first one. This is that it is not immediately obvious that biological learning is ruled out in the period under consideration, because biological evolution could have established a mechanism that is capable of extracting regularities and generalisations from the environment that feeds on its own results. In one version, this says it first extracts regularities and generalisations from sensations of space, colour and so forth, forming such concepts as that of permanent concrete objects that move around in space and have constant properties, such as a constant shape, size and colour, despite such spatial movements. These objects and properties are then taken as the input for a new round of extracting regularities and generalisations. This kind of extraction could result, for instance, in the concept of a class of concrete objects that is united by a common characteristic; based on this we could then extract that of number, which is often defined as a class of classes, as when we say that three is the characteristic of all classes with three members. And so on.

This alternative is far more than an abstract possibility. Suggestions similar to this have a distinguished history in developmental psychology, including the contributions of K. Buhler (1907, 1918), Dirlan (1980), E. J. Gibson (1969), J. J. Gibson (1979) and Piaget (1945, 1965; Piaget & Inhelder, 1969). However, they all have a serious problem that was pointed out by Vygotsky (1931a, p. 55), in a consideration of K. Buhler's version of this idea: 'The main weakness of Buhler's theory is that it attempts to find a psychological equivalent, to the logical operations that produce the development of concepts, in elementary processes, that are common to both perception and thinking' (my trans.). He thinks this is a mistake because the means of forming elementary and more advanced concepts could not be the same, as the two processes are qualitatively different. To put this another way, the extraction mechanisms needed to extract perceptual constancies and the object concept are not at all the same as the extraction processes needed in later periods of development. This being so, biological evolution could not have foreseen what kinds of extraction mechanisms were needed for periods of development that first arose a long time after biological evolution had ceased. The extraction mechanism that was developed under the influence of biological evolution applied only to perception and its immediate successors and could not have served to develop the kinds of concepts that emerged later in the process of cultural evolution.

This problem does not arise for Vygotsky, as he assumes that the use of signs linked to shared activity is the dominant force in the middle period of development. The kind of scaffolding involved both in showing the child forms of shared activity and in showing the child how to talk and use other kinds of signs can mould the child to master forms of behaviour and meaning in a flexible way. This enables cultural learning to adapt itself to the new forms of learning that occur in this period. After this, writing takes over, where the starting point is common ideas, rather than common practical activity, but the moulding influence of adults and older children is still present and still fulfils this function. We can expect that other cultural theories will overcome this problem in ways slightly different from but essentially similar to Vygotsky.

So we can conclude that only cultural theories can explain the child's development beyond about 3 years. This enables us to eliminate from consideration biological theories of development: such as that of Piaget; those of neoPiagetians, such as Pascual-Leone, Case, Halford and Demetriou; the Gibsons; and Fodor (on those other than Piaget see Case, 1988, 1991; Case & Okamoto, 1996; Demetriou, 1998, 2003; Demetriou, Efklides & Platsidou, 1993; Demetriou, Kyriakides, & Avraamidou, 2003; Fodor, 1975, 1983; E. J. Gibson, 1969; J. J. Gibson, 1979; Halford, 1993, 1999a, 1999b; Pascual-Leone and Johnson, 1999, Pascual-Leone, 2000a, 2000b).

Vygotsky's third suggestion is this. Within a cultural approach to cognitive development we cannot hand on sophisticated social practice without signs, because such practice is always moulded by social influence and social influence on cognition, after the age of 3 years, must take the form of signs, for reasons already mentioned (Vygotsky, 1934c, pp. 46–47, 1934e, Lect. 4). To use a central example, although not one used by Vygotsky, the child may learn to sort objects without being spoken to and without being able to put what is done into words. However, to learn sorting without words the child needs either someone to demonstrate what is done or nonspeech feedback during the course of its attempts, such as picking up wrongly assigned items and putting them in the right place. We might be tempted to think of this as the adult's behaviour, so to speak, bumping up against the child's behaviour and thus nudging it to the right path, that is, as a kind of shaping in behaviourist terms (Galperin, 1992). The child receives negative reinforcement, that is, something slightly unpleasant, for part of its efforts and this puts it back on the right track.

However, there is no reason to think that the child finds the modelling or correction inherently unpleasant. It is much more likely to respond to it because it sees it as an attempt to correct its actions. Also, what is learned is likely to be cognitive and not just associations. In this light, the modelling and correction are a communication about what to do. Once we see that they are a communication then they must involve signs, because every communication must involve signs, unless it is done by telepathy.

In the light of this, there is no such thing as higher forms of mental functioning without signs and it is signs that provide the guidance for practice that is guided by conscious processes. This is not to deny that simple imitation and shaping are involved in producing some parts of the child's behaviour, but this is only that which Vygotsky describes as under the control of elementary or lower mental functions (Galperin, 1992). If we think that conscious, higher mental functions also play a key role in the child's development, then this can only come from the meaning conveyed by signs. So signs are everywhere dominant in higher forms of cultural development or higher mental functions.

This third argument is less convincing than the first two. Despite what Vygotsky claims, there is an alternative way in which the child could learn ideas. A. N. Leont'ev (1948, 1960, 1974), in his hugely influential activity theory, with its stress on direct practice, maintained that higher mental functions can arise without the influence of signs. What is passed on to the child is certain ways of doing things and the child generates its own consciousness of these. Although practices may sometimes be passed on by signs, these will often not be those involved in speech and other sophisticated forms of communication, but just gestures and other simple methods of communication. What is true for the child was also true for the historical development of production. This approach is cultural and so is not vulnerable to Vygotsky's critique of noncultural approaches.

However, Vygotsky has a fourth argument, previously called the hurdle argument, that says that signs have the capacity to amplify our natural powers and enable us to exercise abilities we would otherwise not be able to attain (Vygotsky, 1930k, pp. 40–44, 1931b, pp. 60–63, 1934c, pp. 45–50, 126–127). In Chapter 11, we saw that this provides good reason for saying that at successive points in development speech, arithmetical and other scientific signs, writing and concepts all provide significant and necessary amplification of the child's natural capacities (see also Bruner, 1964, 1983, 1990). This does not show that such signs power development, but it does show that they are an indispensable requirement for it. This in turn shows a fatal weakness in Leont'ev's (1948, 1960, 1974) approach, which stresses social practice as against signs.

Distinguishing between cultural-sign approaches

There is a range of approaches to the cultural development of cognition stressing signs, other than that of Vygotsky, including Bruner (1964, 1983, 1990, 1996); Carey and Spelke (Carey, 1995, 1996; Carey & Spelke, 1994, 1996; Spelke, 2000; Spelke & Hermer, 1996; Spelke & Newport, 1998); Galperin (1959, 1965, 1968, 1969, 1992; Galperin & Georgiev, 1969); Harre (1999, 2000, 2002); Newman and Holzman (1993, 1996); Shweder (1996; Shweder & Le Vine, 1984; Stigler, Shweder, & Herdt, 1990); and Wells (1999, 2002).

We can find reasons for rejecting some of these by considering some critical issues that distinguish between them.

Constructivism versus moderate realism One of the main issues that divides cultural-sign theories of development is whether the knowledge gained through signs is realistic or constructed. Some sign-based views of the child's development adopt what is usually called linguistic constructivism, which says that our view of the world reflects the way language structures the world rather than reality. We are trapped within a socially generated illusion that bears no relation to reality. There is a long-standing, but still effective, style of argument against constructivism. This is the one that Hegel directed at Kant, who also proposed a constructivist theory of knowledge (Hegel, 1838, section on Kant).

In constructivist theories based on signs, the understanding achieved by the child is a reflection neither of the world as it is nor of the nature of the person who knows, but of symbolic interaction between the child and others. All the person knows is the result of this interaction, while all the psychologist knows is that there are laws of knowledge, which the psychologist finds out from studying this interaction. So the psychologist and the subject know the results of the interaction, but they know little or nothing about the world itself or about the subject. This means that the universe is now divided into two unknowable parts and a knowable part. The two unknowable parts and the knowable part are obviously radically different. This is therefore a kind of dualism. In much of classical dualism, found in philosophers such as Descartes, the two parts of the universe are mind and matter. Here they are social interaction and what is not such interaction.

The problem here is not in saying that the world and the subject differ from social interaction, which is obvious. The problem is that the two realms, of interaction and noninteraction, have been set up as radically different parts of the universe. Much modern philosophy and science rejects this, as it is contrary to the basic principles of science. These say that in general an economical explanation should be sought for what goes on in the universe that will extend to all its parts. Such dualism also offends against the fundamental principles of science, as the noninteractive part of the universe cannot be explained at all, while science maintains that the whole universe should be explicable. These problems do not exist for Vygotsky and other realists.

The weakness of this refutation of social constructivism is that while many people will agree that dualism is undesirable, they do not think this overrides every other consideration. However, on balance the issue favours Bruner, Galperin, Vygotsky and other realist writers over the constructivism of Harre (1999, 2002), Newman and Holzman (1993, 1996) and Wells (1999, 2002).

Conceptions of the world and logic For Vygotsky, what is learned is primarily a conception of the world that is closely connected to practice, which is different from, but rationally connected to, linguistic logic and meaning.

There have been two main reasons that philosophers and psychologists have thought that we have a separate underlying representation of the world, or naive physics, distinct from logic and the meanings directly attached to logical systems. The first was pointed out by Quine (1951) and is this. Logicism, which Piaget followed, says that every system of logic carries with it its own ontology or view of the world, of which naive physics is one. So, in Piaget's case, the underlying logic of practice carries with it a kind of naive ontology. However, Quine and other logicians have established that common systems of logic can be interpreted in terms of more than one ontology. So there must be a distinction between logic and ontology (Burkhardt & Smith, 1999; Cocciarella, 1987; Randell & Cohn, 1992a, 1992b; Randell, Cui, & Cohn, 1992a, 1992b; Smith, 1982, 1991, 1992, 1995a, 1995b; Smith & Welty, 2001).

Quine has sometimes quite reasonably been referred to as the most influential American philosopher of the second half of the twentieth century; his reputation alone has succeeded in getting this argument considerable airplay and acceptance among psychologists and linguists, as well as philosophers (e.g. Bloom & Keil, 2001; Jackendoff, 1994, 1997, 2002; Keil & Lockhart, 1999; Keil & Wilson, 2000a, 2000b; Neisser, 1976; Wilson & Keil, 2000).

A second argument is that interpreting the meaning of a communication requires an understanding of its context, which requires a representation of the real world, especially when it is not present. This again implies a representation of the world that is not just read off logic (Jackendoff, 1994, 1997, 2002; Keil, 1991a, 1991b; Keil & Lockhart, 1999; Keil & Wilson, 2000a, 2000b; Neisser, 1976; Rieber, 1983). A related point is that designers of artificial intelligence programs, designed to talk to people or other machines in natural language, have found that to say relevant things the programs must represent a naive ontology of the context of the communication (Guarino & Poli, 1995; Poli & Simons, 1996; Smith, 1995a, 1995b; Smith & Casati, 1994; Smith & Welty, 2001).

This is a serious blow to Piaget, as well as for others who have followed him in collapsing the distinction between logic and the world, such as Harre, Newman, Holzman and Wells. However, it also creates problems for Vygotsky. This is because he uses the idea of a close link between a conception of the world and logic to explain how influence moves down, from language and logic, to practice and a conception of the world. If there is no such unique link, it is not immediately clear how this can occur.

One answer, from a Vygotskyan perspective, is that the use of logical words is scaffolded by adults and older children. This tells the child which conception of the world the culture attaches to its logic.

Galperin Of all the alternatives to Vygotsky, that of Galperin (1959, 1965, 1968, 1969, 1977, 1992; Galperin & Elkonin, 1972) deserves particular mention as perhaps the most coherent and detailed. Although Galperin had considerable personal contact with Vygotsky during the latter's lifetime, in the 1930s he was seen as aligned with A. N. Leont'ev after the split between Leont'ev and Vygotsky and joined the former's group at Karkhov, in Ukraine. However, two things suggest that on some fundamental issues he was more aligned with Vygotsky. The first is that he maintained that there are two broad phases in learning during the years 3 to 17: learning to do things without signs and then learning to do the same things guided by signs. As we will see, his analysis of these phases goes beyond Vygotsky, but it does not contradict him in regard to the role of signs. The second point is that Galperin, unlike Leont'ev and his school, published little about his ideas until 1954, probably fearing they would be condemned.

However, on one issue Galperin disagrees with Vygotsky. He thinks that learning on particular topics goes through his phases with only minor reference to stages. After a learning task is presented by an adult, the learner receives a schema representing information about how to perform the actions required by the task. An example is that the child receives wooden blocks and is shown a model built with the blocks. They are to understand that the model is the schema for their actions and these should be to build the model. So, if the model is a building, they are to construct another one like it.

For Vygotsky, this phase of learning occurs largely through imitation and conditioning. So this introduction of learning to use an internal schema to control action is an addition to Vygotsky. However, it is not a contradiction of him, if we take Vygotsky's main message to be that above the age of 3 years the child's learning is both cultural and cognitive and involves the dominant role of signs. In fact, in this preliminary phase of learning we do not need learning to be particularly cognitive, as according to both Vygotsky and Galperin that will be added by the influence of signs in a later phase. Galperin's view is cultural in this early phase and is actually more cognitive than Vygotsky's view, as it involves schemata. The cultural nature of learning is seen both in the presentation of the schema and in other ways that the child is helped to succeed in the task, many of them involving scaffolding by adults.

Galperin (1989; Galperin & Kabylnitskaia, 1974) also argued that, after infancy, the first step in the socialisation of the child's actions and its accommodation to the schema is achieved through the influence that adults have on its attention. This is a problematic idea, as it not clear how the redirection of attention alone can produce learning. To attend to something means to direct the sense organs and their information-gathering power to some thing or things. But for this to produce learning the organism must process the information thus received and this must make a difference to its behaviour. So without some internal processing and pooling of information, merely redirecting attention will not result in learning.

Most approaches to learning deal with attention as part of a whole system of reactions. What Galperin seems to mean is something like Bekhterev's idea that conditioning is achieved through the use of attention. Here, it is assumed that the laws of conditioning will do duty for the internal processing system needed. Some more sophisticated internal processing would explain how the child learns through the redirection of attention in Galperin's situations.

In the next step in learning, actions are separated from the material objects (the wooden blocks) on which they had previously been performed. Now the child can represent such actions as building with blocks internally. Such internal actions are then connected to external speech. So the child might say 'This one's too long' to correct what it had done. This corresponds with Vygotsky's use of external speech in problem solving. This then leads on to whispered egocentric speech and then to inner speech, both of which are used to guide performance in the task.

In the next stage, the schema becomes a mental, internalised psychological tool, controlling performance. This schema is internalised by the learner and used to control both the internal and the external actions needed to make a model building. This turns it into an internal mental scheme that guides the building (Galperin, 1965, 1968, 1969, 1992; Galperin & Georgiev, 1969).

A further difference with Vygotsky is that after the first stage of external action, actions are internalised. So Galperin turns the internalisation of action into a separate process from the internalisation of speech. This was connected with Galperin's great interest in Piaget. He believed that through this assumption he would be able to build a bridge to Piagetian psychology, which relied greatly on the internalisation of action (Galperin & Elkonin, 1972; Galperin & Georgiev, 1969). Galperin's internalised actions, however, are socially directed and shaped actions, as in the case of making a building from blocks, while Piaget's were actions constructed by the individual.

This leads to perhaps the main problem with Galperin, which is that he is inclined to attribute the same degree of logical and mathematical precision and scope to internalised operations as Piaget. Piaget has no coherent explanation as to where these come from. Vygotsky thinks they arise from practices accompanied by the use of signs and that neither internal nor external operations unaccompanied by signs can manifest them. Galperin (Galperin & Elkonin, 1972; Galperin & Georgiev, 1969) thinks they can be manifested in internal actions and his main explanation for this is that the actions are guided by a schema provided by adults and are socially scaffolded. Society had discovered that these procedures lead to insight and success and so hands them on to young children. However, this leads to the problem of what this insight is. Galperin is sometimes tempted to appeal to Piaget's notion of a special kind of logical and mathematical experience; however, he realises that, at least in Piaget's hands, this often leads to assuming what we are trying to prove. We find thought has certain properties and we explain them as due to the properties of logical and mathematical experience. If we look again at such concrete examples as the conservations, we find that Galperin no more has a satisfactory explanation for these as purely the product of internalised action than does Piaget.

So far we have only looked at learning guided by images in the form of schemata. However, with development we find that speech and other signs are used. For an older child, for instance, we might just say 'Can you build me a house?' and here the guiding schema is 'Build me a house'. For younger children this will be interpreted as having a concrete meaning; for adolescents it will be interpreted as having a more abstract meaning, made up of concepts attached to signs proper (Galperin, 1977).

On the issue of the existence of stages, the truth probably lies somewhere closer to Galperin than Vygotsky. Vygotsky's stages are more sharply divided than is consistent with recent research (Flavell, 1985, 1992, 1996; Langford, 1987a); while Galperin's idea that there are also general limitations on what can be taught explains why we cannot teach differential calculus and other abstract conceptions to the average 4 year old.

Limited coverage Some current approaches cover only a limited range of what are usually considered to be central topics in cognitive development. This does not show that they are wrong. They could be trialling their approach on a limited range of topics prior to wider application: In fact they give the impression that this is their strategy. However, it is worth noting that the approaches of both Shweder and Carey & Spelke have this limitation.

Summary Vygotsky's arguments against approaches that do not stress the cultural role of signs were reviewed favourably. Available criteria for distinguishing between cultural-sign theories point in certain directions, without being definitive. The arguments against constructivism and in favour of distinguishing conceptions of the world from logic tell against writers such as Harre, Newman, Holzman and Wells. The most developed approaches remaining are those of Bruner, Galperin and Vygotsky. Both Bruner and Galperin were strongly influenced by Vygotsky. Although the views of Carey & Spelke and Shweder provide less comprehensive views of the topic, they contain material that would need to be integrated into any future synthesis.

Development of motivation and emotion

This is Vygotsky's most vulnerable area. His late approach takes the optimistic, rationalistic view of human nature, but he says little to support his stand here.

Freud

Vygotsky's rationalist view of motivation is in some respects difficult to contrast with opposing views, of which the most obvious would be that of Freud, because any test would require us to convert his qualitative statements into some more precise form. This is not just a problem with his way of stating his views, but with theories in this area generally. For instance, Vygotsky claims that the child can realistically assess the results of its actions at a reasonably early age. But to know what we could actually expect from this, it would need to be made more precise. So in areas of this kind we await more theoretical precision.

However, his particular claim that autistic thinking and motivation follow rather than, as Freud would have it, precede rational thought and motivation seems to have a definite advantage over Freud's approach. As Bleuler (1911, 1927) and Kretschmer (1926) pointed out, before Vygotsky, the Freudian idea that the hallucinatory fulfilment of wishes is the infant's first method of coping with the environment appears contrary to Darwin's theory of evolution. To be able to survive the infant should, as soon as possible, attempt realistic adaptation to the environment.

A second point, however, favours Freud and his followers, as well as many other biologically oriented schools, rather than Vygotsky. Vygotsky advocates Spinoza's idea that the child's main motivation is the development of competence and control. Since his time this has been advocated by others, notably Haworth (1986) and White (1959, 1960, 1972). Both Vygotsky and White appear to mean by this that mastery motivation comes to the fore when other more pressing needs are already met. This has been convincingly challenged for some periods of development (Bozhovich, 1968). It is, for instance, a persistent finding that, while mastery motivation and curiosity are strong in primary schoolchildren in the West, it tapers off rapidly in secondary school (Ausubel, Novak, & Hanesian, 1978; Good & Brophy, 1996; McMeniman, 1989). This suggests a need to modify his more global claims about this form of motivation.

Another point of comparison with Freud and others is that Vygotsky claimed that human nature is naturally social and governed by reason. The pessimists, by contrast, have viewed human nature as antisocial, particularly claiming it is naturally prone to violence and aggression (e.g. Freud, 1920;

Wilson, 1976). We can first of all consider this from a Darwinian point of view. We might think that Darwinian evolution could only select benevolence, as this benefits the species, and not antisocial aggression, as it is injurious to the species. This, however, would be to misunderstand such evolution, which contemporary thinking shows acts at the level of the gene and not at that either of the individual or of the species. Thus, animals will act to promote their own survival, as this promotes the perpetuation of their genes, but they will also act to promote the survival of close relatives, such as their own offspring, as these have relatively similar genes (Dawkins, 1999; Hölldobler & Wilson, 1990; Wilson, 1976, 1992). Male apes, in some species, as well as lions and other mammals, kill the previous offspring of females they have obtained mating rights over, in order to speed the process of creating their own offspring, thus advantaging their own genes. However, this theory also suggests that animals will act in a more diluted way in favour of the survival of any member of their species, as they have many genes in common with these members, provided this does not compete with the survival of their own offspring or close relatives. In the case of the males who kill the offspring of newly acquired females, they are killing gene packets that are less like themselves, in order to create ones more like themselves, which is what the theory predicts. However, helping unrelated members of the species, where there is little cost to the self or the self's projects for reproducing its gene packet, should have some, albeit lower, priority.

Although these are not the primary reasons Freud gives for his conclusions, they provide a stronger rationale for them than the ones he gives, which are couched in terms of general principles from physics rather than biology, particularly the second law of thermodynamics (Freud, 1920). Biology, in the nature of things, is bound to be a closer relative to psychology than physics. Vygotsky, by contrast, is placed in difficulty by this reasoning, which predicts that action in favour of one's own immediate relatives and offspring will predominate in social life, with generalised altruism only a secondary influence.

This problem is particularly acute for Vygotsky, as he has already appealed to Darwinian considerations in his argument against Freud's treatment of the origin of realistic action to achieve goals. Furthermore, we cannot just say that human beings have been subject to a long period of historical evolution following biological evolution and thus the Darwinian view is not operative. According to both Vygotsky and most orthodox biology human biological evolution stopped at or before the point that historical evolution began. If this is so, then we have inherited a biological makeup that is the product of Darwinian evolution and has not been altered since then.

While Vygotsky places most stress on Darwinian arguments in dealing with biological evolution, at times he flirts with the Lamarckian theory of biological evolution and even cites with some approval the use of Lamarckian concepts by K. Buhler (1913) and Lenin (1925) (Vygotsky, 1931b, p. 100). This approach says that evolution takes place because the acquired characteristics of organisms are inherited. So, a giraffe that stretches its neck to reach high foliage will pass genes for a longer neck to its offspring as a result of this stretching; according to Lenin (1925) someone who uses logical arguments frequently will pass this capacity to their offspring. However, Vygotsky was reluctant to place any great emphasis on this approach, which is just as well, as it has not fared well subsequently (Dawkins, 1999). Some evidence has appeared in recent years that the inheritance of acquired characteristics may occur in limited circumstances, but it still seems highly unlikely that this is one of the major mechanisms of biological evolution.

In conclusion, although Vygotsky scores over Freud on the issue of the developmental priority of rationality, he was probably wrong about the dominance of mastery motivation throughout development, while his optimistic view of human nature remains problematic from a Darwinian point of view, as well as from some others.

Existential and Jungian views of the self

The most distinctive aspect of Vygotsky's theory of the development of the self is his claim that, from some time after 7 years, a split develops between the inner and outer selves. His linking this with the appearance of inner speech, the considerable evidence there is for the importance of this at this time, the plausibility of his arguments about it and the additional evidence collected by Bozhovich and her colleagues, give this at least initial plausibility.

Vygotsky's view of the self is social, in that he has it depend on the person's social relations and use of signs, rather than the other way round (Vygotsky, 1933i). The most obvious contrast here is with individualist and idealist views of the self, such as those of Jung (1912), Jaspers (1913), R. D. Laing (1964), Perls (1947, 1973, 1989) and Tillich (1952, 1959).

In Laing, for instance, in development the inherent freedom of the human individual retreats inward in the face of an outer world that often turns people into things, that lack such freedom. For Laing, as for many other existentialists, the self has an essential nature that has not been internalised from outside. Rather, action is prompted by the efforts of the self to extricate itself from the contradictions inherent in its nature. In Laing (1964), the person often constructs a false self that is not free, so that the real self can hide behind it and remain unscathed. The outside world does not want us to be free, but if it can coerce the outer personality into being what social conformity requires, a good student, sister, team player, then it will leave the inner self to be free.

For Vygotsky, the self is rooted in relations with other people and in signs. In addition, he opposed the existential conception of the self as founded on metaphysical freedom (Vygotsky, 1931b, pp. 208–219, 1933l). This is the same Darwinian point that Vygotsky (1930o) and Vygotsky and Luria (1925) used against Freud's conception of the infantile self: That it gives the organism negative survival value to be primarily oriented to a self that begins from the problems of its own nature, rather than with those of living in the world. In addition, to think that we have absolute, metaphysical, freedom is to live in a world of delusion. So, on the same Darwinian ground that we used before, we must reject the idealists' view.

Many idealists, of course, reject Darwin and science in general, but if we are to reject both materialism and science we find ourselves outside the entire framework within which Vygotsky worked and would have to reject his ideas too. If we remain within it, we have to reject idealist views of the self.

Conclusions

Extensions to the theory by a number of authors were considered, namely: Bozhovich, McNeill, Ratner, Bruner and Wood. These all provide valuable additions. Although most can be criticised at points, even here they help to raise awareness about the issues a contemporary Vygotskyan must face.

Although many of the comparisons with other theories produced a positive indication for the revised Vygotskyan approach, none provides a definitive test, because of the lack of certainty about the premises of the arguments involved. However, the overall course of the tests is positive and shows why the theory is widely considered so promising.

In the area of cognitive development, theories that reject Vygotsky's argument that higher cognitive processes must result from cultural learning through signs cannot be favoured. This especially applies to those of Piaget and the neoPiagetians. Theories that accept this, such as those of Bruner, the Carey–Spelke style of modularism and Galperin are less easy to distinguish from him.

Vygotsky's view of the development of the self is preferable to those of Freud and the neoFreudians, on the Darwinian ground that the first self to appear will act to gain gratification in the real world, not an imaginary one.

One difficulty for the late theory is Vygotsky's attachment to the importance of curiosity and mastery motivation throughout development, which is contradicted by more recent research. There are also difficulties in relation to his optimistic view of human nature, although these are less specific.

In short, the greatest potential problems of the revised theory appear to be in the areas of motivation and human nature. I have stopped short of suggesting ways of replacing Vygotsky's assumptions here with alternatives, partly because the issues have not been thoroughly explored and partly because, in some cases, this would arguably produce something that is beyond the pale of what can reasonably be called Vygotskyan. Bozhovich (1968) began the process of amendment here, with her suggestion that the child is motivated by the opinions of others to a greater extent than Vygotsky thought; but further changes may be needed.

Part V

Conclusions

14 Conclusions

Vygotsky claimed it was his mission to develop a Marxist psychology. Although in most areas he did this by adopting Marx's ideas, he also altered them where he believed they were no longer viable. This particularly applies to his idea that there is a downward influence of signs, consciousness and self-consciousness on practice in the middle period of development. This contrasts with Marx's idea that tools and practice are the most important factors driving production forward until late in development.

Vygotsky's posture here leaves it open for him to say, which he does quite frequently, that he thinks the historical development of the forces of production leads that of the relations of work; this is one of the key claims of Marx's historical materialism. This is compatible with his stand on signs and self-consciousness, as, on Marx's own admission, key aspects of signs and self-consciousness are part of the forces of production. This is largely responsible for Vygotsky's frequent claim that his ideas are in accordance with Marx's historical materialism.

As part of his mission to develop a Marxist psychology, Vygotsky did not hesitate to use ideas from elsewhere, to fill out areas where he believed Marx to be weak, particularly in the areas of cognition and language. The main sources of these additional ideas were Hegel and Piaget, although Spinoza also played a significant role.

His attempts to develop such an approach went through two periods in the last years of his life: the third period, 1928–31, and the last period, 1932–34. In both, he used Marx's four levels of organisation in production as a framework: tools; social relations; signs and consciousness; and the self. He was also interested in the relation between the biological and historical development of the human species and the development of the child. Both the child and the human race end up at the same destination, namely the psychology of the modern adult. However, Vygotsky was keen to avoid two common reactions to this. First, the recapitulationism of Hall (1915, 1916, 1921), which is today better known from the more sophisticated version of Piaget (1945, 1965), which says that the child develops through the same series of stages as those found in the development of the species. Second, the idea that the child and history follow completely unrelated routes, which is not really credible if we think in terms of stages, but is compatible with an associationist perspective (e.g. Tylor, 1871).

Vygotsky suggests, rather, that the child and the species develop along the same dimensions, but in different ways. One of the main differences is that history is more devious and at times goes backwards, while the child avoids this.

In the third period, the child's development in infancy begins by recapitulating biological development quite closely. However, before this is fully complete, cultural development begins, which undertakes the same tasks as historical development, but in a different way.

The map of the child's cultural development is closely connected to the map of the original development of production, as analysed by Marx. As a result of the biological immaturity of the child, it passes through local stages of development in a simplified form. The child is said to pass through local stages, as the stages only apply to particular aspects of its development, rather than to its development as a whole. Self-consciousness shifts from partial to global with development and the levels influence one another, downward influences predominating in the middle period of development. His approach to when and how they influence one another lacks detail and definition.

In infancy and the first part of early childhood, the most dynamic feature of the individual's development is practice. After this, until mid-adolescence, the dynamics of the child's social system begins from social relations and then moves to their language and consciousness, then to self-consciousness, then to their practical activity or use of tools via language and consciousness and then back to social relations on a higher level. The most dynamic and creative part of this cycle is the one that involves signs and self-consciousness. Until adolescence, self-consciousness mainly takes the form of partial self-consciousness acting on single functions.

In the last period, the connection between the child and history is less direct and is in part given by the Hegelian contention that in the child the relation between form and content is reversed, compared to historical development. The four levels of organisation are conceived more broadly in the child, covering social activities generally, not just production or production-like activities. The remnants of reflexology found in the previous period are now replaced by such traditional cognitive concepts as propositional content. Self-consciousness is said to originate in infancy (0–1 years). It involves weakly focused consciousness of the external activities of the self, in the period from one to 7 years, although this is already sufficient to play a leading role in development. This is followed by the emergence of progressively better controlled and more sophisticated internal and external selves thereafter, to the end of adolescence. The levels continue to influence one another in a predominantly downward direction, with the whole approach, to when and how they do so, now acquiring more detail and definition.

The dynamic model now puts more stress on the role of self-consciousness in producing holistic changes in psychological systems of functions; and on conscious awareness, of having outgrown existing social relations, in producing periodic crisis-like changes in the relations between the child and adults. However, the sequence of dominant dynamic functions is still similar to that given earlier. There is still a shift, from dynamic functions that stress practice, up to about $2\frac{1}{2}$ years; through those that stress the use of signs, until about 16 years; to advanced concepts synthesising both practice and signs.

Knowledge is realistic in the first of these periods, because it is based on practice. In the second, it is realistic because the increasing independence of the child's social relations and self, with development, lead to context-free communication, which leads to concepts that more accurately reflect reality. In adolescence these sources of accurate knowledge of reality come together.

Vygotsky's views are quite dated today in relation to the rate of cognitive development in the average child. Children in developed countries, before adolescence, are cognitively more advanced, both today and at the time Vygotsky wrote, than he thought. He persistently underestimates them to the extent of about one of his stages. In personality development, the main problem of timing is that he places all the crises from 3 to 13 years of age, between six months and a year too late. These two problems do not cancel one another out, as the alterations needed for the cognitive changes are much greater than those needed for the crises.

Six changes to the theory will at least alleviate these and other problems. First, up to 12 years many cognitive changes appear about one of his stages earlier than he thought, particularly those involving meaning.

Second, the first change needs to be confined to the development of signs, meaning and related cognitive functions. This is because it is here that the problems lie. It can be done without disturbing the theory as a whole because many of the child's achievements in the areas of social relations and personality in the period 0–13 years are not closely tied by the theory to the stages in the development of signs and meaning. The linkage is through the understanding that more advanced cognition will equate to more independent social relations, which is a vague equation. This restriction is needed because other aspects of cognitive development, especially the internalisation of language, cannot so easily be detached from their background in the personality.

Third, the placement of play in the new scheme was reconsidered. Play may not be the main dynamic motor of development, driving the preschool age ($2\frac{1}{2}$–$6\frac{1}{2}$ years), as Vygotsky suggested. The precise use of speech, as found in mathematical and scientific vocabulary, was suggested as an alternative.

Fourth, Vygotsky's approach to the development of meaning assumed that signs proper would necessarily involve decontextualised and abstract meanings. This was questioned, both because there is no logical link here and because signs proper appear to become dominant in the child much younger than he thought, making them coincide with contextualised and concrete meanings.

Fifth, the form of the self found at the start of the first four stages is a modified form of the self from the previous stage, with the new form for the stage not readily detectable until the next stage.

Sixth, one of the main functions fulfilled by the ZPD (zone of proximal development) for Vygotsky in his last period was to cancel out the tendency for the main body of the theory to underestimate spontaneous meanings in the period 7–17 years. Teaching, he claimed, could accelerate cognitive development by slightly more than a complete stage. Within the adjusted version outlined above, this is no longer needed. This turns Vygotsky's supposition here into an unmotivated hypothesis that lacks any supporting evidence, while there is a good reason to reject it. Studies of concept attainment in tasks that do not help the child show that the spontaneous concepts that can be attained in this period are close to the observed level of those the child uses. It was suggested that teaching can in fact achieve an advance of only about one-third of a stage.

Aspects of these suggestions have been made previously by Bruner (1984a), Donaldson (1978, 1993, 1996), Van der Veer (1994, 1998) and Van der Veer and Van Ijzendoorn (1985).

These changes are in the spirit of the original theory and are necessitated by experimental and other empirical studies performed since Vygotsky's day. A more general problem, covered in Chapter 13, is that in his last period he assumes that the human animal is naturally social, in the sense of being altruistic and rational. A range of theoretical alternatives challenge this, including neoDarwinism, and Vygotsky presents no reason why we should accept his view rather than theirs. No attempt was made to adjudicate this issue, in view of the wide-ranging and intractable issues involved. However, two points are worth noting. First, if the Darwinian view, for instance, should be found to prevail, this would necessitate a more fundamental reworking of the theory than any of the points considered above. Second, even in the face of such a catastrophe much could probably be salvaged from the original theory, especially in the area of cognitive development. Brief comparisons between the modified version of Vygotsky and other theories of development were given. Vygotsky's theory can be viewed positively in its modified form, first and foremost because it makes the cultural development of the child through signs and self-consciousness the central focus of the theory. His evolutionary argument in favour of this is convincing, although it was anticipated by Mead (1909, 1910).

A comparison with other cultural-sign theories suggested that, although Vygotsky's is one of the strongest, there is a need to investigate whether some of the characteristics of the others would strengthen it further.

Some particular advantages of the theory are worth noting. It explains the link between historical and individual development in an original way that is more firmly linked to a definite theory of history than any other. A theory that does not do this is lacking an essential dimension. Vygotsky's theory also has the advantage that it is wider in scope than any of its rivals, covering both personality and cognitive development. It is a central principle of science that a successful theory with wider scope is to be preferred to a narrower one.

My main message about Vygotsky's method was that in his last three periods there is a considerable gap between what he *says* about it and what he *does* with it. He often says he will apply it to the data that he and his colleagues or others have produced and from this his theory will emerge. However, at other times, he admits, or we can at least infer, that most of his theoretical ideas came from Hegel, Marx and Spinoza. The idea that he came to his empirical studies with a blank slate is not tenable; in fact, he began with theoretical preconceptions. This is significant, as the blank theoretical slate view of empirical studies has made a comeback in recent years, both in education and in psychology (e.g. Lincoln & Guber, 1985). Although the contemporary view is not based on Vygotsky, having most of its roots in the anthropological methods that anthropologists apply to previously unknown tribes, it has acquired unearned prestige by being incorrectly associated with him.

Next, Vygotsky's educational significance. His greatest influence was in the Soviet Union, where his last writings became one of the main justifications for the centralised, and broadly traditional, system of education, that lasted from 1930 until the fall of the Soviet Union. His writings were used as a justification for this system and the system was widely admired for its high average attainments, as well as for the relatively narrow range of its outcomes.

It is common to hear that Vygotsky has had a huge influence on Western education. However, in reality it is not Vygotsky himself who has had most of this influence, especially in recent years, but a rather diminished version of Vygotsky's social progressivist educational philosophy, drawn from his third period. According to this version, Vygotsky thought that education must as far as possible involve a dialogue between teacher and student. Vygotsky's own view in this period was closer to the classic social progressivism of John Dewey (1897, 1916). A genuine aspect of Vygotsky's educational views has also been influential in the West. This is his stress, in both his last periods, on the need for the teacher to teach. Some interpreters, basing themselves on the third period, have assumed this was just a reference to scaffolding (e.g. Wells, 1999) or to a general shift to more teacher-centred teaching (e.g. Daniels, 1993). Some have recognised the extent of this admonishment in Vygotsky's last period (Karpov & Bransford, 1995). Although many other psychologists have advised the teacher to teach, such as Ausubel, Novak, and Hanesian (1978) and Good and Brophy (1996), Vygotsky's perceived advice to do this had great impact in the West in the 1980s, when the advice, derived from Piaget, to let the child discover, was waning. As Vygotsky was perceived at that time to be replacing Piaget in the estimation of Western educationalists, his slogan, for the teacher to teach, was to replace that of Piaget, for the child to discover. The pattern set in that decade has continued.

It is probably not too fanciful to see the stress on dialogism and scaffolding among Western Vygotskyans as part of an attempt to bridge the gap between the advice not to teach of the Piagetians and full-scale teacher-centred teaching. From this point of view it was and is understandable. What is less understandable is the unwillingness to adopt the real Vygotsky of the third period, the advocate of social progressivism, rather than the fictional Vygotsky of the dialogists. The real Vygotsky had more to offer and could have played this bridging role better.

In many of his educational writings, Vygotsky adopts an absolute rather than a contextual view of learning, especially as applied to the normal child. That is to say, he argues that there is one best way to teach, regardless of circumstances. However, in some circumstances, Vygotsky is far from an absolutist. We see this from his ideas about the child with learning difficulties, where he applies the context principle. However, there is a large amount of empirical evidence to show that the context principle is also true within the normal range (Bourke, 1989; Good & Brophy, 1985, 1996; Langford, 1989). In view of this, we need to modify his stance here to include the normal child.

This means that, in considering whether Vygotsky's social progressivism or modified traditionalism is to be preferred, we should consider the aims and context of the education concerned. Factors favouring each of the two forms of educational strategy were considered earlier. For instance, someone who believes the delivery of a standard or national curriculum is desirable will favour the modified traditional approach. Someone who distrusts the content of a particular centralised curriculum will favour social progressivism.

Turning to a final aspect of Vygotsky's theory: It has already been suggested that his approach to the relation between the child and historical development is a positive aspect of his theory, as it provides a detailed and concrete approach. However, it is not the only way to do this.

For his historical analysis Vygotsky chose Marx's account of the historical development of the productive forces, adapted to stress the role of signs and self-consciousness. His view of signs came largely from Hegel. His blend of Hegel and Marx is not derived from that of other Hegelian Marxists of his time, such as Korsch (1923) and Lukacs (1923). It seems to have arisen mainly from Vygotsky's independent attempts to use Hegel to fill the gaps in Marx.

One key issue in attitudes to Vygotsky is how far we could vary his Marxist view of history and still retain the point of the theory, even in a modified form. Presumably, adherents of Vygotsky's theory about children would not wish to find themselves locked into a theory of history they disagreed with. Although, in practice, many Western followers of Vygotsky simply ignore his historical views, as though they were merely peripheral, this is not an adequate way of coping with the problem.

First, any theory of history that retains the appropriate part of Marx's view of the historical development of the forces of production is compatible with Vygotsky's theory about children. So the whole of Marx's view of the social superstructure could be removed and replaced with something else. Another case would be that of someone who thought that Marx was largely right about history, but largely wrong about the nature of socialism and the future. This would also represent a sustainable historical view that could in broad outline be matched with Vygotsky's approach to child development, as his theory of children makes no use of this last part of historical development. Something close to this second view was held by a number of classical liberal theorists, particularly Adam Smith (1776), as well as by some of their more recent followers.

Another kind of link is vaguer, but seems to have some potential. This is to adopt the view of history of some neoHegelian writers. These retain the succession of forms of historical activity found in historical development, approximately as in Marx, but in theory stress the self as the driving factor in history, not economic production. However, like Hegel himself, they tend to be quite ambivalent about this relation, being tempted at critical points to stress the economic and military aspects of history. Given that Vygotsky's child is already substantially reliant on the self, compared to the corresponding historical processes, we might be able to bridge the gap by stressing the elements of production in the Hegelian accounts. Historical examples of this would be the neoHegelianism of Croce (1906), Green (1885–88) and Natorp (1899, 1904), who all promoted idealist versions of the liberal view of history. In our own time, an outstanding example is Francis Fukuyama, author of *The end of history and the last man* (1992) (see also Fukuyama, 1989, 1999, 2002). His provocative slogan that history has ended means that the development of history towards its end point in liberalism has now been completed, so we have now entered the last stage of history.

These examples are not the only ones possible, but they are sufficiently varied to illustrate my point. This is to avoid thinking that Vygotsky can be paired with any historical theory whatsoever, as well as to avoid thinking that only Vygotsky's slightly unorthodox Marxism will do. There are a range of historical theories that can be paired with him or with modifications of his views. At times Western commentators on Vygotsky seem to have been afraid that if the issue is examined in any detail, the Marxist option will emerge as the only one. These comments should show that this is far from the case, although they are not intended to decide which view of history is correct.

References

Note on Vygotsky references

Vygotsky references are given as the first citations in the bibliography attached to his collected works (Vygotsky, 1982–84, in Russian and Vygotsky, 1987–2000, in English). These have been compiled by the Russian editors on the basis that where an item was not published within about three years of being written the original manuscript is cited. The main reason for doing this is that it gives the best indication of when the items are likely to have been written, which is important for Vygotsky due to his radical changes of stance over short periods. Many publication dates are misleading as they are so different from the date of writing.

English translations are indicated at the end of this note. A Russian bibliography can be found in Volume 6 of the 1982–84 Russian version of the *Collected works* (Moscow: Pedagogika), which is reproduced in the 1987–2000 English version (New York: Kluwer). Updated versions of this can be found in Vygodskaya and Livanova (1996) and on the website of the Russian journal *Voprosy Psykhologii* (www.voppsy.ru/journals).

English translations

L. S. Vygotsky (1987–2000). *The collected works of L. S. Vygotsky. Vols 1–6*. (M. Hall, Trans.). New York: Kluwer. This contains Vygotsky 1925a–c, 1926a, b, e, 1927b, d, 1928d, 1930c, g, k, n, o, q, 1931a–c, 1932b, d, e, 1933a, b, e, f, g, i, j, l, 1934c, g. Also the collection of articles titled *Problems of child development* (1960).

L. S. Vygotsky (1971). *The psychology of art*. Cambridge, MA: MIT Press. An enjoyable translation of Vygotsky 1925a, his most readable major work.

L. S. Vygotsky (1978). *Mind in society*. Cambridge, MA: Harvard. This contains abridged versions of Vygotsky 1935a, d, g.

L. S. Vygotsky (1988). *Thought and language* (A. Kozulin, Trans.). Cambridge, MA: MIT Press. This contains the most readable translation to date of Vygotsky 1934c, although the Hall version in the *Collected works* is accurate if you are prepared for some slight extra work.

L. S. Vygotsky (1997). *Educational psychology* (S. Silverman, Trans.). Boca Raton, FL: St. Lucie Press. This is a translation of Vygotsky 1926c.

Soviet Psychology. This translation journal contains two items that have not otherwise appeared in English. These are 1933m (1987, *26*, 72–77), 1935e (1987, *26*, 78–85).

R. Van der Veer, & A. Valsiner (Eds.). (1994). *The Vygotsky reader*. Oxford: Blackwell.

This contains 1929h, 1930h, a fuller version of parts of 1931a than in the *Collected works*, 1934a, 1934e, Lect. 4.

[Page numbers in the text, where an English translation is available, are those in the English *Collected works*.]

References

Ach, N. (1921). *Über die Begriffbildung. Eine experimentelle Untersuchung* [On learning concepts. An experimental investigation]. Berlin: Bamberg.

Adler, A. (1907). *Studie über Minderwertigkeit von Organen* [Studies on organ inferiority]. Berlin: Urban & Schwarzenberg.

Adler, A. (1927). *Individualpsychologie in der Schule: Vorlesungen für Lehrer und Schuler* [Individual psychology in the school: Lectures for teachers and students]. Frankfurt: Fischer.

Adler, A. (1930a). *The education of children* (B. Ginzburg, Trans.). London: Allen & Unwin.

Adler, A. (1930b). *Guiding the child on the principles of individual psychology* (B. Ginzburg, Trans.). London: Allen & Unwin.

Adler, A., & Furtmuller, C. (1914). *Heilen und Bilden: Ärztlich-pädagogische Arbeiten des Vereins für Individualpsychologie* [Therapy and education: Medico-educational studies based on individual psychology]. Munich: Reinhardt.

Althusser, L. (1970). *On reading Capital*. London: New Left Books.

Apperly, I. A., & Robinson, E. J. (1998). Children's mental representation of referential relations. *Cognition, 67*, 3, 287–309.

Arnold, M. (1869). *Culture and anarchy: An essay in political and social criticism*. London: T. Nelson.

Ault, R. (1977). *Cognitive development*. Oxford: Oxford University Press.

Ausubel, D. P., Novak, J. D., & Hanesian, H. (1978). *Educational psychology: A cognitive view*. New York: Holt, Rinehart & Winston.

Ausubel, D. P., Sullivan, S., & Ives, B. (1980). *Developmental psychology*. New York: Grune and Stratton.

Baillargeon, R. (1998). Infants' understanding of the physical world. In M. Sabourin (Ed.), *Advances in psychological science*. New York: Psychology Press, pp. 503–529.

Baillargeon, R. (2002). The acquisition of physical knowledge in infancy: A summary in eight lessons. In U. Goswami (Ed.), *Blackwell handbook of childhood cognitive development*. Malden, MA: Blackwell, pp. 47–83.

Baillargeon, R., & Wang, S. (2002). Event categorization in infancy. *Trends in Cognitive Sciences, 6*, 2, 85–93.

Bakhtin, M. M. (1981). *The dialogic imagination*. Austin, TX: University of Texas Press.

Baldwin, J. M. (1911–1912). *Mental development of the child as an individual and of the human race. Volumes 1 & 2*. New York: Longman Green.

Bandura, A. (1991). Social-cognitive theory of moral thought and action. In W. M. Kurtines & J. L. Gewirtz (Eds.), *Handbook of moral behaviour and development. Volume 1*. Hillsdale, NJ: Lawrence Erlbaum Associates, Inc.

Bandura, A., & Walters, D. (1964). *Social learning theory*. New York: Nostrand.

Barnes, S., Gutfreund, M., Satterly, D., & Wells, G. (1983). Characteristics of adult speech which predict children's language development. *Journal of Child Language, 10*, 1, 65–84.

Bartlett, F. (1932). *Remembering*. Cambridge: Cambridge University Press.

Bekhterev, V. M. (1904). *Mind and life*. St. Petersburg: K. L. Rikker.

Bekhterev, V. M. (1921). *Kollektivniija refleksologija* [Group reflexology]. St. Petersburg: K. L. Rikker.

Bekhterev, V. M. (1926a). *Obshchie osnovy refleksologii cheloveka* [General fundamentals of human reflexology]. Leningrad: Nauka.

Bekhterev, V. M. (1926b). *Rabota golovnogo morga* [The functioning of the brain]. Leningrad: GIT.

Bennett, N. (1976). *Teaching styles and pupil progress*. Cambridge, MA: Harvard University Press.

Bennett, N., Wood, L., & Rogers, J. (1984). *The quality of pupil learning experiences*. Hillsdale, NJ: Lawrence Erlbaum Associates, Inc.

Berk, L. E. (1992). Children's private speech: An overview of theory and the status of research. In R. M. Diaz and L. E. Berk (Eds.), *Private speech: From social interaction to self-regulation*. Hillsdale, NJ: Lawrence Erlbaum Associates, Inc., pp. 17–53.

Berk, L. E., & Winsler, A. (1999). *Scaffolding children's learning: Vygotsky and early childhood education*. Washington, DC: National Association for the Education of Young Children.

Bernstein, B. (1960). Language and social class. *British Journal of Sociology, 11*, 271–276.

Bernstein, B. (1961). Aspects of language and learning in the genesis of the social process. *Journal of Child Psychology and Psychiatry, 1*, 313–324.

Bernstein, B. (1993). Introduction. In H. Daniels (Ed.), *Charting the agenda: Educational activity after Vygotsky*. London: Routledge.

Bernstein, B. (1994). Oppositional codes and social class relations: Rejoinder. *British Journal of Sociology, 45*, 1, 103–108.

Bernstein, B. (1995). Codes oppositional, reproductive and deficit: A case of red herrings. *British Journal of Sociology, 46*, 1, 133–142.

Bernstein, B. (2001). Symbolic control: Issues of empirical description of agencies and agents. *International Journal of Social Research Methodology: Theory & Practice, 4*, 1, 21–33.

Berry, J. W., Poortinga, Y. H., Segall, M. H., & Dasen, P. R. (1992). *Cross-cultural psychology: Research and applications*. New York: Cambridge University Press.

Bleuler, E. (1911). *Dementia praecox oder Gruppe der Schizophrenien* [Dementia praecox or a group of schizophrenias]. Leipzig and Vienna: Deuticke.

Bleuler, E. (1927). *Autistische Denken* [Autistic thinking]. Munich: Bloch.

Bliss, J. (1987). *A developmental study of children's ability to make inferences*. PhD thesis, University of London.

Bliss, J. (1996). Externalizing thinking through modeling: ESRC tools for exploratory learning research program. In S. Vosniadou, S. De Corte, and E. De Corte (Eds.), *International perspectives on the design of technology-supported learning environments*. Hillsdale, NJ: Lawrence Erlbaum Associates, Inc., pp. 25–40.

Bliss, J., & Ogborn, J. (1989). Tools for exploratory learning. *Journal of Computer Assisted Learning, 5*, 1, 37–50.

Bloom, A. (1987). *The closing of the American mind*. New York: Simon & Schuster.

Bloom, L. (1984). Review of M. Atkinson: 'Explanation in the study of child language development'. *Journal of Child Language, 11*, 215–222.

Bloom, L. (1970). *Language development*. Cambridge, MA: MIT Press.

Bloom, P., & Keil, F. C. (2001). Thinking through language. *Mind and Language, 16*, 4, 351–367.

Bogdanov, A. A. (1920). *Elementi proletarskoi kulturi v razvitii ravochego klassa* [Elements of proletarian culture and the development of the rising class]. Moscow: Organon.

Booth, D. (1975). *Pattern painting by the young child.* MEd thesis, University of Sydney.

Booth, D. (1982). Art education and children's spontaneous pattern painting. *Journal of the Institute of Art Education, 6*, 1–16.

Booth, D. (1984). An experimental study of pattern painting by kindergarten children. *Journal of the Institute of Art Education, 8*, 19–24.

Bountrogianni, M., & Pratt, M. (1990). Dynamic assessment: Implications for classroom consultation, peer tutoring and parent education. In J. A. Siegel (Ed.), *Effective consultation in school psychology*. Kirkland, WA: Hogrefe & Huber, pp. 129–140.

Bourke, S. (1989). Teaching methods. In P. E. Langford (Ed.), *Educational psychology: An Australian perspective*. Melbourne: Longman.

Bower, T. G. R. (1974). *Infancy*. San Francisco: Freeman.

Bowlby, J. (1984). *Attachment and loss, Vol. 1. Attachment* (2nd ed.). London: Hogarth.

Bozhovich, L. I. (1968). *Lichnost i ee formirovanie v detskom vorraste* [Personality and its formation during childhood]. Moscow: Pedagogika.

Bozhovich, L. I. (1977). Kontseptjaia kult'urno-istorichesk razvitiji i ee perspektivy. [The idea of the cultural-historical development of the mind and its subsequent development]. *Voprosy Psikhologii, 24*, 29–39.

Bozhovich, L. I. (1997). Razvitie yzikovoi kompetenii skolnikov [Development of the language competence of schoolchildren]. *Voprosy Psikhologii, 41*, 33–41.

Bozhovich, L. I., & Slavina, L. S. (1979). *Psikhicheska razvitie shkolnyka i ego* [The psychological development of the self in the schoolchild]. Moscow: Znanie.

Brown, A. L. (2002). Patterns of thought and prime factorization. In S. R. Campbell and R. Zazkis (Eds.), *Learning and teaching number theory: Research in cognition and instruction*. Westport, CT: Ablex, pp. 131–137.

Brown, A. L., Campione, J. C., Reeve, R. A., Ferrara, R. A., & Palincsar, A. S. (1991). Interactive learning and individual understanding: The case of reading and mathematics. In L. T. Landsmann (Ed.), *Culture, schooling, and psychological development*. Westport, CT: Ablex, pp. 136–170.

Brown, A. L., & Reeve, R. A. (1987). Bandwidths of competence: The role of supportive contexts in learning and development. In L. S. Liben (Ed.), *Development and learning: Conflict or congruence?* Hillsdale, NJ: Lawrence Erlbaum Associates, Inc., pp. 173–223.

Brown, A. L., Thomas, K., & Tolias, G. (2002). Conceptions of divisibility: Success and understanding. In S. R. Campbell & R. Zazkis (Eds.), *Learning and teaching number theory: Research in cognition and instruction*. Westport, CT: Ablex, pp. 41–82.

Brown, R. (1958). How shall a thing be called? *Psychological Bulletin, 65*, 14–21.

Brown, R. (1973). *A first language: The early stages*. Cambridge, MA: Harvard University Press.

Bruner, J. S. (1964). The course of cognitive growth. *American Psychologist, 19*, 1, 1–15.

Bruner, J. S. (1981a). The social context of language acquisition. *Language and Communication, 1*, 155–178.

Bruner, J. S. (1981b). The pragmatics of acquisition. *Behavioural Development: A Series of Monographs, 1*, 39–55.

Bruner, J. S. (1983). Education as social invention. *Journal of Social Issues*, *39*, 4, 129–141.

Bruner, J. S. (1984a). Vygotsky's zone of proximal development: The hidden agenda. *New Directions for Child Development*, *23*, 93–97.

Bruner, J. S. (1984b). Interaction, communication, and self. *Journal of the American Academy of Child Psychiatry*, *23*, 1, 1–7.

Bruner, J. S. (1987). Prologue. In C. Rieber (Ed.), *Collected Works of L. S. Vygotsky. Vol. 1*. New York: Plenum, pp. 3–15.

Bruner, J. S. (1990). Culture and human development: A new look. *Human Development*, *33*, 6, 344–355.

Bruner, J. S. (1996). *The culture of education*. Cambridge, MA: Harvard University Press.

Bruner, J. S., Goodnow, J., & Austin, G. (1956). *A study of thinking*. New York: Wiley.

Bryant, P. (2002). Children's thoughts about reading and spelling. *Scientific Studies of Reading*, *6*, 2, 199–216.

Bryant, P., & Bradley, B. (1985). *Children's reading problems*. Oxford: Blackwell.

Bryant, P., Nunes, T., & Bindman, M. (2000). The relations between children's linguistic awareness and spelling: The case of the apostrophe. *Reading & Writing*, *12*, 3–4, 253–276.

Buhler, C. (1928). *Kindheit und Jugend*. [Childhood and youth] (4th ed.). Göttingen: Hogrefe.

Buhler, K. (1907). Tatsachen und Probleme zu einer Psychologie der Denkvorgänge [Tasks and problems for a psychology of the process of thinking]. *Archiv für Gesamte Psychologie*, *9*, 12.

Buhler, K. (1913). *Die Gestaltswahrnehmungen. 1. Experimentelle Untersuchungen zur Psychologischen und Asthetischen Analyse der Raum und Zeitanschauung* [Perceiving wholes. 1. Experimental investigations towards the psychological and aesthetic analysis of space and time]. Stuttgart: Schmidt.

Buhler, K. (1918). *Die geistige Entwicklung des Kindes* [The mental development of the child]. Jena: Fischer.

Buhler, K. (1922). *Die Theorie der Perzeption* [The theory of perception]. Jena: Fischer.

Burkhardt, H., & Smith, B. (1999). *Handbook of metaphysics and ontology. Volume 1*. Munich: Philosophia.

Busemann, A. (1925). Kollektive Selbsterziehung in Kindheit und Jugend [Collective self-education in childhood and youth]. *Zeitschrift für Pedagogische Psychologie*, *5*, 102–123.

Busemann, A. (1926). *Die Jugend im Eigenen Worte* [Youth in its own words]. Geneva: Langensalz.

Busemann, A. (1927). Die Erregungsphasen [The periods of crisis]. *Zeitschrift für Kinderforschung*, *1*, 2, 56–72.

Butterworth, G., & Grover, L. (1988). The origins of referential communication in human infancy. In L. Weiskrantz (Ed.), *Thought without language: A Fyssen Foundation symposium*. Oxford: Clarendon.

Butterworth, G., & Grover, L. (1989). Social cognition in infancy. *Revue Internationale de Psychologie Sociale*, *2*, 1, 9–22.

Butterworth, G., & Grover, L. (1990). Attenzione visiva congiunta, gesto dimostrativo e comunicazione preverbale nel lattante [Joint visual attention, demonstrative gestures, and preverbal communication in infants]. *Eta Evolutiva*, *37*, 59–70.

Candland, D. K. (1993). *Feral children and clever animals: Reflections on human nature*. London: Oxford University Press.

Cannon, W. B. (1927a). *The physiology of emotion*. London: Routledge.

Cannon, W. B. (1927b). The James-Lange theory of emotions. A critical examination and an alternative theory. *American Journal of Psychology*, *39*, 189–224.

Cannon, W. B. (1929). *Bodily changes in pain, hunger, fear and rage* (2nd ed.). Boston, MA: Macmillan.

Carey, S. (1995). On the origin of causal understanding. In D. Sperber, D. Premack, & A. J. Premack (Eds.), *Causal cognititon: A multidisciplinary debate*. Oxford: Clarendon, pp. 268–302.

Carey, S. (1996). Cognitive domains as modes of thought. In D. R. Olson & N. Torrance (Eds.), *Modes of thought: Explorations in culture and cognition*. Cambridge: Cambridge University Press, pp. 187–215.

Carey, S., & Spelke, E. (1994). Domain specific knowledge and conceptual change. In L. A. Hirschfield & S. A. Gelman (Eds.), *Mapping the mind: Domain specificity in culture and cognititon*. New York: Cambridge University Press, pp. 169–200.

Carey, S., & Spelke, E. (1996). Science and core knowledge. *Philosophy of Science*, *63*, 515–533.

Carr, E. H. (1954). *The interregnum 1923–24: A history of Soviet Russia*. London: Macmillan.

Carr, E. H., & Davies, R. W. (1969–1978). *Foundations of a planned economy, 1926–1929, Vols 1–3: A history of Soviet Russia*. London: Macmillan.

Carrol, J. (1975). *Breakout from the crystal palace*. London: Routledge.

Case, R. (1988). The whole child: Toward an integrated view of young children's cognitive, social, and emotional development. In A. D. Pellegrini (Ed.), *Psychological bases for early education*. Oxford: Wiley, pp. 155–184.

Case, R. (1991). *The mind's staircase: Exploring the conceptual underpinnings of children's thought and knowledge*. Hillsdale, NJ: Lawrence Erlbaum and Associates, Inc.

Case, R., & Okamoto, Y. (1996). The role of central conceptual structures in the development of children's thought. *Monographs of the Society for Research in Child Development*, *61*, 1–2, 1–265.

Chelpanov, G. I. (1917). V analiticheskom metode v psikhologii [Analytical method in psychology]. *Psikhologicheskoe Obozrenie*, *11*, 36–54.

Chelpanov, G. I. (1924). *Psikhologija i marksizm* [Psychology and Marxism]. Moscow: A. V. Durnov.

Chelpanov, G. I. (1925). *Obelaivnaja psikhologija v Rossii i Amerik*. [An assessment of psychology in Russia and America]. Moscow: A. V. Durnov.

Chelpanov, G. I. (1926). *Sociatnoia psikhologiia di uslovnye refleksy* [Social psychology and conditioned reflexes]. Moscow and Leningrad: A. V. Durnov.

Chomsky, N. (1959). Review of B. F. Skinner's *Verbal Behavior*. *Language*, *35*, 26–58.

Chomsky, N. (1965). *Aspects of the theory of syntax*. New York: Wiley.

Chomsky, N. (1966). *Cartesian linguistics*. New York: Harper & Row.

Chomsky, N. (1980a). *Lectures on government and binding*. Milan: Forint.

Chomsky, N. (1980b). *Rules and representations*. New York: Columbia University Press.

Chomsky, N. (1995). *The minimalist program*. Cambridge, MA: MIT Press.

Clark, H., & Clark, E. (1977). *Psychology and language: An introduction to psycholinguistics*. New York: Harcourt, Brace, Jovanovich.

Clay, M. M., & Cazden, C. B. (1992). A Vygotskian interpretation of reading recovery. In Luis C. Moll (Ed.), *Vygotsky and education: Instructional implications and applications of sociohistorical psychology*. New York: Cambridge University Press, pp. 206–222.

Cocciarella, N. (1987). *Logical studies in early analytic philosophy*. London: Unwin.

Colby, A., & Kohlberg, L. (1987). *The measurement of moral judgement, Vol. 1*. Cambridge: Cambridge University Press.

Cole, M. (1971). *The cultural context of learning and thinking: An exploration in experimental anthropology*. London: Methuen.

Cole, M. (1988). Cross-cultural research in the sociohistorical tradition. *Human Development*, *31*, 137–152.

Cole, M. (1996). *Cultural psychology: The once and future discipline*. New York: UWB.

Cole, M., & Wertsch, J. V. (1996). Beyond the individual-social antinomy in discussions of Piaget and Vygotsky. *Human Development*, *39*, 5, 250–256.

Colletti, L. (1969). *Il marxismo e Hegel* [Marxism and Hegel]. Bari: Laterza.

Colletti, L. (1974). Introduction. In L. Colletti (Ed.), *The young Marx*. Harmondsworth: Penguin.

Colletti, L. (1992). *La logica di Benedetto Croce* [The logic of Benedetto Croce]. Marco: Lungro di Cosenza.

Collis, K. F. (1975). *A study of concrete and formal operations in school mathematics*. Melbourne: ACER.

Collis, K. F. (1989). Assessment. In P. Langford (Ed.), *Educational psychology: An Australian perspective*. Melbourne: Longman.

Comrie, B. (2000). From potential to realization: An episode in the origin of language. *Linguistics*, *38*, 5, 989–1004.

Cornejo, C. (2001). Piaget, Vigotski y Maturana: Tres voces, dos constructivismos [Piaget, Vygotsky and Maturana: Three voices, two constructivisms]. *Revista de la Escuela de Psicologia*, *10*, 2, 87–96.

Crace, J. (2003). Helsinki solutions. *The Guardian*, 3 October, p. 13.

Croce, B. (1906). *What is living and what is dead in the philosophy of Hegel* (G. Ainslie, Trans.). London: Longman Green.

Cross, T. (1978a). Mothers' speech and its association with rate of linguistic development in young children. In N. Waterson & C. E. Snow (Eds.), *Development of communication*. London: Wiley.

Cross, T. (1978b). *Mother–infant interaction in the study of child language development*. PhD thesis, University of Melbourne.

Cummin, C. S. (1999). State schools versus private: Another look. *The Age*, 23 November.

Daniels, H. (1993). Vygotskian theory and special education practice in Russia. *Educational Studies*, *19*, 79–90.

Daniels, H. (2001). *Vygotsky and pedagogy*. London: Routledge.

Darwin, C. (1881). *Observations of the life of a child*. London: Green.

Dasen, P. (1973). Piagetian research in central Australia. In G. E. Kearney, P. R. de Lacey, & G. R. Davidson (Eds.), *The psychology of aboriginal Australians*. Sydney: Wiley.

Dasen, P. R. (1988). Between the universal and the specific: The contribution of the cross-cultural approach. *Archives de Psychologie*, *56*, 219, 265–269.

Dasen, P. R. (1993). Theoretical/conceptual issues in developmental research in Africa. *Journal of Psychology in Africa, South of the Sahara, the Caribbean, and Afro-Latin America*, *1*, 5, 151–158.

Dasen, P. R. (1998). Cadres theoriques en psychologie interculturelle. [Theoretical levels in cross-cultural psychology]. In J. G. Adair and D. Belanger (Eds.), *Advances in psychological science, Vol. 1: Social, personal, and cultural aspects*. Hove, UK: Psychology Press, pp. 205–227.

Dawkins, R. (1999). *The extended phenotype: The long reach of the gene* (2nd ed.). Oxford: Oxford University Press.

De Guerrero, M. C. M., & Villamil, O. S. (1994). Social-cognitive dimensions of interaction in L2 peer revision. *Modern Language Journal*, *78*, 4, 484–496.

De Guerrero, M. C. M., & Villamil, O. S. (2000). Activating the ZPD: Mutual scaffolding in L2 peer revision. *Modern Language Journal*, *84*, 1, 51–68.

de Villiers, J. G., & de Villiers, P. A. (1984). *Language development*. Englewood Cliffs, NJ: Prentice Hall.

de Villiers, J. G., & de Villiers, P. A. (1999). Language development. In M. H. Bornstein and M. E. Lamb (Eds.), *Developmental psychology: An advanced textbook* (4th ed.). Mahwah, NJ: Lawrence Erlbaum Associates, Inc., pp. 313–373.

Deborin, A. M. (1909). Dialekticeskij materializm [Dialectical materialism]. In *Na rubeze. Kriticeskij sbornik* [On the edge. A critical collection]. St. Petersburg: Witsch.

Deborin, A. M. (1923). *Vvedenie v filosofija dialekticheskogo materializma* [Introduction to the philosophy of dialectical materialism]. Moscow: Nauka.

Deborin, A. M. (1929). *Dialektika i estestvoznanie* [Dialectics and natural science]. Moscow and Leningrad: Nauka.

deCharms, R. (1984). Motivational enhancement in educational settings. In R. Ames & C. Ames (Eds.), *Research on motivation in education. Vol. 1: Student motivation*. Orlando, FL: Academic Press.

Delacroix, H. J. (1924a). *Le langage et la pensée* [Language and thought] (1st ed.). Paris: Alcan.

Delacroix, H. J. (1924b). Les conditions psychologiques du langage. [The psychological conditions for language]. *Revue Philosophique*, *97*, 28–66.

Delacroix, H. J. (1926). *L'analyse psychologique de la fonction linguistique* [Psychological analysis of the linguistic function]. Oxford: Clarendon.

Delacroix, H. J. (1930). *Le langage et la pensée* [Language and thought] (2nd ed.). Paris: Alcan.

Demetriou, A. (1998). Nooplasis: 10 + 1 postulates about the formation of mind. *Learning & Instruction*, *8*, 4, 271–287.

Demetriou, A. (2003). Mind, self, and personality: Dynamic interactions from late childhood to early adulthood. *Journal of Adult Development*, *10*, 3, 151–171.

Demetriou, A., Efklides, A., & Platsidou, M. (1993). The architecture and dynamics of developing mind: Experiential structuralism as a frame for unifying cognitive developmental theories. *Monographs of the Society for Research in Child Development*, *58*, 5–6, 1–167.

Demetriou, A., Kyriakides, L., & Avraamidou, C. (2003). The missing link in the relations between intelligence and personality. *Journal of Research in Personality*, *37*, 6, 547–581.

Denham, S. (1998). *Emotional development in young children*. New York: Guilford.

Descartes, R. (1637). *Discours de la methode* [Discourse on method]. Paris: Jacques.

Dewey, J. (1897). My pedagogic creed. *The School Journal*, *54*, 77–80.

Dewey, J. (1915). *The psychology and pedagogy of thinking*. Boston, MA: Longman Green.

Dewey, J. (1916). *Democracy and education*. New York: Macmillan.

Dienes, Z. P. (1960). *Building up mathematics*. New York: Hutchinson.

Dienes, Z. P. (1966). *Mathematics in the primary school*. London: Macmillan.

Dirlan, D. (1980). Categories and development. In S. Modgil & C. Modgil (Eds.), *Towards a theory of psychological development*. Slough, UK: NFER, pp. 246–263.

Donaldson, M. (1978). *Children's minds*. London: Fontana.

Donaldson, M. (1993). *Human minds*. London: Fontana.

Donaldson, M. (1996). Humanly possible: Education and the scope of the mind. In D. R. Olson, and N. Torrance (Eds.), *The handbook of education and human development: New models of learning, teaching and schooling*. Malden, MA: Blackwell, pp. 324–344.

Durkheim, E. (1912). *Les formes elementaires de la vie religieuse* [The elementary forms of the religious life]. Paris: Alcan.

Ehri, L. C., Nunes, S. R., Stahl, S. A., & Willows, D. M. (2001). Systematic phonics instruction helps students learn to read: Evidence from the National Reading Panel's meta-analysis. *Review of Educational Research*, *71*, 3, 393–447.

Eliasberg, W. (1923). General review: Recent work on the psychology of forming concepts. *Psychological Bulletin*, *20*, 427–437.

Eliasberg, W. (1925). *Psychologie und Pathologie der Abstraktion, mit Aphorismen zur Psychologie des fernerstehenden Seelenlebens* [Psychology and pathology of abstraction, with aphorisms on the psychology of the more remote forms of mental life]. Leipzig: Ewig.

Elkind, D. (Ed.) (1991). *Perspectives on early childhood education: Growing with young children toward the 21st century*. Washington, DC: National Education Association.

Elkind, D. (1999). Educational research and the science of education. *Educational Psychology Review*, *11*, 3, 271–287.

Elkind, D. (2000). A quixotic approach to issues in early childhood education. *Human Development*, *43*, 4–5, 279–283.

Elkonin, B. D. (1993). The crisis of childhood and foundations for designing forms of child development. *Journal of Russian & East European Psychology*, *31*, 3, 56–71.

Elkonin, B. D. (1994). Historical crisis of childhood: Developing D. B. Elkonin's concept. In A. Alvarez & P. del Rio (Eds.), *Education as cultural construction*. Madrid: Fundacion Infancia y Aprendizaje, pp. 47–52.

Elkonin, B. D. (1996). L. S. Vygotsky i D. B. Elkonin: Znakovoe oposredstvovanie i sovokupnoe deistvie [L. S. Vygotsky and D. B. Elkonin: Sign mediation]. *Voprosi Psikhologii*, *40*, 57–65.

Elkonin, D. B. (1971). Problema periodizatsii psikhologicheskogo razvitia v detskom vozraste [The problem of the periodisation of development during childhood]. *Voprosi Psikhologii*, *4*, 6–20.

Elkonin, D. B. (1984). Posleslovie [Epilogue]. In L. S. Vygotsky, *Sobranie Sochinenii, Tom. 4* [Collected Works, Vol. 4]. Moscow: Pedagogika, pp. 386–403.

Elkonin, D. B., & Dragunova, T. V. (Eds.) (1967). *Vozrastnye i individual'nye osobemlostimladshikh podrostltov* [Age and the development of individual differences]. Moscow: Prosveschenie.

Engels, F. (1878). *Anti-Dühring*. Leipzig: Vorwärts.

Engels, F. (1879). *Dialectics of nature*. Chicago: Kerr.

Engels, F. (1886). Ludwig Feuerbach und der Ausgang der klassischen Deutschen Philosophie [Ludwig Feuerbach and the end of classical German philososphy]. *Die Neue Zeit*, *4*, 1–16.

Engels, F. (1896). The part played by labour in the transition from ape to man. *Die Neue Zeit*, *14*, 545–556.

Erdmann, J. E. (1902). *Abhandlung über Leib und Seele: Eine Vorschule zu Hegel's Philosophie des Geistes* [A treatment of life and soul: A preliminary course on Hegel's philosophy of spirit]. Leiden: A. H. Adriani.

Erikson, E. (1960). *Childhood and society* (2nd ed.). Harmondsworth: Penguin.

Erikson, E. (1968). *Identity, youth and crisis*. New York: Van Nostrand.

Evans, J. St. B. T. (2002). Logic and human reasoning: An assessment of the deduction paradigm. *Psychological Bulletin*, *128*, 6, 978–996.

Evans, J. St. B. T., & Over, D. (1997). Rationality in reasoning: The problem of deductive competence. *Cahiers de Psychologie Cognitive/Current Psychology of Cognition*, *16*, 1–2, 3–38.

Evans, J. St B. T., Newstead, S. E., & Byrne, R. M. J. (1993). *Human reasoning: The psychology of deduction*. Hove, UK: Lawrence Erlbaum Associates Ltd.

Exner, F. S., Rosenkranz, K., & Erdmann J. E. (1842). *Die Psychologie der Hegelschen Schule, Hefte 1 & 2* [The psychology of the Hegelian school, Vols 1 & 2]. Leipzig: Fischer.

Fabio, R. A. (2005). Dynamic assessment of intelligence is a better reply to adaptive behavior and cognitive plasticity. *Journal of General Psychology*, *132*, 1, 41–64.

Feuerbach, L. (1840). *Der Wesen Christentums* [The essence of Christianity]. Leipzig: Schmidt.

Flavell, J. H. (1985). *Cognitive development*. Englewood Cliffs: Prentice Hall.

Flavell, J. H. (1992). Cognitive development: Past, present, and future. *Developmental Psychology*, *28*, 6, 998–1005.

Flavell, J. H. (1996). Piaget's legacy. *Psychological Science*, *7*, 4, 200–203.

Fodor, J. A. (1975). *The language of thought*. New York: Thomas Y. Crowell.

Fodor, J. A. (1983). *The modularity of mind*. Cambridge, MA: MIT Press.

Forman, E. A., & Cazden, C. B. (1994). Exploring Vygotskian perspectives in education: The cognitive value of peer interaction. In R. B. Ruddell & M. R. Ruddell (Eds.), *Theoretical models and processes of reading* (4th ed.). Newark, DE: International Reading Association, pp. 155–178.

Fraser, C., & Roberts, N. (1975). Mothers' speech to children of four different ages. *Journal of Psycholinguistics*, *4*, 9–16.

Frawley, W. (1992). *Linguistic semantics*. Hillsdale, NJ: Lawrence Erlbaum Associates, Inc.

Frawley, W. (1997). *Vygotsky and cognitive science: Language and the unification of the social and computational mind*. Cambridge, MA: Harvard University Press.

Freeman, N. (1980). *Strategies of representation in young children*. London: Academic Press.

Frege, G. (1888). *Grundlagen der Aritmetik* [Foundations of arithmetic]. Erlangen: Universitäts Erlangen.

Freud, A. (1958). Adolescence. *Psychoanalytic study of the child*, *13*, 255–278.

Freud, S. (1900). *Traumdeutung* [The interpretation of dreams]. Leipzig & Vienna: Deutige.

Freud, S. (1915–16). *Introductory lectures on psychoanlaysis*. London: Hogarth.

Freud, S. (1920). *Beyond the pleasure principle*. London: Hogarth.

Freud, S. (1923). *The ego and the id*. London: Hogarth.

Freud, S. (1933). *New introductory lectures on psychoanalysis*. London: Hogarth.

Freudenthal, H. (1974). *The psychology of mathematics*. Amsterdam: Nijhoff.

Fromkin, V., Rodman, R., & Hyams, N. (2003). *An introduction to language* (5th ed.). Boston: Thomson.

Fukuyama, F. (1989). The end of history. *National Interest*, *27*, 1–36.

Fukuyama, F. (1992). *The end of history and the last man*. London: Hamish Hamilton.

Fukuyama, F. (1999). *The great disruption: Human nature and the reconstitution of social order*. New York: Free Press.

Fukuyama, F. (2002). Has history started again? *Policy*, *18*, 3–28.

Furrow, D., & Nelson, K. (1984). Environmental correlates of individual differences in language acquisition. *Journal of Child Language*, *11*, 3, 523–534.

Furrow, D., & Nelson, K. (1986). A further look at the motherese hypothesis: A reply to Gleitman, Newport, and Gleitman. *Journal of Child Language*, *13*, 1, 163–176.

Furth, H. (1966). *Thinking without language*. New York: Free Press.

Galperin, P. Ia. (1959). Razvitia issledovanogo na obrazovinnie deistvei umstvennie [Development of a programme of research on the formation of mental actions]. *Psychological Science in the USSR*, *1*, 125–146.

Galperin, P. Ia. (1965). *Osnovnye rezultaty issledovanii po probleme formirovanie umstvennykh deistviii i poniatii* [The main results of the study of mental actions and concept formation]. Unpublished manuscript, Moscow State University.

Galperin, P. Ia. (1968). Towards research of the intellectual development of the child. *International Journal of Psychology*, *3*, 4, 257–271.

Galperin, P. Ia. (1969). Die Entwicklung der Untersuchung über die Bildung geistiger Operationen [The development of research on the formation of mental operations]. In H. Hiebsch (Ed.), *Ergebnisse der sowjetischen Psychologie* [Achievements of Soviet psychology]. Stuttgart: Klett, pp. 367–405.

Galperin, P Ia. (1977). Problema deiatel'nosti v sovetskoi psikhologii [The problem of activity in Soviet psychology]. *Tesizi dokladov k 5 vesesoluznomu s'ezesdu Obshchesda Psikhologov* [Condensed papers from the 5th all-union congress of the Association of Psychologists]. Moscow: USSR Academy of Sciences, pp. 19–40.

Galperin, P. Ia. (1989). The problem of attention. *Soviet Psychology*, *27*, 3, 83–92.

Galperin, P. Ia. (1992). Stage-by-stage formation as a method of psychological investigation. *Journal of Russian and East European Psychology*, *30*, 4, 60–80.

Galperin, P. Ia., & Elkonin, D. B. (1972). K teorii J. Piaget o razvitii detskogo myshleniia [On Piaget's theory of the development of the child's thinking]. In J. Flavell, *Geneticheskaia psikhologiia Zhana Piazhe* [The genetic psychology of Jean Piaget]. Moscow: Pedagogika.

Galperin, P. Ia., & Georgiev, L. S. (1969). The formation of elementary mathematical notions. In J. Kilpatrick & I. Wirzup (Eds.), *Soviet studies in the psychology of learning and teaching mathematics*. Chicago: University of Chicago Press, pp. 156–178.

Galperin, P. Ia., & Kabylnitskaia, S. L. (1974). *Eksperimental'noe formirovanie vnimaniia* [The experimental formation of attention]. Moscow: Izdatel'stvo MGU.

Ganzen, V. A., & Golovei, L. A. (1982). A systemic description of human ontogeny. *Soviet Psychology*, *20*, 2, 28–48.

Gaskill, M. N., & Diaz, R. M. (1991). The relation between private speech and cognitive performance. *Infancia y Aprendizaje*, *53*, 45–58.

Gelman, R. (1986). Toward an understanding-based theory of mathematics learning and instruction, or, in praise of Lampert on teaching multiplication. *Cognition & Instruction*, *3*, 4, 349–355.

Gelman, R. (2000). The epigenesis of mathematical thinking. *Journal of Applied Developmental Psychology*, *21*, 1, 27–37.

Gelman, R., & Gallistel, C. R. (1978). *The child's understanding of number*. Cambridge, MA: Harvard University Press.

Gesell, A. (1930). *Intellectual development of the child*. New York: Macmillan.

Gesell, A. (1933). Maturation and the patterning of behaviour. In C. Murchison (Ed.), *A handbook of child psychology*. Worcester, MA: Clark University Press.

Gholson, B. (1980). *The cognitive-developmental basis of human learning*. London: Academic Press.

Gholson, B., & Rosenthal, T. (1984). *Applications of cognitive-developmental theory*. London: Academic Press.

Gibbs, J. (1979). Kohlberg's moral stage theory: A Piagetian reconstruction. *Human Development*, *22*, 89–112.

Gibbs, J., Basinger, K. S., & Fuller, D. (1991). *Moral maturity: Measuring the development of sociomoral reflection*. Hillsdale, NJ: Lawrence Erlbaum Associates, Inc.

Gibson, E. J. (1969). *Principles of perceptual learning and development*. New York: Van Nostrand.

Gibson, J. J. (1979). *The ecological approach to visual perception*. Boston: Houghton Mifflin.

Glasser, W. (1974). *Reality therapy*. New York: Harper & Row.

Gleason, J. (2001). *The development of language* (3rd ed.). Boston, MA: Allyn & Bacon.

Good, T., & Brophy, J. E. (1985). School effects. In M. Wittrock (Ed.), *Handbook of research on teaching*. New York: Macmillan.

Good, T., & Brophy, J. E. (1996). *Educational psychology* (4th ed.). New York: Longman.

Goodenough, F. (1931). Anger in young children. *Institute of Child Welfare Monographs*, *9*, 1–196.

Goodman, K. (1967). Reading: A psycholinguistic guessing game. *Journal of the Reading Specialist*, *6*, 126–135.

Goodman, K. (1985). Unity in reading. In H. Singer & R. B. Ruddell (Eds.), *Theoretical models and processes of reading*. Newark, DE: International Reading Association, pp. 813–840.

Gouin, F. (1880). *L'art d'enseigner et d'etudier les langues* [The art of studying and teaching languages]. Paris: Frederick.

Graham, L. R. (1993). *Science in Russia and the Soviet Union: A short history*. Cambridge: Cambridge University Press.

Graves, D. (1983). *Writing, children and teachers at work*. London: Heinemann.

Graves, D. (1991). *Build a literate classroom*. New York: Heinemann.

Green, T. H. (1885–88). *Works, Vols 1–5*. London: Longman.

Greenberg, G., & Haraway, M. M. (2002). *Principles of comparative psychology*. Needham Heights, MA: Allyn & Bacon.

Greene, J. (1987). *Memory, thinking and language*. London: Methuen.

Greenfield, P. M., & Savage-Rumbhaugh, S. (1990). Processes of grammatical combination in *Pan paniscus*. In S. Parker & K. Gibson (Eds.), *Language and intelligence in monkeys and apes*. New York: Cambridge University Press.

Griffin, D. R. (2001). *Animal minds: Beyond cognition to consciousness*. Chicago, IL: University of Chicago Press.

Grice, H. (1975). Logic and conversation. In P. Cole & J. L. Morgan (Eds.), *Syntax and semantics*. New York: Academic Press.

Grize, J-B. (1960). Du groupement au nombre: Essai de formalisation [From groupings to number: An attempt at formalisation]. In P. Greco, J-B. Grize, & J. Piaget

(Eds.), *Études d'epistemologie genetique, Vol. 11* [Studies in genetic epistemology, Vol. 11]. Paris: Presses Universitaires de France.

Guarino, N., & Poli, R. (Eds.) (1995). *The role of formal ontology in information technology*. London: Academic Press.

Guthke, J., & Stein, H. (1996). Are learning tests the better version of intelligence tests? *European Journal of Psychological Assessment*, *12*, 1, 1–13.

Haenen, J. (1996). *Piotr Galperin. Psychologist in Vygotsky's footsteps*. Commack, NY: Nova Science.

Hakuta, K. (1999). The debate on bilingual education. *Journal of Developmental & Behavioral Pediatrics*, *20*, 1, 36–37.

Halford, G. S. (1993). *Children's understanding: The development of mental models*. Hillsdale, NJ: Lawrence Erlbaum Associates, Inc.

Halford, G. S. (1999a). The development of intelligence includes the capacity to process relations of greater complexity. In M. Anderson (Ed.), *The development of intelligence. Studies in developmental psychology*. Hove, UK: Psychology Press, pp. 193–213.

Halford, G. S. (1999b). The properties of representations used in higher cognitive processes: Developmental implications. In I. E. Sigel (Ed.), *Development of mental representation: Theories and applications*. Mahwah, NJ: Lawrence Erlbaum Associates, Inc., pp. 147–168.

Hall, G. S. (1915). Recreation and reversion. *Pedagogical Seminary*, *22*, 510–520.

Hall, G. S. (1916). What we owe to the tree-life of our ape-like ancestors. *Pedagogical Seminary*, *23*, 94–120.

Hall, G. S. (1921). The dangerous age. *Pedagogical Seminary*, *28*, 275–294.

Hampson, J., & Nelson, K. (1993). The relation of maternal language to variation in rate and style of language acquisition. *Journal of Child Language*, *20*, 2, 313–342.

Harre, R. (1999). The rediscovery of the human mind: The discursive approach. *Asian Journal of Social Psychology*, *2*, 1, 43–62.

Harre, R. (2000). Personalism in the context of a social constructionist psychology: Stern and Vygotsky. *Theory & Psychology*, *10*, 6, 731–748.

Harre, R. (2002). Public sources of the personal mind: Social constructionism in context. *Theory & Psychology*, *12*, 5, 611–623.

Harris, A. J., & Sipay, E. R. (1990). *How to increase reading ability: A guide to developmental and remedial methods*. White Plains, NY: Longman.

Haworth, L. (1986). *Autonomy: An essay in philosophical psychology and ethics*. New Haven, CT: Yale University Press.

Hegel, G. W. F. (1807). *Phänomenologie der Geist* [Phenomenology of spirit]. Berlin: L. Heimann.

Hegel, G. W. F. (1831). *Philosophie des Geistes. Encyklopaedie der philosophischen Wissenschaften im Grundrisse, Teil 3* [Philosophy of mind. Encyclopaedia of the philosophical sciences in outline, Part 3] (3rd ed.). Berlin: L. Heimann.

Hegel, G. W. F. (1837). *Vorlesungen über die Philosophie der Geschichte* [Lectures on the philosophy of history]. Berlin: L. Heimann.

Hegel, G. W. F (1838). *Vorlesungen über die Geschichte der Philosophie* [Lectures on the history of philosophy]. Berlin: L. Heimann.

Herbart, J. F. (1808). *Allgemeine Pedagogik* [General pedagogy]. Königsburg: Klaus.

Heriot, P. (1972). *The psychology of language*. London: Methuen.

Hinde, R. A. (1966). *Animal behavior: A synthesis of ethology and comparative psychology*. New York: McGraw-Hill.

Hirst, P. Q. (1968). *Durkheim*. London: Routledge.

Hölldobler, B., & Wilson, E. O. (1990). *The ants*. Cambridge, MA: Belknap.

Holzkamp, K. (1984). Kritische psychologie und phänomenologishes psychologie [Critical psychology and phenomenological psychology]. *Forum Kritische Psychologie, 14*, 5–55.

Holzkamp, K. (1993). *Lernen. Subjectwissenschaftliche Grundlegung* [Learning. Subjective and scientific foundations]. Frankfurt: Campus Forschung.

Humboldt, W. (1824). *Über die Verschiedenheit des menschlichen Sprachbaues und ihren Einfluss auf die geistige Entwicklung des Menschengeschlechts* [On the difference between human languages and their influence on the mental development of human groups]. Paris: Dondey-Dupré.

Inhelder, B., & Piaget, J. (1958). *The growth of logical thinking from childhood to adolescence*. New York: Basic Books.

Inhelder, B., & Piaget, J. (1964). *The early growth of logic in the child*. London: Routledge & Kegan Paul.

Inhelder, B., Sinclair, H., & Bovet, M. (1974). *Learning and the development of cognition*. London: Routledge & Kegan Paul.

Jackendoff, R. (1994). *Patterns in the mind: Language and human nature*. New York: Basic Books.

Jackendoff, R. (1997). *The architecture of the language faculty*. Cambridge, MA: MIT Press.

Jackendoff, R. (2002). *Foundations of language: Brain, meaning, grammar, evolution*. New York: Oxford University Press.

Jaensch, E. R. (1920). *Einige allgemeine Fragen der Psychologie und Biologie des Denkens* [Some general questions of the psychology and biology of thought]. Leipzig: Schmidt.

Jaensch, E. R. (1925). *Über den Aufbau der Wahmehmungswelt und ihre Strucktur im Jugendalter* [On the construction of the perceptual world and its structure in youth]. Leipzig: Schmidt.

Jaensch, E. R. (1927a). Über Eidetick und die typologische Forschungsmethode [On eidetics and the typological research method]. *Zeitschrift für Psychologie, 102*, 1–28.

Jaensch, E. R. (1927b). *Über den Aufbau der Wahmehmungswelt und die Grundlagen der menschlichen Erkenntnis* [On the construction of the perceptual world and the foundations of human knowledge]. Leipzig: Kenner.

Jaensch, E. R. (1930). *Eidetic Imagery*. New York: Macmillan.

James, W. (1902). *Psychology*. New York: Macmillan.

Jamieson, J. R. (1994). Teaching as transaction: Vygotskian perspectives on deafness and mother–child interaction. *Exceptional Children, 60*, 434–449.

Jamieson, J. R. (1995). Visible thought: Deaf children's use of signed and spoken private speech. *Sign Language Studies, 86*, 63–80.

Janet, P. (1930). *L'evolution psychologique de la personnalité* [The psychological evolution of the personality]. Paris: Alcan.

Jaspers, K. (1913). *Algemeine Psychopathogie* [General psychopathology]. Berlin: Fischer.

Jespersen, O. (1904). *Sprøgundervisning* [Teaching a foreign language]. Copenhagen: Kriss.

Johnson-Laird, P. N. (1970). The interpretation of quantified sentences. In G. B. Flores d'Arcais, & W. J. M. Levelt (Eds.), *Advances in psycholinguistics*. Amsterdam: North Holland, pp. 143–159.

Johnson-Laird, P. N. (1993). Personal communication.
Johnson-Laird, P. N. (1997). Rationality, rules and models. *Cahiers de Psychologie Cognitive*, *16*, 114–123.
Johnson-Laird, P. N., & Bara, B. (1984). Syllogistic reasoning. *Cognition*, *16*, 1–61.
Johnson-Laird, P. N., & Byrne, J. (1990). *Deduction*. Hove, UK: Lawrence Erlbaum Associates Ltd.
Joravsky, D. (1961). *Soviet Marxism and natural science*. Oxford: Oxford University Press.
Joravsky, D. (1987). L. S. Vygotskii: The muffled deity of Soviet psychology. In M. G. Ash & W. R. Woodward (Eds.), *Psychology in twentieth-century thought and society*. New York: Cambridge University Press, pp. 189–211.
Joravsky, D. (1989). *Russian psychology: A critical history*. Oxford: Blackwell.
Jung, C. (1912). Wandlungen und Symbole der Libido [Transformations and symbols of the libido]. *Jahrbuch für Psychoanalytische und Psychopathologische Forschung*, *4*, 1–412.
Jung, C. (1939). Archetypes of the collective unconscious. In C. G. Jung (Ed.), *The integration of the personality* (Stanley Bell, Trans.). New York: Fischer.
Jung, C. G. (1945). On the nature of dreams. In C. G. Jung (Ed.), *The structure and dynamics of the psyche*. New York: Fischer.
Jung, C. G. (1955–56). *Mysterium conjunctionis* [The mystical union]. Zurich: Schmidt.
Kant, I. (1781). *Kritik der reinen Vernuft* [Critique of pure reason] (1st ed.). Leipzig: Voss.
Kant, I. (1787). *Kritik der reinen Vernuft* [Critique of pure reason] (2nd ed.). Leipzig: Voss.
Kant, I. (1790). *Kritik der Urteilskraft* [Critique of judgement]. Leipzig: Voss.
Karpov, Y. V., & Bransford, J. D. (1995).Vygotsky and the doctrine of empirical and theoretical learning. *Educational Psychologist*, *30*, 2, 61–66.
Keil, F. C. (1991a). The emergence of theoretical beliefs as constraints on concepts. In S. Carey & R. Gelman (Eds.), *The epigenesis of mind: Essays on biology and cognition*. Hillsdale, NJ: Lawrence Erlbaum Associates, Inc., pp. 237–256.
Keil, F. C. (1991b). Theories, concepts, and the acquisition of word meaning. In S. A. Gelman & J. P. Byrnes (Eds.), *Perspectives on language and thought: Interrelations in development*. New York: Cambridge University Press, pp. 197–221.
Keil, F. C., & Lockhart, K. (1999). Getting a grip on reality. In E. Winograd & R. Fivush (Eds.), *Ecological approaches to cognition: Essays in honor of Ulric Neisser*. Mahwah, NJ: Lawrence Erlbaum Associates, Inc., pp. 171–192.
Keil, F. C., & Wilson, R. A. (2000a). Explaining explanation. In F. C. Keil & R. A. Wilson (Eds.), *Explanation and cognition*. Cambridge, MA: MIT Press, pp. 1–18.
Keil, F. C., & Wilson, R. A. (Eds.) (2000b). *Explanation and cognition*. Cambridge, MA: MIT Press.
Kelly, M. (1971). Some aspects of conservation of quantity in Papua New Guinea in relation to language, sex and years in school. *Papua New Guinea Journal of Education*, *5*, 55–60.
Klahr, D., & Wallace, J. G. (1975). *Cognitive development*. New York: Wiley.
Kohlberg, L. (1958). *The development of modes of moral thinking and choice in the years 10 to 16 years*. PhD Thesis, University of Chicago.
Kohlberg, L. (1964). The development of moral character and ideology. In M. L. Hoffman & L. W. Hoffman (Eds.), *Review of child development research, Vol. 1*. New York: Russell Sage.

Kohlberg, L. (1984). *The psychology of moral development: The nature and validity of moral stages*. San Francisco: Harper & Row.

Kohlberg, L., Yaeger, J., & Hjertholm, E. (1968). Private speech: Four studies and a review of theories. *Child Development, 39*, 3, 691–736.

Kohler, W. (1917). *Die Mentalität von Grossaffen* [The mentality of apes]. Berlin: Fischer.

Kohler, W. (1920). *Die Physischen Gestalten in Ruhe und in stazionären Zustand* [Physical Gestalts in repose and at rest]. Brunswick: Atman.

Kohler, W. (1929). *Gestalt psychology: An introduction to new concepts in modern psychology*. New York: Greenhill.

Kohler, W. (1932). *Probleme der Psychologie* [The problems of psychology]. Berlin: Appel.

Kornilov, K. N. (1922). *Uchenie o reaktsiakh cheloveka* [The teaching on human reactions]. Moscow: Vatin.

Kornilov, K. N. (1928). Biogeneticheskij princip [The biogenetic principle]. In S. M. Vasilejsky (Ed.), *Osnovnye voprosy pedologii v izbrannykh statyakh* [Selected papers on basic problems of pedology]. Moscow and Leningrad: Nauka.

Korsch, K. (1923). *Marxismus und philosophie* [Marxism and philosophy]. Frankfurt: Europäische Verlaganstalt.

Kozulin, A. (1999). *Vygotsky's psychology: A biography of ideas* (2nd ed.). Cambridge, MA: Harvard University Press.

Kozulin, A., & Garb, E. (2004). Dynamic assessment of literacy: English as a third language. *European Journal of Psychology of Education, 19*, 1, 65–77.

Kretschmer, E. (1926). *Medizinistische Psychologie* [Medical psychology]. Berlin: Thiele.

Kretschmer, E. (1928). *Hysterie* [Hysteria]. Berlin: Forschlag.

Krylov, V. Y., & Ostriakova, T. V. (1995). Novii metodi gruppa analiz osnovat L. S. Vygotskii teoria konzept razvitiia [New methods of cluster analysis based on L. S. Vygotsky's theory of concept development]. *Psikhologicheskiy Zhurnal, 16*, 1, 130–137.

Lacan, J. (1966). Le seminaire sur 'La lettre volée'. In J. Lacan, *Ecrits*. Paris: Editions du Seuil, pp. 11–61.

Laing, R. D. (1964). *The divided self*. Harmondsworth: Penguin.

Lamb, M. E., & Campos, J. J. (1982). *Development in infancy*. New York: Random House.

Landau, B. (1991). Knowledge and its expression in the blind child. In D. P. Keating & H. Rosen (Eds.), *Constructivist perspectives on developmental psychopathology and atypical development*. Hillsdale, NJ: Lawrence Erlbaum Associates, Inc., pp. 173–192.

Langford, P. E. (1981). A longitudinal study of children's understanding of logical laws in arithmetic and Boolean algebra. *Educational Psychology*, 1, 119–139.

Langford, P. E. (1986). *Modern philosophies of human nature*. The Hague: Nijhof.

Langford, P. E. (1987a). *Concept development in the primary school*. Beckenham, UK: Croom Helm.

Langford, P. E. (1987b). *Concept development in the secondary school*. Beckenham, UK: Croom Helm.

Langford, P. E. (1988). A comparison of individualised and traditional instruction in arithmetic. *Australian Journal for Research in Mathematics Education, 4*, 1–16.

Langford, P. E. (1989). The process of learning. In P. E. Langford (Ed.), *Educational psychology: An Australian perspective*. Melbourne: Longman.

Langford, P. E. (1993). Evaluation of conditional and biconditional hypotheses in information use tasks during adolescence. *Journal of Genetic Psychology, 154*, 111–126.

Langford, P. E. (1995). *Approaches to the development of moral reasoning*. Hove, UK: Lawrence Erlbaum Associates Ltd.

Langford, P. E. (1997). Separating judicial from legislative reasoning in moral dilemma interviews. *Child Development, 68*, 1105–1116.

Langford, P. E. (2000). Obligation conditionals in a nonstandard conditional reasoning task. *Psychological Reports, 87*, 1203–1217.

Langford, P. E., & Hunting, R. (1994). A representational communication approach to the development of inductive and deductive logic. In A. Demetriou & A. Efklides (Eds.), *Intelligence, mind and reasoning: Structure and development*. New York: Elsevier Science.

Lenin, V. I. (1909). *Materializma v empriocritikizma* [Materialism and empiriocriticism]. Bern: Sola.

Lenin, V. I. (1921). Tri istochiki i sostavnoi chasti Marksisma [The three sources and component parts of Marxism]. *Prosveshcheniye, 3*, 1–17.

Lenin, V. I. (1925). Filosofskie zapiznai knichkai [Philosophical notebooks]. *Pod Znamenem Markzisma, 3*, 126–223.

Lenin, V. I. (1929). *Lenin smesi, tom 9* [Lenin miscellanies, Vol. 9]. Moscow: Nauka.

Leont'ev, A. A. (1995). Ecce homo. *Journal of Russian and East European Psychology, 33*, 35–46.

Leont'ev, A. N. (1930). Razvitie pamyati [Development of memory]. *Trudy Psikhologicheskoi Akademii Kommunisticheskogo Vospitaniya, 5*, 1–63.

Leont'ev, A. N. (1931). *Razvitie panijad. Eksperimental'noe issledovanie vysshikh psikhocheskikh funktzij* [The development of attention. An experimental study of a psychological function] . Moscow and Leningrad: Uchpedgiz.

Leont'ev, A. N. (1948). *Plan razvitiy psyche* [An outline of the evolution of the psyche]. Moscow: University of Moscow Press.

Leont'ev, A N. (1959). Propos istoriicheskogo podchoda izicheniy lydskogo psyche [A propos of the historical approach to the study of the human psyche]. In *Psikhologicheskaya Nauka v SSSR*. Moscow: Uchpedgiz.

Leont'ev, A. N. (1960). *Problemi razvitiy psichiki* [Problems of developmental psychology]. Moscow: Uchpedgiz.

Leont'ev, A. N. (1974). *Dejatel'nost', soznanie, lichnost'* [Activity, consciousness and personality]. Moscow: Pedagogika.

Leont'ev, A. N. (1982). Izobretatelnii razvitii L. S. Vygotskogo [Vygotsky's creative development]. In *Sobranie sochinenii L. S. Vygotskii* [Collected works of L. S. Vygotsky]. Moscow: Pedagogika.

Leont'ev, A. N. (1983). Karl Marx ja psykhologia [Karl Marx and psychology]. *Psykhologia, 18*, 6, 403–411.

Leont'ev, A. N. (1998). Uchenie o srede i pedalogicheskich rabotax L. S. Vygotskogo [A consideration of the pedological works of L. S. Vygotsky]. *Voprosi Psikhologii, 42*, 126–139.

Levi-Strauss, C. (1955). *Tristes tropiques* [Tropical blues]. Paris: Plon.

Levi-Strauss, C. (1956). La pensée sauvage [Primitive thought]. Paris: Gallimard.

Levi-Stauss, C. (1964–71). *Mythologiques. Vols 1–4* [Mythology. Vols 1–4]. Paris: Plon.

Levy-Bruhl, L. (1910). *Les fonctions mentales dans les societes inferieurs* [Mental functions in lower societies] (1st ed.). Paris: Presses Universitaires de France.

Levy-Bruhl, L. (1922). *La mentalité primitive* [The primitive mind]. Paris: Alcan.

Levy-Bruhl, L. (1927). *La morale et la science des moeurs* [Morality and the science of laws] (3rd ed.). Paris: Alcan.

Lewis, M. M. (1957). *How children learn to speak*. London: Harrap.

Lieberman, A. F. (1993). *The emotional life of the toddler*. New York: Macmillan.

Lieberman, D. A. (1993). *Learning: behavior and cognition*. Pacific Grove, CA: Brooks/Cole.

Lifschitz, M., & Langford, P. E. (1977). The role of counting and measurement in conservation learning. *Archives de Psychologie*, *46*, 1–14.

Lincoln, Y. S., & Guber, E. G. (1985). *Naturalistic inquiry*. Beverly Hills, CA: Sage.

Littlewood, W. (1984). *Foreign and second language learning: Language-acquisition research and its implications for the classroom*. Cambridge: Cambridge University Press.

Littlewood, W. (1992). *Teaching oral communication: A methodological framework*. Oxford: Blackwell.

Luchins, A. S. (1942). Mechanization in problem solving. *Psychological Monographs*, *54*, 6, 1–126.

Luchins, A. S., & Luchins, E. H. (1994a). The water jar experiments and Einstellung effects: I. Early history and surveys of textbook citations. *Gestalt Theory*, *16*, 2, 101–121.

Luchins, A. S., & Luchins, E. H. (1994b). The water jar experiments and Einstellung effects: II. Gestalt psychology and past experience. *Gestalt Theory*, *16*, 2, 222–245.

Lukacs, G. (1923). *Geschichte und Klassenbewusstein* [History and class consciousness]. Budapest: PLC.

Lukacs, G. (1967). *Der junge Hegel* [The young Hegel]. Leipzig: ONC.

Lukes, S. (1973). *Emile Durkheim: His life and work*. London: Allen & Unwin.

Lukes, S. (Ed.). (1983). *Durkheim and the law*. Oxford: Martin Robertson.

Lunacharsky, A. (1919). *Die Kulturaufgaben der Arbeiterklasse* [The cultural tasks of the working class]. Berlin: Wilmersdorf.

Luria, A. R. (1925). Psikhoanaliz, kak sistema monisticheskoj psikhologii [Psychoanalysis and monistic psychology as a system]. In K. N. Komilov (Ed.), *Psikhologija i marksam*. Leningrad: Gosudarstvennoe Izdateltvo, pp. 47–80.

Luria, A. R. (1960). *The mind of a mnemonist*. Harmondsworth: Penguin.

Luria, A. R. (1976). *Cognitive development: Its cultural and social foundations*. Cambridge, MA: Harvard University Press.

Marcia, J. E. (1966). Development and validation of ego identity status. *Journal of Personality and Social Psychology*, *3*, 551–558.

Marcuse, H. (1960). *One dimensional man*. New York: Beacon Press.

Marx, K. (1844). *Economische und philosophische Schriften von 1844* [Economic and philosophical manuscripts of 1844]. Manuscripts from Marx's personal archive.

Marx, K. (1846a). *Die deutsche Ideologie* [The German ideology]. Manuscripts from Marx's personal archive.

Marx, K. (1846b). *Thesen an Feuerbach* [Theses on Feuerbach]. Manuscripts from Marx's personal archive.

Marx, K. (1849). Arbeitslohne und Kapital [Wage labour and capital]. *Neue Rhenische Zeitung*, *5*, 1–47.

Marx, K. (1852). *Der achtzehnte Brumaire des Louis Bonaparte* [The eighteenth Brumaire of Louis Bonaparte]. Berlin: Duncker.

Marx, K. (1859). *Zur Kritik der politischen Ökonomie* [Contribution to a critique of political economy]. Berlin: Duncker.

Marx, K. (1867). *Das Kapital. Bd 1* [Capital. Vol. 1] (1st ed.). Hamburg: Meissner.

Marx, K. (1870). Letter to Engels, 14 April, 1870.

Marx, K. (1872). *Das Kapital. Bd 1* [Capital. Vol. 1] (2nd ed.). Hamburg: Meissner.

Marx, K. (1875). Zur Kritik der Grundsätze Gothas [Critique of the Gotha programme]. Letter to leaders of the Eisenach faction of the German Social Democratic Party.

Marx, K. (1876). *Burgerkrieg in Frankreich* [The civil war in France]. Leipzig: Genossenschaftsbuchdrückerei.

Marx, K. (1886). *Das Kapital. Bd 4* [Capital. Vol. 4]. Hamburg: Meissner.

Marx, K., & Engels, F. (1845). *Die heilige Familie* [The holy family]. Berlin: Duncker.

Marx, K., & Engels, F. (1848). *Manifest der kommunistischen Partei* [The communist manifesto]. London: Fredericks.

McKenzie, B. E. (1990). Early cognitive development: Notions of objects, space, and causality in infancy. In C. E. Hauert (Ed.), *Developmental psychology: Cognitive, perceptuo-motor and neuropsychological perspectives*. Oxford: North-Holland, pp. 43–60.

McMeniman, M. (1989). Motivation to learn. In P. E. Langford (Ed.), *Educational psychology: An Australian perspective*. Melbourne: Longman, pp. 215–239.

McNeill, D. (1970). *Language development*. Englewood Cliffs, NJ: Prentice Hall.

McNeill, D. (1983). The circle from gesture to sign. In M. Marschark & M. D. Clark (Eds.), *Psychological perspectives on deafness*. Hillsdale, NJ: Lawrence Erlbaum Associates, Inc., pp. 153–183.

McNeill, D. (1987). *Psycholinguistics: A new approach*. New York: Harper & Row.

McNeill, D. (1992). *Hand and mind: What gestures reveal about thought*. Chicago, IL: University of Chicago Press.

McNeill, D. (2000). Analogic/analytic representations and cross-linguistic differences in thinking for speaking. *Cognitive Linguistics*, *11*, 1–2, 43–60.

Mead, G. H. (1909). Social psychology as counterpart to physiological psychology. *Psychological Bulletin*, *6*, 401–408.

Mead, G. H. (1910). Social consciousness and the consciousness of meaning. *Psychological Bulletin*, *7*, 397–405.

Meyer, R. (2002). *Phonics exposed: understanding and resisting systematic direct intense phonics instruction*. Mahwah, NJ: Lawrence Erlbaum Associates, Inc.

Mill, J. S. (1846). *Utilitarianism, liberty and representative government*. London: Dent.

Millar, S. (1994). *Understanding and representing space: Theory and evidence from studies with blind and sighted children*. New York: Clarendon.

Minick, N. (1987). The development of Vygotsky's thought: An introduction. In C. Reiber (Ed.), *The collected works of L. S. Vygotsky, Vol. 1*. New York: Plenum, pp. 17–38.

Modgil, S., & Modgil, C. (1976). *Piagetian research: Compilation and summary. Vols 1–8*. Slough, UK: NFER.

Montague, R. (1974). *Formal philosophy: Selected papers of Richard Montague*. New Haven, CT: Yale University Press.

Moro, C., & Rodriguez, C. (2000). La création des representations chez l'enfant au travers des processus de semiosis [The formation of the child's representations through semiotic processes]. *Enfance*, *52*, 3, 287–294.

Mullet, E., & Miroux, R. (1996). Judgment of rectangular areas in children blind from birth. *Cognitive Development, 11*, 1, 123–139.

Natorp, P. (1899). *Sozialpedagogik* [A social approach to pedagogy]. Paderbom: Ferdinand Schoning.

Natorp, P. (1904). *Logik* [Logic]. Marburg: Elwertische Verlagbuchhandlung.

Neisser, U. (1976). *Cognition and reality*. San Francisco: Freeman.

Nelson, K. (1973). Some evidence of the cognitive primacy of categorisation and its functional basis. *Merrill-Palmer Quarterly, 19*, 21–39.

Nelson, K. (1974). Concept, word, and sentence: Interrelations in acquisition and development. *Psychological Review, 81*, 4, 267–285.

Nelson, K. (1990). Language development in context. In E. H. Bendix (Ed.), *The uses of linguistics*. New York: New York Academy of Sciences, pp. 93–108.

Nelson, K. (1996). *Language in cognitive development: Emergence of the mediated mind*. New York: Cambridge University Press.

Nelson, K. (1997). Finding oneself in time. In J. G. Snodgrass & R. L. Thompson (Eds.), *The self across psychology: Self-recognition, self-awareness and the self concept*. New York: New York Academy of Sciences.

Nelson, K. (1999). The developmental psychology of language and thought. In M. Bennett (Ed.), *Developmental psychology: Achievements and prospects*. Philadelphia, PA: Psychology Press, pp. 185–204.

Nelson, K. (2000). Narrative, time and the emergence of the encultured self. *Culture & Psychology, 6*, 2, 183–196.

Nelson, K. (2001). Language and the self: From the 'experiencing I' to the 'continuing me'. In C. Moore & K. Lemmon (Eds.), *The self in time: Developmental perspectives*. Mahwah, NJ: Lawrence Erlbaum Associates, Inc., pp. 15–33.

Newman, F. (2000). The performance of revolution (more thoughts on the postmodernization of Marxism). In L. Holzman & J. Morss (Eds.), *Postmodern psychologies, societal practice, and political life*. New York: Routledge, pp. 165–176.

Newman, F., & Holzman, L. (1993). *Lev Vygotsky: Revolutionary scientist*. London: Routledge.

Newman, F., & Holzman, L. (1996). *Unscientific psychology: A cultural-performatory approach to understanding human life*. Westport, CT: Praeger.

Nielsen, L. (1991). Spatial relations in congenitally blind infants: A study. *Journal of Visual Impairment & Blindness, 85*, 1, 11–16.

O'Connor, M. C. (1996). Managing the intermental: Classroom group discussion and the social context of learning. In D. I. Slobin & J. Gerhardt (Eds.), *Social interaction, social context, and language: Essays in honor of Susan Ervin-Tripp*. Hillsdale, NJ: Lawrence Erlbaum Associates, Inc., pp. 495–509.

OECD (2003a). *Program for international student assessment report*. Geneva: OECD.

OECD (2003b). *Education at a glance*. Geneva: OECD.

Overton, W. S. (1990). Competence and procedures: Constraints on the development of logical reasoning. In W. S. Overton (Ed.), *Reasoning, necessity and logic*. Hillsdale, NJ: Lawrence Erlbaum Associates, Inc.

Oxley, P. (2001). *Russia, 1855–1991: From tsars to commissars*. Oxford: Oxford University Press.

Palmer, H. E. (1921). *The oral method of teaching languages*. Cambridge: Heffer.

Papadopoulos, D. D. (1996). Observations on Vygotsky's reception in academic psychology. In C. W. Tolman & F. Cherry (Eds.), *Problems of theoretical psychology*. North York, ON: Captus Press, pp. 145–155.

Papadopoulos, D. D. (1999). *Lew Wygotsky: Weg und Wirkung* [Lev Vygotsky. Career and influence]. Frankfurt: Campus Forschung.

Parmenter, G. (1976). *An investigation into the language of 2.5 year old children attending daycare centres*. PhD thesis, University of Melbourne.

Pascual-Leone, J. (2000a). Is the French connection neo-Piagetian? Not nearly enough! *Child Development*, *71*, 4, 843–845.

Pascual-Leone, J. (2000b). Reflections on working memory: Are the two models complementary? *Journal of Experimental Child Psychology*, *77*, 2, 138–154.

Pascual-Leone, J., & Johnson, J. (1999). A dialectical constructivist view of representation: Role of mental attention, executives, and symbols. In I. E. Sigel (Ed.), *Development of mental representation: Theories and applications*. Mahwah, NJ: Lawrence Erlbaum Associates, Inc., 169–200.

Pavlov, I. P. (1897). *Lektsii o rabote glavnykh pishchevaritel'nykh zhelez* [Lectures on the functional control of digestive activity]. St. Petersburg: Ministerstva Putei Soobshenia.

Pavlov, I. P. (1926). *Uslovnyi refleks* [Conditioned reflexes]. Moscow: Academii Nauk.

Payne, T. R. (1968). *S. L. Rubinstein and the philosophical foundations of Soviet psychology*. Dordrecht: Reidel.

Peill, E. J. (1975). *Invention and discovery of reality*. London: Wiley.

Peirce, C. S. (1868). Questions concerning certain faculties claimed for man. *Journal of Speculative Philosophy*, *2*, 103–114.

Peirce, C. S. (1892). Man's glassy essence. *The Monist*, *5*, 63–84.

Peirce, C. S. (1923). *Chance, love and logic*. London: Kegan Paul.

Pellegrini, A. (1984). The effect of classroom ecology on preschoolers' use of language. In A. Pellegrini & T. Yawkey (Eds.), *The development of oral and written language in social contexts*. Norwood, NJ: Ablex.

Penuel, W. R., & Wertsch, J. V. (1995). Vygotsky and identity formation: A sociocultural approach. *Educational Psychologist*, *30*, 2, 83–92.

Perez, B. (2004). *Becoming biliterate: A study of two-way bilingual immersion education*. Mahwah, NJ: Lawrence Erlbaum Associates, Inc.

Perls, F. S. (1947). *Ego hunger and aggression*. New York: Random House.

Perls, F. S. (1973). *The Gestalt approach: Eyewitness to therapy*. New York: Bantam.

Perls, F. S. (1989). Theory and technique of personality integration. *TACD Journal*, *17*, 1, 35–52.

Peters, R. S. (1975). A reply to Kohlberg. *Phi Delta Kappan*, *56*, 678–679.

Peterson, C. (1996). *Looking forward through the life span: Developmental psychology*. Sydney: Prentice Hall.

Piaget, J. (1923). *Le langage et la pensée chez l'enfant* [The language and thought of the child]. Neuchâtel: Delachaux et Niestlé.

Piaget, J. (1924). *Le jugement et le raisonnement chez l'enfant* [The judgement and reasoning of the child]. Neuchâtel: Delachaux et Niestlé.

Piaget, J. (1926a). *La representation du monde chez l'enfant* [The child's conception of the world]. Paris: Alcan.

Piaget, J. (1926b). La premiére année de l'enfant [The child's first year]. *British Journal of Psychology*, *18*, 23–56.

Piaget, J. (1930). Les procédés de l'éducation morale: Rapport [The process of moral education: A report]. In *Cinquième congrès international d'éducation morale* [Fifth international congress on moral education]. Paris: Alcan, pp. 182–219.

Piaget, J. (1931). *Le jugement morale chez l'enfant* [The moral judgement of the child]. Paris: Alcan.
Piaget, J. (1936). *Les origines de l'intelligence chez l'enfant* [The origins of intelligence in the child]. Paris: Alcan.
Piaget, J. (1941). *La genése du nombre chez l'enfant* [The child's conception of number]. Neuchâtel and Geneva: Delachaux & Niestlé.
Piaget, J. (1945). *Traite de logique* [Treatise on logic]. Paris: Presses Universitaires de France.
Piaget, J. (1963). Défence de l'epistemologie genetique. In E. Beth, J. B. Grize, J. Martin, R. Matalon, B. Naess, & J. Piaget (Eds.), *Études de l'épistemologie genetique, Vol. 14. La filiation des structures* [Studies in genetic epistemology, Vol. 14. The sequence of structures]. Paris: Presses Universitaires de France.
Piaget, J. (1965). *Sagesse et illusions de philosophie* [Insights and illusions of philosophy]. Paris: Presses Universitaires de France.
Piaget, J. (1967). Mathemathiques: Les donnes genetiques [Mathematics: The genetic basis]. In *Logique et connaissance scientifique: Encyclopaedia de la Pleiade* [Logic and scientific knowledge: Encyclopaedia de la Pleiade]. Paris: Gallimard.
Piaget (1970). *Science of education and the psychology of the child.* London: Longman.
Piaget, J. (1972). Intellectual evolution from adolescence to adulthood. *Human Development, 15*, 1–12.
Piaget, J. (1974). *La prise de conscience* [Entry into consciousness]. Paris: Presses Universitaires de France.
Piaget, J. (1977). *Psychology and epistemology*. Harmondsworth: Penguin.
Piaget, J., & Garcia, R. (1991). *Towards a logic of meanings*. Hillsdale, NJ: Lawrence Erlbaum Associates, Inc.
Piaget, J., & Inhelder, B. (1941). *Le developpement des quantites chez l'enfant* [The child's conception of quantities]. Neuchâtel and Paris: Delachaux & Niestlé.
Piaget, J., & Inhelder, B. (1948). *La representation de l'espace chez l'enfant* [The child's conception of space]. Paris: Presses Universitaires de France.
Piaget, J., & Inhelder, B. (1969). *The psychology of the child.* London: Routledge.
Piaget, J., Inhelder, B., & Szeminska, A. (1948). *La representation de la geometrie chez l'enfant* [The child's conception of geometry]. Paris: Presses Universitaires de France.
Pinker, S. (1984). *Language learnability and language development*. Cambridge, MA: Harvard University Press.
Pinker, S. (1994). *The language instinct*. New York: HarperCollins.
Plekhanov, G. V. (1895). *Razvitii monisti vzglyadi istorii* [The development of the monist view of history]. Moscow: PUP.
Plekhanov, G. V. (1897). *Izbrannye filosofskie proavedenija* [Essays on the philosophy of the advance guard]. Moscow: PUP.
Plekhanov, G. V. (1922a). *Ocherki po istorii materializina* [Studies in the history of materialism] (3rd ed.). Moscow: Kuskov.
Plekhanov, G. V. (1922b). *Iskusstvo* [Essays]. Moscow: SNO.
Plekhanov, G. V. (1922c). *Osnovnye voprosy marksizma* [Fundamental problems of Marxism]. Moscow: Izkusstvo.
Poli, R., & Simons, P. (Eds.). (1996). *Formal ontology*. Dordrecht: Kluwer Academic.
Polivanova, K. N. (1994). A psychological analysis of age-specific developmental crises. *Voprosy Psychologii, 39*, 61–69.
Poole, M. E. (1970). *Language and education*. Melbourne: Australia International Press.

Poole, M. E. (1978). Linguistic code and cognitive style: Interdomain analyses. *Perceptual & Motor Skills*, *46*, 1159–1164.

Poole, M. E. (1979a). Elaboration of linguistic code and verbal-processing strategies: Interdomain analyses. *Psychological Reports*, *45*, 1, 283–296.

Poole, M. E. (1979b). Social class, sex and linguistic coding. *Language & Speech*, *22*, 1, 49–67.

Postman, L., & Crutchfield, R. S. (1952). The interaction of need, set and stimulus structure in a cognitive task. *American Journal of Psychology*, *65*, 196–217.

Potebnya, A. A. (1864). *Myshlie y rech'* [Thought and speech]. Kiev: SINTO.

Potebnya, A. A. (1894). *Iz lektsii po teorii slovesnosti* [Lectures on the theory of the Slavic languages]. Kharkov: K. Schasni.

Pratt, C. (1993). The representation of knowledge and beliefs. In C. Pratt & A. Garton (Eds.), *Systems of representation in children: Development and use*. Oxford: Wiley, pp. 27–47.

Preisler, G. M. (1995). The development of communication in blind and in deaf infants: Similarities and differences. *Child Care, Health & Development*, *21*, 2, 79–110.

Premack, D. (1971). Language in chimpanzees? *Science*, *172*, 88–122.

Preyer, W. (1882). *Die Seele des Kindes* [The child's soul]. Leipzig: Geigen.

Price, R. F. (1977). *Marx and education in Russia and China*. London: Croom Helm.

Quine, W. V. O. (1951). Ontology and ideology. *Philosophical Studies*, *2*, 11–15.

Randell, D. A., & Cohn, A. G. (1992a). Modelling topological and metrical properties in physical processes. In R. J. Brachman (Ed.), *Principles of knowledge representation and reasoning*. Toronto: Aris.

Randell, D. A., & Cohn, A. G. (1992b). Exploiting lattices in a theory of space and time. *Computers and Mathematical Applications*, *23*, 459–476.

Randell, D. A., Cui, Z., & Cohn, A. G. (1992a). A spatial logic based on regions and connection. In B. Nebel (Ed.), *Principles of knowledge representation and reasoning*. Proceedings of the third international conference. Cambridge, MA: MIT Press, pp. 165–176.

Randell, D. A., Cui, Z., & Cohn, A. G. (1992b). An interval logic for space based on connection. In B. Neumann (Ed.), *10th European conference on artificial intelligence*. New York: Wiley, pp. 394–398.

Ratner, C. (1989). A social-constructionist critique of the naturalist theory of the emotions. *Journal of Mind and Behavior*, *10*, 211–230.

Ratner, C. (1991). *Vygotsky's sociohistorical psychology and its contemporary applications*. New York: Plenum.

Ratner, C. (1997). In defense of activity theory. *Culture and Psychology*, *3*, 211–223.

Ratner, C. (1998). Historical and contemporary significance of Vygotsky's sociohistorical psychology. In R. W. Rieber & K. Salzinger (Eds.), *Psychology: Theoretical-historical perspectives* (2nd ed.). Washington, DC: American Psychological Association, pp. 455–473.

Ratner, C. (2000). A cultural-psychological analysis of the psychology of emotions. *Culture and Psychology*, *6*, 5–39.

Redgrave, K. (1987). *Child's play*. Cheadle, UK: Boys & Girls Welfare Society.

Reiff, P. (1959). *Freud: The mind of the moralist*. London: Gollancz.

Resnick, L. B. (1987). *Education and learning to think*. Washington, DC: National Academy Press.

Resnick, L. B. (1992). Assessing the thinking curriculum: New tools for educational reform. In B. R. Gifford & M. C. O'Connor (Eds.), *Changing assessments: Alternative views of aptitude, achievement and instruction*. New York: Kluwer Academic, pp. 37–75.

Reynolds, P. (1988). *A comparison of linguistic interaction in three child care situations at the child's first and second birthdays*. PhD Thesis, La Trobe University, Melbourne.

Ribot, T. A. (1888). *La psychologie de l'attention* [The psychology of attention]. Paris: Alcan.

Ribot, T. A. (1897). *Psychologie des sentiments* [Psychology of feelings]. Paris: Alcan.

Ribot, T. A. (1900). The nature of the creative imagination. *International Monatschrift*, *2*, 1–25.

Ribot, T. A. (1906). *Essay on the creative imagination*. Chicago, IL: Open Court.

Richardson, D. (1992). *Teaching art, craft and design*. Melbourne: Longman.

Ricciuti, H. N. (1965). Objective grouping and selective ordering in infants 12–24 months. *Merrill-Palmer Quarterly*, *11*, 129–148.

Rieber, R. W. (1983). *Dialogues on the psychology of language and thought*. New York: Plenum.

Rips, L. J. (1994). *The psychology of proof: Deductive reasoning in human thinking*. Cambridge, MA: MIT Press.

Robinson, E. J., & Mitchell, P. (1995). Masking of children's early understanding of the representational mind: Backwards explanation versus prediction. *Child Development*, *66*, 4, 1022–1039.

Rodriguez, C., & Moro, C. (1998). El uso convencional tambien hace permanentes a los objetos. [Objects are also made permanent by their conventional use]. *Infancia y Aprendizaje*, *84*, 67–83.

Rogoff, B. (1986). Adult assistance of children's learning. In T. E. Raphael (Ed.), *The contexts of school-based literacy*. New York: Random House.

Rosen, H. (1972). *Language and class*. Bristol, UK: Falling Wall Press.

Rosenkranz, K. (1840). *Kritischen erläuterungen von Hegelschen Systems* [A critical exposition of the Hegelian system]. Königsberg: Bornträger.

Rosenkranz, K. (1870). *Erläuterungen zu Hegel's Encyklopdie der philosophischen Wissenschaften* [Commentary on Hegel's encyclopaedia of the philosophical sciences]. Berlin: L. Heimann.

Rosenthal, D. A., Gurney, R. M., & Moore, S. M. (1981). From trust to intimacy: A new inventory for examining Erikson's stages of psychosocial development. *Journal of Youth & Adolescence*, *10*, 6, 525–537.

Rubinshtein, S. L. (1934). *Osnovi psikhologii* [Fundamentals of psychology]. Moscow: GIV.

Rubinshtein, S. L. (1935). Problema psikhologia v sochelnia Markska [Problems of psychology in the works of Marx]. *Sovetskaia psikhotekhnika*, *6*, 1–84.

Rubinshtein, S. L. (1946). *Osnovi obshchei psikhologii* [Foundations of general psychology]. Moscow: Akademii Nauk.

Rubinshtein, S. L. (1959). *Printzipi i puti razvitiia psikhologii* [Principles and problems of developmental psychology]. Moscow: Akademii Nauk.

Rulcker, T. (1969). *Die Neusprachenunterricht and hoheren Schulen: Zur Geschichte und Kritik seiner Didaktik* [New ways of teaching languages in high schools: On the history and criticism of their teaching methods]. Frankfurt: Diesterweg.

Russell, B. (1926a). *On education*. London: Unwin.

Russell, B. (1926b). *Education and the good life*. New York: Liveright.

Sakharov, L. S. (1930). O metodakh issledovanija ponjatij [Methods for studying concepts]. *Psikhologija*, *3*, 1–98.

Sander, L. W. (1969). The longitudinal course of early child–mother interaction. In B. M. Foss (Ed.), *Determinants of infant behaviour, Vol. 4*. London: Methuen, pp. 189–228.

Saussure, F. de (1916). *Cours de linguistique generale* [Course in general linguistics]. Paris: Payot.

Savage-Rumbhaugh, S., McDonald, K., Sevcik, R. A., Hopkins, W. D., & Robert, H. (1986). Spontaneous symbol acquisition and communicative use in pygmy chimpanzees. *Journal of Experimental Psychology: General, 112*, 211–233.

Schachter, S., & Singer, J. (1963). Cognititive, social and physiological determinants of emotional state. *Psychological Review, 69*, 379–399.

Seagrim, G. (1980). *Furnishing the mind: A comparative study of cognitive development in Central Australian Aborigines*. Sydney and London: Academic Press.

Segall, M. H., Dasen, P. R., Berry, J. W., & Poortinga, Y. H. (1999). *Human behavior in global perspective: An introduction to cross-cultural psychology* (2nd ed.). Needham Heights, MA: Allyn & Bacon.

Serge, V. (1968). *The life of Trotsky*. London: Collins.

Shayer, M. (1980). Adolescent thought. In M. Modgil and C. Modgil (Eds.), *Towards a theory of psychological development*. Slough, UK: NFER, pp. 324–361.

Shayer, M. (1998). How can we use the literature with students in school in mind? *Learning & Instruction, 8*, 4, 387–392.

Shayer, M. (2003). Not just Piaget; not just Vygotsky; and certainly not Vygotsky as alternative to Piaget. *Learning & Instruction, 13*, 5, 465–485.

Shayer, M., & Adey, M. S. (1993). Accelerating the development of formal thinking in middle and high school students: IV. Three years after a two-year intervention. *Journal of Research in Science Teaching, 30*, 4, 351–366.

Sheehan, M. (1993). *Marxism and the philosophy of science: A critical history*. New York: Humanities Press International.

Shotter, J. (1995). In conversation: Joint action, shared intentionality and ethics. *Theory and Psychology, 5*, 49–73.

Shotter, J. (1998). Agency and identity. In A. Campbell & S. Muncer (Eds.), *The social child*. Hove, UK: Psychology Press, pp. 271–291.

Shweder, R. A. (1996). True ethnography: The lore, the law, and the lure. In R. Jessor, A. Colby, & R. Shweder (Eds.), *Ethnography and human development*. Chicago: University of Chicago Press, pp. 15–52.

Shweder, R. A., & LeVine, R. A. (1984). *Culture theory*. Cambridge: Cambridge University Press.

Simons, P. M. (1987). *Parts. A study in ontology*. Oxford: Clarendon.

Skemp, R. (1971). *The psychology of learning mathematics*. Harmondsworth: Penguin.

Slobin, D. I. (1973). Cognitive prerequisites for the development of grammar. In C. A. Ferguson & D. I. Slobin (Eds.), *Studies of child language development*. New York: Holt, Rinehart & Winston.

Slobin, D. I. (1982). Universal and particular in the acquisition of language. In E. Wanner & L. R. Gleitman (Eds.), *Language acquisition: The state of the art*. Cambridge: Cambridge University Press.

Slobin, D. I. (1997). The universal, the typological, and the particular in acquisition. In D. I. Slobin (Ed.), *The crosslinguistic study of language acquisition, Vol. 5: Expanding the contexts*. Mahwah, NJ: Lawrence Erlbaum Associates, Inc.

Smith, A. (1776). *The wealth of nations*. London: Green.

Smith, B. (Ed.). (1982). *Parts and moments. Studies in logic and formal ontology*. Munich: Philosophia.

Smith, B. (1991). Relevance, relatedness and restricted set theory. In G. Schurz & G. J. W. Dorn (Eds.), *Advances in scientific philosophy. Essays in honour of Paul Weingartner*. Amsterdam: Rodolpi, pp. 45–56.

Smith, B. (1992). Characteristica universalis. In K. Mulligan (Ed.), *Language, truth and ontology*. Dordrecht: Kluwer, pp. 50–81.

Smith, B. (1995a). Common sense. In B. Smith & D. W. Smith (Eds.), *The Cambridge companion to Husserl*. New York: Cambridge University Press.

Smith, B. (1995b). Formal ontology, common sense and cognitive science. *International Journal of Human-Computer Studies*, *43*, 641–667.

Smith, B., & Casati, R. (1994). Naive physics: An essay in philosophy. *Philosophical Psychology*, *7*, 225–244.

Smith, B., & Welty, C. (Eds.) (2001). *Formal ontology in information systems*. Ogunquit, ME: Asis.

Smith, L. (1994). Reasoning models and intellectual development. In A. Demetriou & A. Efklides (Eds.), *Intelligence, mind and reasoning: Structure and development*. Amsterdam: Elsevier, pp. 173–190.

Sochor, Z. A. (1988). *Revolution and culture: The Bogdanov–Lenin controversy*. Ithaca, NY: Cornell University Press.

Spelke, E. S. (2000). Nativism, empiricism, and the origins of knowledge. In D. Muir & A. Slater (Eds.), *Infant development: The essential readings*. Malden, MA: Blackwell, pp. 36–51.

Spelke, E. S., & Hermer, L. (1996). In R. Gelman & T. Kit-Fong (Eds.), *Perceptual and cognitive development. Handbook of perception and cognition* (2nd ed.). San Diego, CA: Academic Press, pp. 71–114.

Spelke, E. S., & Newport, E. L. (1998). Nativism, empiricism and the development of knowledge. In W. Damon & R. Lerner (Eds.), *Handbook of child psychology, Vol. 1. Theoretical models of human development* (5th ed.). New York: Wiley, pp. 275–340.

Spinoza, B. de (1688). *Ethica* [Ethics]. Leipzig: Meiner.

Spitz, R. A. (1960). *Die Entstehung der ersten Objectbeziehungen* [The formation of the first object relations]. Stuttgart: Klett.

Spitz, R. A. (1961). Some early prototypes of ego defenses. *Journal of the American Psychoanalytic Association*, *9*, 626–651.

Spranger, E. (1925). *Psychologie des Jugendalters* [The psychology of youth]. Leipzig: Quelle & Meyer.

Spranger, E. (1928). *Kultur und Erziehung. Gesammelte Pedagogische Aufsätze*. [Culture and education. Collected pedagogic writings] (4th ed.). Leipzig: Quelle & Meyer.

Stern, H. H. (1983). *Fundamental concepts of language teaching*. Oxford: Oxford University Press.

Stern, H. H. (1992). *Issues and options in language teaching*. Oxford: Oxford University Press.

Stern, W. (1922). *Psychologie der Kleinkinderheit nach sechs Jahre* [Psychology of early childhood to age six]. Berlin: Fischer.

Stern, W. (1927). *Psychologie der frühen Kindheit* [Psychology of early childhood]. Leipzig: Quelle & Meyer.

Sternberg, R. (1995). *In search of the human mind*. New York: Harcourt Brace.

Sternberg, R. (1999). *Cognitive psychology* (2nd ed.). Fort Worth, TX: Harcourt Brace.

Stigler, J. W., Shweder, R.A., & Herdt, G. (Eds.) (1990). *Essays on comparative human development*. Cambridge: Cambridge University Press.

Storr, A. (1972). *The dynamics of creation*. Harmondsworth: Penguin.

Subbotsky, E. V. (1996). Contseptsii L. S. Vygotscogo o visshich i nizshich psikhicheskich funkshiich i sovremmenie isolvedannie posnavatelnogo razvitii v mladenchestvii [L. S. Vygotsky's distinction between lower and higher mental functions and recent studies on infant cognitive development]. *Voprosy Psikhologii*, *40*, 88–92.

Tarski, A. (1944). The semantic conception of truth. *Philosophy and Phenomenological Research*, *4*, 341–375.

Tartter, V. C. (1986). *Language processes*. New York: Holt, Rinehart & Winston.

Thorndike, E. L. (1902). The experimental method of studying animal intelligence. *International Monatschrift*, *5*, 224–238.

Thorndike, E. L. (1911). *Animal intelligence*. New York: Macmillan.

Thorndike, E. L. (1913). *Educational psychology*. New York: Macmillan.

Thorpe, W. H. (1956). *Learning and instinct in animals*. Cambridge, MA: Harvard University Press.

Tillich, P. (1952). *The courage to be*. New Haven, CT: Yale University Press.

Tillich, P. (1959). *Theology of culture*. New York: Oxford University Press.

Tolman, C. W. (2001). The origins of activity as a category in the philosophies of Kant, Fichte, Hegel and Marx. In S. Chaiklin (Ed.), *The theory and practice of cultural-historical psychology*. Aarhus, Denmark: Aarhus University Press, pp. 84–92.

Tomlinson, P. (1999). Personal communication.

Toomey, D. (1976). Educational inequality. *Australia New Zealand Journal of Sociology*, *17*, 253–269.

Toomey, D. (1989). Equality of opportunity. In P. E. Langford (Ed.), *Educational psychology: An Australian perspective*. Melbourne: Longman.

Trainer, T. (1982). *Dimensions of moral thought*. Sydney: University of New South Wales Press.

Trevarthen, C. (1988). Universal co-operative motives: How infants begin to know the language and culture of their parents. In G. Jahoda & I. M. Lewis (Eds.), *Acquiring culture: Cross cultural studies in child development*. New York: Croom Helm, pp. 37–90.

Trevarthen, C. (1993). The self born in intersubjectivity: The psychology of an infant communicating. In U. Neisser (Ed.), *The perceived self: Ecological and interpersonal sources of self-knowledge*. New York: Cambridge University Press, pp. 121–173.

Trevarthen, C. (1999). What infants' imitations communicate: With mothers, with fathers and with peers. In J. Nadel & G. Butterworth (Eds.), *Imitation in infancy*. New York: Cambridge University Press, pp. 127–185.

Trevarthen, C. (2003a). The infant's world. *Journal of Child Psychology & Psychiatry & Allied Disciplines*, *44*, 1, 154–155.

Trevarthen, C. (2003b). Infant psychology is an evolving culture. *Human Development*, *46*, 4, 233–246.

Trevarthen, C., & Aitken, K. J. (2001). Infant intersubjectivity: Research, theory, and clinical applications. *Journal of Child Psychology & Psychiatry & Allied Disciplines*, *42*, 1, 3–48.

Trotsky, L. (1924). *Literatura i revoliutsiia* [Literature and revolution]. Moscow: Garpod.

Trotsky, L. (1934). *The history of the Russian Revolution* (M. Eastman, Trans.). London: Gollancz.

Tryphon, A., & Voneche, J. (1996). Introduction. In A. Tryphon & J. Voneche (Eds.), *Piaget–Vygotsky: The social genesis of thought*. Oxford: Lawrence Erlbaum Associates Ltd, pp. i–viii.

Tucker, R. C. (1974). Introduction. In R. C. Tucker (Ed.), *Marx and Engels, Selected Works*. New York: Ann Arbor, pp. 1–28.

Tulviste, P. (1989). A comparison of the development of scientific and naturalistic concepts. *Soviet Psychology, 27*, 1, 5–21.

Tulviste, P. (1991). *The cultural-historical development of verbal thinking*. Huntington, NY: Nova Science.

Tulviste, P. (1992). On the historical heterogeneity of verbal thought. *Journal of Russian & East European Psychology, 30*, 1, 77–88.

Tylor, E. (1871). *Primitive culture*. London: Murray.

Tzuriel, D. (2001). *Dynamic assessment of young children*. Dordrecht, Netherlands: Kluwer Academic.

Valsiner, J. (1999). I create you to control me: A glimpse into basic processes of semiotic mediation. *Human Development, 42*, 1, 26–30.

Valsiner, J., & Van der Veer, R. (1988). On the social nature of human cognition. *Journal for the Theory of Social Behavior, 18*, 117–136.

Van der Veer, R. (1986). Vygotsky's developmental psychology. *Psychological Reports, 59*, 527–536.

Van der Veer, R. (1994). The concept of development and the development of concepts. *European Journal of Psychology of Education, 9*, 293–300.

Van der Veer, R. (1996). Vygotsky and Piaget: A collective monologue. *Human Development, 39*, 5, 237–242.

Van der Veer, R. (1998). From concept attainment to knowledge formation. *Mind, Culture, and Activity, 5*, 2, 89–94.

Van der Veer, R. (2001). The idea of units of analysis: Vygotsky's contribution. In S. Chaiklin (Ed.), *The theory and practice of cultural-historical psychology*. Aarhus, Denmark: Aarhus University Press, pp. 93–106.

Van der Veer, R. (2003). Primitive mentality reconsidered. *Culture & Psychology, 9*, 2, 179–184.

Van der Veer, R., & Valsiner, J. (1991). *Understanding Vygotsky. The quest for synthesis*. Oxford: Blackwell.

Van der Veer, R., & Van Ijzendoorn, M. H. (1985). Vygotsky's theory of the higher psychological processes: Some criticisms. *Human Development, 28*, 1, 1–9.

Van Sommers, P. (1984). *Drawing and cognition*. Cambridge: Cambridge University Press.

Vygodskaya, G. L., & Lifanova, T. M. (1996). *Lev Semenovich Vygotsky*. Moscow: SMISL.

Vygotsky, L. S. (1914). *Gamlet* [Hamlet]. Unpublished manuscript.

Vygotsky, L. S. (1925a). *Psikhologija iskusstva* [Psychology of art]. PhD thesis, Moscow University.

Vygotsky, L. S. (1925b). Soznanie kak problema psikhologii povedenija [Consciousness as a problem in the psychology of behavior]. In K. N. Komilov (Ed.), *Psikhologija i marksizm. Tom 1* [Psychology and marxism. Vol. 1]. Moscow, Leningrad: GIZ, pp. 175–198.

Vygotsky, L. S. (1926a). Metodika refleksologicheskogo i psikhologicheskogo issledovanija [Methodology of reflexological and psychological research]. In K. N.

Kornilov (Ed.), *Problemy sovremennoi psikhologii. Bd 2* [Problems of modern psychology. Vol. 2]. Leningrad: Gosudarstvennoe, pp. 264–266.

Vygotsky, L. S. (1926b). Po povodu stat'i K. Koffka o samonabliudenii [Apropos of the paper of K. Koffka on self observation]. In K. N. Kornilov (Ed.), *Problemy sovremennoi psikhologii* [Problems of modern psychology]. Leningrad: Gosudarstvennoe, pp. 176–178.

Vygotsky, L. S. (1926c). *Pedagogicheskaja psikhologija* [Pedagogical psychology]. Moscow: Rabotnik Prosveshchehnija.

Vygotsky, L. S. (1926d). Problema dominantnykh reaktsii [The problem of dominant reactions]. In *Problemy sovremmenoi psikhologii. Bd 2* [Problems of modern psychology. Vol. 2]. Leningrad: GIZ, pp. 100–123.

Vygotsky, L. S. (1927a). Biogeneticheskii zakon v psikhologii i pedagogike [Biogenetic law in psychology and pedagogy]. *BSE* [Great Soviet encyclopedia], *6*, 275–279.

Vygotsky, L. S. (1927b). Defekt i sverkhkompensatsija [Defect and overcompensation]. In *Umstvennaja otstalost', slepota i glukhonemota* [Mental retardation, blindness and deafmuteness]. Moscow: Doloi Negramotnost', pp. 51–76.

Vygotsky, L. S. (1927c). Sovremennaja psikhologija i iskusstvo [Modern psychology and art]. *Sovetskoe Iskusstvo* [Soviet art], *8*, 57–58.

Vygotsky, L. S. (1927d). *Istoricheskii smysl psikhologicheskogo krizisa* [The historical meaning of the crisis in psychology]. Unpublished manuscript.

Vygotsky, L. S. (1928a). K voprosy o dinamike detskogo kharaktera [The problem of the dynamics of child character]. In *Pedologija i vospitanie* [Pedology and education]. Moscow: Rabotnik Prosveshchenija, pp. 99–119.

Vygotsky, L. S. (1928b). Psikhologicheskoe osnovy vospitanija i obuchenija glukhonemogo rebenka [Psychological bases for the rearing and teaching of the deafmute child]. *Pedagogicheskaja Entsiklopedija* [Pedagogical encyclopedia], *2*, 395.

Vygotsky, L. S. (1928c). Psikhologicheskoe osnovy vospitanija i obuchenija slepogo rebenka [Psychological bases for rearing and teaching the blind child]. *Pedagogicheskaja Entsiklopedija* [Pedagogical encyclopedia], *2*, 394–395.

Vygotsky, L. S. (1928d). Razvitie trudnogo rebenka i ego izuchenie [Development and study of the difficult child]. In *Osnovnye problemy pedologii v SSSR* [Basic problems in pedology in the USSR]. Moscow: Rabotnik Prosveshchenija, pp. 132–136.

Vygotsky, L. S. (1928e). Umstvenno otstalye deti [Mentally retarded children]. *Pedagogicheskaja Entsiklopedija* [Pedagogical encyclopedia], *2*, 397–398.

Vygotsky, L. S. (1928f). Vospitanie slepogluknonemykh detei [Education of blind, deafmute children]. *Pedagoigicheskaja Entsiklopedija* [Pedagogical encyclopedia], *2*, 395–396.

Vygotsky, L. S. (1928g). *Pedologija shkol'nogo vozrasta* [Pedology of the school age]. Moscow: BZO.

Vygotsky, L. S. (1928h). Problema kul'turnogo razvitija rebenka [The problem of the cultural development of the child]. *Pedologija* [Pedology], *1*, pp. 58–77.

Vygotsky, L. S. (1929a). Razvitie aktivnogo vnimanija v detskom vozraste [Development of active attention during childhood]. In *Voprosy marksistskoi pedagogiki. Trudy AKV* [Problems in Marxist pedagogy. Proceedings of the academy of communist education]. Moscow: GIZ, pp. 112–114.

Vygotsky, L. S. (1929b). Struktura interesov v perekhodnorn vozraste i interesy rabochego podrostka [The structure of interests during the transitional age and interests of the working adolescent]. In *Voprosy pedologii rabochego podrostka* [Problems in the pedology of the working adolescent]. Moscow: GIV, pp. 25–68.

Vygotsky, L. S. (1929c). Razvitie activnogo vnimanija v detskorn vozraste [Development of active attention during childhood]. In *Voprosy marksistskai pedagogica* [Problems of Marxist pedagogy]. Moscow: IPKP.

Vygotsky, L. S. (1929d). Geneticheskie korni myshlenija i rechi [Genetic roots of thinking and speech]. *Estesvoznanie i Marksizm*, *1*, 106–133.

Vygotsky, L. S. (1929e). K voprosu ob intellekte antropoidov v svjazi s rabotami V. Kelera [The problem of the intellect of anthropoids in connection with the work of W. Kohler]. *Estesvoznanie i Marksizm*, *1*, 106–133.

Vygotsky, L. S. (1929f). Rechenzii N. Dmitrieva, N. Ol'denburg, and L. Perekrestova, *Shkol'naja dramaticheskaja rabota na osnove issledovanija detskogo tvorchestva* [Review of N. Dmitrieva, N. Ol'denburg, and L. Perekrestova, Theatre work in school based on the study of children's creativity]. *Isskustvo v Skhole*, *8*, 29–31.

Vygotsky, L. S. (1929g). Osnovnye polozhenija plana pedologicheskoi issledovatel'skoi raboty v ob trudnogo detstva [Basic assumptions of the plan for pedological research in the area of difficult childhood]. *Pedologija*, *3*, 333.

Vygotsky, L. S. (1929h). The cultural development of the child. *Journal of Genetic Psychology*, *36*, 415–434.

Vygotsky, L. S. (1930a). O syjazi mezhdu trudovoi dejatel'nostju i intellektual'nym razvitiem rebenka [The connection between work activity and intellectual development of the child]. *Pedologija*, *56*, 588–596.

Vygotsky, L. S. (1930b). Biologicheskaja osnova affekta [Biological basis of affect]. *Khochu Vse Znat'*, *15*, 480–481.

Vygotsky, L. S. (1930c). Predislovie [Preface]. In W. Kohler, *Issledovanie intellekta chelovekopodobnykh obezyan* [The mentality of apes]. Moscow: Kommunict Akademii, pp. i–xxix.

Vygotsky, L. S. (1930d). K probleme razvitija interesov v perekhodnorn vozraste [The problem of developing interests during the transitional age], *Robitnicha Osvita*, *78*, 63–81.

Vygotsky, L. S. (1930e). Problema vysshikh intellektual'nykh funktsii v sisterne psikhotekhnicheskogo issledovanija [The problem of higher intellectual functions in the system of psychotechnical research]. *Psikhotekhnika i Psikhophiziologija Truda*, *3*, 374–384.

Vygotsky, L. S. (1930f). Psikhika, soznajnie i bessoznatel'noe [The mind, consciousness and unconsciousness]. In *Elementy obshchei psikhologii* [Elements of general psychology] (4th ed.). Moscow: BZO, pp. 48–61.

Vygotsky, L. S. (1930g). Psikhologicheskikh sistemakh [On psychological systems]. Unpublished manuscript.

Vygotsky, L. S. (1930h). Sotsialisticheskaja peredelka cheloveka [The socialist transformation of man]. *VARNITSO* [Journal of the All Union Association of Workers of Science and Technology for Assistance to the Building of Socialism], *910*, 36–44.

Vygotsky, L. S. (1930i). *Voobrazhenie i tvorchestvo v shkol'nom vozraste* [Imagination and creativity during the school years]. Moscow and Leningrad: GIZ.

Vygotsky, L. S. (1930j). Vstupitel'naja statja [Introductory paper]. In *Ocherk dukhovnogo razvitija rebenka* [Outline of the mental development of the child]. Moscow: Rabotnik Prosveshchenija, pp. 1–14.

Vygotsky, L. S. (1930k). *Orudie i znak* [Tool and sign]. Personal archive of L. S. Vygotsky, manuscript.

Vygotsky, L. S. (1930l). *Voobrazhenie i tvorchestvo v detskom vozraste* [Imagination and creativity during childhood]. Moscow and Leningrad: GIZ.

Vygotsky, L. S. (1930m). Strukturaja psikhologija [Structural psychology]. In L. Vygotsky, S. Gellershtejn, & B. Fingert (Eds.), *Osnovnye techenija sovremennoi psikhologii* [Basic trends in modern psychology]. Moscow and Leningrad: GIZ, pp. 84–125.

Vygotsky, L. S. (1930n). Predislovie [Preface]. In K. Buhler, *Ocherk dukhovnogo razvitija rebenka* [Selected essays on child development]. Moscow: BZO, pp. 1–17.

Vygotsky, L. S. (1930o). Psikhika, soznanie, bessoznatel'noe [Psychology, consciousness, the unconscious]. In *Elementy obshchei psikhologii* [Elements of general psychology]. Moscow: BZO, pp. 48–61.

Vygotsky, L. S. (1930p). K voprosu o rechevom razvitii i vospitanii glukhonemogo rebenka [Problem of speech development and teaching in the deafmute child]. Report to the Second All-Russian Conference of Workers with Deafmute Children and Adolescents.

Vygotsky, L. S. (1931a). *Pedologija Podrostka* [Pedology of the adolescent]. Moscow: BZO.

Vygotsky, L. S. (1931b). *Istorija razvitija vysshikh psikhicheskikh funktsii* [History of the development of higher mental functions]. Unpublished manuscript.

Vygotsky, L. S. (1931c). K voprosu o kompensatornykh protsessakh v razvitii umstvenno otstalogo rebenka [The problem of compensatory processes in the development of the mentally retarded child]. Stenographic record at the Conference of Workers of Supplementary Schools, Leningrad, 23 May 1931.

Vygotsky, L. S. (1931d). K voprosu o pedologii i smezhnykh s neju naukakh [The problem of pedology and allied sciences]. *Pedologija*, *3*, 52–58.

Vygotsky, L. S. (1931e). Kollektiv kak faktor razvitia anomal'nogo rebenka [The group as a factor in the development of the abnormal child]. *Voprosy Defektologii*, *12*, 8–17.

Vygotsky, L. S. (1931f). Pedologija i skmezhnye s neju nauki (okonchanie) [Pedology and allied sciences (conclusion)]. *Pedologija*, *78*, 12–22.

Vygotsky, L. S. (1931g). Predislovie [Preface]. In A N. Leont'ev, *Razvitie pamiati* [The development of attention]. Moscow and Leningrad: GIZ.

Vygotsky, L. S. (1932a). K probleme psikhologii shizofrend. [On the problem of the psychology of schizophrenia]. In *Sovetskaja nevropatologija, psikhiatlija, psikhogigiena*. [Soviet neuropathology, psychiatry and psychohygiene]. St. Petersburg: GIZ.

Vygotsky, L. S. (1932b). Afladencheskii vozrast [Infancy]. Two manuscripts from the personal archive of L. S. Vygotsky. The first is an unfinished book chapter, 78 pp., the second a stenographic record of a lecture, 21 November 1932.

Vygotsky, L. S. (1932c). Problema rechi I myshlenija rebenka v ucheni Zh. Piazhe. [Problems of thinking and speech in the teaching of J. Piaget]. In J. Piaget, *Rech i myshlenie rebenka* [The language and thought of the child]. Moscow and Leningrad: Uchpedgiz.

Vygotsky, L. S. (1932d). Rannee detstvo [Early childhood]. Stenographic record of a lecture, Leningrad Pedagogical Institute, 15 December 1932.

Vygotsky, L. S. (1932e). *Lektsii po psikhologii* [Lectures on psychology]. Stenographic record of a lecture series given in 1932.

Vygotsky, L. S. (1933a). Krizis pervogo goda zhizni [Crisis at age one]. Stenographic record of a lecture at the Leningrad Pedagogical Institute, 21 December 1933.

Vygotsky, L. S. (1933b). Doshkol'nyi vozrast [Preschool age]. Personal archive of L. S. Vygotsky, 15 pp. Stenographic record of a lecture at the Leningrad Pedagogical Institute.

Vygotsky, L. S. (1933c). Predislovie [Preface]. In L. V. Zankov, M. S. Pevzner, & V. F. Shmidt, *Trudnye deti v shkol'noi rabote* [Difficult children and schoolwork]. Moscow and Leningrad: Uchpedgiz, pp. 1–5.

Vygotsky, L. S. (1933d). Igra i ee rol'v psikhicheskom razvitii rebenka [Play and its role in the mental development of the child]. Stenographic record of a lecture at the Leningrad Pedagogical Institute, 1933.

Vygotsky, L. S. (1933e). K voprosu o dinamike umstvennogo razvitija normal'nogo i nenormal'nogo rebenka [The problem of the dynamics of the mental development of the normal and abnormal child]. Personal archive of L. S. Vygotsky. Stenographic record of a lecture at the Bubnov Pedagogical Institute, 23 December 1933.

Vygotsky, L. S. (1933f). Krizis trekh let [Crisis at age three]. Stenographic record of a lecture at the Leningrad Pedagogical Institute, April 1933.

Vygotsky, L. S. (1933g). Negativnaja faza perekhodnogo vozrasta [Negative phase of the transitional age]. Archive of the A. M. Herzen Leningrad Pedagogical Institute, 17 pp. Stenographic record of a lecture at the Leningrad Pedagogical Institute, 26 June 1933.

Vygotsky, L. S. (1933h). Problema soznanija [The problem of consciousness]. In *Psikhologija grammatiki* [The psychology of grammar]. Moscow: Moscow State University.

Vygotsky, L. S. (1933i). Problema vozrasta. Igra [The problem of age. Play]. Stenographic record of concluding address at the seminar, Leningrad Pedagogical Institute, 23 March 1933.

Vygotsky, L. S. (1933j). Krizis semi let [Crisis at age seven]. Stenographic record of a lecture at the Leningrad Pedagogical Institute, April 1933.

Vygotsky, L. S. (1933k). Osnovnye psikhologicheskie osobennosti shkol'nogo vozrasta [Basic psychological features of the school age]. Unpublished manuscript, archive of the A. I. Herzen Leningrad Pedagogical Institute, 43 pp.

Vygotsky, L. S. (1933l). *Uchenie ob emotsijakh. Istorikopsikhologicheskoe issledovanie* [Teachings on the emotions. A historico-psychological study]. Unpublished manuscript, 500 pp.

Vygotsky, L. S. (1933m). Sovremmenaya problema schizofrenii [Contemporary problems of schizophrenia]. Report to a conference on schizophrenia, Moscow, 28 pp.

Vygotsky, L. S. (1934a). *Fashizm v psikhoneurologii* [Fascism in psychoneurology]. Moscow and Leningrad: Biomedgiz.

Vygotsky, L. S. (1934b). Mladenchestvo i rannii vozrast [Infancy and early childhood]. Archive of the A. I. Herzen Leningrad Pedagogical Institute, 24 pp. Stenographic record of a lecture at the Leningrad Pedagogical Institute, 23 February 1934.

Vygotsky, L. S. (1934c). *Myshlenie i rech'* [Thinking and speech]. Moscow and Leningrad: Sotsekgiz.

Vygotsky, L. S. (1934d). Myshlenie shkol'nika [Thinking of the schoolchild]. Archive of the A. I. Herzen Leningrad Pedagogical Institute, 14 pp. Stenographic record of a lecture at the Leningrad Pedagogical Institute, 3 May 1934.

Vygotsky, L. S. (1934e). *Osnovy pedologii* [Fundamentals of pedology]. Moscow: Moscow Medical Institute. Stenographic record of a course of lectures, Second Moscow Medical Institute, 1934, 211 pp.

Vygotsky, L. S. (1934f). Problema vozrasta [The problem of age]. Personal archive of L. S. Vygotsky, 95 pp.

Vygotsky, L. S. (1934g). Psikhologija i uchenhie o lokalizatsii psikhicheskikh funktsii [Psychology and the localization of mental functions]. In *Penyi vseukrainskii s'ezd nevropatologov i psikhiatrov* [First all-Ukraine congress of neuropathologists and psychiatrists]. Karkhov: GIZ, pp. 34–41.

Vygotsky, L. S. (1934h). Shkol'nyi vozrast [School age]. Archive of the A. I. Herzen Leningrad Pedagogical Institute, 61 pp., 25 pp. Stenographic records of a lecture in two parts at the Leningrad Pedagogical Institute, 23 February, 10 March 1934.

Vygotsky, L. S. (1934i). Problema razvitija v struktumcj psikhologii. Kriticheskoe issledovanie [The problem of development in structural psychology. A critical essay]. In K. Koffka, *Oznovy psikhicheskogo razvitija* [Fundamentals of mental development]. Moscow: Sotzegediz, pp. ix–lvi.

Vygotsky, L. S. (1934j). Thought in schizophrenia. *Archives of Neurology and Psychiatry, 31*, 1063–1077.

Vygotsky, L. S. (1934k). Problema razvitija i raspada vysshikh psykhicheskikh funktsii [Problems of the development and dissolution of higher mental functions]. Report to a conference of the Institute of Experimental Medicine, 28 April 1934.

Vygotsky, L. S. (1935a). Predystorija pis'mennoi rechi [Prehistory of written speech]. In L. S. Vygotsky, *Umstvennoe razvitie detei v protsesse obuchenija* [Mental development of children in the process of teaching]. Moscow and Leningrad: Uchpedgiz, pp. 73–95.

Vygotsky, L. S. (1935b). Dinamika umstvennogo razvitija shkol'nika v svjazi s obucheniem [Dynamics of mental development of the schoolchild in connection with teaching]. In L. S. Vygotsky, *Umstvennoe razvitie detei v protsesse obuchenija* [Mental development of children in the process of teaching]. Moscow and Leningrad: GIZ, pp. 33–52.

Vygotsky, L. S. (1935c). K voprosu o razvitii nauchnykh ponjatii v shkol'nom vozraste [The problem of the schoolchild's development of scientific concepts]. In Zh. I. Shif, *Razvitie nauchnykh ponjatii u shkol'nika* [Development of scientific concepts in the schoolchild]. Moscow and Leningrad: Uchpedgiz, pp. 3–17.

Vygotsky, L. S. (1935d). Problema obuchenija i umstvennoe razvitie v shkol'nom vozraste [The problem of teaching and mental development during school age]. In L. S. Vygotsky, *Umstvennoe razvitie detei v protsesse obuchenija* [Mental development of children in the process of teaching]. Moscow and Leningrad: GIZ, pp. 3–19.

Vygotsky, L. S. (1935e). Problema umstvennoi otstalosti [The problem of mental retardation]. In L. S. Vygotsky, *Umstvenno otstalyi rebenok* [The mentally retarded child]. Moscow, Uchpedgiz, pp. 7–34.

Vygotsky, L. S. (1935f). Razvitie zhiteiskikh i nauchnykh ponyatii v shkol'nom vozraste [Development of life and learning concepts during school age]. In L. S. Vygotsky, *Umstvennoe razvitie detei v protsesse obuchenija* [Mental development of children in the process of teaching]. Moscow and Leningrad: GIZ, pp. 96–115.

Vygotsky, L. S. (1935g). O pedologicheskom analise pedagogicheskogo protsessa [Pedological analysis of the pedagogical process]. In L. S. Vygotsky, *Umstvennoe razvitie detei v protsesse obuchenija* [Mental development of children in the process of teaching]. Moscow and Leningrad: GIZ, pp. 116–134.

Vygotsky, L. S. (1960). *Problema razvitiia i respada* [Problems of child development]. Moscow: Akademii Pedagogovo Nauka.

Vygotsky, L. S. (2001). *Lektsii po pedologii* [Lectures on pedology]. Moscow: Ichevsk.

Vygotsky, L. S., & Luria, A. R. (1925). Predislovie [Preface]. In S. Freud, *Po tu storonu principa udovolstviia* [Beyond the pleasure principle]. Moscow: Sovremennye Problemy, pp. i–xv.

Vygotsky, L. S., & Luria, A. R. (1930). *Etjudy po istorii povedenija. (Obezyana. Primitiv. Rebenok)* [Studies in the history of behaviour. (Simian. Primitive Man. Child)]. Moscow and Leningrad: Gosudarstvennoe.

Vurpillot, E. (1976). *The visual world of the child.* Oxford: International University Press.

Weil-Barais, A. (1994). Heuristic value of the notion of zone of proximal development in the study of child and adolescent construction of concepts in physics. *European Journal of Psychology of Education, 9*, 4, 367–383.

Wells, G. (1974). The early development of children's speech. *Child Language, 3*, 46–62.

Wells, G. (1983). Language and learning in the early years. *Early Child Development & Care, 11*, 1, 69–77.

Wells, G. (1987). The negotiation of meaning: Talking and learning at home and at school. In B. Fillion & C. N. Hedley (Eds.), *Home and school: Early language and reading*. Westport, CT: Ablex, pp. 3–25.

Wells, G. (1996). Using the tool-kit of discourse in the activity of learning and teaching. *Mind, Culture, & Activity, 3*, 2, 74–101.

Wells, G. (1999). *Dialogic inquiry: Towards a sociocultural practice and theory of education*. Cambridge: Cambridge University Press.

Wells, G. (2002). The role of dialogue in activity theory. *Mind, Culture, & Activity, 9*, 1, 43–66.

Wells, G., & Claxton, G. (Eds.) (2002). *Learning for life in the 21st century: Sociocultural perspectives on the future of education*. Oxford: Blackwell.

Wertheimer, M. (1922). Untersuchungen zur Lehre von der Gestalt: 1. Prinzipielle Bemerkungen [Studies on the Gestalt doctrine: 1. Principal remarks]. *Psychologisches Forschung, 1*, 1–34.

Wertheimer, M. (1925). *Drei Abhandlungen zur Gestalttheorie* [Three studies of Gestalt theory]. Erlangen: Verlag der philosophischen Akademie.

Wertsch, J. V. (1985). *Vygotsky and the social formation of mind.* Cambridge, MA: Harvard University Press.

Wertsch, J. V. (1990). Dialogue and dialogism in a socio-cultural approach to mind. In I. Markova & K. Foppa (Eds.), *The dynamics of dialogue*. Berkhamstead, UK: Harvester Wheatsheaf, pp. 62–82.

Wertsch, J. V. (1994a). Reclaiming the natural line in Vygotsky's theory of cognitive development. *Human Development, 37*, 6, 343–345.

Wertsch, J. V. (1994b). The primacy of mediated action in sociocultural studies. *Mind, Culture, & Activity, 1*, 4, 202–208.

Wertsch, J. V. (1998). *Mind as action.* New York: Oxford University Press.

Wertsch, J. V. (2000). Intersubjectivity and alterity in human communication. In N. Budwig & I. C. Uzgiris (Eds.), *Communication: An arena of development.* Stamford, CT: Ablex, pp. 17–31.

Wertsch, J. V., & Sohmer, R. (1995). Vygotsky on learning and development. *Human Development, 38*, 6, 332–337.

Wertsch, J. V., & Toma, C. (1995). Discourse and learning in the classroom: A sociocultural approach. In L. P. Steffe & J. E. Gale (Eds.), *Constructivism in education.* Hillsdale, NJ: Lawrence Erlbaum Associates, pp. 159–174.

Westen, D. (1994). Towards an integrative model of affect regulation. *Journal of Personality, 62*, 641–647.

Whitbourne, S. K., & Tesch, S. A. (1985). A comparison of identity and intimacy statuses in college students and alumni. *Developmental Psychology, 21*, 1039–1044.

White, R. W. (1959). Motivation reconsidered: The concept of competence. *Psychological Review*, *66*, 297–333.

White, R. W. (1960). Competence and the psychosexual stages of development. In M. R. Jones (Ed.), *Nebraska symposium on motivation*. Lincoln, NB: University of Nebraska Press, pp. 97–141.

White, R. W. (1972). *The enterprise of living*. New York: Holt, Rinehart & Winston.

Whorf, B. L. (1956). *Language, thought and reality*. Cambridge, MA: MIT Press.

Wilson, E. O. (1976). *Sociobiology*. Boston, MA: Belknap.

Wilson, E. O. (1992). *The diversity of life*. Boston, MA: Belknap.

Wilson, R. A., & Keil, F. C. (2000). The shadows and shallows of explanation. In F. C. Keil & R. A. Wilson (Eds.), *Explanation and cognition*. Cambridge, MA: MIT Press, pp. 87–114.

Wood, D. (1998). *How children think and learn: The social contexts of cognitive development* (2nd ed.). Malden, MA: Blackwell.

Wood, D., & O'Malley, C. (1996). Collaborative learning between peers. *Educational Psychology in Practice*, *11*, 4, 4–9.

Wood, D., Bruner, J. S., & Ross, G. (1976). The role of tutoring in problem solving. *Journal of Child Psychology & Psychiatry*, *17*, 2, 89–100.

y Gasset, O. (1933). *The revolt of the masses*. London: Unwin.

Yaroshevsky, M. G. (1985). *Lev Semenovich Vygotsky*. Moscow: Pedagogika.

Yaroshevsky, M. G. (1989). *Lev Semenovich Vygotsky*. New York: Progress.

Yaroshevsky, M. G. (1998). Traktorka istorii povedenii v nauchnoi shkole Vygotscogo-Lurii [The history of behaviour interpreted by the scientific school of Vygotsky-Luria]. *Voprosy Psikhologii*, *42*, 118–139.

Yaroshevsky, M. G., & Gorsnedze, L. S. (1982). Posleslovie [Epilogue]. In *L. S. Vygotsky, sobranie sochinenii. Tom. 1* [L. S. Vygotsky Collected Works, Vol. 1]. Moscow: Pedagogika.

Yates, F. A. (1964). *The art of memory*. London: Dent.

Zaporozhets, A. V., & Elkonin, D. B. (1971). *The psychology of preschool children* (J. Shybut & S. Simon, Trans.). Oxford: MIT Press.

Author index

Subject index

For Product Safety Concerns and Information please contact our EU representative GPSR@taylorandfrancis.com Taylor & Francis Verlag GmbH, Kaufingerstraße 24, 80331 München, Germany